Depression

Depression provides a valuable and accessible resource for students, practitioners and researchers seeking an up-to-date overview and summary of research-based information about depression. With the help of clinical examples, the authors present chapters covering the hypothesised causes of depression, including genetic and biological factors, life stress, family and interpersonal contributors to depression.

The third edition extensively updates prior coverage to reflect advances in the field. The presumed causes of depression from both a biological perspective as well as from social and cognitive perspectives are explored in detail. Two chapters explore the most recent developments in pharmacological and biological interventions and in psychological treatments, as well as the prevention of depression. This new edition includes an updated discussion about challenges in research, including heterogeneity and diagnosis of depression and proposed solutions, as well as the efficacy and availability of treatments.

Authored by experts in the field who are active researchers and clinicians, *Depression* provides a state-of-the-art primer for final year undergraduate and postgraduate students, clinicians, professionals and researchers seeking a broad reference task that critically evaluates research into depression.

Constance Hammen is a professor and clinical psychologist at UCLA, and a cognitive-behavioural therapist.

Edward Watkins is a chartered clinical psychologist at the Mood Disorders Centre, University of Exeter.

Clinical Psychology: A Modular Course

Clinical Psychology: A Modular Course was designed to overcome the problems faced by the traditional textbook in conveying what psychological disorders are really like. All the books in the series, written by leading scholars and practitioners in the field, can be read as stand-alone texts, but they will also integrate with the other modules to form a comprehensive resource in clinical psychology. Students of psychology, medicine, nursing and social work, as well as busy practitioners in many professions, often need an accessible but thorough introduction to how people experience anxiety, depression, addiction, or other disorders, how common they are, and who is most likely to suffer from them, as well as up-to-date research evidence on the causes and available treatments. The series will appeal to those who want to go deeper into the subject than the traditional textbook will allow, and base their examination answers, research, projects, assignments, or practical decisions on a clearer and more rounded appreciation of the clinical and research evidence.

Chris R. Brewin

Depression

Third Edition

Constance Hammen and Edward Watkins

Routledge
Taylor & Francis Group

LONDON AND NEW YORK

First published 2018
by Routledge
2 Park Square, Milton Park, Abingdon, Oxon OX14 4RN

and by Routledge
711 Third Avenue, New York, NY 10017

Routledge is an imprint of the Taylor & Francis Group, an informa business

British Library Cataloguing-in-Publication Data
A catalogue record for this book is available from the British Library

Library of Congress Cataloging-in-Publication Data
A catalog record for this book has been requested

ISBN: 978-1-138-64616-2 (hbk)
ISBN: 978-1-138-64617-9 (pbk)
ISBN: 978-1-315-54280-5 (ebk)

Typeset in Palatino and Myriad
by Florence Production Ltd, Stoodleigh, Devon, UK

Contents

Tables and figures

1

Defining and diagnosing depression

I had another tortured, sleepless night until nearly dawn and awoke with an instant of calm before I recognised the heaviness in my body and the sense of desolation about the coming day. I pushed myself out of bed and made myself go through the steps of getting ready for work. How can I make my deadened face smile at the boss, I wondered, and manage my tasks when I can barely concentrate? It's hard to imagine that only a couple of months ago I was able to enjoy even the minutiae of the day and looked forward to spending time with friends and the family. Now I can barely remember when the world didn't seem cast in shades of grey, and I felt able to enjoy a sunset or a sip of tea. My doctor tells me that it will get better with time, that depression lifts, but I am not sure that prediction will apply to me. I feel so alone, leaden and empty that I wonder if I can go on.

The words of this individual capture vividly the experience of depression, and its themes have also been echoed in ancient texts of the Bible, Greek, Roman and Chinese classics – as well as Shakespearean plays and Russian novels. Depression is a universal, timeless and ageless human affliction. However, while the personal experience of depression is profoundly painful, it is often misunderstood by others. Individuals in Western societies are often raised to expect to have considerable control over moods, and are exhorted not to let themselves suffer from depression. Thus, it is distressing to others when a loved one or friend does not 'snap out' of depression, and the hopeless, helpless and self-hating attitudes expressed by depressed individuals often seem illogical and irrational, as if the depressed person wilfully and perversely holds onto unreasonable moods and beliefs.

As this book hopes to explore, depression is neither uncommon nor particularly paradoxical – nor is it a failure of willpower and motivation. It is enormously impairing – and even deadly – and its effects on both the afflicted person and his or her family can be profoundly negative. Yet, we also have a number of effective treatments for depression and science is gaining considerable insight into the processes underpinning depression.

Phenomenology of depressive experiences

The term *depression* is used in everyday language to describe a range of experiences from a slightly noticeable and temporary mood decrease to a profoundly impaired and even life-threatening disorder. When used to describe a mood, the term conveys a temporary state of sadness and loss of energy or motivation that may last a few moments, hours, or even a few days. As such, it is usually a normal reaction to an upsetting event, or even an exaggerated description of a typical event ('this weather is depressing'). A young man might feel sad for a few days following a romantic disappointment, or a woman might be discouraged for a few days upon being passed over for a job. Such experiences are not the topic of this book. Rather, the term 'depression' as used here refers to a constellation of experiences including not only mood, but also physical, mental and behavioural experiences that define more prolonged, impairing and severe conditions that may be clinically diagnosable as a syndrome of depression.

The description at the beginning of the chapter may differ from the personal experiences of other depressed people, but all share features of the syndromes of depression. Each sufferer has features from the four different domains that define depressive disorders. The four general domains are affect, cognition, behaviour and physical functioning.

Affective symptoms

Depression is one of several disorders generically called affective disorders, referring to the manifestations of abnormal affect or mood, as a defining feature. Thus, depressed mood, sadness, feeling low, down in the dumps or empty are typical. However, sometimes the most apparent mood is irritability (especially in depressed children). Moreover, not all depressed people manifest sadness or depression as such. Instead, they may report feeling loss of interest or pleasure, a feeling of 'blah', listlessness, apathy. Nothing seems enjoyable – not even experiences that previously elicited positive feelings, including work and recreation, social interactions, sexual activity and the like. Pastimes are no longer enjoyable; even pleasurable relationships with one's family and friends may no longer hold appeal or even be negative, and the individual may find it hard to think of things to do that might help to relieve the depression even temporarily. Even when he or she accomplishes an important task, there is little sense of satisfaction. Some severely depressed people have described the loss of pleasure as seeing the world in black, white and grey with no colour. The experience of loss of interest or pleasure, called anhedonia, is one of the most common features of the depression syndrome, according to many studies of depressed adults and teenagers, from many different countries (reviewed in Klinger, 1993).

George, a middle-aged man of apparent good health, has felt listless and bored for a few weeks. His favourite television programmes are no longer of interest to him in the evenings, and on weekends he can't think of anything to do that he imagines would be pleasurable – in contrast to his formerly active and fun-seeking self. He says his pals are 'boring' and his attitude about seeing his girlfriend is that she doesn't interest him anymore. Fortunately, she is astute enough to suspect that he became depressed ever since someone else got the promotion at work that he hoped for – though George himself would deny that he is depressed.

Cognitive symptoms

Some have called depression a disorder of thinking, as much as it is a disorder of mood. Depressed people typically have negative thoughts about themselves, their worlds and the future. They experience themselves as incompetent, worthless and are relentlessly critical of their own acts and characteristics, and often feel guilty as they dwell on their perceived shortcomings. Low self-esteem is therefore a common attribute of depression. Individuals may feel helpless to manage their lives or resolve problems. They may view their lives and futures as bleak and unrewarding, feeling that change is not only pointless but essentially unattainable. Cognitions reflecting hopelessness about one's ability to control desired outcomes may be common, and the resulting despair may also give rise to thoughts of wanting to die or to take one's own life.

Annette has been increasingly depressed since her boyfriend went off to university. Although he keeps in touch with her, she is consumed with the thoughts that he is trying to meet other women, that she's not good enough to sustain his interest – and indeed, why would anyone ever love her. At work she imagines that she is doing a poor job and expects to be fired – despite her boss's praise for her achievements. When her girlfriends ask her to go out with them she believes that they don't really want her company and are only feeling sorry for her that her boyfriend is away. As she becomes more and more depressed, she believes herself to be a horrible person; tasks at work seem more and more overwhelming so that she believes that she is incompetent and utterly helpless to figure out how to manage projects she used to do with ease.

The cognitive features of depression have been given particular emphasis by some investigators, who note that thinking in such self-critical ways actually makes people more depressed or prolongs their depression. This observation gave rise to Aaron Beck's cognitive model of depression (Beck, 1967; Beck, 1976), which hypothesises an underlying vulnerability to depression due to tendencies to perceive the self, world and future in negative ways. The cognitive model of depression and related models are discussed in Chapter 5.

In addition to negativistic thinking, depression is often marked by difficulties in mental processes involving concentration, decision-making and memory. The depressed person may find it enormously difficult to make even simple decisions, and significant decisions seem beyond one's capacity altogether. Depressed patients often report problems in concentrating, especially when reading or watching television, and memory may be impaired. Memory problems, in fact, often lead depressed people to worry further that their minds are failing, and in older depressed individuals what is actually a treatable memory deficit due to depression may be misinterpreted as a sign of irreversible dementia.

Behavioural symptoms

Consistent with the apathy and diminished motivation of depression, it is common for individuals to withdraw from social activities or reduce typical behaviours. In severe depression, the individual might stay in bed for prolonged periods. Social interactions might be shunned, both because of loss of motivation and interest, and also because depressed people perceive, fairly accurately, that being around them may be aversive to others.

Actual changes in motor behaviour are often observed, taking the form either of being slowed down or agitated and restless. Some depressed individuals may talk and move more slowly, their faces showing little animation with their mouths and eyes seeming to droop as if weighted down, all of which are labelled psychomotor retardation. Their speech is marked by pauses, fewer words, monotone voice and less eye contact (Buyukdura, McClintock and Croarkin, 2011; Schrijvers, Hulstijn and Sabbe, 2008). Other depressed people display psychomotor agitation, indicated by restlessness, hand movements, fidgeting, self-touching, and gesturing. Psychomotor agitation may be more commonly observed in depressed people who are also experiencing anxiety symptoms.

Physical symptoms

In addition to motor behaviour changes that are apparent in some depressed people, there may also be changes in appetite, sleep and energy. Reduced energy is a very frequent complaint. Depressed patients complain of listlessness, lethargy, feeling heavy and leaden, and lacking the physical stamina to undertake or complete tasks.

Sleep disturbance is a particularly important symptom of depression, with the majority (60–84 per cent) of unipolar depressed patients reporting poorer quality of sleep, experienced as a loss of restfulness and/or a reduced duration of sleep (Benca, Obermeyer, Thisted and Gillin, 1992; Kupfer, 1995). Sleep changes can take several forms: difficulty falling asleep, staying asleep or too much sleep. Depressed people sometimes experience what is called 'early morning awakening', a problem of waking an hour or more before the regular awakening time, usually with difficulty falling back asleep.

The relationship between sleep disturbance and depression is a complex one, with a close correspondence existing between regulation of mood and regulation of sleep (Lustberg and Reynolds, 2000). There is robust evidence of a reciprocal relationship between insomnia and depression (Asarnow, Soehner and Harvey, 2014; Herrick and Sateia, 2016). As well as being an important consequence or complication of depression, impaired sleep also often precedes and predicts a subsequent episode of depression (Asarnow et al., 2014; Harvey, 2011).

Patients with depression also experience changes in appetite, typically in the form of decreased appetite with corresponding weight loss. However, some depressed people eat more when depressed, with this pattern often associated with increased sleep.

Implications

The multiplicity of symptoms of depression means that depressed people differ from one another in the manifestations of their disorder and in the particular combination, nature and severity of their symptoms. Such differences may reflect variability in the severity of the depression, as well as suggesting that there may be different forms of depression that have different causes and treatments. The diagnostic systems in use today define several categories that cut across these variabilities, and that represent the major forms of the disorder that are the basis of most research and clinical categorisation. However, there has also been considerable debate about the validity and utility of these diagnostic systems. Thus, this chapter will first present traditional approaches to diagnosis and then discuss their limitations and alternatives.

Diagnosis of depression

The first key diagnostic distinction is between *unipolar* depression and *bipolar* disorder. Unipolar depression, which is the principal focus of this book, includes only depressive conditions occurring in the absence of current or past mania or hypomania, whereas in contrast, *bipolar disorder* is diagnosed when an individual has episodes of mania or hypomania.

Mania is defined as a distinct period of abnormally and persistently elevated, expansive or irritable mood, energy and activity lasting at least one week, in combination with at least three of the following symptoms: inflated self-esteem or grandiosity, decreased need for sleep, increased talkativeness, flight of ideas or racing thoughts, distractibility and poor concentration, increase in goal-directed activity or psychomotor agitation, and excessive involvement in pleasurable but risky activities such as overspending or sexual indiscretions. *Hypomania* is a milder form of mania, lasting four days or more. Thus, whereas depression is typically characterised by reduced arousal and reduced sensitivity to reward and pleasure, mania is typically characterised by increased arousal and increased sensitivity to reward and pleasure.

Unipolar depression

According to the Diagnostic and Statistical Manual of Mental Disorders (DSM), which is a set of agreed guidelines for diagnosis and now on its Fifth Edition-Revised (American Psychiatric Association, 2013; henceforward DSM-5), unipolar depressions basically take one of four forms: major depressive episode, persistent depressive disorder (which includes both chronic major depressive disorder and what was called dysthymia or dysthymic disorder in previous DSM editions), premenstrual dysphoric disorder, or 'depression not otherwise specified' (including several forms of briefer or milder periods of depression). These conditions are briefly described.

Major depressive episode

Table 1.1 compares the diagnostic criteria for major depressive disorder, according to DSM-5 and to the very similar International Classification of Disorders-Version 10 (ICD-10; World Health Organization, 1993). Acknowledging the heterogeneity of depressive presentations, these systems permit individual variability so long as essential features are shared. These essential features include seriously compromised mood (continuous depressed mood or loss of interest/anhedonia) and at least four additional cognitive, behavioural or physical symptoms. Note that individuals must show the symptoms all or most of the day, nearly every day for at least two weeks. Also, in order to be diagnosed, the episode must be clinically significant, in terms of causing distress or impaired functioning in the person's typical, social or occupational roles. Furthermore, alternative causes for the symptoms such as the direct physiological effects of medical illness (e.g., hypothyroidism), medications and substance misuse need to be ruled out before a diagnosis of a major depressive episode can be reached.

Persistent depressive disorder (formerly known as dysthymic disorder)

Persistent depressive disorder would be diagnosed if symptoms of depressed mood occurred for most of the day, for more days than not for at least two years (although there might be brief periods of normal mood lasting no more than two months; at least one year for children and adolescents), regardless of whether major depressive disorder is present. During periods of depressed mood, at least two of the following six symptoms are present: poor appetite or overeating, insomnia or hypersomnia, low energy or fatigue, low self-esteem, poor concentration or difficulty making decisions, or feelings of hopelessness. Additionally, in order to be diagnosed, persistent depressive disorder must be seen to cause significant distress or disruption in the person's major areas of functioning.

Table 1.1 Diagnostic criteria for depressive disorders – comparing DSM-5 (American Psychiatric Association, 2013) and ICD-10 (World Health Organization, 1993)

Major depressive episode

Common criteria	Specific to DSM-5	Specific to ICD-10
Symptoms must be present for at least two weeks continuously and present most of the day and nearly every day. Central symptoms (as indicated by subjective report or observation) are: (a) Depressed mood and/or (b) Loss of interest or pleasure in activities that are normally pleasurable Other symptoms include: (c) Decreased energy or fatigue (d) Disturbed sleep, such as insomnia or hypersomnia (e) Change in appetite (increase or decrease) or associated significant weight loss or gain (f) Psychomotor agitation or retardation (g) Excessive feelings of self-reproach, worthlessness or guilt (h) Poor concentration and/or indecisiveness (i) Recurrent thoughts of death or suicide or any suicidal behaviour Symptoms cause significant distress or impairment in functioning. Symptoms are not due to other possible causes.	At least five symptoms present; at least one needs to be depressed mood or loss of interest/pleasure. Symptoms not due to the direct physiological effects of a drug or medication or a general medical condition.	At least four symptoms for mild episode; at least six for moderate episode; at least nine for severe episode; at least two symptoms need to be depressed mood, loss of interest or decreased energy. Symptoms also include loss of confidence or self-esteem. The person does not meet criteria for mania or hypomania at any time.

Persistent depressive disorder (DSM-5; chronic major depressive disorder; dysthymic disorder)/ Dysthymia (ICD-10).

Common criteria	Specific to DSM-5	Specific to ICD-10
Constant or constantly recurring depressed mood for at least two years. Periods without the symptoms are only brief. When depressed, some of the following symptoms are also present: (a) Disturbed sleep (insomnia or hypersomnia)		

continued...

Table 1.1 Continued

Persistent depressive disorder (DSM-5; chronic major depressive disorder; dysthymic disorder)/Dysthymia (ICD-10).

Common criteria	Specific to DSM-5	Specific to ICD-10
(b) Fatigue or reduced energy (c) Loss of self-confidence or low self-esteem (d) Poor concentration or indecisiveness (e) Feelings of hopelessness or despair There has never been a manic or a hypomanic episode. Symptoms cause significant distress or impairment in functioning. Symptoms are not due to other possible causes (e.g., drug of abuse, medication, medical condition, psychotic disorder).	Most of the day, nearly every day; in children and adolescents can be irritable mood instead of depressed mood, duration at least one year. Never without symptoms for more than two months. Additional symptoms: change in appetite. Requires presence of at least two symptoms in addition to depressed mood. Criteria for a major depressive disorder may be continuously present for two years.	Periods of normal mood last less than a few weeks. Additional symptoms: frequent tearfulness; loss of enjoyment in sex and other pleasurable activities; perceived inability to cope; pessimism about the future or brooding over the past; social withdrawal; reduced talkativeness. Requires at least three symptoms in addition to depressed mood. Few episodes within the two years meet criteria for recurrent depressive episodes.

In previous editions of the DSM, dysthymia was considered a chronic but milder version of depression and treated as distinct from chronic major depression, which is defined as the presence of an episode of major depression lasting continuously for at least two years. The development of the persistent depressive disorder diagnosis reflects the increasing recognition that the chronicity of depression is a major dimension in understanding and treating depression, as further discussed in Chapter 2. Furthermore, the chronicity of elevated depressive symptoms is determined to be more clinically important than whether criteria for major depressive episode are met or not, with few meaningful differences found between chronic major depression and dysthymic disorder in aetiology, presentation or prognosis (Klein, 2008, 2010; Klein and Kotov, 2016).

Premenstrual dysphoric disorder

A new diagnosis in DSM-5, premenstrual dysphoric disorder, is defined as the presence, during most menstrual cycles in the last year, of five or more of the symptoms of depression, with these symptoms emerging during the last week of the luteal phase of the menstrual cycle (pre-menstruation) and remitting a few days after menstruation. As for all depressive disorders, the diagnosis is contingent on the presence of significant impairment or distress. Premenstrual dysphoric disorder appears to be a relatively stable disorder, distinct from depression, which occurs in estimates of between 2–5 per cent of menstruating women (Epperson et al., 2012). Nonetheless, the inclusion of premenstrual dysphoric disorder is not without controversy, with concerns that it may pathologise natural female responses and lead to stigmatisation and discrimination, and queries as to whether symptoms correspond to changes in the menstrual cycle.

Other depression diagnoses

When depressive features are present that do not fit the criteria for major depressive episode or dysthymic disorder, they may fit one of several possible residual categories, including recurrent brief depression, short-duration depression episodes (five or more symptoms less than two weeks) and depressive episode with insufficient symptoms (previously minor depression, at least two weeks of less than five symptoms).

Bipolar disorder

Ronald has just been hospitalised for severe depression and suicidality. Nearly unable to get out of bed, he is dishevelled, weeping and moaning about wishing he were dead. The examining psychiatrist at the hospital determines, however, that in the months before the depression Ronald was extremely euphoric and overactive. He believed he had achieved a breakthrough in his business ideas, and had borrowed huge sums of money to finance new ventures that in retrospect had little chance of success. Sleeping only two or three hours a night, he had worked feverishly on his projects, jumping from one to another without completing any – and had talked incessantly to anyone he could find about how great his ideas were and how important he was about to become. Information from Ronald's family members revealed that he had experienced several such cycles of mania and depression since his early 20s. He was given a diagnosis of bipolar I disorder, and treated with lithium as well as an antidepressant medication.

Bipolar I disorder is diagnosed when an individual has at least one lifetime manic episode. As such, the diagnosis does not require the individual to have had an episode of depression, and, indeed it is possible to have a diagnosis of unipolar mania, i.e., only episodes of mania (Angst and Grobler, 2015). Nonetheless, the majority of individuals with bipolar affective disorder experience cycles of both depression and mania/hypomania, with only 20–30 per cent of individuals with bipolar disorder not experiencing depression (Beesdo et al., 2009). Large epidemiological studies find a prevalence of 1.7–1.8 per cent of pure mania or mania with only mild depression in adolescents and adults (Angst and Grobler, 2015). *Bipolar II disorder* is diagnosed when an individual has met diagnostic criteria for depression along with a history of hypomania.

Bipolar disorder is a chronic problem of recurrent symptoms, often marked not only by extreme mood swings but even by psychotic experiences including delusions and hallucinations. Psychotic features are relatively common in the manic phase of bipolar disorder, presenting in 3–45 per cent of patients (Mazzarini et al., 2010).

Episodes of depression within bipolar disorder (bipolar depression) appear to be similar to episodes of unipolar depression with respect to symptoms, biological features, course and psychosocial antecedents, although bipolar depression is associated with more frequent episodes, more abrupt onsets of depression, more lifetime episodes and more hospital admissions than unipolar depression, suggesting greater dysregulation of mood in bipolar depression (Cuellar, Johnson and Winters, 2005). Furthermore, compared to major depression, one study found that a bipolar depression is characterised by significantly higher rates of psychomotor retardation, difficulty thinking, early morning wakening, morning worsening, delusions and hallucinations (Mitchell et al., 2011).

Individuals with bipolar disorder are considered to have an aetiologically different disorder with a different course from unipolar depression, and to require different types of treatment, including mood stabilising medication. Thus, a clinician must carefully evaluate not only the current symptoms but also the individuals' personal and family history of mood disorders, bearing in mind that research has found that a significant minority of initially depressed people go on to develop bipolar episodes, up to 9 per cent over five years (Bukh, Andersen and Kessing, 2016; Gilman, Dupuy and Perlis, 2012). Thus, because mania or hypomania has not yet been observed, an individual may be diagnosed as suffering from unipolar depression, when over time, it becomes apparent that a more accurate diagnosis is bipolar disorder, especially when the initial diagnosis occurs in adolescence or young adulthood. For example, a ten-year follow-up of 3,000 community participants found that 6 per cent of the initial unipolar major depression cases subsequently developed mania or hypomania, increasing to 9 per cent for those whose depression started before age 17 (Beesdo et al., 2009).

There is also growing evidence that manic symptoms at a level and duration below the diagnostic threshold for hypomania are relatively common in patients who experience recurrent episodes of depression that hitherto would be diagnosed as unipolar depression (Angst et al., 2011; Angst et al., 2010). This is consistent with a view that hypomanic and manic symptoms, like depressive symptoms, can be usefully conceived of occurring on a continuous dimension. It also raises questions as to whether a broader definition and diagnosis categorisation of hypomania and bipolar disorder is required and/or whether sub-threshold hypomanic symptoms are viewed as on the continuum of normal human experience.

Diagnosis of depression in children and adolescents

Although the emphasis of the book is adult depression, there is good evidence that depression is also present in children and adolescents.

Barney is a 10-year-old boy whose irritability and temper tantrums are evident both at home and at school. With little provocation he bursts into tears and yells and throws objects. At home he has been sleeping poorly, and has gained 10 pounds over the past couple of months from constant snacking. At school he seems to have difficulty concentrating and seems easily distracted. Increasingly shunned by his peers, he plays by himself – and at home, spends most of his time in his room watching television. The school psychologist talked with him, and she reports that he is a deeply unhappy child who expresses feelings of worthlessness and hopelessness – and even a wish that he would die. These experiences probably began about six months ago when his father – divorced from the mother for several years – remarried and moved to another town where he spends far less time with Barney.

This case illustrates three key issues about the diagnosis of depression in youngsters. First, the essential phenomenological features of the depression syndrome are similar in both children and adults, and show continuity from childhood through adolescence into adulthood (Luby, 2010; Luby, Gaffrey, Tillman, April and Belden, 2014; Luby, Si, Belden, Tandon and Spitznagel, 2009). Second, because children's externalising or disruptive behaviours attract more attention or are more readily expressed, compared to internal, subjective suffering, depression is sometimes overlooked. It may not be recognised, or it might not be assessed. Childhood depression has a high level of co-existing disorders, especially involving conduct problems and other disruptive behaviours; such patterns gave rise to the erroneous belief that depression is 'masked'. Third, several features of the syndrome of depression, such as irritable mood, are more likely to be typical of children than of adults, leading to age-specific modifications of the diagnostic criteria.

Major depression, therefore, would be diagnosed with adult criteria as in Table 1.1, but permitting irritability instead of depressed mood. Irritability may be substituted for depressed mood because irritability is a common expression of distress in depressed youngsters – as shown in the case of Barney – and because young depressed children may not express subjective negative affect.

The debate as to the nature and extent of developmental differences in the presentation of depression has not yet been fully resolved, with evidence of continuity between pre-school onset depression and depression in later childhood and early adolescence (Luby et al., 2014). Nonetheless, there is some evidence that adolescents with depression report more hopelessness, hyper-somnia, suicidality and weight changes than children with depression, whereas younger depressed children are more likely to have physically unjustified or exaggerated somatic complaints and greater irritability (Bufferd, Dougherty, Carlson, Rose and Klein, 2012; Luby et al., 2014; Luby et al., 2009).

Studies that have compared the symptoms of depressed youngsters and adults find little relationship between age and presentation of depression, with the structure of major depression similar in adolescents and adults (Lamers et al., 2012; Thapar, Collishaw, Pine and Thapar, 2012). However, patterns of comorbidity are likely to be somewhat different at different ages. For instance, depressed children (and young adolescents) are more likely than depressed older adolescents to display separation anxiety disorders, while adolescents report more generalised anxiety disorder, eating disorders and substance use disorders.

Suicidal thoughts and attempts are among the diagnostic criteria for major depression. Suicidal ideation is quite common in depressed youngsters: with rates ranging from 41 per cent to 68 per cent in children and adolescents (e.g., Kovacs, Goldston and Gatsonis, 1993; Lewinsohn, Rohde and Seeley, 1998). Within the National Comorbidity Study – adolescents in the US that sampled over 10,000 adolescents aged 13 to 18, among those with major depressive disorder, nearly 30 per cent reported some suicidality in the last year and 10.8 per cent reported a suicide attempt in the last year (Nock et al., 2013). Of those who reported an attempt, 76 per cent had a lifetime history of major depression or dysthymia.

To address concerns about potential overdiagnosis and overtreatment of bipolar disorder in children (Leibenluft, 2011), a new diagnosis, disruptive mood dysregulation disorder was added in DSM-5. Diagnosis of disruptive mood dysregulation disorder requires chronic and severe irritability as indicated by both severe and frequent temper outbursts (tantrums) occurring at least three times a week for one year across different settings and pervasive irritable or angry mood, in children between 6 and 18 years old. Symptoms consistent with disruptive mood dysregulation disorder prospectively predict increased risk for depressive and anxiety disorders, but less risk for mania and bipolar disorder (Stringaris et al., 2010). These criteria are estimated to apply to 1–3 per cent of school-aged and pre-school children (Copeland, Angold, Costello and Egger, 2013). However, disruptive mood dysregulation disorder has been criticised for being difficult to distinguish from existing childhood diagnoses such as conduct disorder (Axelson et al., 2012).

Subtypes of depression

In addition to the formal diagnostic categories of depression, researchers and clinicians have sought to parse the considerable heterogeneity in how depression clinically presents into distinct subtypes that better predict course and response to treatment. A historic theme cutting across this search has been the idea that there are 'biological' (alternatively called endogenous, autonomous, primary, endogenomorphic) depressions that are diseases arising in the absence of environmental precipitants vs. 'psychological' depressions that stem from personality or situational factors (also called neurotic, reactive, psychogenic). However, despite considerable efforts, there has been little convincing evidence for subtypes of depression that are qualitatively and aetiologically distinct or that reliably predict differential response to treatment (e.g., Harkness and Monroe, 2002; Kendler, 1997; Leventhal and Rehm, 2005).

The most robust distinct symptom profiles for depression are *atypical depression* and *melancholic depression*. *Melancholic* features include anhedonia with lack of responsiveness to pleasurable stimuli, such that even good events, funny stories, or enjoyable experiences do not elicit any (or only a small amount) of positive reaction, excessive or inappropriate guilt, marked psychomotor change (retardation or agitation), and significant loss of appetite and weight. Also, the depression is regularly worse in the morning than evening, with early morning wakening (diurnal variation) (Lamers et al., 2010; Lamers et al., 2012).

Atypical features include mood reactivity in which mood improves in response to positive events, increase in appetite or weight, hypersomnia, heavy and leaden feelings in the arms or legs and a long-standing pattern of increased sensitivity to criticism or rejection from other people (Davidson et al., 1982).

Consistent with these distinctions, a taxometric analysis to determine the latent structure of symptoms within a sample of 818 patients with depression from the Netherlands Study of Depression and Anxiety (NESDA) found three classes of symptom patterns corresponding broadly to a severe melancholic subtype (46.3 per cent prevalence), a severe atypical subtype (24.6 per cent prevalence), and a class of moderate severity (29.1 per cent prevalence) (Lamers et al., 2010; Lamers et al., 2012). Individuals who displayed the melancholic subtype and atypical subtypes and remained depressed showed stability in their clinical presentation over two years (Lamers et al., 2012).

Furthermore, there is evidence of biological differences between the different subtypes of depression within the NESDA sample. Atypical depression was found to be associated with increased body mass index (BMI) and increased rates of metabolic syndrome (characterised by increased waist circumference, lower high-density lipid cholesterol, increased blood pressure, raised triglycerides and increased obesity), all associated with increased risk for cardiac disease and diabetes. There were also elevated rates of inflammatory markers (C-reactive protein, interleukin-6, tumour necrosis factor-α) (Lamers et al., 2013). In contrast, persons with melancholic depression had a higher increase in response on the saliva cortisol awakening curve and higher diurnal slope compared with persons with atypical depression and with controls (see Chapter 4). This pattern of results suggests that inflammatory and metabolic dysregulation is associated with atypical depression, whereas hypothalamic–pituitary–adrenal (HPA) axis hyperactivity is associated with melancholic depression (Lamers et al., 2013).

Nonetheless, the majority of evidence suggests that melancholic, atypical and non-melancholic, and non-atypical depression cannot be distinguished on aetiology, psychosocial or developmental factors (Harkness and Monroe, 2002; Kendler, 1997) or course of the depression (Kessing, 2003; Mulder et al., 2006). A six-year follow-up of the NESDA sample found few significant differences in clinical outcomes between the 'melancholic' and 'atypical' classes, confirming prior findings that these subcategories do not predict course of depression, with severity of symptoms the most important predictor of course (Lamers, Beekman, van Hemert, Schoevers and Penninx, 2016). However, the melancholic class had longer persisting suicidal thoughts throughout the follow-up, whereas the atypical class had worse somatic outcomes, with continuously high BMI and a high rate of metabolic syndrome, even after remission from episodes of major depression.

Furthermore, there is no strong evidence that subtypes of depression predict a differential treatment response to pharmacotherapy when this is examined in large-scale, randomised controlled trials (Bobo et al., 2011; McGrath et al., 2008) and once initial depression severity has been accounted for in analyses (Arnow et al., 2015; Gili et al., 2012).

Ellen dreads the autumn. As the days become shorter and the weather cold and gloomy, her spirits sink. She becomes more and more lethargic, going to bed a bit earlier each night and having trouble getting up in the dark mornings. In contrast to her summer favourites of fruits and vegetables, she finds herself eating heavier foods, with a special interest in rich, thick sauces, oily meats, breads and pastries of any kind. Often, by December she slips into a depressive episode, marked by low energy and inactivity – with sleeping and eating representing her main enjoyments. Although she believes that she will never feel good again and sometimes finds herself wishing for death, she has learned that by March or April she begins to emerge from her gloom and return to her normal life.

Seasonal pattern depressions refer to those that have an apparent regular onset during certain times of the year, and which also disappear at a characteristic time of the year. In the Northern hemisphere, the most common pattern is autumn or winter depressions, remitting in the spring. Depression with a seasonal pattern, also known as Seasonal Affective Disorder (SAD) (Rosenthal et al., 1984), which has a prevalence of approximately 2 per cent in temperate climates, demonstrates some stability in presentation across time and is more common in women (Pjrek et al., 2016; Steinhausen, Gundelfinger and Metzke, 2009). Such depressive episodes are especially marked by low energy, more sleeping, overeating and weight gain, and craving for carbohydrate foods (Jacobsen, Wehr, Sack, James and Rosenthal, 1987). A recent long-term prospective study indicated that a seasonal pattern toward a small increase in depressive symptom burden in the months surrounding the winter solstice (e.g., December–February) was found in a sample of individuals with major depression, suggesting a continuum in seasonal affective response, with individuals with SAD at one extreme (Cobb et al., 2014). Several meta-analyses indicate that SAD can be successfully treated by repeated exposure to bright light in the morning (phototherapy) (Golden et al., 2005; Martensson, Pettersson, Berglund and Ekselius, 2015), although caveats are drawn due to small sample sizes, short-term follow-ups and choice of control conditions in the treatment trials.

Depression with psychotic features is usually a severe depression, and includes presence of either hallucinations or delusions. Typically, such hallucinations or delusions have a depressive theme, such as guilt due to the belief that one has caused a terrible misfortune, belief that one is deserving of punishment or is being punished (e.g., voices accusing one of sins or failures), nihilistic beliefs (delusions about the world ending or that one is going to be killed or is already dead), or somatic delusions reflecting the belief that one is rotting away. Such delusions and hallucinations are described as mood-congruent since they are consistent with the negative, self-critical thinking found in depression. Less often, depressed individuals may have delusions and hallucinations that are not related to depressive or destructive themes (e.g., belief that one's thoughts are being broadcast on the radio, described as mood-incongruent). For a diagnosis of major depression with psychotic features, rather than schizophrenia or schizoaffective disorder, the delusions and hallucinations must only occur in the context of a major depressive episode. Psychotic depression appears to be relatively stable over repeated episodes, such that if a person has a psychotic depression, their future episodes are likely to show psychotic features (Coryell et al., 1996). Psychotic depression is associated with severe psychomotor disturbance (agitation or retardation), increased feelings of worthlessness and guilt, more severe symptoms, increased mortality and a more severe clinical course (Rothschild, 2013).

Postpartum depression

Between 40 and 80 per cent of women develop mild symptoms such as crying, insomnia, poor appetite and mood lability in the period 3–7 days after giving birth; called 'baby blues', these experiences are considered normal responses to the profound shifts in hormones, and typically spontaneously remit after several days. However, when a major depressive episode develops shortly after delivery (the first four weeks after giving birth in DSM-5, although researchers argue for three–six months post-partum), it may be identified as major depression with postpartum onset (O'Hara and McCabe, 2013). Postpartum depression is the most common complication of childbearing, with estimates ranging from 7 per cent to 13 per cent (Banti et al.,

2011; Navarro et al., 2008). Although the prevalence of depression postpartum appears to be similar to the prevalence of depression found in demographically matched, non-child-bearing women (O'Hara and McCabe, 2013), having a baby may increase the risk for depression. In a large US national survey, the likelihood of becoming depressed was 1.5 times greater within one year of being pregnant, relative to when not in a postpartum period after adjusting for sociodemographic characteristics, previous history of depression, overall health and stressful life events (Vesga-Lopez et al., 2008). A recent study examining UK primary care medical records for childbirth, depression diagnoses and antidepressant prescriptions for over 72,000 couples over a 12-year period, estimated that incidence of depression or antidepressant prescription in the first year postpartum for women was c.14 per cent, with this reducing to c.6 per cent annually and remaining stable throughout the study (Dave, Petersen, Sherr and Nazareth, 2010).

Typically, the symptoms of postpartum depression are not different from symptoms of major depressive episode (O'Hara and McCabe, 2013). Prenatal dysphoric disorder, low mood in the first 2–4 days postpartum, experiencing stressful events during pregnancy, low social support and a previous history of depression all predict increased risk for postpartum depression. Women who have experienced complications during pregnancy, including pre-eclampsia, prenatal hospitalisation and emergency caesarean section are at increased risk for being depressed two months postpartum (Blom et al., 2010).

About one woman in 1,000 has a psychotic postpartum depression. These severe episodes commonly involve delusions about the child ('he's the devil') that cause the woman to act in ways that endanger the child's life. Women who have had one such postpartum psychosis have an elevated risk for subsequent postpartum episodes with psychotic features. Such episodes are especially likely to occur among women with histories of bipolar disorder, but may also occur in unipolar depression.

Comorbidity in depression

Depression is often accompanied by other disorders, most commonly anxiety disorders (approximately 60 per cent), particularly generalised anxiety disorder, panic disorder, social phobia and post-traumatic stress disorder (PTSD). In both the original US National Comorbidity Study (NCS) and its replication, of all the community residents who met criteria for lifetime and/or 12-month major depression, approximately 75 per cent had at least one other diagnosis, with only a minority having 'pure' cases of depression (Blazer, Kessler, McGonagle and Swartz, 1994; Kessler et al., 2003). Similarly, in the NESDA study, for patients with a diagnosis of depressive disorder, 67 per cent had a current and 75 per cent had a lifetime comorbid anxiety disorder (Lamers et al., 2011).

Substance abuse and alcoholism and eating disorders are frequently accompanied by depressive disorders in both clinical and community samples. Several large epidemiological studies found rates of 25–30 per cent for co-morbid substance/alcohol abuse with depression (Davis et al., 2005; Melartin et al., 2002). The presence of either alcohol use disorders or major depression doubles the risk of the other disorder (Boden and Fergusson, 2011).

In addition, rates of *personality disorders* are elevated among people diagnosed with depression. Personality disorders refer to a set of patterns of dysfunctional conduct and attitudes that started early in life, are persistent and affect all areas of the person's functioning. Presence of personality disorders, especially borderline personality disorder, predicts the persistence of major depression (Skodol et al., 2011).

Mixtures of disorders raise a number of important implications. First, much research purporting to discuss 'depression' might actually be about the comorbid disorders; since investigators commonly do not report co-existing diagnoses, it is difficult to tell how much the results are influenced by the correlated problems rather than the depressive disorder itself. Second, the presence of comorbidity with depression usually implies worse functioning and a worse course than 'pure' depression. For example, the presence of a comorbid anxiety disorder or of elevated anxiety symptoms predicts a significantly worse course of depression and dysthymia, even over decades (Coryell et al., 2012). Likewise, a comorbid personality disorder predicts a poorer outcome (Holzel, Harter, Reese and Kriston, 2011; Skodol et al., 2011).

Challenges and alternatives to the diagnostic approach

A key benefit of the DSM and ICD systems is that detailed operationalisation of symptoms has substantively improved the reliability of diagnosis, such that there is a high level of agreement between different clinicians and researchers in classifying the presence vs. absence of disorder. Furthermore, by providing a common clinical language and terminology, it has improved communication. However, questions remain about the validity and utility of these diagnostic classifications (Horwitz and Wakefield, 2007; Hyman, 2010; Insel et al., 2010; Sanislow et al., 2010; Wakefield, 2016), especially with respect to predicting the course of illness and response to treatment – and it cannot take into account the very different mixes of symptoms across individuals and the variety of co-existing disorders.

One concern is the high rates of co-morbidity between depression and other disorders. Elevated comorbidity could be an artefact of problems with the diagnostic system itself. For example, the overlap between the symptom criteria for major depression and anxiety disorders has led to suggestions that there may be potential boundary problems in diagnostic classification, with all these diagnoses forming a cluster of disorders characterised by elevated distress (Andrews et al., 2009). There is accumulating evidence that the high levels of comorbidity observed between anxiety and mood disorders may result, in part, from temperamental dimensions common across disorders (Brown and Barlow, 2009). For example, the personality dimension of trait neuroticism, which results in increased subjective emotional distress, is strongly implicated as a vulnerability factor for both depression and anxiety, and predicts worse long-term outcome (Barlow, Ellard, Sauer-Zavala, Bullis and Carl, 2014).

A second concern is the high levels of heterogeneity within the diagnosis: two individuals could both meet criteria for major depression but only share a single common symptom, and have vastly different presentations. These problems of heterogeneity have greatly interfered with scientific progress on understanding core aetiological mechanisms of depression, not to mention barriers to treatment success. It may be that focus on observed symptom clusters rather than on potential underlying mechanisms has limited the development of treatment efficacy (Insel et al., 2010; Sanislow et al., 2010).

A third issue is whether a dimensional approach to symptoms may be at least as valid and useful as the categorical diagnostic one. For example, there is continuity between subsyndromal depression and major depression (Kessler, Zhao, Blazer and Swartz, 1997). In a number of large-scale prospective community samples, with up to 35,000 adults and follow-ups between three and 16 years, subclinical depressive symptoms predicted subsequent major depression, increasing the risk between two and five times relative to those with no symptoms (Fogel, Eaton and Ford, 2006; Judd et al., 1998; Pietrzak et al., 2013). Thus, any individual presenting with mild symptoms is at elevated risk for full-blown depression at a later date. Moreover, mild symptoms also result in significantly impaired functioning in daily life – a topic discussed in Chapter 2.

A fourth concern is how one determines what is an abnormal versus normal response and thereby set the thresholds and criteria for diagnosis. For example, the criteria of two weeks duration for major depression has been critiqued as arbitrary and not having a strong empirical basis regarding its ability to discriminate between normal versus abnormal responses to loss events, with evidence that sadness, especially grief and despair, frequently last several weeks when sampled in a community non-clinical sample (Scherer, 2015).

There is also debate as to what is a normal response to negative events such as bereavement. In earlier versions of DSM, depressive symptoms that lasted for less than two months following the death of a loved one were not considered a major depressive episode but a normal response to bereavement. However, in DSM-5, this 'bereavement exclusion' was removed on the grounds that there are few differences in course, background and treatment response between bereavement-related depression and non-bereavement depression (Zisook et al., 2012). However, others have argued that this makes normal sadness pathological, and, instead that a transient and self-limiting period of low mood and associated symptoms may be a normal and proportional response to a range of difficult life events including bereavement, losing a job or the end of a relationship (Horwitz, 2015; Horwitz and Wakefield, 2007; Wakefield, 2016). These two authors cite evidence that such periods of 'uncomplicated' depression including bereavement-excluded depression do differ from major depression in duration and recurrence (Wakefield and First, 2012; Wakefield and Schmitz, 2013). In this view, major depression is distinguished from normal sadness by emotional responses that are extreme, disproportionate or prolonged in response to context and circumstances (Wakefield and Schmitz, 2014).

On the basis of these concerns, several alternatives to formal diagnostic categories are being explored. One approach involves a focus on processes and mechanisms that are common across diverse disorders (the 'transdiagnostic' approach; Harvey, Watkins, Mansell and Shafran, 2004). For example, repetitive negative thinking (rumination or worry) is a cognitive process common across depression and anxiety disorders, which has been causally implicated in their onset and maintenance (Nolen-Hoeksema and Watkins, 2011). Similarly, stress, early abuse, negative life events, trauma and having a parent who has a mental health problem, all predict future risk for a range of mental health problems, without specifically predicting what disorder(s) the individual will develop (Conway, Starr, Espejo, Brennan and Hammen, 2016). Likewise, genetic risks for psychopathology are not uniquely related to specific disorders but apply across traditional diagnostic boundaries (Buckholtz and Meyer-Lindenberg, 2012).

A related approach is to find and study the separate units within disorders – the intermediate phenotypes or endophenotypes, which are not the disorders themselves but instead precursor components such as biomarkers or cognitive markers that are considered to be heritable and that are associated with and present at a higher rate in individuals with the disorder, and thus provide a step between genes and clinical phenotypes. Endophenotypes include behaviours and cognitive processes such as anhedonia, trait neuroticism, poor working memory, but also neural and biological processes such as sustained amygdala reactivity and decreased dorsolateral prefrontal cortex activity and hypothalamic–pituitary–adrenal axis dysregulation (Goldstein and Klein, 2014).

One specific instantiation of these approaches is the Research Domain Criteria Initiative from the US National Institute of Mental Health (RDoC) (Cuthbert and Insel, 2013; Cuthbert and Kozak, 2013; Insel et al., 2010; Sanislow et al., 2010), which aims to 'develop new ways of classifying disorders based on dimensions of observable behaviours and brain functions' rather than by diagnosis (Sanislow et al., 2010, p. 631). RDoC adopts both a transdiagnostic and a dimensional approach, reflecting processes that are shared across traditional diagnostic categories and span the range from normal to abnormal function. The goal is to define the basic dimensions of functioning to be studied across genetic, neurobiological and psychological levels-of-analysis, by examining putative endophenotypes. These are organised together into constructs where they repeatedly co-occur and change together as a shared cluster, for example, in depression, a putative construct is Loss, involving associated molecular mechanisms (e.g., inflammatory processes), neural activity (e.g., sustained amygdala reactivity), physiological activation (e.g., HPA axis dysregulation) and behaviours such as rumination, withdrawal, crying and sadness. RDoC aims to classify on homogeneity in the presentation and clustering of these biological and psychological mechanisms, and to ascertain the impact of this approach for improving understanding and treatment of psychiatric disorders. This is an ambitious and long-term project, and we don't yet know whether it is achievable. As a classification tool, it will be judged on the same criteria as existing diagnostic systems, namely, reliability, validity and utility.

An alternative transdiagnostic and dimensional approach proposes that the structure of disorders such as depression is best described as a complex network of components that interact in dynamic ways (Borsboom and Cramer, 2013). These network approaches argue that instead of depressive symptoms (e.g., insomnia, low mood) all resulting from a single underlying syndrome (i.e., major depression), they can instead be described as a complex network of interacting components, which influence each other in dynamic and reciprocal loops, for example, poor sleep leads to tiredness, which leads to low mood, which impairs sleep (Kendler, Zachar and Craver, 2011). In this model, there is not a single disorder per se, but individuals differ in the strength of the causal connections between symptoms and mental states, and thus in the risk that they interact to produce a vicious spiral that results in a grouping of severe symptoms versus occasional or short-lived symptoms (Wichers, 2014). Consistent with this model, using experience sampling methods, self-rated momentary mental states (e.g., 'down', 'insecure'), completed randomly ten times a day for five days, were more strongly connected moment-to-moment in individuals with a diagnosis of depression than in individuals with no diagnosis (Wigman et al., 2015).

Assessing depression

Both clinical description and research on depression rely on two types of methods: those that measure the severity of depressive experiences, and those that measure the presence of diagnosable conditions. This section briefly describes the most frequently used procedures, acknowledging that many more exist than will be discussed.

Diagnostic methods

Applying the DSM or ICD criteria for major depression and dysthymia requires interviewing the individual (or an appropriate informant). For research purposes it is highly desirable to use standardised interviews in which the relevant questions are asked in the same way each time by each interviewer. Such procedures ensure comparability and communicability across different studies purporting to investigate similar clinical conditions.

The principal interview to cover the DSM diagnostic criteria is the Structured Clinical Interview for DSM (SCID) (current version, DSM-5), which covers all the major diagnostic categories (First, Williams, Karg and Spitzer , 2015; Spitzer, Williams, Gibbon and First, 1996). (A child version of the Schedule for Affective Disorders and Schizophrenia (SADS), called the Kiddie-SADS, continues to be widely used for juvenile populations.) The semi-structured probes of the SCID are intended to cover both current and lifetime history of disorders, and clinical judgements are required so that it is assumed that interviewers have had clinical training. Field trials have indicated adequate reliability for major diagnoses. The following is an example of a probe for symptoms of major depressive episode:

In the last month . . . has there been a period of time when you were feeling depressed or down most of the day nearly every day? (What was that like?)

IF YES: How long did it last? (As long as two weeks?)

Likewise, the Composite International Diagnostic Interview (CIDI); (Robins et al., 1988) is a standardised diagnostic interview commonly used for epidemiological research. Likewise, the Composite International Diagnostic Interview (CIDI; Robins et al., 1988) is a structured diagnostic interview that can be administered by trained nonclinical staff, and is thus suitable for use in large epidemiological research samples.

Assessing severity of depression

Several methods are commonly used to evaluate the severity of current depression separate from diagnosis. One approach is interview-based, such as the Hamilton Rating Scale for Depression (HRSD; Hamilton, 1960). It remains the most frequently used interviewer rated measure of depression, and contains 21 items covering mood, behavioural, somatic and cognitive symptoms. By convention, only 17 of the original 21 items are typically scored. For the 17-item version, total scores of 0–7 indicate no depression, 8–17 mild depression, 18–25 moderate depression and scores of 26 plus severe depression (Williams, 1998). The HRSD has been shown to be sensitive to change in the severity of depressive symptomatology over time, and consequently, is useful as a measure of the efficacy of therapy.

There are numerous self-report questionnaires designed to measure depression or depressed affect including the Beck Depression Inventory (BDI, original version, Beck, Ward, Mendelson, Mock and Erbaugh, 1961; revised version, BDI-II, Beck, Steer and Brown, 1996) and the Patient Health Questionnaire (PHQ-9; Spitzer, Kroenke, Williams and Patient Health Questionnaire Primary Care Study Group, 1999). The BDI-II consists of 21 items selected to represent the affective, cognitive, motivational and physiological symptoms of depression, with patients reporting how they have been feeling over the past two weeks on a graded series of four alternative statements, ranging from neutral (e.g., 'I do not feel sad') scored 0, to a maximum level of severity scored 3 (e.g., 'I am so sad or unhappy that I can't stand it'), giving a range of scores from 0 to 63. Scores of 0–13 indicate no depression, 14–19 mild depression, 20–28 moderate depression and scores of 29–63 severe depression.

The PHQ-9 consists of nine items that each correspond to the DSM-5 criteria for major depression, and respondents indicate for each symptom how much it has bothered them in the past two weeks (0 'not at all', 1 'several days', 2 'more than half the days', 3 'nearly every day'). It has been used both as an index of levels of symptoms and also as a screening tool for diagnosis: a meta-analysis of 17 validation studies concluded that it has good diagnostic properties for depression (Gilbody, Richards, Brealey and Hewitt, 2007). It is now part of the minimum data set that is collected after every treatment session for depression in the NHS Improving Access to Psychological Treatment service in the UK.

Summary

◆ Depression ranges from a normal sad mood lasting only moments to a profoundly impairing condition that may be life threatening.
◆ To be clinically significant, depression involves changes in mood, cognitive functioning, behaviour and bodily states, and must persist over time and interfere with normal behaviour.
◆ A crucial distinction must be made between unipolar and bipolar depression, due to different causes, course and treatment.
◆ Both children and adults may be diagnosed with major depression or persistent depressive disorder.
◆ Depression presents many faces and may co-exist with other disorders.
◆ The diagnostic system has been criticised with respect to validity, utility and heterogeneity; alternative approaches that have been proposed include transdiagnostic, dimensional and endophenotype systems of organising clinical presentations.
◆ Different instruments are available to measure depression diagnoses and severity of depressive symptoms.

References

American Psychiatric Association. (2013). *Diagnostic and statistical manual of mental disorders (5th edn.)*. Washington, DC: Author.

Andrews, G., Goldberg, D. P., Krueger, R. F., Carpenter, W. T., Hyman, S. E., Sachdev, P. and Pine, D. S. (2009). Exploring the feasibility of a meta-structure for DSM-V and ICD-11: could it improve utility and validity? *Psychological Medicine, 39*(12), 1993–2000.

Angst, J., Azorin, J. M., Bowden, C. L., Perugi, G., Vieta, E., Gamma, A. and Young, A. (2011). Prevalence and characteristics of undiagnosed bipolar disorders in patients with a major depressive episode: the BRIDGE Study. *Archives of General Psychiatry, 68*(8), 791–799.

Angst, J., Cui, L. H., Swendsen, J., Rothen, S., Cravchik, A. and Merikangas, K. R. (2010). Major depressive disorder with subthreshold bipolarity in the National

Comorbidity Survey Replication. *American Journal of Psychiatry, 167*(10), 1194–1201.

Angst, J. and Grobler, C. (2015). Unipolar mania: a necessary diagnostic concept. *European Archives of Psychiatry and Clinical Neuroscience, 265*(4), 273–280.

Arnow, B. A., Blasey, C., Williams, L. M., Palmer, D. M., Rekshan, W., Schatzberg, A. F., . . . Rush, A. J. (2015). Depression subtypes in predicting antidepressant response: a report from the iSPOT-D Trial. *American Journal of Psychiatry, 172*(8), 743–750.

Asarnow, L. D., Soehner, A. M. and Harvey, A. G. (2014). Basic sleep and circadian science as building blocks for behavioral interventions: a translational approach for mood disorders. *Behavioral Neuroscience, 128*(3), 360–370.

Axelson, D., Findling, R. L., Fristad, M. A., Kowatch, R. A., Youngstrom, E. A., Horwitz, S. M., . . . Birmaher, B. (2012). Examining the proposed Disruptive Mood Dysregulation Disorder diagnosis in children in the Longitudinal Assessment of Manic Symptoms Study. *Journal of Clinical Psychiatry, 73*(10), 1342–1350.

Banti, S., Mauri, M., Oppo, A., Borri, C., Rambelli, C., Ramacciotti, D., . . . Cassano, G. B. (2011). From the third month of pregnancy to 1 year postpartum. Prevalence, incidence, recurrence, and new onset of depression. Results from the Perinatal Depression-Research and Screening Unit study. *Comprehensive Psychiatry, 52*(4), 343–351.

Barlow, D. H., Ellard, K. K., Sauer-Zavala, S., Bullis, J. R. and Carl, J. R. (2014). The origins of neuroticism. *Perspectives on Psychological Science, 9*(5), 481–496.

Beck, A. T. (1967). *Depression: clinical, experimental and theoretical aspects.* New York: Harper and Row.

Beck, A. T. (1976). *Cognitive therapy and emotional disorders.* New York: Meridian.

Beck, A. T., Steer, R. A. and Brown, G. K. (1996). *The Beck Depression Inventory – Second Edition.* San Antonio, TX: The Psychological Corporation.

Beck, A. T., Ward, C. H., Mendelson, M., Mock, J. and Erbaugh, J. (1961). An inventory for measuring depression. *Archives of General Psychiatry, 4*, 561–574.

Beesdo, K., Hofler, M., Leibenluft, E., Lieb, R., Bauer, M. and Pfennig, A. (2009). Mood episodes and mood disorders: patterns of incidence and conversion in the first three decades of life. *Bipolar Disorders, 11*(6), 637–649.

Benca, R. M., Obermeyer, W. H., Thisted, R. A. and Gillin, J. C. (1992). Sleep and psychiatric-disorders – a meta-analysis. *Archives of General Psychiatry, 49*, 651–668.

Blazer, D. G., Kessler, R. C., McGonagle, K. A. and Swartz, M. S. (1994). The prevalence and distribution of major depression in a national community sample – the National Comorbidity Survey. *American Journal of Psychiatry, 151*, 979–986.

Blom, E. A., Jansen, P. W., Verhulst, F. C., Hofman, A., Raat, H., Jaddoe, V. W. V., . . . Tiemeier, H. (2010). Perinatal complications increase the risk of postpartum depression. The Generation R Study. *BJOG: an International Journal of Obstetrics and Gynaecology, 117*(11), 1390–1398.

Bobo, W. V., Chen, H., Trivedi, M. H., Stewart, J. W., Nierenberg, A. A., Fava, M., . . . Shelton, R. C. (2011). Randomized comparison of selective serotonin reuptake inhibitor (escitalopram) monotherapy and antidepressant combination pharmacotherapy for major depressive disorder with melancholic features: a CO-MED report. *Journal of Affective Disorders*, *133*(3), 467–476.

Boden, J. M. and Fergusson, D. M. (2011). Alcohol and depression. *Addiction*, *106*(5), 906–914.

Borsboom, D. and Cramer, A. O. J. (2013). Network analysis: An integrative approach to the structure of psychopathology. *Annual Review of Clinical Psychology*, *9*, 91–121.

Brown, T. A. and Barlow, D. H. (2009). A proposal for a dimensional classification system based on the shared features of the DSM-IV anxiety and mood disorders: implications for assessment and treatment. *Psychological Assessment*, *21*(3), 256–271.

Buckholtz, J. W. and Meyer-Lindenberg, A. (2012). Psychopathology and the human connectome: toward a transdiagnostic model of risk for mental illness. *Neuron*, *74*(6), 990–1004.

Bufferd, S. J., Dougherty, L. R., Carlson, G. A., Rose, S. and Klein, D. N. (2012). Psychiatric disorders in preschoolers: continuity from ages 3 to 6. *American Journal of Psychiatry*, *169*(11), 1157–1164.

Bukh, J. D., Andersen, P. K. and Kessing, L. V. (2016). Rates and predictors of remission, recurrence and conversion to bipolar disorder after the first lifetime episode of depression – a prospective 5-year follow-up study. *Psychological Medicine*, *46*(6), 1151–1161.

Buyukdura, J. S., McClintock, S. M. and Croarkin, P. E. (2011). Psychomotor retardation in depression: biological underpinnings, measurement, and treatment. *Progress in Neuro-Psychopharmacology and Biological Psychiatry*, *35*(2), 395–409.

Cobb, B. S., Coryell, W. H., Cavanaugh, J., Keller, M., Solomon, D. A., Endicott, J., . . . Fiedorowicz, J. G. (2014). Seasonal variation of depressive symptoms in unipolar major depressive disorder. *Comprehensive Psychiatry*, *55*(8), 1891–1899.

Conway, C. C., Starr, L. R., Espejo, E. P., Brennan, P. A. and Hammen, C. (2016). Stress responsivity and the structure of common mental disorders: transdiagnostic internalizing and externalizing dimensions are associated with contrasting stress appraisal biases. *Journal of Abnormal Psychology*, *125*(8), 1079–1089.

Copeland, W. E., Angold, A., Costello, E. J. and Egger, H. (2013). Prevalence, comorbidity, and correlates of DSM-5 proposed Disruptive Mood Dysregulation Disorder. *American Journal of Psychiatry*, *170*(2), 173–179.

Coryell, W., Fiedorowicz, J. G., Solomon, D., Leon, A. C., Rice, J. P. and Keller, M. B. (2012). Effects of anxiety on the long-term course of depressive disorders. *British Journal of Psychiatry*, *200*(3), 210–215.

Coryell, W., Leon, A., Winokur, G., Endicott, J., Keller, M., Akiskal, H., Solomon, D. (1996). Importance of psychotic features to long-term course in major depressive disorder. *American Journal of Psychiatry*, *153*, 483–489.

Cuellar, A. K., Johnson, S. L. and Winters, R. (2005). Distinctions between bipolar and unipolar depression. *Clinical Psychology Review*, *25*, 307–339.

Cuthbert, B. N. and Insel, T. R. (2013). Toward the future of psychiatric diagnosis: the seven pillars of RDoC. *BMC Medicine, 11.*

Cuthbert, B. N. and Kozak, M. J. (2013). Constructing constructs for psychopathology: the NIMH Research Domain Criteria. *Journal of Abnormal Psychology, 122*(3), 928–937.

Dave, S., Petersen, I., Sherr, L. and Nazareth, I. (2010). Incidence of maternal and paternal depression in primary care. *Archives of Pediatrics and Adolescent Medicine, 164*(11), 1038–1044.

Davidson, J. R. T., Miller, R. D., Turnbull, C. D. and Sullivan, J. L. (1982). Atypical depression. *Archives of General Psychiatry, 39,* 527–534.

Davis, L. L., Rush, J. A., Wisniewski, S. R., Rice, K., Cassano, P., Jewell, M. E. . . . McGrath, P. J. (2005). Substance use disorder comorbidity in major depressive disorder: an exploratory analysis of the Sequenced Treatment Alternatives to Relieve Depression cohort. *Comprehensive Psychiatry, 46,* 81–89.

Epperson, C. N., Steiner, M., Hartlage, S. A., Eriksson, E., Schmidt, P. J., Jones, I. and Yonkers, K. A. (2012). Premenstrual Dysphoric Disorder: evidence for a new category for DSM-5. *American Journal of Psychiatry, 169*(5), 465–475.

First, M.B., Williams, J. B. W., Karg, R. S. and Spitzer, R. L. (2015). *Structured Clinical Interview for DSM-V (SCID).* Arlington VA: American Psychiatric Association.

Fogel, J., Eaton, W. W. and Ford, D. E. (2006). Minor depression as a predictor of the first onset of major depressive disorder over a 15-year follow-up. *Acta Psychiatrica Scandinavica, 113,* 36–43.

Gilbody, S., Richards, D., Brealey, S. and Hewitt, C. (2007). Screening for depression in medical settings with the Patient Health Questionnaire (PHQ): a diagnostic meta-analysis. *Journal of General Internal Medicine, 22*(11), 1596–1602.

Gili, M., Roca, M., Armengol, S., Asensio, D., Garcia-Campayo, J. and Parker, G. (2012). Clinical patterns and treatment outcome in patients with melancholic, atypical and non-melancholic depressions. *PLOS One, 7*(10), 8.

Gilman, S. E., Dupuy, J. M. and Perlis, R. H. (2012). Risks for the transition from major depressive disorder to bipolar disorder in the National Epidemiologic Survey on Alcohol and Related Conditions. *Journal of Clinical Psychiatry, 73*(6), 829–836.

Golden, R. N., Gaynes, B. N., Ekstrom, R. D., Hamer, R. M., Jacobsen, F. M., Suppes, T. . . . Nemeroff, C. B. (2005). The efficacy of light therapy in the treatment of mood disorders: a review and meta-analysis of the evidence. *American Journal of Psychiatry, 162,* 656–662.

Goldstein, B. L. and Klein, D. N. (2014). A review of selected candidate endophenotypes for depression. *Clinical Psychology Review, 34,* 417–427.

Hamilton, M. (1960). A rating scale for depression. *Journal of Neurology Neurosurgery and Psychiatry, 12,* 52–62.

Harkness, K. L. and Monroe, S. M. (2002). Childhood adversity and the endogenous versus nonendogenous distinction in women with major depression. *American Journal of Psychiatry, 159,* 387–393.

Harvey, A. G. (2011). Sleep and circadian functioning: critical mechanisms in the mood disorders? *Annual Review of Clinical Psychology, 7,* 297–319.

Harvey, A. G., Watkins, E., Mansell, W. and Shafran, R. (2004). *Cognitive behavioural processes across psychological disorders.* Oxford: Oxford University Press.

Herrick, D. D. and Sateia, M. J. (2016). Insomnia and depression: a reciprocal relationship. *Psychiatric Annals, 46*(3), 164–172.

Holzel, L., Harter, M., Reese, C. and Kriston, L. (2011). Risk factors for chronic depression – a systematic review. *Journal of Affective Disorders, 129*(1–3), 1–13.

Horwitz, A. V. (2015). The DSM-5 and the continuing transformation of normal sadness into depressive disorder. *Emotion Review, 7*(3), 209–215.

Horwitz, A. V. and Wakefield, J. C. (2007). *The loss of sadness: how psychiatry transformed normal sorrow into depressive disorder.* New York: Oxford University Press.

Hyman, S. E. (2010). The diagnosis of mental disorders: the problem of reification. *Annual Review of Clinical Psychology, 6,* 155–179.

Insel, T., Cuthbert, B., Garvey, M., Heinssen, R., Pine, D. S., Quinn, K., . . . Wang, P. (2010). Research Domain Criteria (RDoC): toward a new classification framework for research on mental disorders. *American Journal of Psychiatry, 167*(7), 748–751.

Jacobsen, F. M., Wehr, T. A., Sack, D. A., James, S. P. and Rosenthal, N. E. (1987). Seasonal Affective-Disorder – a review of the syndrome and its public-health implications. *American Journal of Public Health, 77,* 57–60.

Judd, L. L., Akiskal, H. S., Maser, J. D., Zeller, P. J., Endicott, J., Coryell, W. . . . Keller, M. B. (1998). A prospective 12-year study of subsyndromal and syndromal depressive symptoms in unipolar major depressive disorders. *Archives of General Psychiatry, 55,* 694–700.

Kendler, K. S. (1997). The diagnostic validity of melancholic major depression in a population-based sample of female twins. *Archives of General Psychiatry, 54,* 299–304.

Kendler, K. S., Zachar, P. and Craver, C. (2011). What kinds of things are psychiatric disorders? *Psychological Medicine, 41*(6), 1143–1150.

Kessler, R. C., Berglund, P., Demler, O., Jin, R., Koretz, D., Merikangas, K. R. . . . Wang, P. S. (2003). The epidemiology of major depressive disorder – results from the National Comorbidity Survey Replication (NCS-R). *JAMA-Journal of the American Medical Association, 289,* 3095–3105.

Kessler, R. C., Zhao, S. Y., Blazer, D. G. and Swartz, M. (1997). Prevalence, correlates, and course of minor depression and major depression in the national comorbidity survey. *Journal of Affective Disorders, 45,* 19–30.

Klein, D. N. (2008). Classification of depressive disorders in the DSM-V: Proposal for a two-dimension system. *Journal of Abnormal Psychology, 117*(3), 552–560.

Klein, D. N. (2010). Chronic depression: diagnosis and classification. *Current Directions in Psychological Science, 19*(2), 96–100

Klein, D. N. and Kotov, R. (2016). Course of depression in a 10-year pospective study: evidence for qualitatively distinct subgroups. *Journal of Abnormal Psychology, 125*(3), 337–348.

Klinger, E. (1993). Loss of interest. In C.G. Costello (ed.), *Symptoms of depression* (pp. 43–62). New York: Wiley.

Kovacs, M., Goldston, D. and Gatsonis, C. (1993). Suicidal behaviors and childhood-onset depressive disorders – a longitudinal investigation. *Journal of the American Academy of Child and Adolescent Psychiatry, 32*, 8–20.

Kupfer, D. J. (1995). Sleep research in depressive illness – clinical implications: a tasting menu. *Biological Psychiatry, 38*, 391–403.

Lamers, F., Beekman, A. T. F., van Hemert, A. M., Schoevers, R. A. and Penninx, B. (2016). Six-year longitudinal course and outcomes of subtypes of depression. *British Journal of Psychiatry, 208*(1), 62–68.

Lamers, F., Burstein, M., He, J. P., Avenevoli, S., Angst, J. and Merikangas, K. R. (2012). Structure of major depressive disorder in adolescents and adults in the US general population. *British Journal of Psychiatry, 201*(2), 143–150.

Lamers, F., de Jonge, P., Nolen, W. A., Smit, J. H., Zitman, F. G., Beekman, A. T. F. and Penninx, B. (2010). Identifying depressive subtypes in a large cohort study: results from the Netherlands Study of Depression and Anxiety (NESDA). *Journal of Clinical Psychiatry, 71*(12), 1582–1589.

Lamers, F., Rhebergen, D., Merikangas, K. R., de Jonge, P., Beekman, A. T. F. and Penninx, B. (2012). Stability and transitions of depressive subtypes over a 2-year follow-up. *Psychological Medicine, 42*(10), 2083–2093.

Lamers, F., van Oppen, P., Comijs, H. C., Smit, J. H., Spinhoven, P., van Balkom, A. . . . Penninx, B. (2011). Comorbidity patterns of anxiety and depressive disorders in a large cohort study: the Netherlands Study of Depression and Anxiety (NESDA). *Journal of Clinical Psychiatry, 72*(3), 341–348.

Lamers, F., Vogelzangs, N., Merikangas, K. R., de Jonge, P., Beekman, A. T. F. and Penninx, B. (2013). Evidence for a differential role of HPA-axis function, inflammation and metabolic syndrome in melancholic versus atypical depression. *Molecular Psychiatry, 18*(6), 692–699.

Leibenluft, E. (2011). Severe mood dysregulation, irritability, and the diagnostic boundaries of bipolar disorder in youths. *American Journal of Psychiatry, 168*(2), 129–142.

Leventhal, A. M. and Rehm, L. P. (2005). The empirical status of melancholia: implications for psychology. *Clinical Psychology Review, 25*(1), 25–44.

Lewinsohn, P. M., Rohde, P. and Seeley, J. R. (1998). Major depressive disorder in older adolescents: Prevalence, risk factors, and clinical implications. *Clinical Psychology Review, 18*, 765–794.

Luby, J. L. (2010). Preschool depression: the importance of identification of depression early in development. *Current Directions in Psychological Science, 19*(2), 91–95.

Luby, J. L., Gaffrey, M. S., Tillman, R., April, L. M. and Belden, A. C. (2014). Trajectories of preschool disorders to full DSM depression at school age and early adolescence: continuity of preschool depression. *American Journal of Psychiatry, 171*(7), 768–776.

Luby, J. L., Si, X., Belden, A. C., Tandon, M. and Spitznagel, E. (2009). Preschool depression homotypic continuity and course over 24 months. *Archives of General Psychiatry, 66*(8), 897–905.

Lustberg, L. and Reynolds, C. F. (2000). Depression and insomnia: questions of cause and effect. *Sleep Medicine Reviews*, *4*, 253–262.

Martensson, B., Pettersson, A., Berglund, L. and Ekselius, L. (2015). Bright white light therapy in depression: a critical review of the evidence. *Journal of Affective Disorders*, *182*, 1–7.

Mazzarini, L., Colom, F., Pacchiarotti, I., Nivoli, A. M. A., Murru, A., Bonnin, C. M. . . . Vieta, E. (2010). Psychotic versus non-psychotic bipolar II disorder. *Journal of Affective Disorders*, *126*(1–2), 55–60.

McGrath, P. J., Khan, A. Y., Trivedi, M. H., Stewart, J. W., Morris, D. W., Wisniewski, S. R. . . . Rush, A. J. (2008). Response to a selective serotonin reuptake inhibitor (Citalopram) in major depressive disorder with melancholic features: A STAR*D Report. *Journal of Clinical Psychiatry*, *69*(12), 1847–1855.

Melartin, T. K., Rytsala, H. J., Leskela, U. S., Lestela-Mielonen, P. S., Sokero, T. P. and Isometsa, E. T. (2002). Current comorbidity of psychiatric disorders among DSM-IV major depressive disorder patients in psychiatric care in the Vantaa Depression Study. *Journal of Clinical Psychiatry*, *63*, 126–134.

Mitchell, P. B., Frankland, A., Hadzi-Pavlovic, D., Roberts, G., Corry, J., Wright, A. . . . Breakspear, M. (2011). Comparison of depressive episodes in bipolar disorder and in major depressive disorder within bipolar disorder pedigrees. *British Journal of Psychiatry*, *199*(4), 303–309.

Mulder, R. T., Joyce, P. R., Frampton, C. M. A., Luty, S. E. and Sullivan, P. F. (2006). Six months of treatment for depression: Outcome and predictors of the course of illness. *American Journal of Psychiatry*, *163*, 95–100.

Navarro, P., Garcia-Esteve, L., Ascaso, C., Aguado, J., Gelabert, E. and Martin-Santos, R. (2008). Non-psychotic psychiatric disorders after childbirth: prevalence and comorbidity in a community sample. *Journal of Affective Disorders*, *109*(1–2), 171–176.

Nock, M. K., Green, J. G., Hwang, I., McLaughlin, K. A., Sampson, N. A., Zaslavsky, A. M. and Kessler, R. C. (2013). Prevalence, correlates, and treatment of lifetime suicidal behavior among adolescents: results from the National Comorbidity Survey Replication Adolescent Supplement. *JAMA Psychiatry*, *70*(3), 300–310.

Nolen-Hoeksema, S. and Watkins, E. R. (2011). A heuristic for developing trans-diagnostic models of psychopathology: explaining multifinality and divergent trajectories. *Perspectives on Psychological Science*, *6*(6), 589–609.

O'Hara, M. W. and McCabe, J. E. (2013). Postpartum depression: current status and future directions. *Annual Review of Clinical Psychology*, *9*, 379–407.

Pietrzak, R. H., Kinley, J., Afifi, T. O., Enns, M. W., Fawcett, J. and Sareen, J. (2013). Subsyndromal depression in the United States: prevalence, course, and risk for incident psychiatric outcomes. *Psychological Medicine*, *43*(7), 1401–1414.

Pjrek, E., Baldinger-Melich, P., Spies, M., Papageorgiou, K., Kasper, S. and Winkler, D. (2016). Epidemiology and socioeconomic impact of seasonal affective disorder in Austria. *European Psychiatry*, *32*, 28–33.

Robins, L. N., Wing, J., Wittchen, H. U., Helzer, J. E., Babor, T. F., Burke, J. . . . Towle, L. H. (1988). The Composite International Diagnostic Interview – an epidemiologic instrument suitable for use in conjunction with different diagnostic systems and in different cultures. *Archives of General Psychiatry, 45,* 1069–1077.

Rosenthal, N. E., Sack, D. A., Gillin, J. C., Lewy, A. J., Goodwin, F. K., Davenport, Y. . . . Wehr, T. A. (1984). Seasonal affective disorder – a description of the syndrome and preliminary findings with light therapy. *Archives of General Psychiatry, 41,* 72–80.

Rothschild, A. J. (2013). Challenges in the treatment of major depressive disorder with psychotic features. *Schizophrenia Bulletin, 39*(4), 787–796.

Sanislow, C. A., Pine, D. S., Quinn, K. J., Kozak, M. J., Garvey, M. A., Heinssen, R. K. . . . Cuthbert, B. N. (2010). Developing constructs for psychopathology research: Research Domain Criteria. *Journal of Abnormal Psychology, 119*(4), 631–639.

Scherer, K. R. (2015). When and why are emotions disturbed? Suggestions based on theory and data from emotion research. *Emotion Review, 7*(3), 238–249.

Schrijvers, D., Hulstijn, W. and Sabbe, B. G. C. (2008). Psychomotor symptoms in depression: a diagnostic, pathophysiological and therapeutic tool. *Journal of Affective Disorders, 109*(1–2), 1–20.

Skodol, A. E., Grilo, C. M., Keyes, K. M., Geier, T., Grant, B. F. and Hasin, D. S. (2011). Relationship of personality disorders to the course of major depressive disorder in a nationally representative sample. *American Journal of Psychiatry, 168*(3), 257–264.

Spitzer, R. L., Kroenke, K., Williams, J. B. and Patient Health Questionnaire Primary Care Study Group. (1999). Validation and utility of a self-report version of PRIME-MD: The PHQ primary care study. *JAMA, 282*(18), 1737–1744.

Spitzer, R. L., Williams, J. B. W., Gibbon, M. and First, M. B. (1996). *Structured Clinical Interview for DSM-IV (SCID).* Washington DC: American Psychiatric Association.

Steinhausen, H. C., Gundelfinger, R. and Metzke, C. W. (2009). Prevalence of self-reported seasonal affective disorders and the validity of the seasonal pattern assessment questionnaire in young adults Findings from a Swiss community study. *Journal of Affective Disorders, 115*(3), 347–354.

Stringaris, A., Baroni, A., Haimm, C., Brotman, M., Lowe, C. H., Myers, F. . . . Leibenluft, E. (2010). Pediatric bipolar disorder versus severe mood dysregulation: risk for manic episodes on follow-up. *Journal of the American Academy of Child and Adolescent Psychiatry, 49*(4), 397–405.

Thapar, A., Collishaw, S., Pine, D. S. and Thapar, A. K. (2012). Depression in adolescence. *Lancet, 379*(9820), 1056–1067.

Vesga-Lopez, O., Blanco, C., Keyes, K., Olfson, M., Grant, B. F. and Hasin, D. S. (2008). Psychiatric disorders in pregnant and postpartum women in the United States. *Archives of General Psychiatry, 65*(7), 805–815.

Wakefield, J. C. (2016). Diagnostic issues and controversies in DSM-5: return of the false positives problem. *Annual Review of Clinical Psychology, 12,* 105–132.

Wakefield, J. C. and First, M. B. (2012). Validity of the bereavement exclusion to major depression: does the empirical evidence support the proposal to eliminate the exclusion in DSM-5? *World Psychiatry, 11*(1), 3–10.

Wakefield, J. C. and Schmitz, M. F. (2013). Normal vs. disordered bereavement-related depression: are the differences real or tautological? *Acta Psychiatrica Scandinavica, 127*(2), 159–168.

Wakefield, J. C. and Schmitz, M. F. (2014). Predictive validation of single-episode uncomplicated depression as a benign subtype of unipolar major depression. *Acta Psychiatrica Scandinavica, 129*(6), 445–457.

Wichers, M. (2014). The dynamic nature of depression: a new micro-level perspective of mental disorder that meets current challenges. *Psychological Medicine, 44*(7), 1349–1360.

Wigman, J. T. W., van Os, J., Borsboom, D., Wardenaar, K. J., Epskamp, S., Klippel, A. . . . Merge. (2015). Exploring the underlying structure of mental disorders: cross-diagnostic differences and similarities from a network perspective using both a top-down and a bottom-up approach. *Psychological Medicine, 45*(11), 2375–2387.

Williams, J. (1998). A structured clinical interview guide for the Hamilton Depression Rating Scale. *Archives of General Psychiatry, 45*, 742–747.

World Health Organization (1993). *The ICD-10 classification of mental and behavioural disorders: diagnostic criteria for research.* Geneva, Switzerland: WHO.

Zisook, S., Corruble, E., Duan, N. H., Iglewicz, A., Karam, E. G., Lanuoette, N. . . . Young, I. T. (2012). The bereavement exclusion and DSM-5. *Depression and Anxiety, 29*(5), 425–443.

2

Course and consequences
of depression

While depression has sometimes been called the 'common cold' of psychological disorders, the label is misleading because it implies that suffering from depression is merely a bothersome but brief and mild inconvenience. Unfortunately, nothing could be farther from the truth. Depression may be so severe as to be lethal, and for many if not most sufferers, it is a recurring or even chronic disorder. Moreover, its effects may be devastating to the individual – not only in suffering, but also in terms of the damaging effects on one's work, family, marital relations and physical health. Indeed, the consequences to the lives of depressed people may even create environmental conditions that increase the likelihood that depression will continue or recur. Therefore, in this chapter we explore the features of the course of depression, including its impairing consequences.

Course of unipolar major depressive disorder

Age of onset of depression

Depression is increasingly recognised as a disorder of relatively young onset. Once viewed as a disorder of middle age, today's researchers observe that adolescence and early adulthood are the most typical periods when clinically significant depression emerges. Kessler and Bromet (2013) reviewed findings from epidemiological surveys sponsored by the World Health

Organization in ten high income and eight low–middle income countries. They found that the median age of onset of depressive disorders was in the mid-20s, with smaller increases of first onset in mid-adulthood and older adulthood. McGorry, Purcell, Goldstone and Amminger (2011) similarly found in their review that high-frequency disorders such as depression, as well as anxiety and substance abuse, have onsets that appear by age 25 in 75 per cent of cases. Young adulthood also emerged as the period of most elevated depressive symptoms in a longitudinal study of adults, decreasing across middle adulthood and then trending upward in older ages (Sutin et al., 2013).

Studies specifically based on adolescent samples such as the US National Comorbidity Survey Adolescent Supplement found that 14 per cent of youth between ages 13 and 18 met criteria for major depression or dysthymic disorder, with rates increasing two-fold between 13–14 and 17–18 (Merikangas et al., 2010). Beesdo, Pine, Lieb and Wittchen (2010) also observed elevated rates of onset of depression in a large German sample of adolescents. Their study additionally highlighted the commonly observed high level of co-occurrence between anxiety disorders (with earlier onset) and depressive disorders (later in adolescence).

It should be emphasised that age of onset may portend potentially important differences between groups. Recent evidence suggests that depression with first onset in childhood, adolescence, adulthood and older adulthood may have somewhat different implications in terms of aetiology and clinical course. Core differences between the age groups are briefly noted in this chapter and Chapter 3. Note that many studies of depression's causes and treatments, including many reviewed in this book, often have not distinguished samples by onset age and therefore may not generalise to studies differing in study populations.

Clinical implications of age of onset

With exceptions to be noted, earlier age of onset of depression generally is associated with a worse course of depression, with greater chances of recurrence, chronicity and impairment in role functioning (e.g., Hollon et al., 2006; Zisook et al., 2004).

There are at least two explanations for worse outcomes. One is that earlier age of onset may reflect a more persisting or debilitating form of depression with more risk factors, such as genetic predisposition and family/environmental disruption and adversity. Several studies have reported an association between early onset depression and depressive disorders in close relatives (e.g., Kendler, Gatz, Gardner and Pedersen, 2005), with numerous studies reporting early onset depression among offspring of depressed parents (e.g., Hammen, Brennan, Keenan-Miller and Herr, 2008; Weissman, Fendrich, Warner and Wickramaratne, 1992). Studies also consistently indicate that exposure to early adverse conditions such as maltreatment and maladaptive family functioning portends early onset and persistence of disorders, including depression (McLaughlin et al., 2010, 2012; Teicher, Samson, Polcari and Andersen, 2009; Tunnard et al., 2014) and greater depression recurrence, chronicity and poorer response to treatment (Nanni, Uher and Danese, 2012). Exposure to parental depression and childhood adversity as risk factors for depressive disorders are explored in greater detail in Chapter 6.

A second hypothesis about the impact of age is that early onset of depression causes disruption of the developmentally significant processes of acquiring important adaptive skills and managing life transitions. It is likely that early onset of depression interferes with healthy development and acquisition of problem-solving skills and positive views of the self and others. Such impairments may contribute to challenging life conditions (or to failure to resolve them) and to the occurrence of negative life events that the person cannot cope with effectively. Thus, depression may recur as individuals with early onset fail to acquire appropriate beliefs and skills to manage stressors in their lives.

Duration and severity of major depressive episodes

By definition, major depressive episodes must last at least two weeks to meet diagnostic criteria. Apart from this minimum, there is considerable variability in the length and severity of depressive episodes. If one suffers from major depression, research reveals both good news and bad news. The good news is that most people recover from major depression within three–six months and eventually recover whether treated or not. A good many major depressive episodes are relatively brief and not substantially impairing. However, the bad news is that many people do not fully recover and continue to have persisting low levels of symptoms or will experience multiple recurring episodes of depression accompanied by significant functional disability. Furthermore, epidemiological surveys in US community samples indicate that 38 per cent of those diagnosed with major depression in the past year were classified as seriously or severely depressed (Kessler, Merikangas and Wang, 2007).

In classic long term follow-up studies of depressed patients, investigators found that the majority recovered within six months of entering the study (Coryell et al., 1994; Keller, Shapiro, Lavori and Wolfe, 1982). Studies of community samples (not in treatment) have found similar but somewhat faster recovery times. For instance, the Netherlands Mental Health Survey and Incidence Study of 7,000 people reported a median duration of major depression of three months, with 63 per cent recovery within six months (Spijker et al., 2002). The US National Comorbidity Survey Replication reported a mean duration of major depression of four months (Kessler et al., 2003), although the largest US survey reported a median duration of six months (Hasin, Goodwin, Stinson and Grant, 2005).

Predictors of episode duration of major depression include severity, with longer duration associated with more severe symptoms (Hollon et al., 2006; Richards, 2011; Spijker et al., 2002, 2004). Also, these same studies agree that first episodes are typically longer in duration than recurrent episodes.

Most studies that have reported on duration of episodes and rates of 'recovery' have commonly defined the terms by the absence of full symptom criteria for major depressive disorder, or they have been cross-sectional studies that did not investigate the natural course of symptomatology over time and between depressive episodes. It has been easy to assume, therefore, that individuals not in diagnosable episodes are 'free' of depression. However, such an assumption is far from accurate for many depressed patients. In their classic longitudinal study, Judd and colleagues (1998) studied the weekly symptom course over a period of up to 12 years in a population seeking treatment for major depression. They found that patients were entirely symptom-free an average of only 41 per cent of weeks of follow-up. While it is not surprising that individuals with histories of multiple major depressive episodes or with 'double depression' (major depressive episode plus dysthymic disorder) were frequently symptomatic, even those with first-episode depression had only 54 per cent of weeks symptom-free. Most individuals reported highly fluctuating courses over time, in and out of periods varying in symptom severity – typically below diagnostic threshold but nonetheless debilitating. Thus, for many individuals depression resembles a chronic disease with a fluctuating course but with some levels of persisting symptoms, rather than a disorder in which acute episodes are followed by long stretches of normal good mood.

Recurrence and chronicity of depression
The former view of depression as a largely remitting and episodic disorder has now been altered by the recognition that for many individuals it is a chronic condition. Changes in diagnostic criteria in the DSM-5, as noted in Chapter 1, highlight the distinction between chronic and nonchronic depression. Klein (2010), for example, proposed a 2 x 2 classification according to chronic/nonchronic, and mild vs. moderate/severe, and such distinctions

may now be captured in DSM-5 criteria. Thus, individuals with mild, chronic depression (dysthymia) or with chronic major depression may now be diagnosed as persistent depressive disorder, which can also apply to those with episodes of major depression on top of mild, chronic depression.

In part the classification changes reflect the fact that the majority of those who have an episode of major depression will have multiple episodes. And for a substantial minority, their depressions persist for long periods or even indefinitely – varying in severity but never going away entirely. In this section we first discuss recurrent depression and then chronic depression, but it is important to bear in mind that many of the studies analysed below have not made the distinctions between chronic and nonchronic depression that are now required by DSM-5.

Among patients seeking treatment for depression, early longitudinal studies reported that between 50 per cent and 85 per cent with one major depressive episode had at least one additional episode (Keller, 1985). Judd (1997), reporting on data from a longitudinal study conducted in the modern era of antidepressant medications, found that the median number of episodes in a treatment sample was four. A review of longitudinal studies found the risk of major depression recurrence among treatment-seeking patients was 60 per cent in five years and 85 per cent in up to 15 years of follow-up, compared with a lower rate of 35–50 per cent recurrence in the general population (Hardeveld, Spijker, De Graaf, Nolen and Beekman, 2010; Monroe and Harkness, 2011). Note that the studies in these reports used strict definitions of recurrence in which the individual experiences a new episode following a period of recovery.

Notably, there is some evidence that the risk for recurrence progressively increases with each episode of major depression – and decreases as the period of recovery is longer. For instance, Solomon et al. (2000) reported that among depressed patients followed over a ten-year period, the probability of recurrence increased 16 per cent with each successive episode. These investigators also found that episodes come closer together over time, as illustrated in Figure 2.1. Similar results were reported by Kessing, Andersen, Mortensen and Bolwig (1998). Theories about underlying psychobiological processes potentially responsible for progressive recurrence are discussed in later chapters.

Because most depressions are recurrent, most clinical and research samples of depression contain mostly individuals who are experiencing recurrent episodes rather than first onset episodes (e.g., Kessler, 1997). This is an important reminder, because studies that have compared predictors of first vs. recurrent episodes have generally found different predictors (e.g., Daley,

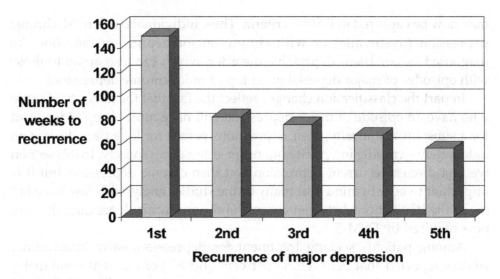

Figure 2.1 Decreasing intervals between successive episodes of depression

Adapted from Solomon, et al., (2000). Multiple recurrences of major depressive disorder. *American Journal of Psychiatry*, *157*, 229–233.

Hammen and Rao, 2000; Lewinsohn, Allen, Seeley and Gotlib, 1999). Post (1992) suggested, for example, that stressors are more predictive of first rather than later episodes of depression, reflecting a process of 'sensitisation'. If depression is a progressive disorder as naturalistic studies have suggested, there may be neurobiological and psychological vulnerabilities that are altered with successive episodes – which could have different treatment implications compared to first episodes. Therefore, studies that do not account for the stage of illness of participants may not result in findings that are widely generalisable.

Predictors of recurrence

In general, a more severe first episode predicts greater likelihood of continuing depression, according to a Danish ten-year longitudinal study that followed patients treated for major depression (Musliner et al., 2016). Most studies have also found that more prior episodes predict greater likelihood of recurrence (e.g., Bockting et al., 2006; Kessing, Hansen, Andersen and Angst, 2004). Furthermore, as noted above, a higher number of previous episodes predicts more rapid recurrence of major depression after recovery. Additional *clinical* predictors of recurrence include residual symptoms of depression (Bockting et al., 2006; Melartin et al., 2004), as well as presence of comorbid psychiatric disorders such as anxiety and substance use disorders (e.g., Melartin et al., 2004; Musliner et al., 2016).

In general, demographic predictors of recurrence are less definitive, with some suggesting women are more susceptible to recurrence or at least seek treatment for recurrence (e.g., Musliner et al., 2016; Richards, 2011), while others find no sex differences (e.g., Kessing et al., 2004). As noted above, younger age of onset is also typically associated with greater likelihood of recurrent depressive episodes, especially if severe and persisting depression.

A number of psychosocial factors such as stressful life events, personality and cognitive vulnerabilities, and poor social support have been studied as predictors of depression – mostly of recurrent episodes. A full review of these factors is presented in later chapters.

Chronicity of depression

As DSM-5 indicates, there are now various presentations of persistent depressive disorder, including mild chronic depression (dysthymic disorder), recurrent depression with incomplete recovery, moderate to severe chronic depression (chronic major depression) or combinations of chronic mild depression with superimposed episodes of major depression (once called 'double depression'). It has been estimated that about 20–25 per cent of depressions have a chronic course (e.g., Spijker et al., 2002). Research has consistently shown that chronicity, compared to non-chronic depression, predicts worse outcomes. A longitudinal study by Klein and Kotov (2016) found that throughout the ten years of follow-up, the chronic group had more depressive symptoms, poorer social and general functioning, and higher rates of suicidal behaviour and hospitalisation. Moreover, there is consensus that the correlates and presumed risk factors include younger age of onset, comorbid anxiety and personality disorders, family history of dysthymic disorder, histories of poorer parenting and childhood sexual abuse, and social maladjustment (Hölzel, Härter, Reese and Kriston, 2011; Klein and Kotov, 2016).

Nature and course of depression in children, adolescents and older adults

Depression is a heterogeneous disorder with different aetiological and clinical features. As noted, research has suggested that it is important to distinguish between childhood, adolescent and adult onset. For instance, biological and genetic contributions may be different for childhood and adolescent onset. Thapar and Rice (2006) report evidence suggesting that adolescent-onset depression is more likely associated with genetic factors than is childhood onset. Weissman and colleagues (Weissman et al., 1999) found that in contrast to the earlier assumption that childhood onset of depression likely predicted further depression continuing into adulthood, depression onset before puberty was associated with *less* continuity of depression than was adolescent onset depression. Carballo et al. (2011) also found less homotypic continuity of depression (depression predicting later depression) among those with childhood onset in a longitudinal sample diagnosed and treated in Madrid.

Also, there is growing evidence that late-adult onset of depression may also reflect different aetiological factors, such as greater likelihood of neurological disorders predicting depression in older populations. Therefore, the following sections will present a few key clinical features of each age-of-onset group, mindful that new developments may increasingly alter our understanding.

Childhood onset depression

Chapter 1 briefly discussed symptoms of depression in children, noting that younger samples typically complain less directly about low mood and display less evidence of negative cognitions, and may focus more on somatic symptoms. Luby and colleagues have particularly studied very young children (ages 3–6) and modified inclusion criteria to feature excess guilt, changes in sleep and activity level, and evidence of decreased pleasure in play and activities. They also noted that young children with depression rarely display the full two weeks or more of persistent symptoms required by DSM-5 and therefore the investigators permitted diagnosis based on recurrent but brief periods of depression manifestations. In Luby and colleagues' longitudinal study, such children and comparison nondepressed preschoolers were followed for up to six years, with preschool depression symptomatology robustly predicting DSM-5 major depressive disorder between ages 6–12 in 51 per cent, compared to 24 per cent in children who were not depressed between ages 3–6 (Luby, Gaffrey, Tillman, April and Belden, 2014). Luby et al. (2014) also found a strong predictive relationship between nonsupportive parenting, early depression and school age major depression. Thus, depression in very young children might be difficult to detect (by parents and teachers) but portends a pernicious, recurring depression with a strong 'environmental' component (harsh and unsupportive parenting).

Most research on childhood onset depression has studied school-age children, approximately ages 6–12 (also called prepubertal depression). Weissman and her colleagues (1999) conducted one of the few long-term longitudinal studies of children diagnosed with major depressive disorder who were then followed up in adulthood ten–15 years later. The majority of the sample had adverse outcomes with considerable psychiatric and psychosocial difficulties in adulthood; thus, overall, childhood onset of depression predicted generally maladaptive functioning over time. However, an especially notable result was the varied outcomes of the depressed children. The long-term study identified three subgroups: a) those with apparently 'true' early-onset depression that recurred into adulthood (homotypic continuity); b) those who did not have further depression but did have other significant psychopathology such as conduct disorder and substance abuse – similar to Carballo et al. (2011); c) those who went on to show eventual evidence of bipolar disorder. Each of these groups is described briefly.

'True' childhood onset unipolar depression is relatively rare, but appears to be associated with a high risk of recurrence (e.g., Luby et al., 2014). It is particularly likely to be associated with anxiety disorders especially in girls (e.g., Costello, Mustillo, Erkanli, Keeler and Angold, 2003; Rohde, Lewinsohn, Klein, Seeley and Gau, 2013). Several studies have found a strong association between childhood anxiety symptoms and inhibited or withdrawn behaviour, and later anxiety and depressive disorders (e.g., Goodwin, Fergusson and Horwood, 2004; Katz, Conway, Hammen, Brennan and Najman, 2011), suggesting that presence of anxious withdrawn symptomatology itself might be a predictor of eventual major depressive disorder. Rohde et al. (2013) also reported that childhood onset was associated with longer episodes than adolescent onset, consistent with findings that many have early onset dys-thymic disorder, possibly followed by major depression (Kovacs, Akiskal, Gatsonis and Parrone, 1994) and high rates of depressive disorders in relatives (e.g., Kovacs, Devlin, Pollock, Richards and Mukerji, 1997; Weissman et al., 1999). Childhood onset depression is commonly associated with considerable family stress, parental disorder, impaired parenting and exposure to adverse conditions (e.g., Jaffee et al., 2002; Klein and Kotov, 2016), although genetic factors cannot be ruled out in light of elevated rates of parental depression and other disorders. It may be speculated that these 'true' depressives will have substantial risk for life-long depression.

The second group of depressed children identified in the Weissman et al. (1999) childhood depression follow-up study, appears to be those with early depression and comorbid behavioural problems that eventuate over time in conduct disorders, substance use disorders, and considerable impairment and social maladjustment. The depression does not recur as such; instead its early appearance along with behavioural disorders seems to foretell the emergence of a variety of other psychiatric and social problems in adolescence and adulthood (e.g., Costello et al., 2003; Harrington, Fudge, Rutter, Pickles and Hill, 1991; Hofstra, van der Ende and Verhulst, 2000).

In their third group, the Weissman follow-up study also found that several of the formerly depressed children developed bipolar disorder by adulthood. Studies subsequently have indicated that a significant portion of children diagnosed with depression in clinical settings eventually evidence the hypomania or mania that define bipolar disorders (e.g., reviewed in Kovacs, 1996). For instance, Kovacs et al. (1994) found that 13 per cent of their depressed sample 'switched' to bipolar disorder. Geller and colleagues (2001) found that 33 per cent of their sample of 72 children with severe major depression had diagnoses of bipolar I disorder when followed up in adulthood. Predictors of eventual mania were having a parent or grandparent with mania. Thus, family history of bipolar disorder is a warning sign in the presence of childhood onset depression, but more general clinical predictors have not yet been validated to determine which depressed children might need to be treated for an underlying bipolar disorder.

Adolescent onset depression

There has been a substantial increase in research on adolescent depression in recent years for the simple reason that it became clear that adolescence (and transition to adulthood through mid-20s) is one of the most common periods of onset of major depressive disorder globally (e.g., Kessler and Bromet, 2013). Rates of depression among adolescents are as high or higher than in adulthood – 8.2 per cent 12-month prevalence of major depression or dysthymic disorder in the US National Comorbidity Survey Adolescent Supplement (Kessler et al., 2012a). Rates of depression onset expand considerably in early adolescence around age 12–13 and continue to increase throughout the transition to adulthood (Costello et al., 2003).

Moreover, investigators began to realise that adolescent distress should not simply be minimised as 'teenage turmoil' but is in fact the prototype of what we think of as adult depression, with all its clinical implications for recurrence and for disruption and impairment. Diagnosed depression in epidemiological surveys of adolescents in the US was rated as serious or moderate in severity in two-thirds of cases (Kessler et al., 2012b). Suicide and suicidal attempts are also higher than in most other age groups (e.g., Rohde et al., 2013). Implications of impairment due to youth depression are potentially enormous, given occurrence during a period of development, which is crucial to establishing autonomy, life skills, educational and occupational attainment, and formation of close relationships outside of their family of origin. Depressed adolescents, notably, have elevated rates of academic failure, teen pregnancy, intimate partner violence, health problems and various social difficulties, as well as suicidal behaviour (e.g., Hammen,

Brennan and Le Brocque, 2011; Katz, Hammen and Brennan, 2013; Keenan-Miller, Hammen and Brennan, 2007a,b; Kessler, Foster, Saunders and Stang, 1995).

Another noteworthy feature of adolescent onset of depression besides the elevated rates and clinical and functional implications is the emergence of gender differences. It is in adolescence that male and female rates of depression diverge significantly such that women's rates exceed those of men by 2:1 as discussed further in Chapter 3.

It should be mentioned that even subclinical levels of depression symptoms may be significant, and it is increasingly recommended that we view depression as a continuum of severity, rather than rely only on diagnostic classification (Hankin, Fraley, Lahey and Waldman, 2005). Symptoms predict clinical and functional outcomes. In a youth sample, subclinical depression at ages 17–18 predicted elevated rates of major depression and depressive symptoms and other disorders, as well as treatment-seeking in two subsequent follow-ups to age 25, compared to those without depressive symptoms (Fergusson, Horwood, Ritter and Beautrais, 2005; see also Shankman, Lewinsohn, Klein, Small, Seeley and Altman, 2009).

Because adolescent depression is essentially the beginning of adult depression, recurrence is a consideration in the likely course of illness. Clinical samples suggest that about 60 per cent or more adolescents have recurrences depending on the duration of follow-up (Emslie et al., 1997; Harrington, Fudge, Rutter, Pickles and Hill, 1990; Weissman et al., 1999). Community samples, presumably more representative of adolescent depressive experiences in general, report between 25–45 per cent recurrence over varying periods of time (Bardone, Moffitt, Caspi, Dickson and Silva, 1996; Lewinsohn, Rohde, Klein and Seeley, 1999; Pine, Cohen, Gurley, Brook and Ma, 1998; Rao, Hammen and Daley, 1999; Hammen, Brennan and Keenan-Miller, 2008). In general, roughly half of adolescent depressions will portend continuity into adulthood, while the others do not recur, possibly suggesting a temporary response to the developmentally typical challenges of adolescence. Those with recurrent depression have clinical courses and functional outcomes as described earlier in the chapter.

Finally, it is emphasised that adolescent depression, and indeed most depression, has high levels of comorbidity, commonly accompanying (or following/preceding) anxiety disorders, alcohol and drug use disorders, disruptive behaviour disorders and eating disorders (e.g., Costello et al., 2003; Kessler et al., 2012a). Such comorbid conditions typically worsen the functional impairments the youth experiences, and may portend more severe and prolonged depression and poorer treatment outcomes.

For all of the reasons noted: high rates, severity and impairment, disruption of normal developmental accomplishments and the prospect of continuing recurrence and symptomatology, experts note the importance of early intervention for treating – and even preventing – the pernicious consequences of adolescent depression (e.g., Costello et al., 2003; Gladstone, Beardslee and O'Connor, 2011; Kessler et al., 2012a,b).

Late life depression

Considerable interest in recent years has focused on characteristics of depression in the elderly that might be different from those of younger adult samples. As we will discuss in Chapter 3, there has been some disagreement about whether rates of depression decline in older samples – and whether there might in fact be an uptick in rates for those in their eighties. Clinically, depression in later life may be overlooked, misunderstood or even misattributed, because its symptoms often overlap with those of medical problems – for instance, loss of appetite and sleep problems, decreased energy, diminished pleasure and involvement, difficulties in memory and concentration. Some suggest that while many depressive symptoms in older samples are the classical syndrome of depression, there may be subtle differences: more psychomotor changes such as agitation or slowing, somatic complaints and less expression of guilt (e.g., Hegeman, Kok, van de Mast and Giltay, 2012). Thus, a treatable disorder such as depression might be mislabeled as dementia or other chronic medical illness, or ignored altogether as less important than medical difficulties.

In general, much of what is known or emerging about late life depression, including course and clinical features, depends on making distinctions about whether depression occurring in late life actually first occurred in older years or whether earlier episodes in younger adulthood preceded late life depression. Unfortunately, many studies of depression in late life do not make a distinction about age of onset, potentially obscuring important patterns or yielding inconsistent findings, and studies specifically of late-life first onset are rare. It has been speculated that about half of the cases of old age depression are first onsets (e.g., Comijs et al., 2015). Comijs and colleagues (2015) studied 285 elderly Dutch men and women who were recruited from mental health care or primary care and diagnosed with depression, and a non-depressed comparison group (overall mean age 70.6) and followed them for two years. 61 per cent had chronic depression through the two years, but even those who improved generally had residual symptoms. The predictors of chronic depression, unsurprisingly, were earlier age of first onset, dysthymic disorder and more chronic medical diseases.

An important implication of age of onset differences concerns aetiological factors. Late life depression may often reflect in part the effects of vascular changes in the brain or other older age dementing disorders such as Alzheimer's disease or Parkinson's (e.g., Blazer, 2003), or result from biological changes associated with certain diseases, such as a stroke. For instance, Köhler, Thomas, Barnett and O'Brien (2010) tested older patients with depression several times over four years and found cognitive impairments were present even after depressive symptoms dissipated, suggesting stable brain changes. Depression symptoms in older adults may in fact sometimes mark the early warning signs of dementia (Blazer, 2003). Depression occurring in the context of vascular and brain changes may be accompanied by more cognitive impairment, psychomotor slowing and reduced interest in typical activities (Blazer, 2003).

Late life depression, whether with early- or late first-onset, often occurs in the context of co-existing medical problems, increased use of medical services (e.g., Husain et al., 2005) and may be accompanied by mobility limitations and social isolation. Rates of suicide in older samples are the highest of all ages for both genders, but markedly so among males globally, although rates differ by culture/religion and are highly associated with depression and physical disability (Bertolote and Fleischmann, 2002; Kaskie, Leung and Kaplan, 2016).

Impaired functioning and consequences of depression

Depression significantly disrupts the normal performance of expected roles, and it is widely misunderstood in most cultures, often viewed as a character weakness – or as a bodily malady. The low mood, reduced energy, pessimism and lack of motivation associated with moderate and severe depression obviously interfere with a person's ability to work, perform chores and relate positively to family and friends. At depression's worst, the afflicted person may spend hours in bed or staring into space, or aimlessly pacing and brooding – often finding it difficult to manage even minimal tasks such as bathing or getting dressed. The negativism, hopelessness and lack of motivation are often a source of incredulity or even of frustration and impatience in others, because depression is often erroneously viewed (even by the afflicted) as failure, weakness, a lack of willpower or low strength of character. Because depression is a globally common, and often a recurring or chronic problem, its consequences can add up to enormous proportions. There has been increasing recognition across the globe that depression is not 'all in your head' but in fact is at least as impairing or even more associated with disability than many chronic medical diseases – even in relatively mild forms (e.g., Johnson, Weissman and Klerman,1992; Wells et al., 1989).

Research has documented at least three specific areas in which depression causes significantly impaired functioning: work, family and marital/inter-personal relationships. A fourth area will also be described separately: the emerging study of the relations between depression and medical conditions. In the following sections the emphasis is on the consequences of depression – how depression has a negative impact on performance in typical roles. It is important to acknowledge, of course, that the relationship between depression and functioning in important roles is bidirectional, since problems in adjustment may cause or exacerbate depressive conditions. The contribution of stressors, family and marital difficulties as causes of depression will be covered in later chapters.

Global burden of depression

The Global Burden of Disease studies by the World Health Organization (WHO) regularly compute the impact of different diseases in terms of 'dis-ability-adjusted life years' according to statistical projections based on factors such as severity of health loss and premature death, across both developed and less-developed nations. Ferrari et al. (2013; see also Whiteford et al., 2013) reported that in 2010, consistent with earlier studies, depression is a leading cause of burden in the world. Figures differ from region to region, but overall the most affected were women, and those of young adult working age. The level of burden has increased substantially over the past ten years due to aging and population growth (Ferrari et al., 2013). Chisholm et al. (2016) projected that if treatments for depression were expanded and scaled up to address the global burden of depression, the net gain would be an estimated $310 billion over the costs of treatment, based on projected costs of diminished work productivity and health care expenses, and would also increase the invaluable social contributions due to healthy life years.

Effects of depression on work

Studies clearly indicate that depression is associated with costly absenteeism from work. For example, Hendriks et al. (2015) studied more than 1,600 Dutch workers over a longitudinal course, and found that depression – especially when comorbid with anxiety – predicted continuing and long-term work disability and absenteeism over a four-year period. Depression also creates what has been called 'presenteeism', the reduction in the quality and productivity of work even when the person is present in the workplace.

In a study by Stewart, Ricci, Chee, Hahn and Morganstein (2003) interviewers asked workers who had been selected because of presence or absence of depression how often they lost concentration, repeated a job, or worked more slowly than usual. An index of 'lost productive time' was calculated, indicating 8.4 hours/week for those with major depression compared to 1.5 hours/week for the nondepressed. The authors estimated the potential loss of billions of dollars due to unproductive time associated with depression. Another study collected 'moment in time' data by electronically signaling workers at five random times per day to write about their work performance (Wang et al., 2004). Those with major depression had decrements in task focus and performance that were calculated to approximate the equivalent of 2.3 days of absence of work per month attributable to depression.

It might be assumed that those in student roles would suffer similar problems with decreased academic effectiveness. Studies generally indicate that depression is associated with poorer academic performance in children and adolescents (e.g., Jaycox et al., 2009), typically a bidirectional relationship, especially for girls (Verboom, Sijtsema, Verhulst, Penninx and Ormel, 2014). Depression is significantly associated with increased rates of failure to complete high school, failure to enter college and failure to complete college (Kessler, Foster, Saunders and Stang, 1995).

Effects of depression on parent–child relations

Studies of family relationships have indicated significant impairment of the parental role when a person is depressed. Depressed parents typically want to be good parents, but the depression takes an enormous toll on their energy, interest, patience and mood – all of which doubtless impair their abilities to sustain positive, supportive and attentive relationships with their children (Psychogiou and Parry, 2014; see also Stein et al., 2014). Depressive symptoms, as well as parents' underlying emotional, cognitive and social vulnerabilities impede parental warmth, responsiveness, monitoring and discipline that undermine children's well-being and effectiveness. In a review and meta-analysis, Lovejoy, Graczyk, O'Hare and Neuman (2000) found that overall, depressed mothers displayed more negative and disengaged behaviours, and were also less positive, compared to nondepressed mothers. Similarly, a review of fathers' parenting behaviour also indicated more negativity and less positive interactions among depressed fathers and their children (Wilson and Durbin, 2010). Common patterns observed among depressed women interacting with their infants include intrusive (harsh, irritated) or withdrawn (disengaged) styles, or mixtures of both styles (Field, Diego and Hernandez-Reif, 2006).

Negative parenting is a mediator of the association between parental depression and child depression (e.g., Goodman, 2007; Stein et al., 2014). A review by McLeod, Weisz and Wood (2007) indicated that parental rejection and hostility were particularly associated with children's depression. In Chapter 6, we present more details on parent–child problems occurring in the families of depressed parents – and the risk to the offspring of developing depression and other maladjustment.

Effects of depression on marital relationships

Depression may also take a toll on marital relationships. As with work and parenting, difficulties in marriages may cause or contribute to depression, but often it is the depression that causes marital problems (see Chapter 6), sometimes leading to divorce. Studies have indicated a strong association between depression and presence of marital distress (Whisman, 2007; 2013; Zlotnick, Kohn, Keitner and Della Grotta, 2000). Not surprisingly, longitudinal studies examining relationships between marital quality and depression over time find bidirectional effects, with each predicting increases in the other (e.g., Najman et al., 2014). Observational studies find higher rates of negative and lower rates of positive communication among couples with depression compared to couples without depression (Rehman, Gollan and Mortimer, 2008).

The symptoms of a spouse or parent's depression may be difficult for families to cope with. Also, of course, depressed spouses are often viewed as a great burden to their partners, causing worry, sharing fewer pleasurable activities and failing to respond to encouragement and support. Indeed, in a classic study, a survey of partners of depressed individuals found that they were troubled by these and numerous other complaints, to the extent that 40 per cent of the partners were sufficiently distressed by their depressed partners to warrant treatment themselves (Coyne et al., 1987).

Depression, death and health

Depression and suicide

Depression is one of the few psychological disorders that can be said to be fatal. Of all of the consequences, suicide is, of course, the starkest consequence of an individual's feelings of hopelessness and depletion. Contributors to suicide vary widely by culture, demographic and social characteristics, and access to lethal means. There are extensive differences in rates of suicide across the globe, although comparisons are hampered by limitations in accurate reporting of cause of death, largely due to cultural beliefs and practices. Rates in the UK and US range from approximately 8 to 12 per 100,000, but may be much higher in Eastern European and some Asian countries (Hawton and van Heeringen, 2009).

While there are many potential contributors to suicide, depression emerges as a strong correlate and presumed causal factor. Hawton and van Heeringen (2009) report that more than 50 per cent of those who die by suicide met criteria for current major depression, although rates vary by country. These authors also note that approximately 4 per cent of people with depression die by suicide. According to meta-analyses of 19 studies, Hawton, Casañas i Comabella, Haw and Saunders (2013) found the following predictors of suicide among individuals with depression: male gender, family psychiatric history, previous suicide attempt, more severe depression, hopelessness and comorbid psychological disorders especially anxiety disorders and substance misuse (especially alcohol). Suicide is also a major public health problem for adolescents worldwide, and is overall the second leading cause of death in youth (ranking first for females and third for males after vehicle crashes and violence) (Hawton, Saunders and O'Connor, 2012). Many of the risk factors are similar to those of adults, although it is noted that personality factors such as impulsivity and psychosocial difficulties, such as family conflict, plus access to lethal methods, often play a substantial role – as does 'contagion' transmitted through media coverage of teen or celebrity suicides.

Suicidal behaviours are often triggered by severe negative psychosocial life events. Suicidal thoughts are commonly consequences of negativistic thinking characteristic of depression: a sense of futility; a view that the future is bleak and bad conditions are unchangeable; that there is nothing one can do to relieve the pain of depressive feelings; and the belief that one is worthless and that others would be better off without them. Such attitudes, when assessed on a scale measuring 'hopelessness', have been found to be associated with a greater likelihood of eventual suicide in outpatients (Beck, Brown and Steer, 1989). Brown, Beck, Steer and Grisham (2000) found that hopelessness, along with severity of depression and suicidal ideation were significant predictors of eventual suicide in a sample of nearly 7,000 psychiatric outpatients.

An important distinction has been made between predictors of suicidal ideation and suicide attempts, with the development of suicidal thoughts and the transition from suicidal thoughts to suicidal attempts seen as distinct processes (Klonsky, May and Saffer, 2016). For example, whereas depression predicts suicidal ideation, it is less clear that depression alone can distinguish between those who have considered suicide relative to those who have attempted suicide. In contrast, disorders of anxiety, agitation and impulse control may be more associated with transitioning from thoughts to attempts. Recent theories have distinguished between factors that drive increased suicidal ideation, such as hopelessness, a sense of defeat and feelings of being trapped, from those that may drive attempts, such as exposure to others' suicidal behaviour, and access to means (O'Connor and Nock, 2014).

Depression and medical morbidity

An expanding and influential body of research focuses on the associations between depression (and other disorders) and health and medical problems (e.g., see Scott et al. (2016) for a global perspective). Depression is increasingly viewed not only as a potential consequence of illness, but also as a cause or contributor to the course and consequences of disease. The implications are enormous: depression is bad for your health, and medical professionals need to recognise and treat or prevent depression as a way to improve health. There are several aspects of the depression–health association.

First, depression may be a psychological consequence of disease and disability, because long-term illness may be severely stressful and distressing. Unfortunately, the symptoms of depression are highly likely to interfere with patients' energy, sense of effectiveness and motivation to comply with necessary treatment, and may add increased impairment of functioning and reduced quality of life beyond that caused by the disease itself (e.g., Katon, 2003). Depressed patients are likely to have poorer compliance with treatment, poorer response to treatments and higher rates of complications. Such outcomes may translate into increased costs of medical care – more primary care visits, more emergency room, pharmacy, laboratory and hospitalisation costs. For example, Katon, Lin, Russo and Unutzer (2003) found that total costs of medical services were significantly higher in the past six months among depressed compared to nondepressed older adults, after controlling for chronic medical illness. Egede and Ellis (2010) reviewed studies of diabetes and depression, and found poorer metabolic control and more complications among the depressed patients, adding to disability and lessened quality of life.

Second, there is growing evidence that depression may have an effect on development or worsening of medical conditions through maladaptive health behaviours, such as smoking, excessive alcohol use, lack of exercise, poor nutrition and being overweight, and poor sleep habits. When people are depressed they may lack the motivation, focus and positive expectations necessary to engage in efforts to sustain healthy lifestyles or desist from unhealthy habits. For example, maladaptive health behaviours such as being sedentary are associated with various poor health outcomes (Thorp, Owen, Neuhaus and Dunstan, 2011), and the effects of smoking and consumption of excess calories are well known. It is also known that depression is associated with smoking and difficulties quitting (Weinberger, Pilver, Desai, Mazure and McKee, 2012).

Third, there is increasing evidence that depression may exert direct bio-logical effects on illness, likely operating through inflammatory mechanisms, which themselves are modified by genetic, stress and environmental influences, and through the deleterious effects of stress on the hypothalamic-pituitary-adrenal (HPA) axis. For instance, metabolic syndrome is a combination of obesity, high blood pressure, low levels of high-density lipoprotein cholesterol (HDL-C), hyperglycemia and elevated triglycerides. Individuals with major depressive disorder, compared with non-depressed individuals, have signi-ficantly higher rates of these markers for risk for cardiovascular disease and diabetes, independent of demographic factors and smoking (e.g., Vancamfort et al., 2014).

There is mounting evidence of bidirectional effects between depression and heart disease, obesity, diabetes and asthma, among other diseases. Even controlling for negative health behaviours and demographic factors such as age, gender and education, a survey by Strine et al. (2008) found that cardio-vascular disease, asthma and diabetes are significantly associated with current or past depression. Longitudinal studies show that depression predicts development or exacerbation of these health conditions and also the medical conditions predict depression (Egede and Ellis, 2010; Luppino et al., 2010; Jiang, Qin and Yang, 2014). In part such effects operate through depression's negative effect on health behaviours, but it is suspected that complex biological mechanisms are also in play, and these are discussed more fully in Chapter 4 (Biological aspects of depression). A particularly dramatic example is the effect of depression on cardiac mortality. A number of longitudinal studies have now reported that more individuals with coronary heart disease with depression and anxiety will die during the follow-up period than those not depressed but equally ill (Watkins et al., 2013; see also Leung et al., 2012). Reviews of studies of people who were healthy at baseline and followed up over periods ranging from four to 15 years, found that depression increased the risk of death by heart disease or of having a heart attack (myocardial infarction) by a factor of 1.64 (Rugulies, 2002).

Depression's impairment: the implications

Unfortunately depression is awful enough by itself, but its consequences – especially in the context of chronic/recurrent depression – are highly likely to add to the debility, stress and helplessness in the face of difficult family relationships, work and health issues. In this sense depression begets depression, contributing to life circumstances that may overwhelm individuals' resources for coping. The clear implications are the need for effective, aggressive treatment to mitigate its effects, education to institutions and communities about the meaning and costs of depression, and even preventive interventions in high-risk situations. Treatment issues are discussed in later chapters.

Summary

◆ Depressive disorders typically start in adolescence or young adulthood, with major depression usually lasting four–six months even if untreated. Depressions are commonly but not inevitably recurrent, and many individuals have a fairly chronic course.

◆ Earlier onset of depressive disorder generally portends more severe and recurrent depression with greater impairment.

◆ Depressions may differ in their aetiology, course, and treatment implications depending on whether they first begin in childhood, adolescence, adulthood or older adulthood.

◆ The consequences of depression – even at fairly mild levels – on work, marriage, parenting and health may be considerably negative, not just for the individuals involved but also for the family and society. Depression is one of the major sources of global burden of cost and loss of benefits to society.

◆ Health, marital, parental and work impairments due to depression may contribute to further depression in a vicious cycle if untreated. Further, a bidirectional relationship between many medical problems and depression is coming to light, suggesting the need for greater awareness of depression and its role in aetiology and treatment of disease.

References

Bardone, A., Moffitt, T., Caspi, A., Dickson, N. and Silva, P. (1996). Adult mental health and social outcomes of adolescent girls with depression and conduct disorder. *Development and Psychopathology*, *8*, 811–829.

Beck, A. T., Brown, G. and Steer, R. A. (1989). Prediction of eventual suicide in psychiatric inpatients by clinical ratings of hopelessness. *Journal of Consulting and Clinical Psychology, 57*(2), 309–310.

Beesdo, K., Pine, D. S., Lieb, R. and Wittchen, H. U. (2010). Incidence and risk patterns of anxiety and depressive disorders and categorization of generalised anxiety disorder. *Archives of General Psychiatry, 67*(1), 47–57.

Bertolote, J. M. and Fleischmann, A. (2002). Suicide and psychiatric diagnosis: a worldwide perspective. *World Psychiatry, 1*(3), 181–185.

Blazer, D. G. (2003). Depression in late life: review and commentary. *Journal of Gerontology, 58A*, 249–265.

Bockting, C. L., Spinhoven, P., Koeter, M. W., Wouters, L. F., Schene, A. H. and Depression Evaluation Longitudinal Therapy Assessment Study Group. (2006). Prediction of recurrence in recurrent depression and the influence of consecutive episode on vulnerability for depression: a 2-year prospective study. *Journal of Clinical Psychiatry, 67*, 747–755.

Brown, G. K., Beck, A. T., Steer, R. A. and Grisham, J. R. (2000). Risk factors for suicide in psychiatric outpatients: a 20-year prospective study. *Journal of Consulting and Clinical Psychology, 68*, 371–377.

Carballo, J. J., Muñoz-Lorenzo, L., Blasco-Fontecilla, H., Lopez-Castroman, J., García-Nieto, R., Dervic, K., . . . Baca-García, E. (2011). Continuity of depressive disorders from childhood and adolescence to adulthood: a naturalistic study in community mental health centers. *The Primary Care Companion to CNS Disorders, 13*(5). doi: *10.4088/PCC.11m01150*

Chisholm, D., Sweeny, K., Sheehan, P., Rasmussen, B., Smit, F., Cuijpers, P. and Saxena, S. (2016). Scaling-up treatment of depression and anxiety: a global return on investment analysis. *The Lancet Psychiatry, 3*(5), 415–424.

Comijs, H. C., Nieuwesteeg, J., Kok, R., van Marwijk, H. W., van der Mast, R. C., Naarding, P., . . . and Stek, M. L. (2015). The two-year course of late-life depression; results from the Netherlands study of depression in older persons. *BMC Psychiatry, 15*(20). doi: *10.1186/s12888–015–0401–5*

Coryell, W., Akiskal, H. S., Leon, A. C., Winokur, G., Maser, J. D., Mueller, T. I. and Keller, M. B. (1994). The time course of nonchronic major depressive disorder: uniformity across episodes and samples. *Archives of General Psychiatry, 51*(5), 405–410.

Costello, E. J., Mustillo, S., Erkanli, A., Keeler, G. and Angold, A. (2003). Prevalence and development of psychiatric disorders in childhood and adolescence. *Archives of General Psychiatry, 60*, 837–844.

Coyne, J. C., Kessler, R. C., Tal, M., Turnbull, J., Wortman, C. B. and Greden, J. F. (1987). Living with a depressed person. *Journal of Consulting and Clinical Psychology, 55*(3), 347–352.

Daley, S. E., Hammen, C. and Rao, U. (2000). Predictors of first onset and recurrence of major depression in young women during the 5 years following high school graduation. *Journal of Abnormal Psychology, 109*, 525–533.

Egede, L. E. and Ellis, C. (2010). Diabetes and depression: global perspectives. *Diabetes Research and Clinical Practice, 87*(3), 302–312.

Emslie, G. J., Rush, A. J., Weinberg, W. A., Kowatch, R. A., Hughes, C. W., Carmody, T., and Rintelmnn, J. (1997). A double-blind, randomised, placebo-controlled trial of fluoxetine in children and adolescents with depression. *Archives of General Psychiatry, 54*, 1031–1037.

Ferrari, A. J., Charlson, F. J., Norman, R. E., Patten, S. B., Freedman, G., Murray, C. J., . . . Whiteford, H. A. (2013). Burden of depressive disorders by country, sex, age, and year: findings from the global burden of disease study 2010. *PLOS Medicine, 10*(11), e1001547.

Fergusson, D. M., Horwood, L. J., Ritter, E. M. and Beautrais, A. L. (2005). Sub-threshold depression in adolescence and mental health outcomes in adulthood. *Archives of General Psychiatry, 62*, 66–72.

Field, T., Diego, M. and Hernandez-Reif, M. (2006). Prenatal depression effects on the fetus and newborn: a review. *Infant Behaviour and Development, 29*(3), 445–455.

Geller, B., Zimerman, B., Williams, M., Bolhofner, K. and Craney, J. L. (2001). Bipolar disorder at prospective follow-up of adults who had prepubertal major depressive disorder. *American Journal of Psychiatry, 158*(1), 125–127.

Gladstone, T. R., Beardslee, W. R. and O'Connor, E. E. (2011). The prevention of adolescent depression. *Psychiatric Clinics of North America, 34*(1), 35–52.

Goodman, S. (2007). Depression in mothers. *Annual Review of Clinical Psychology, 3,* 107–135.

Goodwin, R. D., Fergusson, D. M. and Horwood, L. J. (2004). Early anxious/with-drawn behaviours predict later internalising disorders. *Journal of Child Psychology and Psychiatry, 45*(4), 874–883.

Hammen, C., Brennan, P., Keenan-Miller, D. and Herr, N. (2008). Early onset recurrent subtype of adolescent depression: clinical and psychosocial correlates. *Journal of Child Psychology and Psychiatry, 49*, 433–440.

Hammen, C. Brennan, P. and Le Brocque, R. (2011). Youth depression and early childrearing: stress generation and intergenerational transmission of depression. *Journal of Consulting and Clinical Psychology, 79*, 353–363.

Hankin, B. L., Fraley, R. C., Lahey, B. B. and Waldman, I. D. (2005). Is depression best viewed as a continuum or discrete category? A taxometric analysis of childhood and adolescent depression in a population-based sample. *Journal of Abnormal Psychology, 114*(1), 96–110.

Hardeveld, F., Spijker, J., De Graaf, R., Nolen, W. A. and Beekman, A. T. F. (2010). Prevalence and predictors of recurrence of major depressive disorder in the adult population. *Acta Psychiatrica Scandinavica, 122*(3), 184–191.

Harrington, R., Fudge, H., Rutter, M., Pickles, A. and Hill, J. (1990). Adult outcomes of childhood and adolescent depression: I. Psychiatric status. *Archives of General Psychiatry, 47*(5), 465–473.

Harrington, R., Fudge, H., Rutter, M., Pickles, A. and Hill, J. (1991). Adult outcomes of childhood and adolescent depression: II. Links with antisocial disorders. *Journal of the American Academy of Child and Adolescent Psychiatry, 30*(3), 434–439.

Hasin, D. S., Goodwin, R. D., Stinson, F. S. and Grant, B. F. (2005). Epidemiology of major depressive disorder: results from the National Epidemiologic Survey on Alcoholism and Related Conditions. *Archives of General Psychiatry, 62*(10), 1097–1106.

Hawton, K., Casañas i Comabella, C. C., Haw, C. and Saunders, K. (2013). Risk factors for suicide in individuals with depression: a systematic review. *Journal of Affective Disorders, 147*(1), 17–28.

Hawton, K., Saunders, K. E. and O'Connor, R. C. (2012). Self-harm and suicide in adolescents. *The Lancet, 379*(9834), 2373–2382.

Hawton, K. and van Heeringen, K. (2009). Suicide. *Lancet, 373*, 1372–1381.

Hegeman, J. M., Kok, R. M., Van der Mast, R. C. and Giltay, E. J. (2012). Phenomenology of depression in older compared with younger adults: meta-analysis. *The British Journal of Psychiatry, 200*(4), 275–281.

Hendricks, S. M., Spijker, J., Licht, C. M., Hardeveld, F., de Graaf, R., Batelaan, N. M., . . . Beckman, A. T. (2015). Long-term work disability and absenteeism in anxiety and depressive disorders. *Journal of Affective Disorders, 178*, 121–130.

Hofstra, M. B., Van der Ende, J. and Verhulst, F. C. (2000). Continuity and change of psychopathology from childhood into adulthood: a 14-year follow-up study. *Journal of the Academy of Child and Adolescent Psychiatry, 39*, 850–858.

Hollon, S. D., Shelton, R. C., Wisniewski, S., Warden, D., Biggs, M. M., Friedman, E. S., . . . Rush, A. J. (2006). Presenting characteristics of depressed outpatients as a function of recurrence: preliminary findings from the STAR*D clinical trial. *Journal of Psychiatric Research, 40*, 59–69.

Hölzel, L., Härter, M., Reese, C. and Kriston, L. (2011). Risk factors for chronic depression – a systematic review. *Journal of Affective Disorders, 129*(1), 1–13.

Husain, M. M., Rush, A. J., Sackeim, H. A., Wisniewski, S. R., McClintock, S. M., Craven, N., . . . Hauger, R. (2005). Age-related characteristics of depression: a preliminary STAR*D report. *American Journal of Geriatric Psychiatry, 13*, 852–860.

Jaffee, S. R., Moffitt, T. E., Caspi, A., Fombonne, E., Poulton, R. and Martin, J. (2002). Differences in early childhood risk factors for juvenile-onset and adult-onset depression. *Archives of General Psychiatry, 59*, 215–222.

Jaycox, L. H., Stein, B. D., Paddock, S., Miles, J. N., Chandra, A., Meredith, L. S., . . . Burnam, M. A. (2009). Impact of teen depression on academic, social, and physical functioning. *Pediatrics, 124*(4), e596-e605.

Jiang, M., Qin, P. and Yang, X. (2014). Comorbidity between depression and asthma via immune-inflammatory pathways: a meta-analysis. *Journal of Affective Disorders, 166*, 22–29.

Johnson, J., Weissman, M. M. and Klerman, G. (1992). Service utilization and social morbidity associated with depressive symptoms in the community. *Journal of the American Medical Association, 267*, 1478–1483.

Judd, L. L. (1997). The clinical course of unipolar major depressive disorders. *Archives of General Psychiatry*, *54*, 989–991.

Judd, L. L., Akiskal, H. S., Maser, J. D., Zeller, P. J., Endicott, J., Coryell, W., . . . Keller, M. B. (1998). A prospective 12-year study of subsyndromal and syndromal depressive symptoms in unipolar major depressive disorders. *Archives of General Psychiatry*, *55*, 694–700.

Kaskie, B. P., Leung, C. and Kaplan, M. S. (2016). Deploying an ecological model to stem the rising tide of firearm suicide in older age. *Journal of Ageing and Social Policy*, http://dx.doi.org/10.1080/08959420.2016.1167512

Katon, W. J. (2003). Clinical and health services relationships between major depression, depressive symptoms, and general medical illness. *Biological Psychiatry*, *54*, 216–226.

Katon, W. J., Lin, E. H., Russo, J. E. and Unutzer, J. (2003). Increased medical costs of a population-based sample of depressed elderly patients. *Archives of General Psychiatry*, *60*, 897–903.

Katz, S., Conway, C., Hammen, C., Brennan, P. and Najman, J. (2011). Childhood social withdrawal, interpersonal impairment, and young adult depression: a mediational model. *Journal of Abnormal Child Psychology*, *39*(8), 1227–1238.

Katz, S., Hammen, C. and Brennan, P. (2013). Maternal depression and the intergenerational transmission of relational impairment. *Journal of Family Psychology*, *27*, 86–95.

Keenan-Miller, D., Hammen, C. and Brennan, P. (2007a). Adolescent psychosocial risk factors for severe intimate partner violence in young adulthood. *Journal of Consulting and Clinical Psychology*, *75*, 456–463.

Keenan-Miller, D., Hammen, C. and Brennan, P. (2007b). Health outcomes related to early adolescent depression. *Journal of Adolescent Health*, *42*, 256–262.

Keller, M. B. (1985). Chronic and recurrent affective disorders: incidence, course, and influencing factors. *Advances in Biochemical Psychopharmacology*, *40*, 111–120.

Keller, M. B., Shapiro, R. W., Lavori, P. W. and Wolfe, N. (1982). Recovery in major depressive disorder: analysis with the life table and regression models. *Archives of General Psychiatry*, *39*, 905–910.

Kendler, K. S., Gatz, M., Gardner, C. O. and Pedersen, N. L. (2005). Age at onset and familial risk for major depression in a Swedish national twin sample. *Psychological Medicine*, *35*, 1–7.

Kessing, L. V., Andersen, P. K., Mortensen, P. B. and Bolwig, T. G. (1998). Recurrence in affective disorder. I. Case register study. *The British Journal of Psychiatry*, *172*(1), 23–28.

Kessing, L. V., Hansen, M. G., Andersen, P. K. and Angst, J. (2004). The predictive effect of episodes on the risk of recurrence in depressive and bipolar disorders: a life-long perspective. *Acta Psychiatrica Scandinavica*, *109*, 339–344.

Kessler, R. C. (1997). The effects of stressful life events on depression. *Annual Review of Psychology*, *48*, 191–214.

Kessler, R. C., Avenevoli, S., Costello, E. J., Georgiades, K., Green, J. G., Gruber, M. J., . . . Sampson, N. A. (2012a). Prevalence, persistence, and sociodemographic correlates of DSM-IV disorders in the national comorbidity survey replication adolescent supplement. *Archives of General Psychiatry, 69*(4), 372–380.

Kessler, R. C., Avenevoli, S., Costello, J., Green, J. G., Gruber, M. J., McLaughlin, K. A., . . . Merikangas, K. R. (2012b). Severity of 12-month DSM-IV disorders in the National Comorbidity Survey Replication Adolescent Supplement. *Archives of General Psychiatry, 69*(4), 381–389.

Kessler, R. C., Berglund, P., Demler, O., Jin, R., Koretz, D., Merikangas, K. R., . . . Wang, P. S. (2003). The epidemiology of major depressive disorder: results from the National Comorbidity Survey Replication (NCS-R). *JAMA, 289*(23), 3095–3105.

Kessler, R. C. and Bromet, E. J. (2013). The epidemiology of depression across cultures. *Annual Review of Public Health, 34*, 119–138.

Kessler, R. C., Foster, C. L., Saunders, W. B. and Stang, P. E. (1995). Social consequences of psychiatric disorders, I: educational attainment. *American Journal of Psychiatry, 152*(7), 1026–1032.

Kessler, R. C., Merikangas, K. R. and Wang, P. S. (2007). Prevalence, comorbidity, and service utilization for mood disorders in the United States at the beginning of the twenty-first century. *Annual Review of Clinical Psychology, 3*, 137–158.

Klein, D. N. (2010). Chronic depression diagnosis and classification. *Current Directions in Psychological Science, 19*(2), 96–100.

Klein, D. N. and Kotov, R. (2016). Course of depression in a 10-year prospective study: evidence for qualitatively distinct subgroups. *Journal of Abnormal Psychology, 125*(3), 337–348.

Klonsky, E. D., May, A. M. and Saffer, B. Y. (2016). Suicide, suicide attempts, and suicidal ideation. *Annual Review of Clinical Psychology, 12*, 307–330.

Köhler, S., Thomas. A. J., Barnett, N. and O'Brien, J. T. (2010). The pattern and course of cognitive impairment in late-life depression. *Psychological Medicine, 40*, 591–602.

Kovacs, M. (1996). Presentation and course of major depressive disorder during childhood and later years of the life span. *Journal of the American Academy of Child and Adolescent Psychiatry, 35*, 705–715.

Kovacs, M., Akiskal, H. S., Gatsonis, C. and Parrone, P. L. (1994). Childhood-onset dysthymic disorder: clinical features and prospective naturalistic outcome. *Archives of General Psychiatry, 51*, 365–374.

Kovacs, M., Devlin, B., Pollock, M., Richards, C. and Mukerji, P. (1997). A controlled family history study of childhood-onset depressive disorder. *Archives of General Psychiatry, 54*, 613–623.

Leung, Y. W., Flora, D. B., Gravely, S., Irvine, J., Carney, R. M. and Grace, S. L. (2012). The impact of pre-morbid and post-morbid depression onset on mortality and cardiac morbidity among coronary heart disease patients: a meta-analysis. *Psychosomatic Medicine, 74*(8), 786–801.

Lewinsohn, P. M., Allen, N. B., Seeley, J. R. and Gotlib, I. H. (1999). First onset versus recurrence of depression: differential processes of psychosocial risk. *Journal of Abnormal Psychology*, *108*, 483–489.

Lewinsohn, P. M., Rohde, P., Klein, D. N. and Seeley, J. R. (1999). Natural course of adolescent major depressive disorder: I. Continuity into young adulthood. *Journal of the American Academy of Child and Adolescent Psychiatry*, *38*(1), 56–63.

Lovejoy, M. C., Graczyk, P. A., O'Hare, E. and Neuman, G. (2000). Maternal depression and parenting behaviour: a meta-analytic review. *Clinical Psychology Review*, *20*, 561–592.

Luby, J. L., Gaffrey, M. S., Tillman, R., April, L. M. and Belden, A. C. (2014). Trajectories of preschool disorders to full DSM depression at school age and early adolescence: continuity of preschool depression. *American Journal of Psychiatry*, *171*, 768–776.

Luppino, F. S., de Wit, L. M., Bouvy, P. F., Stijnen, T., Cuijpers, P., Penninx, B. W. and Zitman, F. G. (2010). Overweight, obesity, and depression: a systematic review and meta-analysis of longitudinal studies. *Archives of General Psychiatry*, *67*(3), 220–229.

McGorry, P. D., Purcell, R., Goldstone, S. and Amminger, G. P. (2011). Age of onset and timing of treatment for mental and substance use disorders: implications for preventive intervention strategies and models of care. *Current Opinion in Psychiatry*, *24*(4), 301–306.

McLaughlin, K. A., Green, J. G., Gruber, M. J., Sampson, N. A., Zaslavsky, A. M. and Kessler, R. C. (2010). Childhood adversities and adult psychiatric disorders in the national comorbidity survey replication II: associations with persistence of DSM-IV disorders. *Archives of Psychiatry*, *67*(2), 124–132.

McLaughlin, K. A., Green, J. G., Gruber, M. J., Sampson, N. A., Zaslavsky, A. M. and Kessler, R. C. (2012). Childhood adversities and first onset of psychiatric disorders in a national sample of US adolescents. *Archives of General Psychiatry*, *69*(11), 1151–1160.

McLeod, B. D., Weisz, J. R. and Wood, J. J. (2007). Examining the association between parenting and childhood depression: a meta-analysis. *Clinical Psychology Review*, *27*(8), 986–1003.

Melartin, T. K., Rytsala, H. J., Leskela, U. S., Lestela-Mielonen, P. S., Sokero, T. P. and Isometsa, E. T. (2004). Severity and comorbidity predict episode duration and recurrence of DSM-IV major depressive disorder. *Journal of Clinical Psychiatry*, *65*, 810–819.

Merikangas, K., He, J. P., Burstein, M., Swanson, S., Avenevoli, S., Cui, L., . . . Swendsen, J. (2010). Lifetime prevalence of mental disorders in US adolescents: results from the National Comorbidity Survey Replication–Adolescent Supplement (NCS-A). *Journal of the American Academy of Child and Adolescent Psychiatry*, *49*(10), 980–989.

Monroe, S. M. and Harkness, K. L. (2011). Recurrence in major depression: a conceptual analysis. *Psychological review*, *118*(4), 655–674.

Musliner, K. L., Munk-Olsen, T., Laursen, T. M., Eaton, W. W., Zandi, P. P. and Mortensen, P. B. (2016). Heterogeneity in 10-year course trajectories of moderate to severe major depressive disorder: a Danish national register-based study. *JAMA Psychiatry*, *73*(4), 346–353.

Najman, J. M., Khatun, M., Mamun, A., Clavarino, A., Williams, G., Scott, J., . . . Alati, R. (2014). Does depression experienced by mothers leads to a decline in marital quality: a 21-year longitudinal study. *Social Psychiatry and Psychiatric Epidemiology*, *49*(1), 121–132.

Nanni, V., Uher, R. and Danese, A. (2012). Childhood maltreatment predicts unfavorable course of illness and treatment outcome in depression: a meta-analysis. *American Journal of Psychiatry*, *169*, 141–151.

O'Connor, R. C. and Nock, M. K. (2014). The psychology of suicidal behaviour. *The Lancet Psychiatry*, *1*(1), 73–85.

Pine, D. S., Cohen, P., Gurley, D., Brook, J. S. and Ma, Y. (1998). The risk for early-adulthood anxiety and depressive disorders in adolescents with anxiety and depressive disorders. *Archives of General Psychiatry*, *55*, 56–64.

Post, R. M. (1992). Transduction of psychosocial stress into the neurobiology of recurrent affective disorder. *American Journal of Psychiatry*, *149*, 999–1010.

Psychogiou, L. and Parry, E. (2014). Why do depressed individuals have difficulty in their parenting role? *Psychological Medicine*, *44*, 1347–1347.

Rao, U., Hammen, C. and Daley, S. (1999). Continuity of depression during the transition to adulthood: a 5-year longitudinal study of young women. *Journal of the American Academy of Child and Adolescent Psychiatry*, *38*, 908–915.

Rehman, U. S., Gollan, J. and Mortimer, A. R. (2008). The marital context of depression: research, limitations, and new directions. *Clinical Psychology Review*, *28*(2), 179–198.

Richards, D. (2011). Prevalence and clinical course of depression: a review. *Clinical Psychology Review*, *31*(7), 1117–1125.

Rohde, P., Lewinsohn, P. M., Klein, D. N., Seeley, J. R. and Gau, J. M. (2013). Key characteristics of major depressive disorder occurring in childhood, adolescence, emerging adulthood, and adulthood. *Clinical Psychological Science*, *1*, 41–53.

Rugulies, R. (2002). Depression as a predictor for coronary heart disease: a review and meta-analysis. *American Journal of Preventive Medicine*, *23*, 51–61.

Scott, K. M., Lim, C., Al-Hamzawi, A., Alonso, J., Bruffaerts, R., Caldas-de-Almeida, J. M., . . . Kawakami, N. (2016). Association of mental disorders with subsequent chronic physical conditions: World Mental Health Surveys from 17 Countries. *JAMA Psychiatry*, *73*, 150–158.

Shankman, S. A., Lewinsohn, P. M., Klein, D. N., Small, J. W., Seeley, J. R. and Altman, S. E. (2009). Subthreshold conditions as precursors for full syndrome disorders: a 15-year longitudinal study of multiple diagnostic classes. *Journal of Child Psychology and Psychiatry*, *50*(12), 1485–1494.

Solomon, D. A., Keller, M. B., Leon, A. C., Mueller, T. I., Lavori, P. W., Shea, M. T., . . . Endicott, J. (2000). Multiple recurrences of major depressive disorder. *American Journal of Psychiatry*, *157*(2), 229–233.

Spijker, J., de Graaf, R., Bijl, R. V., Beekman, A. T., Ormel, J. and Nolen, W. A. (2002). Duration of major depressive episodes in the general population: results from the Netherlands Mental Health Survey and Incidence Study (NEMESIS). *British Journal of Psychiatry, 181*, 208–213.

Spijker, J., de Graaf, R., Bijl, R. V., Beekman, A. T., Ormel, J. and Nolen, W. A. (2004). Determinants of persistence of major depressive episodes in the general population: results from the Netherlands Mental Health Survey and Incidence Study (NEMESIS). *Journal of Affective Disorders, 81*, 231–240.

Stein, A., Pearson, R., Goodman, S., Rapa, E., Rahman, A., McCallum, M., . . . Pariante, C. (2014). Effects of perinatal mental disorders on the fetus and child. *The Lancet, 384*, 1800–1819.

Stewart, W. F., Ricci, J. A., Chee, E., Hahn, S. R. and Morganstein, D. (2003). Cost of lost productive work time among US workers with depression. *Journal of the American Medical Association, 289*, 3135–3144.

Strine, T. W., Mokdad, A. H., Balluz, L. S., Gonzalez, O., Crider, R., Berry, J. T. and Kroenke, K. (2008). Depression and anxiety in the United States: findings from the 2006 behavioural risk factor surveillance system. *Psychiatric Services, 59*, 1383–1390.

Sutin, A. R., Terracciano, A., Milaneschi, Y., An, Y., Ferrucci, L. and Zonderman, A. B. (2013). The trajectory of depressive symptoms across the adult life span. *JAMA Psychiatry, 70*(8), 803–811.

Teicher, M. H., Samson, J. A., Polcari, A. and Andersen, S. L. (2009). Length of time between onset of childhood sexual abuse and emergence of depression in a young adult sample. *The Journal of Clinical Psychiatry, 70*(5), 684–691.

Thapar, A. and Rice, F. (2006). Twin studies in pediatric depression. *Child and Adolescent Psychiatric Clinics of North America, 15*(4), 869–881.

Thorp, A. A., Owen, N., Neuhaus, M. and Dunstan, D. W. (2011). Sedentary behaviours and subsequent health outcomes in adults: a systematic review of longitudinal studies, 1996–2011. *American Journal of Preventive Medicine, 41*(2), 207–215.

Tunnard, C., Rane, L. J., Wooderson, S. C., Markopoulou, K., Poon, L., Fekadu, A. . . . Cleare, A. J. (2014). The impact of childhood adversity on suicidality and clinical course in treatment-resistant depression. *Journal of Affective Disorders, 152*, 122–130.

Vancampfort, D., Correll, C. U., Wampers, M., Sienaert, P., Mitchell, A. J., De Herdt, A. . . . De Hert, M. (2014). Metabolic syndrome and metabolic abnormalities in patients with major depressive disorder: a meta-analysis of prevalences and moderating variables. *Psychological Medicine, 44*(10), 2017–2028.

Verboom, C., Sijtsema, J., Verhulst, F., Penninx, B. and Ormel, J. (2014). Longitudinal associations between depressive problems, academic performance, and social functioning in adolescent boys and girls. *Developmental Psychology, 50*(1), 247–257.

Wang, P. S., Beck, A. L., Berglund, P., McKenas, D. K., Pronk, N. P., Simon, G. E. and Kessler, R. C. (2004). Effects of major depression on moment-in-time work performance. *American Journal of Psychiatry, 161*, 1885–1891.

Watkins, L. L., Koch, G. G., Sherwood, A., Blumenthal, J. A., Davidson, J. R., O'Connor, C. and Sketch, M. H. (2013). Association of anxiety and depression with all-cause mortality in individuals with coronary heart disease. *Journal of the American Heart Association*, 2(2), e000068.

Weinberger, A. H., Pilver, C. E., Desai, R. A., Mazure, C. M. and McKee, S. A. (2012). The relationship of major depressive disorder and gender to changes in smoking for current and former smokers: longitudinal evaluation in the US population. *Addiction*, 107(10), 1847–1856.

Weissman, M., Fendrich, M., Warner, V. and Wickramaratne, P. (1992). Incidence of psychiatric disorder in offspring at high and low risk for depression. *Journal of the American Academy of Child and Adolescent Psychiatry*, 31, 640–648.

Weissman, M., Wolk, S., Wickramaratne, P., Goldstein, R.B., Adams, P., Greenwald, S., . . . Steinberg, D. (1999). Children with prepubertal-onset major depressive disorder and anxiety grown up. *Archives of General Psychiatry*, 56, 794–801.

Wells, K. B., Stewart, A., Hays, R. D., Burnam, M. A., Rogers, W., Daniels, M., . . . Ware, J. (1989). The functioning and well-being of depressed patients: results from the Medical Outcomes Study. *JAMA*, 262(7), 914–919.

Whisman, M. A. (2007). Marital distress and DSM-IV psychiatric disorders in a population based national survey. *Journal of Abnormal Psychology*, 116, 638–643.

Whisman, M. A. (2013). Relationship discord and the prevalence, incidence, and treatment of psychopathology. *Journal of Social and Personal Relationships*, 30(2), 163–170.

Whiteford, H. A., Degenhardt, L., Rehm, J., Baxter, A. J., Ferrari, A. J., Erskine, H. E., . . . Burstein, R. (2013). Global burden of disease attributable to mental and substance use disorders: findings from the Global Burden of Disease Study 2010. *The Lancet*, 382(9904), 1575–1586.

Wilson, S. and Durbin, C. E. (2010). Effects of paternal depression on fathers' parenting behaviours: a meta-analytic review. *Clinical Psychology Review*, 30(2), 167–180.

Zisook, S., Rush, A. J., Albala, A., Alpert, J., Balasubramani, G. K., Fava, M., . . . Wisniewski, S. (2004). Factors that differentiate early vs. later onset of major depression disorder. *Psychiatry Research*, 129(2), 127–140.

Zlotnick, C., Kohn, R., Keitner, G. and Della Grotta, S. A. (2000). The relationship between quality of interpersonal relationships and major depressive disorder: findings from the National Comorbidity Survey. *Journal of Affective Disorders*, 59, 205–215.

Continued on earlier pages on the next page.

Watkins, L. L., Koch, C. G., Sherwood, A., Blumenthal, J. A., Davidson, J. R., O'Connor, C., and Sketch, M. H. (2013). Association of anxiety and depression with all-cause mortality in individuals with coronary heart disease. Journal of the American Heart Association, 2(2), e000068.

Weinberger, A. H., Pilver, C. E., Desai, R. A., Mazure, C. M., and McKee, S. A. (2012). The relationship of major depressive disorder and gender to changes in smoking for current and former smokers: longitudinal evaluation in the US population. Addiction, 107(10), 1847-1856.

Weissman, M., Bruce, M. L., Warner, V., and Wickramaratne, P. (1992). Epidemiology of psychiatric disorder in childhood at high and low risk for depression. Journal of the American Academy of Child and Adolescent Psychiatry, 31, 640-648.

Wittchen, H. U., Reed, V., Wunderlich, U., Oldehinkel, P., and Greenwald (1999). Prospective onset with prepubertal onset of major depressive disorder and anxiety: a follow-up. Archives of General Psychiatry, 56, 794-801.

Weich, S., Blanchard, M., Prince, M., Burton, E., Erens, B., and Sproston, K. (2002). Mental health and the built environment: cross-sectional survey of individual and contextual risk factors for depression. British Journal of Psychiatry, 180, 428-433.

Weich, S., Twigg, L., and Lewis, G. (2006). Rural/non-rural differences in rates of common mental disorders in Britain: prospective multilevel cohort study. British Journal of Psychiatry, 188, 51-57.

Welle, R. E., Siegel, J. A., Hays, R. D., Stewart, M. A., Rogers, W., Daniels, M., Ware, J. (1989). The functioning and well-being of depressed patients: result from the Medical Outcomes Study. JAMA, 262(7), 914-919.

Wittchen, H. U. (2002). Multiple disorders and DSM-IV psychiatric disorders in a population-based national survey. Journal of Abnormal Psychology, 111, 645-655.

Whisman, M. A. (2013). Relationship discord and the prevalence, incidence, and treatment of psychopathology. Journal of Social and Personal Relationships, 30(2), 163-170.

Whiteford, H. A., Degenhardt, L., Rehm, J., Baxter, A. J., Ferrari, A. J., Erskine, H. E., Vos, T. (2013). Global burden of disease attributable to mental and substance use disorders: findings from the Global Burden of Disease Study 2010. The Lancet, 382(9904), 1575-1586.

Wang, S., and Deal, R. (2010). Linkers of parental depression to children's internalizing behaviour: a meta-analytic review. Clinical Psychology Review, 30(2), 152-150.

Zisook, S., Rush, A. J., Albala, A., Alpert, J., Balasubramani, G. K., Fava, M., Wisniewski, S. (2004). Factors that differentiate early vs. later onset of major depression disorder. Psychiatry Research, 129(2), 127-140.

Zlotnick, C., Kohn, R., Keitner, G., and Della Grotta, S. A. (2000). The relationship between quality of interpersonal relationships and major depressive disorder: findings from the National Comorbidity Survey. Journal of Affective Disorders, 59, 205-215.

3
Who is affected by depression?

Depression is universal. It is seen in all cultures, all age groups, and all segments of society, rich or poor. In this chapter we explore three issues. First, how common is depression and what proportion of the population is affected? Second, are some segments of the population more prone to depression than others? The third issue is *why* some groups are more depression-prone than others, and what might be the implications for understanding depression.

Prevalence of depression

One of the greatest challenges of depression is that it is common, afflicting large portions of the population. Indeed, its frequency is the reason that it has been termed the 'common cold' of psychological disorders. When considering how frequent depressive disorders may be, it is helpful to consider two measures, one concerning how many depressed people there are in a given period, and the other indicating how many people experience significant depression in their lifetimes.

The most valid method of estimating the frequency of depression, either in a given period or over a lifetime, is a survey of representative adult community members who are systematically interviewed using standard criteria for diagnosing depressive disorders. Despite efforts to standardise methods, variations in procedures have affected rates of reported depression including ages of the population sampled, changes in the diagnostic criteria for disorders over time, as well as alterations in interview methods (Kessler et al., 2003). Moreover, only in recent years has there been increasing standardisation of methods across nations, using the World Health Organization (WHO) Composite International Diagnostic Interview (CIDI), which itself has gone through several revisions. The use of the WHO-CIDI in randomly selected adult samples permits calculation of population rates of disorders, facilitates cross-national comparisons and helps to identify mental health needs within diverse communities. The studies below all have used WHO-CIDI methods except where noted.

12-Month prevalence of depression in adults

Using the diagnosis of major depressive episode according to DSM-IV criteria as the unit of measurement, one common measure is the rate of depression in the past year. In the largest available survey, carried out with assistance from the WHO World Mental Health (WMH) Survey Initiative, Kessler and colleagues collected epidemiological data from 18 countries involving 89,000 representative adults. In their report, Bromet et al. (2011) found that across 10 high income countries, the average 12-month prevalence of major depressive episode was 5.5 per cent, and the mean rate across 8 low-to-middle income countries was 5.9 per cent – a nonsignificant difference. Notably, rates in high income countries ranged from 2.2 per cent (Japan) to 8.3 per cent (US). In the lower income nations, rates ranged between 3.8 per cent in Shenzen, China and 10.4 per cent in São Paulo, Brazil (see Table 3.1). As Bromet and colleagues note, varying rates raise questions about the reasons for differences that cannot yet be answered. For instance, there may be effects of different kinds of stressful social conditions across countries contributing to depression. Also, there are likely methodological issues reflecting limitations in representativeness of samples in some countries. It is also important to consider the effects of cultural factors on accurately defining and capturing depression experiences, as well as influencing respondents' willingness to express them in the face-to-face interviews. Risk factors contributing to depression occurrence are presented in various chapters of this book.

The largest single national epidemiological survey covering 43,000 adults representing all segments of the population in the US used DSM-IV criteria but a slightly different interview than the WMH study. The authors reported a 12-month major depressive episode prevalence of 5.3 per cent (Hasin, Goodwin, Stinson and Grant, 2005).

Table 3.1 Proportion of adults with diagnosis of major depression in past 12 months by country

	% with DSM-IV major depression in 12 months
High-income countries	
Belgium	5.0
France	5.9
Germany	3.0
Israel	6.1
Italy	3.0
Japan	2.2
Netherlands	4.9
New Zealand	6.6
Spain	4.0
United States	8.3
Total	*5.5*
Low-to-middle-income countries	
Sao Paulo, Brazil	10.4
Columbia	6.2
Pondicherry, India	4.5
Lebanon	5.5
Mexico	4.0
Shenzen, China	3.8
South Africa	4.9
Ukraine	8.4
Total	*5.9*

Adapted from Bromet, E., Andrade, L., Hwang, I., Sampson, N., Alonso, J., de Girolamo, G., Kessler, R.C. (2011). Cross-national epidemiology of DSM-IV major depressive episode. *BMC Medicine 9*, 90.

Increasingly there is recognition that depression is best thought of as occurring on a continuum of severity in which distress and impairment occur even if an individual does not meet full diagnostic criteria for a major depressive episode (e.g., Rodríguez, Nuevo, Chatterji and Ayuso-Mateos, 2012; Ruscio and Ruscio, 2000). For example, Kessler and colleagues (1997) reported that in addition to the lifetime rate of major depression, another 10 per cent of the US adult population had experienced minor depressive disorder with impairment at some point. Thus, elevated rates of depressive symptoms are typically found in community and primary care medical samples, reminding us that the true scope of debility due to depression is much higher than approximately 6 per cent of diagnosed major depression in a given year (e.g., Van de Velde, Bracke and Levecque, 2010).

Although 'happiness' is a construct that is not the opposite of depression, readers may also be interested in variations in happiness and perceived well-being around the globe. Findings are presented country by country, and analyses of the social conditions that may influence perceived well-being are evaluated including such concepts as safety, income fairness/inequality, health, education, and government (see Helliwell, Layard and Sachs, 2015).

Lifetime diagnoses of depression in adults

Not only is depression fairly common at any given moment or within the past year, but its lifetime prevalence shows that a substantial segment of the population experiences a major depressive episode at least once. The WHO study mentioned above reported a rate of 14.6 per cent among high income countries (range 6.6 per cent in Japan and 21 per cent in France), and 11.1 per cent in low-middle income countries, ranging from 6.5 per cent in Shenzen and 18.4 per cent in São Paulo (Bromet et al., 2011).

Two additional points about the epidemiology of depression warrant mention. One is that whether current or lifetime depressive disorders are highly likely to co-occur with other psychological disorders (more than 70 per cent have comorbidity; Kessler et al., 2003). Such disorders, as noted in Chapter 1, occur either concurrently, or most commonly other disorders occur historically prior to depressive disorders. Depressive disorders most often co-occur with anxiety disorders (e.g., Kessler et al., 2011), but also with elevated rates of behavioural and substance use disorders (e.g., Hasin et al., 2005).

Sociodemographic correlates of depression

As we have noted, depression occurs in all segments of society worldwide. However, some categories of people seem to be more susceptible than others. Two of the most-studied differences are age and gender, but we must also consider additional characteristics such as culture/ethnicity, socioeconomic status, and social characteristics such as marital status.

Ethnicity and cultural differences

The WHO cross-national study of 18 nations noted earlier, hints at cultural and ethnic sources of variance in rates of depression. Cross-cultural differences, where they do exist, are especially pronounced between Western and non-Western cultures. However, caution is needed in drawing firm conclusions that Western rates are actually higher, because the methods for defining depression in different cultures may not be fully comparable despite use of standardised assessment instruments. The expression of depressive symptoms, for example, may vary by culture, so that the same measurement instruments may not be equally appropriate. One important cultural difference is the extent to which individuals distinguish between emotional and somatic experiences. Western thinking makes a distinction between mind and body that most of the non-Western world would find strange (Markus and Kitayama, 1991). Westerners emphasise self-expression, promotion of autonomy, uniqueness and openness to emotional expression, with depression often focused on individual subjective, self-oriented distress ('I'm a loser', 'I feel worthless'). In contrast, non-Western expressions of emotional distress more commonly focus on bodily complaints and relational problems. The diagnostic criteria for depression are largely Western, and might fail to capture non-Western expressions. Similarly, cultures differ in the extent to which it is desirable and acceptable to admit certain experiences, such as suicidal thoughts, which might affect the diagnosis of depressive conditions. Thus, the meaning of different rates of depression in different cultures requires cautious interpretation.

Within the US, extensive studies have been conducted on ethnic subgroups, permitting evaluation of possible cultural differences separate from socio-economic status. The National Comorbidity Survey-Replication, sampling English-speaking households, found that Hispanics and Blacks both had lower rates of lifetime major depression than did Whites (Breslau, Aguilar-Gaxiola, Kendler, Su, Williams and Kessler, 2005) as well as lower rates of current major depression (Riolo, Nguyen, Greden and King, 2005), although the latter investigators reported higher rates of dysthymic disorder (mild persistent depression) in specific subgroups; Mexican Americans and African Americans, compared to Whites. In an adolescent sample from the National Comorbidity Survey, there were no differences between race groups in major depression after adjusting for income, sex, and age (Avenevoli, Swendsen, He, Burstein and Merikangas, 2015).

In US samples, ethnic differences may be affected by immigrant status. A study comparing US and foreign-born Mexican Americans and Whites found that foreign-born groups were at significantly lower risk for mood disorders compared to US-born groups (Grant, Stinson, Hasin, Dawson, Chou and Anderson, 2004). However, US-born Mexican-Americans had higher rates of depression than foreign-born Mexican-Americans (the 'immigrant paradox'), suggesting a negative effect of acculturation on mental health, although their rates of depression were lower than those of US-born Whites. Overall, studies of differences in patterns of depression among subgroups within a population can be explored to clarify the cultural beliefs and customs, socioeconomic and stress factors that affect rates of depression.

Immigration status has emerged as an important public policy and health topic in Europe in recent years, inasmuch nearly 9 per cent of the population in 2010 were foreign-born – and of course, far more today. A mental health survey of depressive symptoms was conducted by the European Social Survey 2006/7 involving 37,000 representative members of the general population (including 5,400 immigrants) residing in 20 European countries. Levecque and Van Rossem (2015) found that non-EU migrants were especially susceptible to elevated symptoms, particularly first-generation migrants. The effects were largely due to the investigators' measures of experienced discrimination and host countries' policies representing barriers to socioeconomic integration, including type of welfare supports. Self-perceived membership in an ethnic minority group was not in itself predictive of depression.

Socioeconomic status

In many of the classic epidemiological surveys conducted in the US, low income and lower educational attainment are consistently associated with higher rates of major depressive episodes (Hasin et al., 2005; Kessler et al., 2003). Similarly, in the WHO WMH Survey higher income nations overall also showed an association between low income and depression (Bromet et al., 2011). However, in low-middle income countries, varying levels of income were not significantly associated with depression. Associations of depression with education levels were generally not significant overall, and in some countries high educational attainment was associated with depression, while in others depression was more likely among the less educated. It can be speculated that the context in which poverty and low education occur is critically important, with depression likely depending on stress-inducing barriers – both psychological and material – that low socioeconomic status creates.

Marital status

Marital condition is one of the strongest demographic correlates of major depression in nearly all major epidemiological surveys. Notably, in the WHO study of 18 nations, Bromet and colleagues (2011) found that in high-income countries, being separated or never married had the highest association with major depressive episode, while in low-middle income countries the highest association was with being divorced or widowed. Countries varied considerably, presumably reflecting to some extent the cultural meaning of the different marital situations and the extent of marginalisation of the non-married person, plus likely the accompanying economic hardship and availability of alternative sources of financial support. However, interactions with gender and income status were not specifically reported.

As we will explore in more detail in Chapter 6, marital status confers protection from depression – at least in Western high income countries – only when the quality of the marriage is good. Poor quality relationships lacking in closeness and high in conflict are highly predictive of depressive reactions.

Overall, the demographic correlates of depression – such as age and social status – help point in the direction of causal factors. Clearly, any biological model of depression must acknowledge the tremendously important social factors that shape distributions of depressive disorders. Psychological models of depression also must be able to account for the concentration of depressions among women, the young, and the disadvantaged.

Age and depression

Of all the demographic features especially associated with depression, particular attention needs to be focused on age and gender. For many years, depression was considered a disorder of middle age or older. However, as we explore in Chapter 2 on age of onset of depression, it is now apparent that the common age of onset of depression is in late adolescence and early adulthood. Thus, it is not surprising to observe that the proportions of people with current or recent major depression are higher among younger individuals and trending downward after about age 50 in US samples (Kessler, Birnbaum, Bromet, Hwang, Sampson and Shahly, 2010). In the international study, the effect of earlier ages of one-year prevalence was true especially for the higher income nations, but less consistent in the lower-middle income countries (Kessler, Birnbaum, Shayley et al., 2010).

Several additional issues regarding age of depression are explored further below.

Increasing rates of depression among the young

Young adult and teenage onset and prevalence of depression appears to reflect a true change in patterns of depression that started occurring in the latter part of the twentieth century. Marking a change from eras when clinically significant depression was mostly seen in middle-aged and older adults, Klerman and Weissman (1989) were among the first to propose that depression was increasing among the young. They noted that rates of depressive disorder were relatively higher in those born more recently, based on retrospective reports from US populations born in different eras. What they termed a 'birth cohort effect' was substantiated in an international study. The Cross National Collaborative Group (1992) employed standardised methods of assessing retrospective reports of depression in various US cities, Paris, Beirut, Alberta (Canada), Puerto Rico, Munich, New Zealand, Taiwan and Florence (Italy). Respondents were classified by decade of birth, and in all but the Florence sample, rates of major depression were highest by age 25 among those born since 1955 compared to those born earlier. The US NCS-R study has also documented significantly increased rates of depression among those in younger birth cohorts, with higher levels by age 20 among those born more recently (Kessler et al., 2003). A number of smaller-scale studies also reported similar trends, and particularly indicated relatively high rates of depressive disorders and symptoms in adolescents (e.g., Lewinsohn, Rohde, Seeley and Fischer, 1993; Oldehinkel, Wittchen and Schuster, 1999). The US National Comorbidity Survey-Adolescent Supplement of youth 13–18 found an overall lifetime prevalence of major depressive episode or dysthymia of 11.7 per cent (and 17–18 year-olds reported a lifetime rate of 15.4 per cent) (Merikangas et al., 2010; see also Oldehinkel et al., 1999 in a Dutch sample).

To confirm the birth cohort effect, it is especially informative to have samples using similar methods assessed at different time points, but such research designs have been rare. An example is a study of two representative national samples of English youth, one studied in 1986 and one studied in 2006. The authors found that twice as many 16–17-year-old girls reported frequent experiences of depressive and anxious symptoms in 2006 (approximately 20 per cent) as in 1986 (approximately 9 per cent), and boys also showed increases (Collishaw, Maughan, Natarajan and Pickles, 2010). In the US, investigators compared scores on a well-known measure of symptomatology and personality features across several decades of testing on college students and high school students (Twenge, Gentile, DeWall, Ma, Lacefield and Schurtz, 2010). The authors found significant increases over time on proportions scoring in the 'clinical' range, including scores on the Depression Scale. These results are paralleled by clear evidence of greatly increased help-seeking for depression among college students over recent years (e.g., Hunt and Eisenberg, 2010). However, the increase in treatment-seeking may reflect changing attitudes of greater acceptance of treatment, and the findings do not directly validate an increased occurrence of depression in those born more recently.

What could account for this seeming trend toward more depression among the young? Is there an epidemic of depression in Western nations? This is a challenging problem. Are results skewed by method artifacts?

As noted, few studies are available that used identical methods given multiple times over the years. Most of the studies of the birth cohort effect have relied on retrospective reports of lifetime depression, but such information requires not only memory accuracy, but also awareness and accurate labelling of personal experiences. Some have argued that young people nowadays have greater perception of and willingness to acknowledge and even seek help for depressive experiences than in previous generations. This is probably accurate, but should not be taken to imply that they exaggerate minor problems that become mislabelled as depressive disorders. Indeed, suicide rates for young people dramatically increased until around 1990 in the US, suggesting true – not exaggerated – distress and debility. Regarding memory artifacts, more distal experiences may be more easily forgotten compared to younger people's more recent experiences, and thus there may be some merit to the argument that birth cohort increases in depression may be an artifact of memory issues (Paykel, Brugha and Fryers, 2005). A different approach to avoid memory artifact is to rely only on assessment of current depression. Costello, Erklani and Angold (2006) examined epidemiological studies of child and adolescent depression over the period 1965 and 1995. They found similar rates of current diagnoses of depression across the samples at different times, thus partially disputing the notion of a growing epidemic of depression among younger participants.

Although there may be some method artifacts at play in accounting for some of the dramatic birth cohort differences in depression, investigators have also noted significant social and cultural shifts over the years that might contribute to greater depression. It has been suggested that evidence of increased instability in the family (such as divorce) and increasing social mobility, are not only potential sources of depression but might also reduce the available resources for helping individuals cope with stressful situations that cause depression. Some have argued that cultural shifts emphasising values of materialism and personal attainment, to the relative de-emphasis on serving God, community, and broader social goals, have left young people with greater pressure for success and less opportunity for fulfillment and sense of meaning (e.g., Hunt and Eisenberg, 2010; Seligman, Reivich, Jaycox and Gillham, 1995; Twenge et al., 2010). In later chapters we review various theories of the causes of depression that explore the role of stress, family and interpersonal relations, social support, and beliefs about the self and the future as they pertain to depression. The bottom line on age of onset of depression is that for any theory of depression to be credible, it must be capable of helping to account for the apparently increased rates of depression in young people.

Epidemiology of depression in children and adolescents

Most epidemiological surveys have included only adults of 18 and older and excluded children and youth. Estimates of childhood depression, for example, are based on limited surveys. Before the 1980s depression was conceptualised as a disorder that children could not experience directly because they were not developmentally mature enough. That view changed radically, however, in ensuing decades, and age-adjusted criteria can be applied reliably even to very young children. However, depression in children younger than about 12 is relatively rare, affecting an estimated 2–3 per cent of the population or less (e.g., Costello, Mustillo, Erkanli, Keeler and Angold, 2003; Egger and Angold, 2006). Clinically significant depression in preschool age children apparently occurs in around 1 per cent (Stalets and Luby, 2006), and is predictive of school-age depression and substantial functional impairment (Luby, 2010).

The great majority of major depressive episodes in adolescents occur after about age 13. As noted earlier, the US National Comorbidity Survey-Adolescent Supplement of 13–18-year-olds found an overall lifetime prevalence of major depressive episode or dysthymia of 11.7 per cent and one-year prevalence of 7.5 per cent (Avenevoli, Swendsen, He, Burstein and Merikangas, 2015; Merikangas et al., 2010), accompanied by significant levels of severity, comorbidity, suicidality, and impairment of functioning. A review of various studies of youth depression including international samples shows a range of rates of major depression, but they generally agree that median rates of prevalence rise steadily throughout adolescence and reach or exceed those of adults by mid-to-late adolescence (Thapar, Collishaw, Pine and Thapar, 2012). In later chapters the course, correlates, dysfunctions, and risk factors for adolescent depression are discussed. Because of the high rates of recurrence of adolescent depression during adulthood, its features largely define the prototype of typical adult depression.

Depression in older adults

Depression among the older segments of the population has often been misunderstood. Sometimes its manifestations as problems of memory and loss of energy and other bodily symptoms are misinterpreted as senescence, an irreversible decline in mental and physical capabilities. Also, depression may be misperceived, mistaken as medical complaints such as fatigue, loss of appetite, low energy, insomnia and reduced mobility. Thus, depression that can be treated might be misdiagnosed as a largely untreatable problem, or missed altogether. Nowadays, however, there is increasing attention to late life depression, particularly as it may affect quality of life and capacity to cope with medical illnesses, and also because it may often be a symptom and warning sign of degenerative neurological conditions.

In the US and other higher income countries, major depression is significantly lower in individuals 65 and above compared to younger samples (e.g., Bromet et al., 2011; Kessler et al., 2010). In low-middle income nations the rates are relatively higher in late life, although in both income groups of nations there is considerable variability. However, many epidemiological studies have not included representative samples that live in institutional care or other facilities in which depression is likely higher than among community-dwelling residents. Also, when continuous measures of depressive symptomatology, rather than only diagnoses are assessed, some studies show increases in depression in older samples generally. In the Canadian Study of Health and Aging, for example, individuals of 65 and older who represented both community-dwelling and seniors in chronic care and nursing home facilities were studied longitudinally over ten years, and regularly evaluated for both depressive diagnoses and symptomatology (Wu, Schimmele and Chappell, 2012). Average depressive symptom scores increased linearly from age 65 on – largely correlated with increases in medical comorbidity. However, diagnoses of depression showed a U-shaped pattern with age, declining after age 65 but rising after about age 85. The Baltimore Longitudinal Study of Aging studied individuals aged 19–95 over a longitudinal course using a continuous measure of depressive symptoms (Sutin, Terracciano, Milaneschi, An, Ferrucci and Zonderman, 2013). Results of this study also showed a U-shaped curve, with symptoms highest at younger ages, then declining to about age 60 and then trending upward significantly to age 90 – and not due solely to increased somatic complaints. Thus, patterns of depression in late life vary with the design of the study, the representativeness of the sample and methods of assessment – as well as cultural variations in the meaning and social consequences of ageing. In wealthier, Western-oriented nations, depression is largely a problem of younger citizens, but possibly shows upticks in late life.

Gender differences in depression

In addition to age differences in who is affected by depression, one of the most striking characteristics of depression is that it is far more common among women than men. Across different methods of study and different countries of the world, with few exceptions, studies report approximately a 2:1 rate of depression diagnoses for women compared to men (e.g., Bromet et al., 2011).

For example, in the largest US epidemiological survey, lifetime rate of major depressive disorder was 17.1 per cent for women and 9 per cent for men, and one-year prevalence was 6.9 per cent for women and 3.6 per cent for men (Hasin et al., 2005). Also, the level of depressive symptoms in women was higher in women than men in all 25 countries of the European Social Survey (3rd wave), and statistically significantly higher in 23 countries (Van de Velde, Bracke, Levecque and Meuleman, 2010). Moreover, depression is accompanied by high levels of comorbid conditions as we have noted, and depressed women in particular experience high levels of anxiety disorders (e.g., Kessler, 2003) compared to men.

Lifetime rates of diagnosed depression for US adolescent women were 15.9 per cent, and 7.7 per cent for men (Merikangas et al., 2010). Interestingly, in general there are no significant gender differences in rates of depression in children, as boys generally show the same or even higher rates of diagnoses and symptoms as girls (e.g., Angold, Erkanli, Silberg, Eaves and Costello, 2002; Luby, Gaffrey, Tillman, April and Belden, 2014). Notably, however, girls' rates of depression tend to accelerate around age 12 or 13 and are similar to adult women's rates during adolescence, and continue higher than men's rates through the lifespan, while boys' depression rates remain relatively stable at a lower level compared to girls (e.g., Angold et al., 2002; Hankin and Abramson, 2001). These patterns raise two important questions: why more depression in females, and why does the gender difference emerge in adolescence?

Why more depression in women?

Numerous efforts have been devoted to explaining sex differences in depression (e.g., Hankin and Abramson, 2001; Kessler, 2003; Kuehner, 2016; Nolen-Hoeksema, 1990; 2002), hypothesising multiple contributing factors. The gender differences appear in virtually every culture studied, and in nearly every age group except preadolescent children. Some have argued that the gender effects may be partly due to 'artifacts' of sex role differences that affect individuals' perceptions, symptom expressions and reports rather than 'actual' differences. To some extent, it is likely that the excess of depression in women may stem partly from perceptions that depression represents emotional 'weakness' and is therefore shunned by males as unacceptable behaviour. Males may experience depression but express their symptoms differently (e.g., by emphasising physical complaints or work difficulties rather than subjective distress, possibly leading to different diagnostic outcomes – or, deal with depression by excessive use of alcohol and drugs that obscure feelings). Martin, Neighbors, and Griffith (2013) proposed that 'alternative depressive symptoms' such as irritability, aggression, risk-taking, and drug use correlate significantly with traditional depression, and may thus represent male depression. These authors found that when the alternative and traditional symptoms were both included in diagnostic procedures for depression, the rate of depression in men and women was similar – but further studies are needed to validate their alternative criteria.

While differences in male and female role socialisation and symptom expression may contribute somewhat to gender differences in the experience and expression of diagnosable depression, most major explanations have focused on biological, social and psychosocial differences between women and men.

Biological differences

The first thing most people think of to explain sex differences in depression is female biology. However, bear in mind that the marked increase in rates of depression in both men and women in recent decades cannot reasonably be attributed to rapid changes in sex hormones. Rapid changes aside, hormonal fluctuations associated with pregnancy and the postpartum period, menstrual cycles and menopause may seem like strong candidates as explanations for gender differences in depression. However, as we review in Chapter 4 on the biology of depression, studies of hormone–depression associations are complex, have small effects even when major hormonal shifts occur and have effects that likely depend on contributing processes of various psychological and contextual factors. We discuss later in the chapter the specific question of pubertal changes and the emergence of depression in adolescent women.

Another biological 'suspect' concerns effects of stress. Growing emphasis on abnormalities of the stress response system in depression (Chapter 4) may have implications for women to the extent that stress responses are affected by hormones – and because of women's apparently greater exposure and reactivity to stressors. Moreover, complex associations among stress, hormonal activity and depression may also be affected by genetic contributions as we discuss further in Chapter 4.

Social and environmental conditions

There are several variants of the idea that women experience greater stress than men do, and that it is the stress (or stress interacting with some predisposing vulnerability) that causes depression. One version is that in general, women's lives are more chronically stressful due to diminished opportunity and lower status than males – that women are poorer, have less power to control their own destinies, have lower status jobs or roles or pay and have less access to sources of acclaim and reward than men do. As we have discussed earlier in this chapter, women's social status – lower income, less education, widowed or divorced marital conditions – all predict higher levels of depression (although no segment of the population is protected from depression). It has also been hypothesised that women also may be at risk for depression to the extent that their lives include chronically stressful 'dual roles' such as worker and parent that might be in conflict, or hold dual roles that may be more demanding than those of men (e.g., spouse and worker; single working parent). Support for the negative effects of dual roles for women was reported in a classic study by Aneshensel, Frerichs and Clark (1981) based on a large epidemiological survey. They found that among people who were both married and employed, women were more depressed than men – but among unmarried respondents with no children, working men and women did not differ. Poverty and raising children alone may be highly stressful, but in addition, more women than men serve as the primary caregivers for ill relatives such as elderly parents and children with disabilities, although in the very oldest age groups men are often caretakers (e.g., Dahlberg, Demack and Bambra, 2007; Talley and Crewes, 2007).

A second approach to stress has focused on occurrence of stressful life events, suggesting that women are exposed to greater levels of acute stress than men are. Reviews of gender differences in exposure to stressful life events have yielded somewhat mixed findings with most but not all finding that women report high rates of recent stressors than men do (e.g., reviewed in Hammen, 2005; Shih, Eberhart, Hammen and Brennan, 2006). More consistently, women report more stressors with interpersonal content, such as relationship problems, conflicts and losses. Also, women are socialised, and possibly biologically programmed, to spend more time and effort and be more oriented to caregiving and nurturing roles with children, family and friend networks. They are more likely to base their sense of self-worth on close connections with loved ones, compared to men who are more likely oriented to instrumental and achievement roles as sources of self-worth. Accordingly, women are therefore tuned into and more negatively affected by stressful events happening not only to themselves but also to others in their networks (such as illness/accidents and crises happening to family members and close friends). As noted above, women commonly serve more often in stressful caregiving roles, such as responsibilities for helping elderly and ill parents, or caring for children with disabilities. In addition to the chronic stress of managing such responsibilities, there is susceptibility to acute stressful life events associated with such roles, such as medical emergencies, and handling crises involving access to relevant services.

A third type of stress concerns trauma exposure. Men may be more likely exposed to certain types of trauma than women, such as combat, violence and some types of accidents, and such experiences may promote maladaptive reactions and behaviours such as post traumatic stress disorder, elevated rates of drug and alcohol abuse and sometimes suicidality. Relevant to depression, women worldwide are exposed to significantly higher rates of sexual assault in childhood and adolescence than men are (Barth, Bermetz, Heim, Trelle and Tonia, 2013; Finkelhor, Shattuck, Turner and Hamby, 2014). For example Barth et al. (2013) reported average rates of forced intercourse in 9 per cent of girls and 3 per cent in boys based on reviews of studies in 24 countries. In a US telephone survey of youth aged 15–17, rates increased with age such that at 17 years old, 26.6 per cent of girls reported sexual abuse or assault, compared with 5.1 per cent for boys (Finkelhor et al., 2014). Exposure to sexual abuse during childhood and adolescence is strongly predictive of adult depressive disorders and suicidality. For example, in the largest US epidemiological survey, childhood (before age 18) sexual abuse or assault predicted double the rate of major depressive disorder (30 per cent) than among those with no sexual abuse (Pérez-Fuentes, Olfson, Villegas, Morcillo, Wang and Blanco, 2013). In addition to childhood sexual abuse, women and girls are also more likely experience rape, female genital mutilation, sex trafficking, forced marriage and honour killings in some parts of the world, although the effects of these kinds of sexual violence on depression have rarely been studied (Kuehner, 2016).

Finally, research generally supports the idea that females may not only experience higher levels of negative conditions and certain kinds of stressful life events, but also suggests that women are more emotionally reactive to stress in the form of depressive states than men are. For example, Shih, Eberhart, Hammen and Brennan (2006) found that when adolescent girls and boys experienced similar high levels of recent stressful experiences, the girls had significantly higher levels of depression than the boys did. It is also the case that chronic and acute stressors with interpersonal content (such as conflicts, relationship breakups, social isolation) are especially likely to trigger depression reactions compared to stressors with non-interpersonal content (Shih et al., 2006; Teo, Choi and Valenstein, 2013; Vrshek-Schallhorn et al., 2014).

Thus, across various realms of stressful experiences, there is evidence of women's greater stress exposure and association between the exposure and depression. However, it must be emphasised that the link between stress and depression varies considerably as modified by numerous factors such as the person's coping skills and resources, interpretations of the meaning of the stressor, temperament and neurobiological and genetic processes – all of which are discussed in greater detail in later chapters. We discuss coping factors as one of the major focuses of sex differences in depression.

Coping factors

Some investigators have suggested that instead of, or in addition to, social and stress factors that promote depression, women might engage in fewer of the effective coping resources necessary to battle stress and depression than men do. Certainly, disadvantaged women exposed to chronic adversities simultaneously experience the reduction of material coping resources, such as financial and direct help, and may lack stable supportive marital relationships. Although they may have family and social networks, emotional support might itself be reduced if the others are also taxed by their own adversities associated with disadvantaged status (e.g., Belle, 1990).

Women may also have characteristic ways of coping with depression that might actually intensify the dysphoria. In 1991 Susan Nolen-Hoeksema first proposed that when experiencing emotional distress, women display a response style that emphasises rumination, self-focus, and over-analysis of the problems and of their own emotions ('why do I feel this way?'). In contrast, men use more distraction (such as physical activity, sports) and active, direct problem solving – although they may also use dysfunctional coping such as alcohol misuse. When ruminative responses are employed, they tend to intensify negative, self-focused thinking and to interfere with active problem solving – hence deepening or prolonging the symptoms of depression. Taking problem-solving steps or distracting oneself by activity, by contrast, might help to reduce and shorten the depressive experiences. Nolen-Hoeksema argues that sex role socialisation sets the stage for gender differences in coping styles, with boys being discouraged from showing and talking about emotionality and being encouraged to learn to take action, while girls are given license to express emotions and even encouraged to analyze them and discuss them with others. Over the years a large body of studies has demonstrated support for these hypotheses, including gender differences in coping style and the association of ruminative coping with depression (e.g., Johnson and Whisman, 2013; Lyubomirsky, Layous, Chancellor and Nelson, 2015; Michl, McLaughlin, Shepherd, Nolen-Hoeksema, 2013; Nolen-Hoeksema, 2012). In later chapters we discuss associations between depressive cognitions and ruminative response style, as well as rumination-focused treatments for depression (Watkins, 2016).

Why do gender differences emerge in early adolescence?

Explanations of the large increase in girls' depression levels beginning in early adolescence generally focus on the pubertal transition, including biological, social, environmental and psychological factors associated with maturation. As Mendle (2014) and Rudolph (2014) note, puberty is marked by dramatic transformations in youths' lives – some positive and some not, such as major changes in social roles affecting relationships with peers, parents and romantic partners, potentially experiencing changes in body image and self-esteem, as well as likely increasing desire and pressure for autonomy. All young people, boys as well as girls, experience marked increases in symptomatology across a wide variety of disorders. Girls especially show more depression, panic attacks and disordered eating, along with aggression, conduct problems and rule-breaking, while boys are especially likely to show increases in aggression and conduct issues including substance use and rule-breaking.

Biologically, pubertal development involves changes in gonadal hormone levels and effects, although Mendle (2014) notes that the direct associations between hormonal changes such as estradiol and testosterone and psychopathology are not well understood. Also during adolescent development, the brain is experiencing neural maturation. As Rudolph (2014; see also Ladouceur, 2012) notes, developmental neuroscience research has established that there is inconsistent maturation across parts of the brain, such that areas of the prefrontal cortex relevant to cognitive control (such as judgment and executive functions) are less fully developed in adolescence, compared to areas such as subcortical limbic regions including the amygdala and hippocampus that regulate emotion, arousal and motivation. This disjuncture may lead to emotion dysregulation, such as heightened and prolonged emotional reactivity to social-emotional stimuli, with less availability of brain maturation in areas promoting cognitive control and coping.

In particular, pubertal timing – early maturation compared to peers – is associated with more depression in girls (reviewed in Mendle, 2014; Rudolph, 2014). The precise mechanisms by which girls' early pubertal development results in depression are not yet clear, but likely there are both biological and psychosocial/contextual contributors. Biologically, to a significant extent timing is under genetic control, but in addition, it has been shown that early pubertal development in adolescents is especially associated with adverse environmental conditions such as harsh parenting, maltreatment, poverty and family instability (Ellis, 2004). This means that early-maturing youth may face the potentially exciting but also confusing changes of puberty within more stress-filled life contexts, perhaps armed with less effective supports and

behavioural coping strategies. At the same time, disjunctures in brain development noted above may promote heightened emotional reactivity to stressors
but less well-developed control mechanisms for cognitive, behavioural and
emotional coping.

Additional psychological and social issues that affect girls, in particular,
at puberty, have also been shown to be predictive of depression. Early-
maturing girls, for example, often have lower self-esteem and concerns about
body image and weight gain, whereas for boys early maturity is generally
perceived as positive and advantageous (reviewed in Rudolph, 2014). While
there may be some social advantages associated with girls' maturation (more
attention from boys), research has shown that physical maturation may also
have costs, such as teasing, relational aggression and sexual harassment
(Rudolph, 2014). Moreover, to the extent that pubertal maturation is often
accompanied by girls' increased interest in romantic relationships, there is
significant evidence that such early relationships are commonly associated
with depression in the face of instability, break-ups, disappointments, sexual
issues, conflicts and the like – not to mention potentially negative reactions
from parents and peers (reviewed in Davila, 2008). Further, a longitudinal
study of adolescent girls suggested that those with early pubertal development were especially likely to develop ruminative style, and that rumination
helped to account for the association between early pubertal status and
depressive symptoms (Alloy, Hamilton, Hamlat and Abramson, 2016).

In sum, depression in young women in the adolescent transition to
adulthood sets the stage for increasing rates of depression to double those of
depression in men, persisting throughout the adult child-bearing years. The
factors that contribute to the emergence of depression in young people are
some of the core variables that shape the enormous burden of depression, as
discussed more fully in Chapter 2.

Summary

- Major depression is highly prevalent throughout the world,
  affecting an average of one in seven adults in high income
  countries and one in nine in lower-to-middle income countries.
  Additionally, many additional thousands of individuals
  experience significant depressive symptoms that do not reach
  full criteria for a major episode.
- Depression mainly affects adolescents and young adults, with
  evidence of increasing rates among young people born in more

recent decades compared to older generations. There is some evidence that rates are also elevated in elderly populations.

◆ Women are twice as likely to experience major depression as men, and significant gender differences occur across most cultures.

◆ Besides age and gender, additional sociodemographic factors are associated with elevated rates of depression, including social disadvantage, cultural differences and marital status. Thus, theories of the origins of depression must be able to account for diverse social factors that determine who is affected.

◆ Women's elevated rates of depression emerge in adolescence and explanations focus on biological factors such as female hormones, women's apparent greater exposure to stressors and gender differences in coping styles and resources.

References

Alloy, L. B., Hamilton, J. L., Hamlat, E. J. and Abramson, L. Y. (2016). Pubertal development emotion regulatory styles, and the emergence of sex differences in internalising disorders and symptoms in adolescence. *Clinical Psychological Science*, 4, 867–881.

Aneshensel, C. S., Frerichs, R. R. and Clark, V. A. (1981). Family roles and sex differences in depression. *Journal of Health and Social Behaviour*, 22, 379–393.

Angold, A., Erkanli, A., Silberg, J., Eaves, L. and Costello, E. J. (2002). Depression scale scores in 8–17-year-olds: effects of age and gender. *Journal of Child Psychology and Psychiatry*, 43(8), 1052–1063.

Avenevoli, S., Swendsen, J., He, J. P., Burstein, M. and Merikangas, K. R. (2015). Major depression in the National Comorbidity Survey–Adolescent Supplement: prevalence, correlates, and treatment. *Journal of the American Academy of Child and Adolescent Psychiatry*, 54(1), 37–44.

Barth, J., Bermetz, L., Heim, E., Trelle, S. and Tonia, T. (2013). The current prevalence of child sexual abuse worldwide: a systematic review and meta-analysis. *International Journal of Public Health*, 58(3), 469–483.

Belle, D. (1990). Poverty and women's mental health. *American Psychologist*, 45(3), 385–389.

Breslau, J., Aguilar-Gaxiola, S., Kendler, K. S., Su, M., Williams, D. and Kessler, R. C. (2005). Specifying race-ethnic differences in risk for psychiatric disorder in a USA national sample. *Psychological Medicine*, 35, 1–12.

Bromet, E., Andrade, L., Hwang, I., Sampson, N., Alonso, J., de Girolamo, G., . . . Kessler, R.C. (2011). Cross-national epidemiology of DSM-IV major depressive episode. *BMC Medicine*, 9, 90.

Collishaw, S., Maughan, B., Natarajan, L. and Pickles, A. (2010). Trends in adolescent emotional problems in England: a comparison of two national cohorts twenty years apart. *Journal of Child Psychology and Psychiatry*, 51(8), 885–894.

Costello, E., Erkanli, A. and Angold, A. (2006). Is there an epidemic of child or adolescent depression? *Journal of Child Psychology and Psychiatry*, 47(12), 1263–1271.

Costello, E. J., Mustillo, S., Erkanli, A., Keeler, G. and Angold, A. (2003). Prevalence and development of psychiatric disorders in childhood and adolescence. *Archives of General Psychiatry*, 60, 837–844.

Cross National Collaborative Group. (1992). The changing rate of major depression: cross-national comparisons. *Journal of the American Medical Association*, 268, 3098–3105.

Dahlberg, L., Demack, S. and Bambra, C. (2007). Age and gender of informal carers: a population-based study in the UK. *Health and Social Care in the Community*, 15(5), 439–445.

Davila, J. (2008). Depressive symptoms and adolescent romance: theory, research, and implications. *Child Development Perspectives*, 2(1), 26–31.

Egger, H. L. and Angold, A. (2006). Common emotional and behavioural disorders in preschool children: presentation, nosology, and epidemiology. *Journal of Child Psychology and Psychiatry*, 47(3–4), 313–337.

Ellis, B. J. (2004). Timing of pubertal maturation in girls: an integrated life history approach. *Psychological Bulletin*, 130(6), 920–958.

Finkelhor, D., Shattuck, A., Turner, H. A. and Hamby, S. L. (2014). The lifetime prevalence of child sexual abuse and sexual assault assessed in late adolescence. *Journal of Adolescent Health*, 55(3), 329–333.

Grant, B. F., Stinson, F. S., Hasin, D. S., Dawson, D. A., Chou, S. P. and Anderson, K. (2004). Immigration and lifetime prevalence of DSM-IV psychiatric disorders among Mexican Americans and non-Hispanic Whites in the United States. *Archives of General Psychiatry*, 61, 1226–1233.

Hammen, C. (2005). Stress and depression. *Annual Review of Clinical Psychology*, 1, 293–319.

Hankin, B. L. and Abramson, L. Y. (2001). Development of gender differences in depression: an elaborated cognitive vulnerability–transactional stress theory. *Psychological Bulletin*, 127, 773–796.

Hasin, D. S., Goodwin, R. D., Stinson, F. S. and Grant, B. F. (2005). Epidemiology of major depressive disorder: results from the National Epidemiologic Survey on Alcoholism and Related Conditions. *Archives of General Psychiatry*, 62(10), 1097–1106.

Helliwell, J. F., Layard, R. and Sachs, J. (eds). (2015). *World Happiness Report 2015*. New York: Sustainable Development Solutions Network. Download from website http://worldhappiness.report/ed/2015/ and the World Happiness Report 2016 Update is on the website http://worldhappiness.report/

Hunt, J. and Eisenberg, D. (2010). Mental health problems and help-seeking behaviour among college students. *Journal of Adolescent Health*, 46(1), 3–10.

Johnson, D. P. and Whisman, M. A. (2013). Gender differences in rumination: a meta-analysis. *Personality and Individual Differences, 55*(4), 367–374.

Kessler, R. C. (2003). Epidemiology of women and depression. *Journal of Affective Disorders, 74*(1), 5–13.

Kessler, R. C., Berglund, P., Demler, O., Jin, R., Koretz, D., Merikangas, K. R., . . . Wang, P. S. (2003). The epidemiology of major depressive disorder: results from the National Comorbidity Survey Replication (NCS-R). *Journal of the American Medical Association, 289*(23), 3095–3105.

Kessler, R. C., Birnbaum, H., Bromet, E., Hwang, I., Sampson, N. and Shahly, V. (2010). Age differences in major depression: results from the National Comorbidity Survey Replication (NCS-R). *Psychological Medicine, 40*(02), 225–237.

Kessler, R. C., Birnbaum, H. G., Shahly, V., Bromet, E., Hwang, I., McLaughlin, K. A., . . . Stein, D. (2010). Age differences in the prevalence and co-morbidity of DSM-IV major depressive episodes: results from the WHO World Mental Health Survey Initiative. *Depression and Anxiety, 27*(4), 351–364.

Kessler, R. C., Ormel, J., Petukhova, M., McLaughlin, K. A., Green, J. G., Russo, L. J., . . . and Andrade, L. (2011). Development of lifetime comorbidity in the World Health Organization world mental health surveys. *Archives of General Psychiatry, 68*(1), 90–100.

Kessler, R. C., Zhao, S. Y., Blazer, D. G. and Swartz, M. (1997). Prevalence, correlates, and course of minor depression and major depression in the national comorbidity survey. *Journal of Affective Disorders, 45*, 19–30.

Klerman, G. L. and Weissman, M. M. (1989). Increasing rates of depression. *Journal of the American Medical Association, 261*, 2229–2235.

Kuehner, C. (2016). Why is depression more common among women than among men? *The Lancet Psychiatry, 4*, 146–158.

Ladouceur, C. D. (2012). Neural systems supporting cognitive-affective interactions in adolescence: the role of puberty and implications for affective disorders. *Frontiers in Integrative Neuroscience, 6*, 65. http://dx.doi.org/10.3389/fnint.2012.00065

Levecque, K. and Van Rossem, R. (2015). Depression in Europe: does migrant integration have mental health payoffs? A cross-national comparison of 20 European countries. *Ethnicity and Health, 20*(1), 49–65.

Lewinsohn, P. M., Rohde, P., Seeley, J. R. and Fischer, S. A. (1993). Age-cohort changes in the lifetime occurrence of depression and other mental disorders. *Journal of Abnormal Psychology, 102*(1), 110–120.

Luby, J. L. (2010). Preschool depression the importance of identification of depression early in development. *Current Directions in Psychological Science, 19*(2), 91–95.

Luby, J. L., Gaffrey, M. S., Tillman, R., April, L. M. and Belden, A. C. (2014). Trajectories of preschool disorders to full DSM depression at school age and early adolescence: continuity of preschool depression. *American Journal of Psychiatry, 171*, 768–776.

Lyubomirsky, S., Layous, K., Chancellor, J. and Nelson, S. K. (2015). Thinking about rumination: the scholarly contributions and intellectual legacy of Susan Nolen-Hoeksema. *Annual Review of Clinical Psychology, 11*, 1–22.

Markus, H. R. and Kitayama, S. (1991). Culture and the self: implications for cognition, emotion, and motivation. *Psychological Review*, *98*(2), 224–253.

Martin, L. A., Neighbors, H. W. and Griffith, D. M. (2013). The experience of symptoms of depression in men vs women: analysis of the National Comorbidity Survey Replication. *JAMA Psychiatry*, *70*(10), 1100–1106.

Mendle, J. (2014). Why puberty matters for psychopathology. *Child Development Perspectives*, *8*(4), 218–222.

Merikangas, K. R., He, J. P., Burstein, M., Swanson, S. A., Avenevoli, S., Cui, L., . . . Swendsen, J. (2010). Lifetime prevalence of mental disorders in US adolescents: results from the National Comorbidity Survey Replication–Adolescent Supplement (NCS-A). *Journal of the American Academy of Child and Adolescent Psychiatry*, *49*(10), 980–989.

Michl, L. C., McLaughlin, K. A., Shepherd, K. and Nolen-Hoeksema, S. (2013). Rumination as a mechanism linking stressful life events to symptoms of depression and anxiety: longitudinal evidence in early adolescents and adults. *Journal of Abnormal Psychology*, *122*(2), 339–352.

Nolen-Hoeksema, S. (1990). *Sex differences in depression*. Stanford, CA: Stanford University Press.

Nolen-Hoeksema, S. (2002). Gender differences in depression. In I. H. Gotlib and C. L. Hammen (eds), *Handbook of depression* (pp. 492–509). New York: Guilford Press.

Nolen-Hoeksema, S. (2012). Emotion regulation and psychopathology: the role of gender. *Annual Review of Clinical Psychology*, *8*, 161–187.

Oldehinkel, A. J., Wittchen, H. U. and Schuster, P. (1999). Prevalence, 20-month incidence and outcome of unipolar depressive disorders in a community sample of adolescents. *Psychological Medicine*, *29*(03), 655–668.

Paykel, E. S., Brugha, T. and Fryers, T. (2005). Size and burden of depressive disorders in Europe. *European Neuropsychopharmacology*, *15*(4), 411–423.

Pérez-Fuentes, G., Olfson, M., Villegas, L., Morcillo, C., Wang, S. and Blanco, C. (2013). Prevalence and correlates of child sexual abuse: a national study. *Comprehensive Psychiatry*, *54*(1), 16–27.

Riolo, S. A., Nguyen, T. A., Greden, J. F. and King, C. A. (2005). Prevalence of depression by race/ethnicity: findings from the National Health and Nutrition Examination Survey III. *American Journal of Public Health*, *95*(6), 998–1000.

Rodríguez, M. R., Nuevo, R., Chatterji, S. and Ayuso-Mateos, J. L. (2012). Definitions and factors associated with subthreshold depressive conditions: a systematic review. *BMC Psychiatry*, *12*(1), 181. doi: 10.1186/1471-244X-12-181

Rudolph, K. D. (2014). Puberty as a developmental context of risk for psychopathology. In M. Lewis and K. D. Rudolph (eds), *Handbook of developmental psychology* (3rd edn, pp. 331–354). New York: Springer.

Ruscio, J. and Ruscio, A. M. (2000). Informing the continuity controversy: a taxometric analysis of depression. *Journal of Abnormal Psychology*, *109*(3), 473–487.

Seligman, M. E. P., Reivich, K., Jaycox, L. and Gillham, J. (1995). *The optimistic child*. New York: Houghton Mifflin.

Shih, J. H., Eberhart, N., Hammen, C. and Brennan, P. A. (2006). Differential exposure and reactivity to interpersonal stress predict sex differences in adolescent depression. *Journal of Clinical Child and Adolescent Psychology*, *35*, 103–115.

Stalets, M. M. and Luby, J. L. (2006). Preschool depression. *Child and Adolescent Psychiatric Clinics of North America*, *15*(4), 899–917.

Sutin, A. R., Terracciano, A., Milaneschi, Y., An, Y., Ferrucci, L. and Zonderman, A. B. (2013). The trajectory of depressive symptoms across the adult life span. *JAMA Psychiatry*, *70*(8), 803–811.

Talley, R. C. and Crews, J. E. (2007). Framing the public health of caregiving. *American Journal of Public Health*, *97*(2), 224–228.

Teo, A., Choi, H. and Valenstein, M. (2013) Social relationships and depression: ten-year follow-up from a nationally representative study. *PLOS One 8*(4): e62396. doi: 10.1371/journal.pone.0062396

Thapar, A., Collishaw, S., Pine, D. S. and Thapar, A. K. (2012). Depression in adolescence. *The Lancet*, *379*(9820), 1056–1067.

Twenge, J. M., Gentile, B., DeWall, C. N., Ma, D., Lacefield, K. and Schurtz, D. R. (2010). Birth cohort increases in psychopathology among young Americans, 1938–2007: a cross-temporal meta-analysis of the MMPI. *Clinical Psychology Review*, *30*(2), 145–154.

Van de Velde, S., Bracke, P. and Levecque, K. (2010). Gender differences in depression in 23 European countries. Cross-national variation in the gender gap in depression. *Social Science and Medicine*, *71*(2), 305–313.

Van de Velde, S., Bracke, P., Levecque, K. and Meuleman, B. (2010). Gender differences in depression in 25 European countries after eliminating measurement bias in the CES-D 8. *Social Science Research*, *39*(3), 396–404.

Vrshek-Schallhorn, S., Mineka, S., Zinbarg, R. E., Craske, M. G., Griffith, J. W., Sutton, J., . . . Adam, E. K. (2014). Refining the candidate environment interpersonal stress, the serotonin transporter polymorphism, and gene-environment interactions in major depression. *Clinical Psychological Science*, *2*(3), 235–248.

Watkins, E. R. (2016). *Rumination-focused cognitive-behavioural therapy for depression*. New York: Guilford Press.

Wu, Z., Schimmele, C. M. and Chappell, N. L. (2012). Ageing and late-life depression. *Journal of Ageing and Health*, *24*(1), 3–28.

4

Biological aspects of depression

For decades many have characterised the causes of depression as fundamentally biological while others have emphasised primarily psychological causes. Those who have emphasised biological/genetic origins point to the fact that depression seems to run in families, the effectiveness of antidepressant medications and that depression often involves biological symptoms such as changes in sleep, appetite, energy and activity level. None of these arguments is necessarily logically or empirically compelling as evidence for biological causation. More than ever before, however, scientific breakthroughs in knowledge and technology in genetics and studies of the brain have powered much of the research in psychopathology. This chapter attempts to characterise the current state of the rapidly-evolving understanding of depression from the biological perspective.

Conceptual issues in the biology of depressive disorders

Before discussing the current understanding of the genetics and neurobiology of depression, several issues affect our understanding of the purpose, research design and interpretation of biological research. These are themes to employ when evaluating the quality and significance of research.

Complexity

Scientific advances in the past 25 years or so have opened the door to every level of analysis from intracellular and molecular genetic aspects of brain function to the activities of whole regions of the brain operating together as circuits. Research involves many levels of the workings of normal and impaired human emotional and behavioural functioning including genetic, hormonal, cellular and intracellular, structural and functional aspects of the brain. Further, it is understood that such activities interact with each other in unimaginably complex ways – and that those activities are strongly shaped by environmental (including cultural) factors as well as the unfolding of these processes and outcomes over the course of normal and aberrant development starting from gestation. The term 'multiple levels of analysis' has been promoted by many (Cicchetti and Dawson, 2002; Hankin, 2015) to attempt to capture genetic, neural, endocrinological and environmental processes at the individual, family and community level, and to explore their changing effects over the process of development. For some, the concept is a mandate for 'team' efforts linking environment, development and multiple biological/genetic factors, but clearly such efforts are extraordinarily complex, expensive and necessitate multidisciplinary groups of experts. Others are moved to go deeper into narrower topics. In this chapter and throughout the book we try to highlight some attempts at multiple levels of analysis but such efforts are clearly at a nascent stage.

Causality vs. correlation

When depressed and nondepressed groups are compared and found to differ on a biological factor such as neural or chemical activity, what is the appropriate conclusion? Frequently, the conclusion or implication drawn is that the factor is of aetiological significance – that is, it is the underlying *cause* of the depression. However, it is conceivable, even likely, that many biological 'differences' simply reflect *consequences* of depression due to concurrent changes in sleep or activity level, or emotional distress. Or, they may be *correlates* of some other unknown process, such as stress, but in themselves have little aetiological significance. Aetiological questions require research designs capable of demonstrating causality, and it is rare that experimental studies, involving random assignment and exposure to procedures intended to produce effects, are either ethical or feasible or credible. The increasing use of longitudinal studies that examine depressed people during and after depressive episodes will help to determine which biological parameters are merely 'state dependent' and simply reflect depression-related changes, and which are more stable. However, even if stable, it may still be difficult to conclude that the biological parameter has causal significance, because it may reflect a residual of the depressive episode itself (a 'scar'). Therefore, designs that are not only longitudinal but identify potential subjects at risk for depression *before* they actually experience episodes may be needed to help elucidate the status of the biological factor. It is further necessary to keep in mind that a putative 'marker' or indicator of risk or vulnerability may itself not have causal significance but may simply be a correlate or indicator of some other process that has aetiological features (Kraemer, Stice, Kazdin, Offord and Kupfer, 2001). This is not to say that 'markers' or 'correlates' are unimportant to study. They may indeed help to clarify the pathophysiological process that occurs when depression is instigated for whatever reason. As such, they may play some important role in understanding the course or indicating a treatment mechanism. Unfortunately, however, risk factors are often assigned causal significance not warranted by the design or data.

Static vs. transactional models

Another conceptual challenge concerns the nature of the theoretical model of biological effects in depression. Some investigators appear to subscribe to simple 'main effects' models, such as genetic defects or neuroendocrine dysregulation, implying that such factors are necessary and sufficient causes of depression. However, existing evidence best supports a diathesis–stress model, requiring a pathophysiological diathesis (vulnerability), which must be triggered by some environmental or physical stressor. As noted earlier, to date there has simply been insufficient attention to an integration of biological and stress or psychosocial factors – or, investigators hypothesise but do not actually measure the triggering effect of stress.

Another difficulty is that diathesis–stress models may tend to be static, focused on the interaction of the two factors but disregarding the possibility that the factors have effects and relations with each other that change over time and experience. In the chapter on stress effects, examples will be reported in which it is clear that the effects of stress on depression are not static and not one-directional but are dynamic over time and transactional (depression and stress affecting each other).

Reductionism

The essence of this term is the goal of reducing complex phenomena to their simplest and most basic elements, and in many uses, it implies explanatory or causal status. Biological models of psychopathology often tend toward reductionism, especially when terms such as 'biological underpinnings' or 'genetic basis' or 'neural substrates' of depression are used. Sometimes it is simply sloppy language, but in other cases, the causal implications are intended. Both laypeople and scientific thought leaders are likely to say things like 'mental disorders are diseases of the brain' and provide funding for looking at 'fundamental causes' (presumed to be located in the brain and genes). While a few eminent geneticists have come clean and clearly stated that 'there is no gene for . . .' depression (Kendler, 2005; Flint and Kendler, 2014), many neuroscientists have not been so circumspect and commonly imply that their neuroimaging methods have identified structural or functional brain characteristics that 'underlie' (implying 'cause') depression. A full discussion of this complex issue – as well as the costs to science and consumers – is beyond the scope of this chapter, but see Miller (2010).

Developmental issues

There is increasing awareness among researchers that the brain and most biological processes differ with age and experience across the lifespan, and that the processes of development are not linear but may have sensitive periods of increased activity and involving different challenges and outcomes. Healthy processes of growth may be progressive, but abnormalities and irregularities in development may impede advancement to more complex forms of activity. Obviously, we understand the effects of growth and ageing in general, but there is increasing attention to the ideas that certain brain or genetic functions are especially impacted at certain epochs of development, like the influence of gonadal hormones on brain functioning at puberty, or synaptic pruning of the brain occurring in adolescence, or maturation of greater executive functioning not completed until the late teens/early twenties. Developmentally informed research helps us to understand how maternal prenatal stress affects infant development, or why most depressions onset in adolescence but less in childhood, or why many forms of depression in older adults may reflect different brain changes than those depressions experienced in young adulthood. Developmental considerations argue against comparing groups of depressed people whose depression began at different stages of development, and imply that certain treatments may need to be tailored to acknowledge age and developmental processes. Specialists called *developmental psychopathologists* are particularly focused on understanding the origins and processes of lifespan issues in psychological disorders and many are promoting discovery of new knowledge linking environmental experiences, such as childhood trauma to abnormal brain development and subsequent cognitive and behavioural dysfunctions – some of these efforts are described in sections to follow.

Emerging strategies for defining targets of study

As noted in Chapter 1, researchers have become increasingly dissatisfied with current diagnostic classification methods, largely because they identify individuals who may share a diagnosis but differ enormously in symptomatology and course features, and commonly have multiple additional diagnoses (comorbidity). The resulting heterogeneity – which is extremely pronounced in samples with depressive disorders – impedes progress in research on aetiological processes and treatments. Decades of research have failed to identify, and replicate, basic causes of depressive disorders. Scientists have called for use of alternative strategies for redefining the characteristics of samples, as Chapter 1 describes. Examples include focus on endophenotypes (or intermediate phenotypes, potential mechanisms that might be shared by different disorders), or greater use of broad but statistically coherent sets of symptoms (transdiagnostic latent variables), or specific domains of behaviours examined across multiple units of analysis such as cellular, genetic, neural and others (Research Domain Criteria, RdoC; Insel et al., 2010). Endophenotypes for depression might include markers of depression such as negative cognitive biases, neuroticism, increased stress reactivity or impaired reward processing (e.g., Goldstein and Klein, 2014; Hasler, Drevets, Manji and Charney, 2004). Transdiagnostic approaches focus on samples scoring high on a broad 'internalising' factor, sharing negative emotional symptoms characteristic of depression and anxiety disorders (e.g., Krueger and Markon, 2006). Use of the RdoC, for example, promotes studies of reward processing deficits such as anhedonia, which cuts across disorders but may be prominent in some forms of depression (e.g., Pizzagalli, 2014). The current chapter largely focuses on the traditional approach of studying individuals at risk for or who have diagnoses of DSM-defined depressive disorders, but examples of recent research using the alternative models are sprinkled throughout this volume.

Genetic research in depression

Approaching the issue of genetic contributions to depression requires introducing several essential principles that are generally relevant to the study of complex behaviours such as depression. Unlike a few medical illnesses and conditions, there is no single gene for depression (Kendler, 2005). Instead, as Plomin, DeFries, Knopik and Neiderhiser (2016) summarise across many years of study of behavioural genetics, heritability is due to many genes with small effects (see also Flint and Kendler, 2014) – implying that many additional factors, including environmental effects, play large roles. At the same time, as Plomin et al. (2016) remind us, most measures of the environment, such as parenting and the occurrence of stressful life events, show significant genetic influence (e.g., Kendler and Baker, 2007). This is presumed to be largely due to the influence of genetics on personality traits (Plomin et al., 2016). Therefore, the key questions regarding depression are: what is the evidence for genetic contributions, what is it that is genetically transmitted, and how do we understand the relationships between genes and environments? The answers to these questions are complex, continuously developing and are particularly likely to be important to issues of intervention and treatment.

What is the evidence?

Family studies

It is well known that depression runs in families; examining diagnoses within families shows that significantly more major depression occurs in close relatives of a participant with major depressive disorder than in families of individuals without depression (Sullivan, Neale and Kendler, 2000). It is estimated that the rate of major depression in family members of depressed people is 10–25 per cent, which is about three times higher than rates for healthy controls; also, heritability appears to be most apparent in depressions with early onset and recurrent course (Levinson, 2006). There is also evidence that depressions that are chronic or more severe and impairing, are particularly likely to indicate heritable patterns in families (Levinson, 2006; Mondimore et al., 2006). Also, there is evidence from twin studies that depression is more heritable in women than men (Kendler, Gatz, Gardner and Pedersen, 2006).

Research on the children of depressed parents represents an often-studied version of family patterns of depression. Overall, such research indicates that by the late teens, children of a depressed parent have approximately a 50 per cent chance of developing a disorder of some kind, with possibly 20–40 per cent becoming depressed (e.g., Beardslee, Versage and Gladstone, 1998). A meta-analysis of 193 studies that included both clinical (treated) and community (untreated) samples found significantly elevated rates of disorders and depression among children of depressed women (Goodman et al., 2011).

Family and offspring studies blur the boundaries between genetic and environmental effects on depression, because the influence of the quality of family life, parent–child relations and other environmental factors may contribute to disorders. The effects of psychological and interpersonal factors on depression are explored in Chapter 6. Different genetic designs have attempted to clarify the role of heritability, as follows.

Twin studies

Because of the confound of genes and environments in family studies, twin studies were seen as an improvement because twins are presumed to share the same environment while varying in genetic similarity, comparing identical twins (monozygotic, sharing 100 per cent of genes), with fraternal twins (dizygotic, sharing about 50 per cent of genes). Complex statistical procedures are used to compare the concordance rates for depression among twin pairs and the degree to which similarity and differences may be ascribed to genetic or nongenetic sources. For example, Kendler and Prescott (1999) studied 3,790 monozygotic and dizygotic male and female twins, and found significantly greater major depression concordance in monozygotic than dizygotic twins, affirming a genetic contribution to depression. In a meta-analysis of well-designed twin studies, Sullivan and colleagues (2000) estimated that the heritability of major depression is in the range of 31–42 per cent, which may be characterised as a moderate effect of genetic factors. The statistical results also suggested that the influence of individual environmental factors, such as personal stressful events, is an additional and somewhat larger contributor to depression than shared family environment. It is largely due to the twin study findings that researchers generally accept the idea that depression is moderately heritable, with a substantial contribution due to environmental factors (although as noted earlier, some 'environmental' factors may have genetic components). Kendler, Aggen and Neale (2013) have reported that twin data also indicate that different symptoms of the depression syndrome have different heritability patterns, and strongly argue for improvements in assessment and subtyping of depression to provide more homogeneous samples for advancements in genetic research.

Genome-wide association studies

In recent years the investigation of genetic contributions to psychological disorders has taken advantage of substantial scientific breakthroughs. The focus is now on the molecular genetic bases or 'gene finding' across the entire human genome. Currently considerable research funding supports genome-wide association studies (GWAS) that analyse DNA sequences. A single nucleotide polymorphism, called a SNP (snip) represents a difference in a single DNA building block, called a nucleotide; SNPs are the most common type of genetic variation among people. They occur within and between genes, and can be thought of as markers for comparing the genomes of individuals who have a particular disorder ('cases' such as major depression) and those who do not have the disorder ('controls'). Genome-wide association studies look for patterns of differences in commonly shared variants among the millions of SNPs. Studies need thousands of individuals to provide DNA for analysis, in order to be sufficiently sized to detect statistically significant differences.

While GWAS studies have yielded important findings in some medical conditions, and even some findings relevant to major mental illness such as schizophrenia, they have proven to be somewhat unproductive with respect to depressive disorders. Over a dozen GWAS studies on depression have been reported and results summarised by Dunn et al. (2015). Essentially, findings included results that were detected but were not replicated, or some studies found no significant differences, or a few differences were detected but in regions lacking protein-coding sequences and of unknown biological function. As a result of disappointing yields, experts have proposed several improvements in research methods and designs: include much larger samples to detect the very small effects that likely account for differences; include focus on rare variants and not just common SNPs; include systematic analyses of environmental characteristics that might moderate the small effects of genetic parameters; and greatly refine the phenotypes by which depression samples are defined, thus reducing the enormous heterogeneity of depression (e.g., Cohen-Woods, Craig and McGuffin, 2013; Flint and Kendler, 2014; Wray et al., 2012). Most of these improvements are underway. For instance, the CONVERGE Consortium (Cai et al., 2015) studied over 5,000 Chinese women with severe recurrent depressive disorders and more than 5,000 comparison women in a whole-genome-wide sequencing study. The study identified and also replicated findings of two SNPs that distinguished between groups. A further analysis with an even more refined phenotype of severe melancholic type depression increased the signal of one of the SNPs, a variant that may be related to mitochondrial DNA inherited through the maternal line. It is suspected that this particular SNP is more prevalent and therefore more detectable in the Chinese compared to typically Western samples. The use of a narrow phenotype of severe melancholic subtype depression in women likely removes considerable 'noise' from GWAS searches compared to broad 'major depression' phenotypes, but likely additional subtypes will need to be pursued.

What is transmitted?

As noted earlier, there is no expectation that a particular gene is 'the' depression gene that causes depression as a disease state (e.g., Kendler, 2005).

Instead, it is apparent that countless genes of very small effects contribute to the vulnerability to depression. Such genes likely affect neural and neuroendocrine mechanisms that determine how individuals dysfunctionally interpret, respond to and cope with life stressors that eventuate in depressive reactions, or that confer particular traits and behavioural tendencies that contribute to depression (a few examples might be insecure attachment, negative cognitive style, neuroticism, ruminative response style, dysfunctional conflict resolution tendencies). In short, virtually every facet of personality and stress reactivity is likely to have heritable components – but how they work together to produce depression is likely very complex indeed. Obviously, genetically regulated processes are strongly modified by environmental, prenatal and childhood experiences and their impact on neural/biological and social development (see discussion in Relationships Between Genes and Environments).

Candidate gene studies

Candidate gene studies focus on genes with known function plausibly related to mechanisms of depression. Neurotransmitter systems, especially the mono-amines such as those linked to pharmacologic treatment of depression, or hypothalamic–pituitary–adrenal axis and stress reactivity systems, have been implicated in depression, and their genetic characteristics have recently been the focus of research. There has been a large volume of research on candidate genes such as the monoamine oxidase type A (MAOA), the serotonin transporter (5HTT) and its serotonin-transporter-linked polymorphic region, 5-HTTLPR. Serotonin receptor genes, and tryptophan hydroxylase (TPH) genes have been investigated, as well as those controlling dopamine receptors and dopamine transport; all have generally yielded inconsistent or weak findings when cases and controls are compared (Cohen-Woods, Craig and McGuffin, 2013). Interest in genes that regulate responses to stressors has also driven research in recent years, largely to identify new targets for drug development in light of the known association of depression with stressful life event precipitants. Similarly, chronic stress has been found to reduce brain-derived neurotrophic factor (BDNF) gene expression in hippocampal neurons, but Cohen-Woods et al. (2013) have reported few consistent findings of these stress-related gene differences in studies of depression.

As we explore in the next section, a consistent and continuing criticism of many studies of genetic differences between depressed and nondepressed samples is their failure to consider that the effects of genes may be modified by environmental exposures and current conditions. Efforts to address such issues are explored next.

The relationships between genes and environments in depression

What do we mean by 'environment' and why is it important in considering genetics of depression? Environmental influences may apply broadly to any biological or psychological experiences that the individual is exposed to that have the potential for altering something about the person – ranging from pesticides to quality of parenting. Such experiences may literally sculpt the brain, alter or turn on gene functioning and lead to complex patterns of effective or impaired learning and behaviour. Ignoring the critical impact of environmental exposures on biological processes greatly limits our ability to optimise understanding, prediction and change of psychological disorders.

Nevertheless, with respect to genetics, the relations between genes and environments are complex and elusive. At least three types of relationships are considered below, each described briefly in relation to depression.

Gene–environment interactions (G x E)

Some of the strongest predictors of depression are 'environmental' exposures such as child abuse, having a depressed mother or having a recent major stressful life event – as explored in later chapters. Traditionally, most theories of psychopathology, especially depression, have been framed as 'diathesis-stress' models in which both the vulnerability factor (diathesis) and stress (environmental factor) are required (interact) to trigger a depressive episode. That is, most people who have a stressor will not get depressed unless they also have certain vulnerabilities including genetic characteristics (and the reverse is also theoretically true – vulnerable individuals will not usually become depressed in the absence of personally meaningful stressors). Twin studies using statistical modeling of similarities (in depression) among those who share all or half of their genes have long supported gene by environment interactions (G x E; e.g., Kendler et al., 1995).

Candidate gene by environment interactions were first demonstrated for depression by Caspi et al. (2003) using a specific functional polymorphism in the serotonin system, 5-HTTLPR; every individual has one of three different polymorphisms, s/s, s/l, l/l. As shown in Figure 4.1, the authors found that each of four different measures of depression or suicidality were higher in individuals who reported larger numbers of recent stressful life events, but the amount of increase was significantly stronger for carriers of the s/s polymorphism of the serotonin transporter gene (with much less effect for those with the l/l polymorphism). Not shown in the figure, the authors also found a similar effect when the stress was measured as childhood maltreatment. It appears that stress is a trigger of depression, mainly for those who carry at least one s allele of this particular candidate gene. These findings are a power-

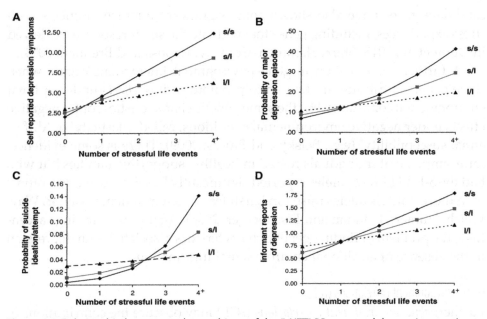

Figure 4.1 Relationship between polymorphisms of the 5-HTTLPR gene and depressive reactions to stressful life events

Source: Caspi, A., Sugden, K., Moffitt, T. E., Taylor, A., Craig, I. W., Harrington, H., . . . Poulton, R. (2003). Influence of life stress on depression: moderation by a polymorphism in the 5-HTT gene. *Science, 301*, 386–389. Reprinted with permission from AAAS.

ful example of the likelihood that for many genetic diatheses, the effects of genes may not be evident except under adverse environmental conditions. Thus, GWAS or main effects models of candidate gene comparisons of depressed and nondepressed cases may fail to show genetic differences, but the two groups may actually differ in some other characteristic that is not measured (such as stress exposure) that triggers depression in those with certain genetic features (gene–environment interaction).

A number of studies have subsequently conducted similar G x E analyses, and the gene by environment interaction designs with the 5-HTTLPR variants have been very controversial because some researchers found results similar to Caspi and colleagues but others did not (e.g., see meta-analyses by Karg, Burmeister, Shedden and Sen, 2011; Risch et al., 2009; also Dunn et al., 2015). The controversy may turn on design and methodology issues, such as sample size, quality of measures of stress and stress content, with indications that the best quality of stress measurement is more likely to reveal G x E associations (Karg et al., 2011). Although the serotonin transporter gene has been the focus of most such research – also bolstered by evidence showing variation in amygdala activity associated with 5-HTTLPR (Hariri et al., 2002) – other candidate genes have also shown some significant interaction effects with stress experiences, including genes that regulate the stress response (reviewed in Dunn et al., 2015; Starr, Hammen, Conway, Raposa and Brennan, 2014).

A further complication in gene–environment interactions occurs when some genetic attributes are known to promote *positive effects* under optimal environmental conditions, but the same genetic characteristics confer negative effects under negative environmental conditions, called 'plasticity' or 'differential susceptibility' (e.g., Belsky and Pluess, 2009). There is some evidence, for example, that individuals reared in healthy, supportive families but who had the 5-HTTLPR *s/s* alleles reported significantly less depressive symptoms than those with *s/s* alleles raised in harsh family environments (Taylor, Way, Welch, Hilmert, Lehman and Eisenberger, 2006). Again, such findings accentuate the problem of finding genetic characteristics associated with depression in the absence of additional environmental information.

Gene–environment correlations (rGE)

Further, *gene–environment correlations* (*r*GE) may obscure the contributions of both genes and environment because the genes and environments co-occur, and leading to errors in interpretations about causal factors. Plomin, DeFries and Loehlin (1977) described three types. An example of 'passive' gene–environment correlation relevant to depression is the likelihood that having depressed parents results in the transmission to the child of genetic causes of depression, plus the influence of problematic parenting styles that are also influenced by parents' genetic characteristics. The child's maladaptive outcomes may be erroneously attributed to the parenting environment when it is at least partly genetically determined. Another type of gene–environment correlation is 'evocative' (or reactive): the individual's heritable traits and temperaments may elicit reactions from the environment. A withdrawn child with shy and fearful heritable traits may elicit rejection or even bullying from peers, and develop low self-esteem and depressed mood. The fundamental causes may be both genetic and environmental, and not solely one or the other. Finally, gene–environment correlations may be called 'active' in the cases where an individual seeks environmental exposure due to heritable traits. For instance, a depression-vulnerable person with heritable traits of fearfulness and low positive affect may seek out social experiences that are perceived as 'safe', but may be very unrewarding or unfulfilling and ultimately likely to trigger loneliness and depression.

Many studies using twin methodologies have demonstrated gene–environment correlations affecting, for example, marital relationships, parenting relations, social support and the occurrence of stressful life events (particularly those not due to 'fate' but are to some extent under the individual's control) and similar social behaviours (Kendler and Baker, 2007). Jaffee and Price (2007) described molecular genetic approaches to *r*GE, although there are few to date and most are not about depression. The key point to be made is the necessity for drawing appropriate causal conclusions, primarily about environmental vs. genetic 'causes' of maladaptive outcomes.

Epigenetics

A relatively new field of genetic studies, epigenetics refers to the study of biological processes (chemical processes involving methylation and histone proteins) typically resulting from environmental events (including stressful experiences, exposure to toxins, nutrition, parenting quality and many others) that affect the functioning of DNA and regulate the switching on and off and the operation of genes. The analogy has been used of a movie that is based on the enactment of a script (genes) that is interpreted by the actions of a director (epigenetics). The genes themselves (script) are not altered by environmental inputs, but different epigenetic experiences (different directors) will emphasise some aspects and delete others or elicit different interpretations of the same words and characters. A light but useful video helps to illustrate the meaning and implications of epigenetic processes (SciShow, 2012).

Epigenetic studies suggest that stressor-induced DNA methylation may alter gene expression in the brain related to HPA axis functions, neurotransmission and neuroplasticity – processes with effects relevant to mental health (Hing, Gardner and Potash, 2014). Environmentally (stress) induced DNA methylation has been shown to have both short-term and long-term effects and in some instances *intergenerational* effects. It appears that epigenetic effects and processes may differ by type of stress (e.g., chronic or acute) as well as severity (Griffiths and Hunger, 2014). As an example, one study found effects of mothers' prenatal depression on methylation in specific genes in the infant that were associated with the infants' abnormal cortisol responses in response to stress stimuli at three months of age (e.g., Oberlander et al., 2008). There is considerable interest in the evolving body of research on evidence of methylation in relation to exposure to early life stress, and findings of epigenetic changes in individuals with major depressive disorder – findings that might imply future use of epigenetic biomarkers to improve diagnosis and suggest targets of pharmacological treatment (Dalton, Kolshus and McLoughlin, 2014). Epigenetic studies with candidate genes will increasingly be supplemented by genome-wide DNA methylation studies (Hing et al., 2014).

Brain and neuroendocrine functioning and depression

Depression is essentially a disorder of negative perceptions (cognitions) and emotions, typically in response to stressors that are interpreted as loss and inadequacy of the sense of self, but also negatively affecting thoughts about others, the world and the future. In many current models, depression is a prolonged and severe dysphoric reaction to stress. Many scientists describe the brain as the main organ of reactions to stress (McEwan, Gray and Nasca, 2015). It is in the brain, which is extensively governed and shaped by thousands of genes, and by experience and development, that scientists have looked at processes that control perception, emotional reactions, stress perception and coping with stressful situations. Dysfunctional reactions include a seeming tendency to interpret situations excessively negatively, and inability to effectively control the content, persistence and severity of the negative thoughts and feelings about the self and circumstances. Consequently, a large body of biological research on depression, driven by advances in basic knowledge and technology, has focused on the emotional, cognitive and stress-responsive neural and neuroendocrine mechanisms describing emotion regulation and cognitive control. This voluminous research includes both animal and human studies and is too vast to cover in detail, but key issues, current understanding and future goals are highlighted. We focus mostly on neuroendocrine functioning in response to perceived stress, and aspects of brain structure and function particularly relevant to depressive emotional states.

Neuroendocrine functioning: hypothalamic–pituitary–adrenal axis abnormalities in response to stress

As discussed in Chapter 5, stressful life events precede and are presumed to precipitate a depressive episode in the great majority of cases of depression. However, most people who experience significant life events do not get depressed. Therefore, much of the emphasis in research on the aetiology of depression is the search for why some people, but not others, become depressed following personally meaningful stressors. A number of genetic, family functioning, cognitive, personality and demographic factors that contribute to risk and vulnerability to depression are discussed in different chapters, but here we discuss the biological research on potential abnormalities of the biological stress-response system in the brain, especially in the hypothalamic–pituitary–adrenal axis (HPA axis), that represent some of the mechanisms that account for depressive responses to stressful experiences.

The HPA axis in humans evolved to enable responses to stressful situations (such as danger from predators, hunger), involving complex biological systems working together serving survival needs, while also temporarily inhibiting systems less essential to survival, thus supporting focused attention, physiological activation (such as for 'fight' or 'flight'), promoting the execution of relevant behaviours and sustaining energy necessary to perform actions and protect the body. When the stressor threat is no longer salient, the body returns to its normal levels and patterns of functioning (homeostasis). However, it has long been known that sustained biological responses to stress may have negative consequences, leading to physiological changes that result in illnesses and psychological disorders.

Depression is associated with several abnormalities of the HPA axis associated with high levels of cortisol. Cortisol has a normal diurnal pattern – generally highest in the morning with a peak about 30 minutes after awakening (cortisol awakening response; CAR) and then a decline throughout the day to low levels at night and during sleeping. Thus, measurement of cortisol may occur at a single time point such as evening, or CAR, or over the course of a day, or in response to a stressful experimental 'challenge', and unsurprisingly there have been many conflicting findings. However, a few general trends have emerged. Medical diseases that cause excessive cortisol show elevated rates of depression in patients. Many studies have shown that depressed individuals commonly display elevated levels of cortisol, and show abnormal daily patterns (Frodl and O'Keane, 2013; Pariante and Lightman, 2008). Testing the hypothesis of abnormal HPA axis involvement in depression, early studies demonstrated that administration of a synthetic form of cortisol (dexamethasone) elicited different patterns of response in depressed patients and healthy controls. Healthy individuals typically display a temporary suppression of real cortisol but return to normal levels over a period of hours. However, patients displayed greater resistance to cortisol suppression and earlier 'escape' from suppression, consistent with abnormal levels and diminished homeostatic processes.

Stetler and Miller (2011) analysed several hundred studies comparing depressed and nondepressed patients on indicators of various HPA axis hormones, and found significantly higher levels of cortisol among depressed patients. Older and more severely depressed hospitalised patients were especially likely to show HPA hyperactivity. Burke, Davis, Otte and Mohr (2005) reported a meta-analysis of studies comparing depressed and non-depressed adults on stress 'challenge' tests such as public speaking or cognitive performance tasks. They found that depressed individuals were more likely to show abnormal patterns of cortisol reactivity and recovery, specifically indicating blunted reactivity (largely due to high baseline levels) and longer time to recovery or less recovery. Consistent with Stetler and Miller (2011), poor recovery was observed in those with more severe depression.

While much of the research has compared groups who are already depressed or not, and other studies have examined short-term patterns in response to naturally occurring stress, it is important for research to look for particular markers or indicators that might predict *future* depression. For example, some investigators have focused on level of cortisol shortly after awakening (CAR). Vrshek-Schallhorn and colleagues (2013) found that in a young adult sample, elevated CAR at baseline statistically predicted increased risk of onset of major depression for up to two and a half years, beyond the triggering effects of stressful life event occurrence. CAR also predicted recurrences of major depressive episode more strongly than first episodes. Furthermore, different types of designs have looked at prediction in those who have never been depressed but might be considered at risk. Several such studies have shown that offspring of depressed parents have higher levels of cortisol reactivity than healthy control offspring, and that higher levels of offspring cortisol predicted future depression (Azar, Pacquette, Zoccolillo, Baltzer and Tremblay, 2007; Halligan, Herbert, Goodyer and Murray, 2007; Lupien et al., 2011; Mackrell, et al., 2014). Presumably such effects in high-risk populations operate through both genetic and environmental pathways.

Prediction studies, to a greater extent than comparative studies, suggest that abnormal cortisol and HPA axis functioning may thus be causal contributors to depression, rather than simply consequences of stress and depression. What are the presumed mechanisms causing abnormal HPA axis activity? There is no definitive answer yet. There is particular interest in the role of environmental stress in shaping HPA axis functioning. For instance, a number of studies have examined early life exposure to adversity and stress (e.g., Frodl and O'Keane, 2013; Pariante and Lightman, 2008). Frodl and O'Keane (2013) summarised research that found evidence of abnormal levels of cortisol in samples of adults and children with histories of maltreatment and other forms of early childhood adversity. Also, genetic characteristics – and epigenetic factors – may determine the extent to which an individual experiences abnormal HPA axis processes including sustained high cortisol (e.g., Frodl and O'Keane, 2013). Evidence suggests, for example, that polymorphisms of glucocorticoid receptor genes (GR) are associated with increased risk of developing major depression (van Rossum et al., 2006), and differences in response to treatment for depression (e.g., Brouwer et al., 2006; van Rossum et al., 2006). Indeed, human and animal studies strongly indicate epigenetic effects on GR and multiple genes stemming from environmental effects of early childhood adversity, and such effects increase HPA respons- ivity to stress (Turecki and Meaney, 2016). Stress reactivity is also highly likely to be related to temperament, cognitive styles and other personal experiential factors that are discussed in different chapters. Moreover, abnormalities of the HPA axis itself affect the brain structure and circuitry associated with emotional and cognitive control relevant to depression, as we discuss in the next section.

Finally, it should be noted that the voluminous amount of research on HPA axis functioning in depression has yielded general trends but consider- able inconsistency in outcomes, across both human and animal research. Significant differences are likely due to variations in methods, samples, definitions and measures of depression and comorbid conditions, age groups, types and age of stress occurrence, and cortisol methodologies. In light of methodological variations, and in response to rapidly emerging understand- ing of basic neuroendocrinological and neural processes, there is considerable further work to be done to clarify causal mechanisms sufficient to improve clinical prediction, prevention and treatment.

Neural aspects of depression

Although earlier biological research on depression focused extensively on neurotransmitter systems, development of modern imaging techniques, along with basic experimental animal research, has revolutionised research on understanding both normal and abnormal structural and functional properties of the brain. With the voluminous number of studies published in recent years has come fuller appreciation of the enormous complexity of the brain at every level from intracellular to anatomical structure, including interactions among genetic, neuroendocrine, neurotransmitter, hormonal and neural circuits. Adding to the complexity are processes of normal and abnormal development of the brain, and the effect of environmental–experiential factors on the brain.

With respect to depression, much of the emphasis has been on neural areas and functions that support perceptions and interpretations of the self and environment, and the areas and functions responsible for emotional reactions and emotional regulation. Thus, the topics of great interest in depression involve brain regions and processes that account for biased attention to negative stimuli, heightened emotional reactivity and reduced cognitive control (e.g., Disner, Beevers, Haigh and Beck, 2011). More specifically, subcortical areas of the brain that comprise the limbic system (including the amygdala and hippocampus) that regulate emotion, motivation, learning and memory, and their reciprocal connectivity with the prefrontal cortex and related areas, have been particular focuses of research on depression (Price and Drevets, 2012).

The hippocampus is a small structure located under the cerebral cortex and serves many functions including those related to learning and memory (and their relevance to one's sense of self and encoding and retrieval of negative information and memories). It is known to be highly susceptible to the damaging effects of excessive stress-related glucocorticoids, resulting in impaired learning and memory. Excessive glucocorticoid production also causes impairment of feedback mechanisms that inhibit cortisol, thus leading to further exposure to glucocorticoids resulting in neuronal atrophy and cell death and loss of synaptic plasticity in the hippocampus (e.g., Frodl and O'Keane, 2013). Many imaging studies have shown that depressed individuals – especially those who have had early-onset or prolonged or recurrent depression – demonstrate smaller hippocampal volumes (reflecting less cell growth and more cell death) than those without depression or with a single episode (e.g., McKinnon, Yucel, Nazarov and MacQueen, 2009). It appears that reductions of hippocampal volumes are depressive-state-dependent (potentially reversible) but also progressive in the context of recurrent episodes (e.g., Ahdidan et al., 2011). A study remarkable for combining neuroimaging data across multiple sites with nearly 2,000 patients with major depression compared to over 7,000 controls, concluded that earlier onset and recurrent depression, compared with single episodes, were associated with the most robust reductions of hippocampal volumes (Schmaal and the ENIGMA Major Depressive Disorder Working Group, 2015). Thus, hippocampal dysfunction appears to be a result of depression rather than a cause, but suggests the necessity of effective treatment to prevent progressive effects. However, because smaller hippocampal volumes may result from both genetic factors and exposure to early life adversity (e.g., review in Frodl and O'Keane, 2013), some individuals may be at elevated risk for hippocampal impairment.

Adjacent to the hippocampus and mutually involved in processing and interpretation of emotional stimuli, is the amygdala. In keeping with models of abnormalities in cognitive information-processing and memory formation and retrieval as central to depression (as discussed in Chapter 5), many studies have used functional imaging techniques to observe the neural activity of depressed compared to nondepressed individuals when they are shown stimuli with negative content (e.g., Hamilton et al., 2012). Specifically, consistent with well-known depressive bias toward negative content, many studies have used an experimental paradigm in which individuals' amygdala activity is monitored during the presentation of images of sad (or happy) faces. Stuhrman, Suslow and Dannlowsky (2011) reviewed multiple functional magnetic resonance studies and found strong evidence of amygdala hyper-activity among depressed individuals compared to nondepressive, and some evidence that they also showed less amygdala reactivity to positive facial stimuli (see also Disner, Beevers, Haigh and Beck, 2011 review). Stuhrman et al. (2011) also note that several studies of depressed individuals in remission and in children at risk for depression have shown amygdala hyperactivity to sad faces, suggesting that the neural activity may be a stable characteristic indicating vulnerability for depression, rather than a state-dependent effect that is absent when the individual is not depressed – although further studies are needed to confirm.

In terms of structural volume of the amygdala rather than reactivity, some studies have reported that depressed individuals have smaller amygdalae suggestive of effects of neurotoxicity similar to those of cortisol-exposed hippocampal volume. For instance, Hamilton, Siemer and Gotlib (2008) performed meta-analyses of studies and found smaller volumes in unmedi-cated patients, whereas there were no differences in sizes of amygdalae in medicated patients compared to healthy controls. Schmaal and the ENIGMA Major Depressive Disorder Working Group (2015) found a tendency – but not statistically robust – for depressed individuals to have smaller amygdala volumes.

Beyond the assessment of specific aspects of brain function, an important development is the study of transactions between different areas, e.g., neural circuits connecting different structures and functions. Specifically, functional connectivity between the subcortical areas and cortical areas has been the focus of considerable interest in depression, and there is an enormous amount of research using different neuroscience methodologies and techniques. Although there is considerable complexity in the findings of specific con-nections and regions, a general theme is that depressed individuals display neural patterns of both heightened activity of limbic areas involved in the selective detection, elaboration and expression of negative emotion, along with decreased activity in cortical areas to which they are connected (such as the dorsolateral prefrontal cortex) that are involved in cognitive control (e.g., Disner et al., 2011; Hamilton et al., 2012). Thus, when depressed, individuals display selective attention to negative stimuli and overemotional reactions, and at the same time show diminished cognitive control defined as processes of distraction, disengagement or other methods of cognitive 'mood repair' such as activation of positive memories or effective problem-solving (e.g., Disner et al., 2011; Gotlib and Joormann, 2010; Hamilton et al., 2012; see also Kaiser, Andrews-Hanna, Wager and Pizzagalli, 2015). An example is depres-sive rumination (e.g., Lyubomirsky, Layous, Chancellor and Nelson, 2015), in which the person's brain is highly emotionally reactive but the cognitive control mechanisms of the frontal cortical areas are insufficiently active or effective in ways that could promote useful problem-solving. Numerous studies have contributed to, and are pursuing, an understanding of the complexities of relations between depressive cognitive styles and neural activities (e.g., Hamilton, Farmer, Fogelman and Gotlib, 2015; Mandell, Siegle, Shutt, Feldmiller and Thase, 2014). A great deal of additional research is needed to determine the extent to which such processes may indicate markers of vulnerability before an individual develops depression (e.g., Joormann, Cooney, Henry and Gotlib, 2012), whether they are stable or mood-state dependent patterns, and what kinds of treatments may effectively alter the dysfunctional mechanisms.

It is important to note that neural processes are highly dependent on chemical messaging systems such as neurotransmitters, and are greatly affected by genetic factors. In a classic study, individuals who had one or two copies of the short (s) allele of the serotonin transporter promoter polymorphism (5-HTTLRP), an allele associated with negative emotionality and anxiety responses, showed greater amygdala reactivity to the presentation of fearful faces, compared to those without the genetic characteristic (Hariri et al., 2002; see also a meta-analysis by Munafò, Brown and Hariri, 2008). In a further example of 'multiple levels of analysis', Pagliaccio et al. (2015) examined resting state fMRI (scanning while the person is not engaged in a task) functional connectivity between limbic and cortical areas in a sample of 9–14-year-olds. The investigators were particularly interested in whether weakened connectivity between the amygdala and anterior cingulate cortex is increased among children who had been exposed to higher levels of stressful events and who had higher levels of genetic markers of several HPA-Axis-related genes. As predicted, they found more dysfunctional (weakened) connectivity in high-stress children with more risky genetic profiles. Moreover, weakened connectivity predicted more internalising (depression, anxiety) symptoms and poorer emotion regulation skills approximately one year later. These results hint about the role of environmental events and genetic predisposition in sculpting neural patterns that underlie negative emotionality and emotion regulation, but further research over a longer developmental span will be necessary.

Depression and the immune system

The strong association between stress and depression has promoted considerable interest in the possibility that some forms of depression may be linked to dysfunctions in the immune system and inflammatory processes. Cortisol and the immune system interact with each other. For example, cortisol acts to suppress release of substances of the immune reaction that cause inflammation, and inflammation may promote cortisol secretion. While cortisol normally suppresses inflammation, under some conditions such as persistent exposure to stress, abnormal levels of inflammation may occur. Thus, chronic stress can trigger significant inflammatory reactions, and inflammation can have many effects on the body. The immune system is crucial to the body's response to illness and injury, with circulating cells that detect pathogens, resulting in triggering a variety processes intended to promote healing, including expression of proinflammatory genes that produce cytokines, which are cell-signaling proteins. Those that increase inflammation are called pro-inflammatory cytokines, such as interleukin-1 (IL-1), interleukin-6 (IL-6), and tumor necrosis factor-α (TNF-α). Under normal conditions these processes are essential to health, but in the case of excessive inflammatory activity, adverse outcomes may occur.

Several observations have influenced the view that some forms of depression may be related to inflammatory processes. First, in addition to their wound-healing and disease-fighting consequences, normal inflammatory processes in response to illness, injuries and infectious diseases commonly promote 'sickness behaviours' that are depression-like, such as sad mood, loss of pleasure, fatigue, social withdrawal and psychomotor slowing, all in the service of marshalling resources for recovery and disease containment. Typically such sickness behaviours are mild and temporary, but it has been hypothesised that for some individuals, their inflammatory system responds to stress with excessive, prolonged reactions, including over-reactivity to perceived social environmental stressors (e.g., Slavich and Irwin, 2014).

A second observation is that many people who have medical illnesses that are known to have a substantial inflammatory component, such as asthma, diabetes, arthritis and heart disease, also meet criteria for depression (Anderson, Freedland, Clouse and Lustman, 2001; Kinder, Carnethon, Palaniappan, King and Fortmann, 2004; Miller and Blackwell, 2006). Increasingly, such studies indicate that inflammatory processes are centrally involved in the progression of medical diseases (e.g., Nemeroff and Goldschmidt-Clermont, 2012). For example, individuals with coronary heart disease who are depressed and anxious were significantly more likely to die during the three-year follow-up than those who were equally ill but did not have elevated depressive/anxiety symptoms (Watkins et al., 2013). A meta-analysis by Leung et al. (2012) suggested that depression after a heart attack, especially if combined with prior depression, is especially predictive of cardiac mortality.

Third, while the pathophysiology of the link between depression and disease is not entirely understood, it appears that individuals with elevated depression have higher levels of markers of inflammation (e.g., Dowlati et al., 2010). For example, C-reactive protein (CRP), a molecule produced in response to the proinflammatory cytokine IL-6, is higher in those with depression than in comparison groups, controlling for relevant health factors such as smoking and obesity (Furtado and Katzman, 2015; Nemeroff and Goldschmidt-Clermont, 2012). Further, certain types of medication appear to induce depression-like symptoms, and therefore, a number of controlled studies have established the induction of depression or depression-like symptoms by administration of cytokines as treatment for certain viral infections and some cancers (immune activation treatments; Felger and Lotrich, 2013; Slavich and Irwin, 2014). All of these findings provide suggestive evidence of a link between inflammation and depression. Although the nature of a causal relationship is not fully known, and whether only a subgroup of people of individuals show inflammation-related depression, remains to be determined.

The issue of how abnormal inflammatory processes arise is far from resolved, although emerging research suggests both environmental (stress) and genetic processes. Regarding stress exposure, for example, considerable research has shown that naturally occurring acute and chronic stressors in adults, as well as exposure to mild stress in laboratory experiments, elicit elevations in inflammatory biomarkers (reviewed in Slavich and Irwin, 2014). Moreover, Slavich and Irwin (2014) highlight evidence suggesting that social stressors (such as rejection, social exclusion; e.g., Murphy, Slavich, Rohleder and Miller, 2013) promote markers of inflammatory activity. They argue that in the modern world in which predator threat is rare, humans have adapted to respond especially to social threats. These authors show that life events involving personal rejection significantly increase the risk of depressive reactions, compared to non-rejection life events (e.g., Slavich, Thornton, Torres, Monroe and Gotlib, 2009). Thus, they argue for a social stress basis for depression associated with maladaptive inflammatory processes.

There is also a growing body of research suggesting that childhood exposure to high levels of stress may be particularly likely to predict high levels of inflammatory markers and depression. Miller and Cole (2012) studied adolescent girls over a two-and-a-half-year longitudinal course, mapping the associations between inflammatory biomarkers such as CRP and IL-6 and depression. They found that elevations occurring in both the biomarkers and depression occurred in the girls who experienced high levels of adverse childhood experiences (such as poverty, parental mental health issues, parental separation), but not in girls with low levels of adversity. Miller and Cole argue that the 'coupling' of depression and inflammation may be unique to highly stress-exposed samples. The authors noted that they and others found that elevated inflammation lingered after the depression resolved, potentially heightening vulnerability to further depression and possible medical complications.

Genetic factors doubtless play a role in the links among stress, maladaptive inflammatory processes and depression. A growing body of research has demonstrated that certain polymorphisms relevant to cytokine production seem to make some individuals more vulnerable to the effects of stress. For example, Tartter, Hammen, Bower, Brennan and Cole (2015) showed that polymorphisms of the IL-6 and IL-1β genes expressing higher levels of proinflammatory cytokines predicted higher levels of depression in youth who recently experienced chronic interpersonal stress, compared to those with lower expressing polymorphisms. Thus, it is proposed that genetic features may interact with environmental stress exposure to predict higher levels of inflammation-related depression. A related line of research studied the interaction of cytokine treatment with genes that code for expression of pro-inflammatory cytokines. In those studies, for example, depressive symptoms were induced by the treatment of the hepatitis-C virus; patients with certain polymorphisms of genes such as interleukin-6 and tumor necrosis factor-α that affect transcription of cytokines were generally likely to display higher levels, or certain types, of depression symptoms (reviewed in Felger and Lotrich, 2013). It should be noted that while environmental and genetic factors may affect inflammation and inflammation-related depression, Felger and Lotrich (2013) also note that cytokine production has wide-ranging effects on neurotransmitters and neural circuits and neuropeptides, and thus abnormal levels of cytokines may affect depression through numerous complex processes.

The role of female hormones in depression

In view of the robust gender differences in depression as noted in Chapter 3, it has been common to speculate that female hormones likely play an important role in women's greater incidence of depressive disorders. There are four hormonally-relevant phases of women's reproductive life that have been linked to depression: the emergence of the gender difference around the time of puberty; premenstrual dysphoric disorder and mood shifts during the premenstrual phase; postpartum depression; and depression during menopause and perimenopause. Attributing depression in women to hormonal causes has been fraught with controversy over the years in part due to sociopolitical considerations, and the research examining the linkages has been marred by imprecise methods of assessing hormones, overly simplistic models, small sample sizes or generally questionable methods of measuring moods. However, new discoveries about brain–hormone relationships, methods of measuring hormones and improved research designs have contributed promising leads. Unfortunately, we have learned that the extremely complex associations among neurotransmitter and neuroendocrine systems and fluctuating levels of gonadal hormones do not yield a clear understanding of their link to depression in women. Moreover, a host of potential genetic and environmental factors appear to modify the associations among hormones, neurobiological variables and depression. Thus, while increasing evidence points to a role for gonadal hormones in some forms of depression, the effects are generally small and work in complex ways with neuroregulatory circuits in currently uncharted processes that are modified by psychosocial variables.

Pubertal changes and depression

Given the dramatic divergence of rates of depression in males and females beginning in early adolescence, many investigators have suspected that hormonal changes occurring during pubertal development are causally related to depression. In contrast, others have pointed to pubertal timing, rather than pubertal status, arguing that the social and psychological changes accompanying puberty, rather than puberty as such, are challenging and stressful, and may lead to depression. Thus, some have proposed direct effects between hormonal changes and depression (e.g., Angold, Costello, Erkanli and Worthman, 1999), while others have hypothesised intervening effects of life circumstances or bidirectional effects between hormonal changes and stressful circumstances.

Research consistently shows that girls who reach puberty earlier than their peers are more likely to experience depression, and other psychological and adjustment difficulties throughout puberty and possibly beyond (Graber, 2013; Graber, Seeley, Brooks-Gunn and Lewinsohn, 2004; Mendle, Turkheimer and Emery, 2007; Rudolph, 2014). It has been further hypothesised that depression is especially likely in early-maturing girls who also experience stressful negative conditions, especially in family and peer relationships. There is considerable evidence that negative family conditions such as lack of parental warmth, parent–child and marital disruption may not only predict child depression and maladjustment, but also poor family conditions predict earlier onset of puberty in girls (Graber, 2013). Additionally, girls appear to be more susceptible than boys to stressful experiences in close relationships including family as well as peer and romantic relationships. Thus, it has been shown that the effects of early pubertal development on depression are greater when girls have experienced recent family stress or stress in peer relationships (Conley and Rudolph, 2009; Rudolph and Troop-Gordon, 2010).

The complete picture of how hormones work to increase adolescent girls' likelihood of depression is far from clear. Fluctuating levels of gonadal hormones introduce changes in other systems such as the HPA axis, requiring adjustments and maturation of the feedback mechanisms that might alter responsiveness to stress (Steiner, Dunn and Born, 2003). Such complex stress-regulatory systems may play an important role in girls' increased depression given the solid evidence that adolescent girls' rates of exposure to stressors, especially interpersonal, are higher than those of boys (e.g., Cyranowski, Frank, Young and Shear, 2000; Shih, Eberhart, Hammen and Brennan, 2006). Also, it is well-established that adolescence is associated with changes in brain morphology and function that have enormous implications for mood reactivity, motivational and cognitive control functions (e.g., Goddings et al., 2014). Given the role of limbic and cortical processes for experiences of depression as reviewed in earlier sections, there is increasing interest in potential associations among pubertal hormonal processes and brain development in depression-relevant neural circuits. For example, Blanton et al. (2012) found that among girls ages 9–15, pubertal status, but not age, was associated with differences in right hippocampus and amygdala volumes that predict vulnerability to depression. Clearly, further research is needed to develop complete models linking hormonal, neuroendocrine, environmental and psychological processes in susceptibility to onset of depression in adolescence.

Premenstrual dysphoric disorder

Premenstrual dysphoric disorder, noted in Chapter 1, describes a severe, recurring and impairing form of the milder and more common premenstrual syndrome, or PMS. Both are defined by negative affect, moodiness, irritability and physical symptoms whose occurrence is limited to the luteal (post-ovulatory) phase of the menstrual cycle, remitting soon after the menstrual cycle begins. Research findings are consistent with understanding these conditions as biological in nature, rather than as sociopolitical labels demeaning of women or as mood instability due mainly to personality or psychological vulnerability. For instance, there appears to be a heritable component to premenstrual disorders (Kendler, Karkowski, Corey and Neale, 1998), and symptoms are eliminated with medical or surgical interventions (e.g., Steiner et al., 2003). Research has not yet clarified the mechanisms involved, but studies suggest that sufferers of premenstrual dysphoric disorder have normal hormonal levels and activities, but possibly abnormal sensitivity to the serotonergic system that operates in a close reciprocal relationship with gonadal hormones (Steiner et al., 2003). Consistent with a possible role of the serotonergic neurotransmitter system, selective serotonin reuptake inhibiter (SSRI) antidepressants appear to be effective treatments for the symptoms of PMS or premenstrual dysphoric disorder (Steiner and Born, 2000). Moreover, SSRI antidepressant medications work substantially faster and are still effective when administered intermittently only during the premenstrual phase in premenstrual dysphoric disorder but not in major depression (Steiner, 2000).

Postpartum depression

Postpartum depression may refer to three distinct phenomena, 'baby blues', major depression and postpartum psychosis. Postpartum blues occur in a substantial percentage of women in the first few days after birth, and include symptoms of crying, sadness and upset that are short-lived and rarely treated. Postpartum major depression, on the other hand, fulfills criteria for major depressive episode occurring either during pregnancy or within the four weeks following delivery, and may occur in 3–6 per cent of women (half have onset before delivery). Since only a minority of women experiences such depressions, they are clearly not an inevitable response to hormonal changes in pregnancy and birth. Indeed, comparisons between groups of pregnant and nonpregnant women do not necessarily indicate heightened rates of depression in the postpartum period compared to other times in the woman's life (O'Hara and McCabe, 2013). On the other hand, there may be a subgroup of women who are vulnerable to become depressed during the peripartum period.

About one woman in 1,000 has a psychotic postpartum depression with delusions (postpartum psychosis) with rapid onset after childbirth. Women who have had one such postpartum psychosis have an elevated risk for subsequent such episodes. It is believed that most such cases occur among women with bipolar disorder. Extreme forms of such psychotic depressions may include the risk of suicide or infanticide. However, the rarity of the disorder has resulted in limited research on its mechanisms.

Research on biological causal factors notes that many reproductive hormones and neuroendocrines such as estradiol, progesterone and cortisol that support pregnancy, fetal development and delivery may involve very high levels that drop precipitously after birth. The hormone withdrawal theory has been weakly supported in certain respects for some hormones but not others. However, it is likely that reproductive hormones and stress hormones interact in complex ways with each other and modulate effects of neurotransmitter systems (e.g., Yim et al., 2015). Therefore, more integrative studies of mechanisms are required. Fairly strong evidence exists implicating the same stress and social factors that predict depression in women more generally: prior history of depression, depressive and anxiety symptoms, neuroticism, stressful life events and chronic stress, interpersonal difficulties including marital instability and low social support (O'Hara and McCabe, 2013; Yim et al., 2015). Hormonal and other biological mechanisms such as genetic, epigenetic and inflammatory processes may play important roles in postpartum depression in individuals who are at risk for depression because of adverse environmental and psychological characteristics.

Depression associated with menopausal changes

Clinical lore has long promoted the idea that a woman's chances of depression increase when she is going through menopausal changes in midlife. Most longitudinal research on women shows that they have higher levels of depression and depressive symptoms during the perimenopausal/menopausal phase of midlife compared to the nonmenopausal stage – although the majority of women do not experience depression during menopause (Bromberger et al., 2003; Cohen et al., 2006; Freeman, Sammel, Lin and Nelson, 2006). It appears that one of the strongest predictors is history of past depression. A 13-year follow-up study of midlife women found that rates of major depression were much higher among individuals with previous episodes (59 per cent) than among never-depressed women (28 per cent) (Bromberger, Schott, Kravitz and Joffe, 2015). Also, the predictors of depression were different for the first-onset compared to recurrent depressed women. First-onset predictors were presence of health problems and perceived health-related limitations as well as menopausal vasomotor symptoms (night sweats, hot flashes), whereas recurrence in previously depressed women was most strongly associated with post-menopausal status and personality features, such as anxiety traits, ruminative self-focus and self-perceived emotional difficulties. In general, many of these risk factors have been replicated across various cross-sectional and longitudinal studies (e.g., reviewed in Gibbs, Lee and Kulkarni, 2012).

Most studies have found no consistent evidence of a direct role of level of gonadal hormones on midlife/menopausal depression (e.g., Bromberger et al., 2015). However, as with depression associated with other stages of female reproductive life, there is a strong suggestion that the complex interplay between reproductive hormones and other biological and psychosocial factors may play a role in midlife depression. In particular, Gibbs et al. (2012) review evidence that suggests that some women are vulnerable to hormonal *fluctuations*, developing depressive symptoms in response to significant endocrine changes occurring during puberty, pregnancy and birth, and perimenopause. Co-acting risk factors are likely to be genetic, neuroendocrine and stress processes, cognitive styles, health status and health behaviours, and personality and coping resources. Gibbs and colleagues observed that a significant risk factor for perimenopausal depression is past history of depressive reactions to reproductive phases, such as premenstrual syndrome and postpartum depression.

Taken together, research on puberty, premenstrual mood changes, postpartum depression and menopausal depression all indicate some evidence that depression rates may be associated with changes and fluctuations in hormonal activity that occur throughout women's lives. However, the findings also implicate complex interactions among hormones, neurobiological processes and stress processes that make it difficult to attribute depression to hormones as such. Moreover, Steiner et al. (2003) note that since hormonal changes occur in all women while mood disorders occur in only a minority, genetic factors may also contribute to individual differences in how the hormones affect the body's reactions to stresses in the environment. Hormonal issues may add to the excess rates of depression in women compared to men, but are among multiple contributing factors with complex interactions.

Summary

◆ There is no definitive biological theory of the cause of depression. However, a large and increasing body of biological research demonstrates that depression is associated with genetic vulnerability, dysregulation in the stress-response HPA axis and brain abnormalities in structure and function that are particularly associated with limbic and cortical areas responsible for the integration of emotional responding to stressful stimuli and experiences, and cognitive control.

◆ Increased understanding of the brain clearly implicates highly complex interactions among different circuits and networks, and neurohormones and neurotransmitters, from the level of anatomical structure down to molecular processes – and requires further knowledge of brain development and how it is shaped by genetic and environmental processes. Definitive models of the causes of depression will require integration of multiple levels of analysis to understand the complex mechanisms involved. Also, research advances are more likely to occur when the target being studied is a highly refined characteristic, such as an aspect of a disorder (intermediate phenotype) or other well-developed measure, rather than a DSM-5 diagnosis.

◆ Rapid advances in genetic research methods have affirmed that depression is moderately heritable, but that effects of individual genes are very small and inconclusive, and findings obscured by diagnostic heterogeneity. Moreover, the relationships between genes and environment are complex, bidirectional and dynamic – suggesting many avenues of research yet to be pursued.

◆ Abnormal levels and regulation of cortisol and related hormones suggest that depression is often related to defects in the stress response system, likely amplified by childhood exposure to adverse conditions that sculpt the brain and modify genetic mechanisms.

◆ There is growing interest in inflammatory processes and their relation to depression as well as to physical health, with increasing evidence that some depressions are associated with higher levels of inflammation.

◆ Female hormones have been hypothesised as a crucial factor in the higher rates of depression in women. However, hormonal changes and fluctuations appear to affect only some women, and their effects likely depend on multiple additional factors including genetics, life circumstances and coping strategies.

References

Ahdidan, J., Hviid, L. B., Chakravarty, M. M., Ravnkilde, B., Rosenberg, R., Rodell, A., . . . Videbech, P. (2011). Longitudinal MR study of brain structure and hippocampus volume in major depressive disorder. *Acta Psychiatrica Scandinavica*, *123*(3), 211–219.

Anderson, R. J., Freedland, K. E., Clouse, R. E. and Lustman, P. J. (2001). The prevalence of comorbid depression in adults with diabetes a meta-analysis. *Diabetes Care*, *24*(6), 1069–1078.

Angold, A., Costello, E. J., Erkanli, A. and Worthman, C. M. (1999). Pubertal changes in hormone levels and depression in girls. *Psychological Medicine*, *29*, 1043–1053.

Azar, R., Paquette, D., Zoccolillo, M., Baltzer, F. and Tremblay, R. E. (2007). The association of major depression, conduct disorder, and maternal overcontrol with a failure to show a cortisol buffered response in 4-month-old infants of teenage mothers. *Biological Psychiatry*, *62*, 573–579.

Blanton, R. E., Cooney, R. E., Joormann, J., Eugène, F., Glover, G. H. and Gotlib, I. H. (2012). Pubertal stage and brain anatomy in girls. *Neuroscience*, *217*, 105–112.

Beardslee, W. R., Versage, E. M. and Gladstone, T. R. (1998). Children of affectively ill parents: a review of the past 10 years. *Journal of the American Academy of Child and Adolescent Psychiatry*, *37*(11), 1134–1141.

Belsky, J. and Pluess, M. (2009). Beyond diathesis stress: differential susceptibility to environmental influences. *Psychological Bulletin*, *135*(6), 885–908.

Bromberger, J. T., Assmann, S. F., Avis, N. E., Schocken, M., Kravitz, H. M. and Cordal, A. (2003). Persistent mood symptoms in a multiethnic community cohort of pre- and peri-menopausal women. *American Journal of Epidemiology*, *158*, 347–356.

Bromberger, J. T., Schott, L., Kravitz, H. M. and Joffe, H. (2015). Risk factors for major depression during midlife among a community sample of women with and without prior major depression: are they the same or different? *Psychological Medicine*, *45*(08), 1653–1664.

Brouwer, J. P., Appelhof, B. C., van Rossum, E. F., Koper, J. W., Fliers, E., Huyser, J., . . . Wiersinga, W. M. (2006). Prediction of treatment response by HPA-axis and glucocorticoid receptor polymorphisms in major depression. *Psychoneuroendocrinology*, *31*(10), 1154–1163.

Burke, H. M., Davis, M. C., Otte, C. and Mohr, D. C. (2005). Depression and cortisol responses to psychological stress: a meta-analysis. Psychoneuroendocrinology, *30*(9), 846–856.

Cai, N., Bigdeli, T. B., Kretzschmar, W., Li, Y., Liang, J., Song, L., . . . Wang, G. (2015). Sparse whole-genome sequencing identifies two loci for major depressive disorder. *Nature*, *523*, 588–591.

Caspi, A., Sugden, K., Moffitt, T. E., Taylor, A., Craig, I. W., Harrington, H., . . . Poulton, R. (2003). Influence of life stress on depression: moderation by a polymorphism in the 5-HTT gene. *Science*, *301*, 386–389.

Cicchetti, D. and Dawson, G. (2002). Editorial: multiple levels of analysis. *Development and Psychopathology*, *14*(03), 417–420.

Cohen, L. S., Soares, C. N., Vitonis, A. F., Otto, M. W. and Harlow, B. L. (2006). Risk for new onset of depression during the menopausal transition. *Archives of General Psychiatry*, *63*, 385–390.

Cohen-Woods, S., Craig, I. W. and McGuffin, P. (2013). The current state of play on the molecular genetics of depression. *Psychological Medicine*, *43*, 673–687.

Conley, C. S. and Rudolph, K. D. (2009). The emerging sex difference in adolescent depression: interacting contributions of puberty and peer stress. *Development and Psychopathology*, *21*, 593–620.

Cyranowski, J. M., Frank, E., Young, E. and Shear, K. (2000). Adolescent onset of the gender difference in lifetime rates of major depression. *Archives of General Psychiatry*, *57*, 21–27.

Dalton, V. S., Kolshus, E. and McLoughlin, D. M. (2014). Epigenetics and depression: return of the repressed. *Journal of Affective Disorders*, *155*, 1–12.

Disner, S., Beevers, C., Haigh, E. and Beck, A. (2011). Neural mechanisms of the cognitive model of depression. *Nature Reviews Neuroscience*, *12*, 467–477.

Dowlati, Y., Herrmann, N., Swardfager, W., Liu, H., Sham, L., Reim, E. K. and Lanctôt, K. L. (2010). A meta-analysis of cytokines in major depression. *Biological Psychiatry*, *67*(5), 446–457.

Dunn, E. C., Brown, R. C., Dai, Y., Rosand, J., Nugent, N. R., Amstadter, A. B. and Smoller, J. W. (2015). Genetic determinants of depression: recent findings and future directions. *Harvard Review of Psychiatry*, *23*, 1–18.

Felger, J. C. and Lotrich, F. E. (2013). Inflammatory cytokines in depression: neurobiological mechanisms and therapeutic implications. *Neuroscience*, *246*, 199–229.

Flint, J. and Kendler, K. S. (2014). The genetics of major depression. *Neuron*, *81*(3), 484–503.

Freeman, E. W., Sammel, M. D., Lin, H. and Nelson, D. B. (2006). Associations of hormones and menopausal status with depressed mood in women with no history of depression. *Archives of General Psychiatry*, *63*, 375–382.

Frodl, T. and O'Keane, V. (2013). How does the brain deal with cumulative stress? A review with focus on developmental stress, HPA axis function and hippocampal structure in humans. *Neurobiology of Disease*, *52*, 24–37.

Furtado, M. and Katzman, M. A. (2015). Examining the role of neuroinflammation in major depression. *Psychiatry Research*, *229*(1), 27–36.

Gibbs, Z., Lee, S. and Kulkarni, J. (2012). What factors determine whether a woman becomes depressed during the perimenopause? *Archives of Women's Mental Health*, *15*(5), 323–332.

Goddings, A. L., Mills, K. L., Clasen, L. S., Giedd, J. N., Viner, R. M. and Blakemore, S. J. (2014). The influence of puberty on subcortical brain development. *Neuroimage*, *88*, 242–251.

Goldstein, B. L. and Klein, D. N. (2014). A review of selected candidate endophenotypes for depression. *Clinical Psychology Review*, *34*(5), 417–427.

Goodman, S. H., Rouse, M. H., Connell, A. M., Broth, M. R., Hall, C. M. and Heyward, D. (2011). Maternal depression and child psychopathology: a meta-analytic review. *Clinical Child and Family Psychology Review*, *14*(1), 1–27.

Gotlib, I. H. and Joormann, J. (2010). Cognition and depression: current status and future directions. *Annual Review of Clinical Psychology*, *6*, 285–312.

Graber, J. A. (2013). Pubertal timing and the development of psychopathology in adolescence and beyond. *Hormones and Behaviour*, *64*, 262–269.

Graber, J. A., Seeley, J. R., Brooks-Gunn, J. and Lewinsohn, P. M. (2004). Is pubertal timing associated with psychopathology in young adulthood? *Journal of the American Academy of Child and Adolescent Psychiatry*, *43*(6), 718–726.

Griffiths, B. and Hunger, R. (2014). Neuroepigenetics of stress. *Neuroscience, 275*, 420–435.

Halligan, S. L., Herbert, J., Goodyer, I. and Murray, L. (2007). Disturbances in morning cortisol secretion in association with maternal postnatal depression predict subsequent depressive symptomatology in adolescents. *Biological Psychiatry, 62*(1), 40–46.

Hamilton, J. P., Etkin, A., Furman, D. J., Lemus, M. G., Johnson, R. F. and Gotlib, I. H. (2012). Functional neuroimaging of major depressive disorder: a meta-analysis and new integration of baseline activation and neural response data. *American Journal of Psychiatry, 169*, 693–703.

Hamilton, J. P., Farmer, M., Fogelman, P. and Gotlib, I. H. (2015). Depressive rumination, the default-mode network, and the dark matter of clinical neuroscience. *Biological Psychiatry, 78*(4), 224–230.

Hamilton, J. P., Siemer, M. and Gotlib, I. H. (2008). Amygdala volume in major depressive disorder: a meta-analysis of magnetic resonance imaging studies. *Molecular Psychiatry, 13*(11), 993–1000.

Hankin, B. L. (2015). Depression from childhood through adolescence: risk mechanisms across multiple systems and levels of analysis. *Current Opinion in Psychology, 4*, 13–20.

Hariri, A. R., Mattay, V. S., Tessitore, A., Kolachana, B., Fera, F., Goldman, D., . . . Weinberger, D. R. (2002). Serotonin transporter genetic variation and the response of the human amygdala. *Science, 297*(5580), 400–403.

Hasler, G., Drevets, W. C., Manji, H. K. and Charney, D. S. (2004). Discovering endophenotypes for major depression. *Neuropsychopharmacology, 29*(10), 1765–1781.

Hing, B., Gardner, C. and Potash, J. (2014). Effects of negative stressors on DNA methylation in the brain: implications for mood and anxiety disorders. *American Journal of Medical Genetics B. 165B*, 541–554.

Insel, T., Cuthbert, B., Garvey, M., Heinssen, R., Pine, D. S., Quinn, K., . . . Wang, P. (2010). Research Domain Criteria (RDoC): toward a new classification framework for research on mental disorders. *American Journal of Psychiatry, 167*, 748–751.

Jaffee, S. R. and Price, T. S. (2007). Gene-environment correlations: a review of the evidence and implications for prevention of mental illness. *Molecular Psychiatry, 12*, 432–442.

Joormann, J., Cooney, R. E., Henry, M. L. and Gotlib, I. H. (2012). Neural correlates of automatic mood regulation in girls at high risk for depression. *Journal of Abnormal Psychology, 121*(1), 61–72.

Kaiser, R. H., Andrews-Hanna, J. R., Wager, T. D. and Pizzagalli, D. A. (2015). Large-scale network dysfunction in major depressive disorder: a meta-analysis of resting-state functional connectivity. *JAMA Psychiatry, 72*(6), 603–611.

Karg, K., Burmeister, M., Shedden, K. and Sen, S. (2011). The serotonin transporter promoter variant (5-HTTLPR), stress, and depression meta-analysis revisited: evidence of genetic moderation. *Archives of General Psychiatry, 68*(5), 444–454.

Kendler, K. S. (2005). 'A gene for . . .': the nature of gene action in psychiatric disorders. *American Journal of Psychiatry*, 162(7), 1243–1252.

Kendler, K. S., Aggen, S. H. and Neale, M. C. (2013). Evidence for multiple genetic factors underlying DSM-IV criteria for major depression. *JAMA Psychiatry*, 70(6), 599–607.

Kendler, K. S. and Baker, J. H. (2007). Genetic influences on measures of the environment: a systematic review. *Psychological Medicine*, 37, 615–626.

Kendler, K. S., Gatz, M., Gardner, C. O. and Pedersen, N. L. (2006). A Swedish national twin study of lifetime major depression. *American Journal of Psychiatry*, 163, 109–114.

Kendler, K. S., Karkowski, L. M., Corey, L. A. and Neale, M. C. (1998). Longitudinal population-based twin study of retrospectively reported premenstrual symptoms and lifetime major depression. *American Journal of Psychiatry*, 155, 1234–1240.

Kendler, K. S., Kessler, R., Walters, E., MacLean, C., Neale, M., Heath, A. and Eaves, L. (1995). Stressful life events, genetic liability, and onset of an episode of major depression in women. *American Journal of Psychiatry*, 152, 833–842.

Kendler, K. S. and Prescott, C. A. (1999). A population-based twin study of lifetime major depression in men and women. *Archives of General Psychiatry*, 56(1), 39–44.

Kendler, K. S., Walters, E. E., Neale, M. C., Kessler, R. C., Heath, A. C. and Eaves, L. J. (1995). The structure of the genetic and environmental risk factors for six major psychiatric disorders in women: phobia, generalised anxiety disorder, panic disorder, bulimia, major depression, and alcoholism. *Archives of General Psychiatry*, 52(5), 374–383.

Kinder, L. S., Carnethon, M. R., Palaniappan, L. P., King, A. C. and Fortmann, S. P. (2004). Depression and the metabolic syndrome in young adults: findings from the Third National Health and Nutrition Examination Survey. *Psychosomatic Medicine*, 66(3), 316–322.

Kraemer, H. C., Stice, E., Kazdin, A., Offord, D. and Kupfer, D. (2001). How do risk factors work together? Mediators, moderators, and independent, overlapping, and proxy risk factors. *American Journal of Psychiatry*, 158, 848–856.

Krueger, R. F. and Markon, K. E. (2006). Reinterpreting comorbidity: a model-based approach to understanding and classifying psychopathology. *Annual Review of Clinical Psychology*, 2, 111–133.

Levinson, D. F. (2006). The genetics of depression: a review. *Biological Psychiatry*, 60(2), 84–92.

Leung, Y. W., Flora, D. B., Gravely, S., Irvine, J., Carney, R. M. and Grace, S. L. (2012). The impact of pre-morbid and post-morbid depression onset on mortality and cardiac morbidity among coronary heart disease patients: a meta-analysis. *Psychosomatic Medicine*, 74(8), 786–801.

Lupien, S. J., Parent, S., Evans, A. C., Tremblay, R. E., Zelazo, P. D., Corbo, V., . . . Séguin, J. R. (2011). Larger amygdala but no change in hippocampal volume in 10-year-old children exposed to maternal depressive symptomatology since birth. *Proceedings of the National Academy of Sciences*, 108, 14324–14329.

Lyubomirsky, S., Layous, K., Chancellor, J. and Nelson, S. K. (2015). Thinking about rumination: the scholarly contributions and intellectual legacy of Susan Nolen-Hoeksema. *Annual Review of Clinical Psychology, 11*, 1–22.

McEwen, B. S., Gray, J. D. and Nasca, C. (2015). Recognising resilience: learning from the effects of stress on the brain. *Neurobiology of Stress, 1*, 1–11.

McKinnon, M., Yucel, K., Nazarov, A. and MacQueen, G. M. (2009). A meta-analysis examining clinical predictors of hippocampal volume in patients with major depressive disorder. *Journal of Psychiatry and Neuroscience, 34*(1), 41–54.

Mackrell, S. V., Sheikh, H. I., Kotelnikova, Y., Kryski, K., Jordan, P., Singh, S. M. and Hayden, E. (2014). Child temperament and parental depression predict cortisol reactivity to stress in middle childhood. *Journal of Abnormal Psychology, 123*, 106–116.

Mandell, D., Siegle, G. J., Shutt, L., Feldmiller, J. and Thase, M. E. (2014). Neural substrates of trait ruminations in depression. *Journal of Abnormal Psychology, 123*(1), 35–48.

Mendle, J., Turkheimer, E. and Emery, R. E. (2007). Detrimental psychological outcomes associated with early pubertal timing in adolescent girls. *Developmental Review, 27*(2), 151–171.

Miller, G. A. (2010). Mistreating psychology in the decades of the brain. *Perspectives on Psychological Science, 5*(6), 716–743.

Miller, G. E. and Blackwell, E. (2006). Turning up the heat: inflammation as a mechanism linking chronic stress, depression, and heart disease. *Current Directions in Psychological Science, 15*(6), 269–272.

Miller, G. E. and Cole, S. W. (2012). Clustering of depression and inflammation in adolescents previously exposed to childhood adversity. *Biological Psychiatry, 72*(1), 34–40.

Mondimore, F. M., Zandi, P. P., MacKinnon, D. F., McInnis, M. G., Miller, E. B., Crowe, R. P., . . . Murphy-Ebenez, K. P. (2006). Familial aggregation of illness chronicity in recurrent, early-onset major depression pedigrees. *American Journal of Psychiatry, 163*, 1554–1560.

Munafò, M. R., Brown, S. M. and Hariri, A. R. (2008). Serotonin transporter (5-HTTLPR) genotype and amygdala activation: a meta-analysis. *Biological Psychiatry, 63*(9), 852–857.

Murphy, M. L., Slavich, G. M., Rohleder, N. and Miller, G. E. (2013). Targeted rejection triggers differential pro-and anti-inflammatory gene expression in adolescents as a function of social status. *Clinical Psychological Science, 1*, 30–40.

Nemeroff, C. B. and Goldschmidt-Clermont, P. J. (2012). Heartache and heartbreak – the link between depression and cardiovascular disease. *Nature Reviews Cardiology, 9*(9), 526–539.

Oberlander, T. F., Weinberg, J., Papsdorf, M., Grunau, R., Misri, S. and Devlin, A. M. (2008). Prenatal exposure to maternal depression, neonatal methylation of human glucocorticoid receptor gene (NR3C1) and infant cortisol stress responses. *Epigenetics, 3*(2), 97–106.

O'Hara, M. W. and McCabe, J. E. (2013). Postpartum depression: current status and future directions. *Annual Review of Clinical Psychology, 9*, 379–407.

Pagliaccio, D., Luby, J. L., Bogdan, R., Agrawal, A., Gaffrey, M. S., Belden, A. C., . . . Barch, D. M. (2015). Amygdala functional connectivity, HPA axis genetic variation, and life stress in children and relations to anxiety and emotion regulation. *Journal of Abnormal Psychology, 124*(4), 817–833.

Pariante, C. M. and Lightman, S. L. (2008). The HPA axis in major depression: classical theories and new developments. *Trends in Neurosciences, 31*(9), 464–468.

Pizzagalli, D. A. (2014). Depression, stress, and anhedonia: Toward a synthesis and integrated model. *Annual Review of Clinical Psychology, 10*, 393–423.

Plomin, R., DeFries, J. C., Knopik, V. S. and Neiderhiser, J. M. (2016). Top 10 replicated findings from behavioural genetics. *Perspectives on Psychological Science, 11*(1), 3–23.

Plomin, R., DeFries, J. C. and Loehlin, J. C. (1977). Genotype-environment interaction and correlation in the analysis of human behaviour. *Psychological Bulletin, 84*, 309–322.

Price, J. L., and Drevets, W. C. (2012). Neural circuits underlying the patholphysiology of mood disorders. *Trends in Cognitive Sciences, 16*(1), 61–71.

Risch, N., Herrell, R., Lehner, T., Liang, K., Eaves, L., Hoh, J., . . . Merikangas, K. (2009). Interaction between the serotonin transporter gene (5-HTTLPR), stressful life events, and risk of depression: a meta-analysis. *Journal of the American Medical Association, 301*, 2462–2471.

Rudolph, K. D. (2014). Puberty as a developmental context of risk for psycho-pathology. In M. Lewis and K. D. Rudolph (eds), *Handbook of Developmental Psychology* (3rd edn, pp. 331–354). New York: Springer.

Rudolph, K. D. and Troop-Gordon, W. (2010). Personal-accentuation and contextual-amplification models of pubertal timing: predicting youth depression. *Development and Psychopathology, 22*, 433–451.

Schmaal, L., Veltman, D. J., van Erp, T. G., Sämann, P. G., Frodl, T., Jahanshad, N., . . . Vernooij, M. W. (2015). Subcortical brain alterations in major depressive disorder: findings from The ENIGMA Major Depressive Disorder working group. *Molecular Psychiatry*, 1–7. doi: 10.1038/mp.2015.69

SciShow (2012). Epigenetics explained. https://youtu.be/kp1bZEUgqVI

Shih, J. H., Eberhart, N., Hammen, C. and Brennan, P. A. (2006). Differential exposure and reactivity to interpersonal stress predict sex differences in adolescent depression. *Journal of Clinical Child and Adolescent Psychology, 35*, 103–115.

Slavich, G. M. and Irwin, M. R. (2014). From stress to inflammation and major depressive disorder: a social signal transduction theory of depression. *Psychological Bulletin, 140*, 774–815.

Slavich, G. M., Thornton, T., Torres, L. D., Monroe, S. M. and Gotlib, I. H. (2009). Targeted rejection predicts hastened onset of major depression. *Journal of Social and Clinical Psychology, 28*, 223–243.

Starr, L., Hammen, C., Conway, C., Raposa, E. and Brennan, P. (2014). Sensitising effect of early adversity on depressive reactions to later proximal stress: moderation by polymorphisms in serotonin transporter and corticotropin releasing hormone receptor genes in a 20-year longitudinal study. *Development and Psychopathology, 26,* 1241–1254.

Steiner, M. (2000). Premenstrual syndrome and premenstrual dysphoric disorder: guidelines for management. *Journal of Psychiatry and Neuroscience, 25,* 459–468.

Steiner, M. and Born, L. (2000). Advances in the diagnosis and treatment of premenstrual dysphoria. *CNS Drugs, 13,* 286–304.

Steiner, M., Dunn, E. and Born, L. (2003). Hormones and mood: from menarche to menopause and beyond. *Journal of Affective Disorders, 74,* 67–83.

Stetler, C. and Miller, G. E. (2011). Depression and Hypothalamic–Pituitary–Adrenal activation: a quantitative summary of four decades of research. *Psychosomatic Medicine, 73,* 114–126.

Stuhrmann, A., Suslow, T. and Dannlowski, U. (2011). Facial emotion processing in major depression: systematic review of neuroimaging findings. *Biology of Mood and Anxiety Disorders, 1,* 10.

Sullivan, P. F., Neale, M. C. and Kendler, K. S. (2000). Genetic epidemiology of major depression: review and meta-analysis. *American Journal of Psychiatry, 10,* 1552–1562.

Tartter, M., Hammen, C., Bower, J. E., Brennan, P. A. and Cole, S. (2015). Effects of chronic interpersonal stress exposure on depressive symptoms are moderated by genetic variation at IL6 and IL1β in youth. *Brain, Behaviour, and Immunity, 46,* 104–111.

Taylor, S. E., Way, B. M., Welch, W. T., Hilmert, C. J., Lehman, B. J. and Eisenberger, N. I. (2006). Early family environment, current adversity, the serotonin transporter promoter polymorphism, and depressive symptomatology. *Biological Psychiatry, 60*(7), 671–676.

Turecki, G. and Meaney, M. J. (2016). Effects of the social environment and stress on glucocorticoid receptor gene methylation: a systematic review. *Biological Psychiatry, 79*(2), 87–96.

van Rossum, E. F., Binder, E. B., Majer, M., Koper, J. W., Ising, M., Modell, S., . . . Holsboer, F. (2006). Polymorphisms of the glucocorticoid receptor gene and major depression. *Biological Psychiatry, 59*(8), 681–688.

Vrshek-Schallhorn, S., Doane, L. D., Mineka, S., Zinbarg, R. E., Craske, M. G. and Adam, E. K. (2013). The cortisol awakening response predicts major depression: predictive stability over a 4-year follow-up and effect of depression history. *Psychological Medicine, 43*(03), 483–493.

Watkins, L. L., Koch, G. G., Sherwood, A., Blumenthal, J. A., Davidson, J. R., O'Connor, C. and Sketch, M. H. (2013). Association of anxiety and depression with all-cause mortality in individuals with coronary heart disease. *Journal of the American Heart Association, 2*(2), e000068.

Wray, N. R., Pergadia, M. L., Blackwood, D. H. R., Penninx, B. W. J. H., Gordon, S. D., Nyholt, D. R., . . . Smit, J. H. (2012). Genome-wide association study of major depressive disorder: New results, meta-analysis, and lessons learned. *Molecular Psychiatry*, *17*(1), 36–48.

Yim, I. S., Stapleton, L. R. T., Guardino, C. M., Hahn-Holbrook, J. and Schetter, C. D. (2015). Biological and psychosocial predictors of postpartum depression: systematic review and call for integration. *Clinical Psychology*, *11*(1), 99–137.

5

Cognitive and life stress approaches to depression

Sarah sips her coffee as she gazes out the window onto the busy street. She watches men and women walk briskly toward their destinations, and imagines that their lives are filled with purpose and meaning – but believes that hers will never be – no interesting job to go to, no eager completion of tasks, no important goal to pursue for the future. She watches couples pass the window, laughing and conversing, and feels a pang of loss. 'I'll never have a relationship again', she thinks, 'no one would want me, and I'll always be alone'. As she often does these days, she leaves the coffee shop unrefreshed and feeling even worse than when she came in.

Sarah's reveries are typical of those of depressed people: a relentless focus on the negative aspects of herself, the world and her future. Such thoughts are usually exaggerations or misperceptions of reality, but invariably they leave the person feeling overwhelmed and hopeless, accentuating or prolonging the symptoms of their depression. Many theorists argue that such negative thinking is not only part of the syndrome of depression, but may indeed reveal a vulnerability to develop depression or to experience recurrences – to the extent that such negativity of thinking is part of the person's typical way of perceiving the self and the world. In this chapter, several of these models that emphasise primarily *cognitive* causes of depression are reviewed and evaluated.

Suppose that we also discover that Sarah's life changed dramatically a month ago, when her fiancé broke off their relationship. She had dreamed of their life together, and was overwhelmed with hurt and anger when he told her he had found someone else. Her feelings rapidly turned into depression. As with Sarah, many people who experience major depressive episodes are reacting to undesirable negative life events. The role of stressful events and adverse life conditions has long been recognised as a contributor to depression, and in the second part of this chapter, we analyse this approach to understanding depression.

Cognitive and information-processing models of depression

Among psychological models of depression, no approach has stimulated more research in the last 50 years than the cognitive model of Aaron Beck (Beck, 1967; 1976) and several subsequent cognitive approaches (for reviews see Beck, 2008; Clark, Beck and Alford, 1999; Beck and Haigh, 2014). Although trained in the psychoanalytic perspective on depression that viewed the condition as introjected anger toward a lost relationship, more than anything Beck was struck by the negative thinking of his patients, the expressions of self-criticism and blame, the exaggeration of misfortune and the beliefs about personal helplessness and futility. He observed that such thoughts were dysfunctional – representing apparent distortions of reality and serving to prolong or exacerbate the symptoms of depression. Therefore, he formulated a cognitive model of depression with three key elements: the *'cognitive triad'*, *faulty information processing* and *negative self-schemas*.

The *cognitive triad* refers to characteristic thinking that emphasises negative expectations, interpretations, perceptions and memories about the self, the world and the future. Defeated, self-critical and hopeless thoughts were believed to contribute to the mood, behavioural, physiological and motivational deficits in depression. Moreover, Beck argued that depressive thinking is typically distorted, that individuals selectively attend to the negative even when alternative positive events and interpretations are plausible, and greatly overgeneralise and magnify adversity while minimising or misinterpreting positive information. These *information processing errors in attention and reasoning* are not deliberate or conscious, but rather they happen spontaneously and *automatically*. As in the example of Sarah earlier, there is no basis for her to conclude that she will never have a meaningful career or relationship – but her mood colours her thoughts in distorted ways, always emphasising the negative.

The third component of Beck's model is the idea of a *negative self-schema*. The schema concept has a long history in psychology, generally referring to organised representations of experiences in memory that serve as a kind of mental filter, guiding the selection, interpretation and recall of information. Schemas are essential to all human information processing, serving the goals of speed and efficiency so that attention can be directed to 'meaningful' information instead of laboriously processing all available information. Thus, by selectively attending to or interpreting certain information, schemas help to fill in 'missing' information based on what is 'expected'. A schema about 'John' for example (tall, dark hair) helps us to rapidly spot him in a crowd, without seeing his face and without inspecting each and every person. Because they are like pre-existing filters or theories, however, errors are possible (e.g., we stop searching for John when we spot a tall, dark-haired man, but later discover that it wasn't John, who was actually sitting down so that we 'ignored' him in our search for tall, dark-haired men).

A *self-schema* refers to organised beliefs and propositions about the self, and according to Beck, the depression-prone person holds negative beliefs (or a mixture of negative and positive). These beliefs may be acquired in child-hood, possibly as a result of critical or rejecting parents, and because the schema is selective in 'taking in' only confirmatory negative information, beliefs are retained despite accumulated evidence to the contrary. That is, a person who believes that it is terribly important to be perfect at all times and believes that he is basically incompetent is likely to pay attention to examples that support this belief while ignoring disconfirming information.

Situations that are stressful and remind the individual of circumstances that were originally responsible for the acquisition of negative self-views are especially likely to activate the negative schema. Thus, a child often scolded for making mistakes might react to a poor exam performance with the 'incom-petence' self-schema. When activated, it directs his attention to any perceived flaws and exaggerates their significance, makes memories available that remind him of past shortcomings, and leads to thoughts about the future that include expectations of failure.

Other cognitive models of depression

In addition to Beck's seminal model of depression, several variants of cognitive theories have been developed over the last 30 years.

Helplessness and hopelessness models of depression

Martin Seligman and his colleagues originally observed that animals that had been exposed to uncontrollable aversive conditions failed to take action to escape such situations when outcomes were no longer uncontrollable, as if they had learned to be helpless. Seligman applied this hypothesis to human depression, suggesting that when one has erroneous expectations that no control is possible (in obtaining desirable outcomes or preventing undesirable ones), one fails to take action and experiences depressive symptoms. Later, the model was refined to include the individual's perceptions of the *causes* of uncontrollable outcomes. Abramson, Seligman and Teasdale (1978) developed the *attributional model* that linked depression to the tendency to ascribe the causes of negative events to qualities of the self that are perceived to be unchanging and pervasive. In contrast, negative outcomes attributed to unstable or specific causes would produce less negative responses. It was further argued that some people characteristically show a 'negative explanatory style' of stable, global and internal causal attributions for negative events, and transient, local and external causal attributions for positive events (Abramson, Seligman and Teasdale, 1978). That is, when something bad or undesirable happens, those vulnerable to depression are more likely to believe that it was caused by global and persisting qualities of themselves that presumably are undesirable and unchangeable. This 'negative explanatory style' is contrasted with the more typical 'self-serving attributional style', where people make more internal, stable and global attributions for positive events than for negative events. A meta-analysis indicates that in healthy controls there is a large self-serving attributional bias, which is reduced in groups with psychopathology, most particularly in patients with depression (Mezulis, Abramson, Hyde and Hankin, 2004).

A further variant of the attributional model is the *hopelessness model* of depression (Abramson, Metalsky and Alloy, 1989; Alloy et al., 1999). In this model, hopelessness (consisting both of negative expectations about the occurrence of a highly valued outcome and perceptions of helplessness to change the likelihood of the outcomes) is the cognition that immediately causes depressive reactions. In turn, hopelessness is the outcome of negative life events that are interpreted negatively, in terms of stable and global causal attributions for the event, or inferred negative consequences of the event and/or inferred negative characteristics of the self, given the event's occurrence. The increased use of negative cognitive styles such as hopelessness and the negative explanatory style has been linked to childhood sexual and emotional maltreatment, personality disorders and more severe depression (Gibb, 2002; Gibb et al., 2001; Rose, Abramson, Hodulik, Halberstadt and Leff, 1994).

Rumination and self-focus models

Several investigators have noted that depressed people tend to repetitively focus in on themselves and on their feelings, with negative consequences for their mood. People with depression exhibit increased *self-focused* attention (Ingram, 1990; Pyszczynski and Greenberg, 1987), which magnifies negative appraisals and the perceived negative consequences of undesirable events and potentially interferes with appropriate social and adaptive functioning, contributing to a vicious cycle. Consistent with this, a meta-analysis of experimental and longitudinal studies of self-focus confirmed the negative consequences on affect of self-focus during sad mood (Mor and Winquist, 2002).

Susan Nolen-Hoeksema further elaborated on this initial work, as noted in Chapter 3 as an explanation for sex differences in depression, and as a theory about vulnerability to depression. She proposed that a *ruminative* response to depression, characterised by repeated focus on self, feelings, symptoms and the causes, meanings and consequences of these symptoms and feelings, is a typically passive style of responding to dysphoric feelings that leads to the exacerbation of symptoms. This theory proposes that rumination is unhelpful because it exacerbates existing negative affect, impairs problem solving, increases selective focus on negative interpretations and impairs motivation to engage in helpful, instrumental actions.

Consistent with this theory, a large and robust evidence base now indicates that rumination is one of the major cognitive vulnerabilities for the onset and maintenance of depression (Lyubomirsky, Layous, Chancellor and Nelson, 2015; Nolen-Hoeksema and Watkins, 2011; Nolen-Hoeksema, Wisco and Lyubomirsky, 2008; Watkins, 2008). In experimental studies, manipulating rumination (compared with distraction) causally exacerbates existing negative affect and negative thinking about the self and future and impairs problem solving (Watkins, 2008). Rumination has no effect on mood and cognition in individuals with normal mood; rather it serves to exacerbate an individual's response to existing stress and difficulties.

In large-scale longitudinal studies, rumination prospectively predicts the onset of major depressive episodes in non-depressed and the maintenance of depressive symptoms in currently depressed individuals, and mediates the effects of other major risk factors on depression in children, adolescents and adults, including past history of depression, neuroticism and family history of depression (Abela et al., 2011; Nolen-Hoeksema, 2000; Spasojevic and Alloy, 2001). For example, in a large general population sample (32,837 people), a structural equation model found family history of mental health diffculties, social deprivation and traumatic or abusive life experiences were all strongly associated with higher levels of anxiety and depression, but that these relationships were largely mediated by rumination (Kinderman, Schwannauer, Pontin and Tai, 2013). Rumination has also been found to be a mechanism that mediates the effects of stressful life events on depression and anxiety (Michl, McLaughlin, Shephard and Nolen-Hoeksema, 2013; Ruscio, Gentes, Jones, Hallion, Coleman and Swendsen, 2015) and that mediates the relationship between cognitive biases in interpretation and memory and depressed symptoms (Wisco, Gilbert and Marroquin, 2014) and between low self-esteem and subsequent depression (Kuster, Orth and Meier, 2012).

Importantly, research has suggested that there are distinct subtypes or styles of processing involved in rumination, with only the more abstract, evaluative and self-judgemental form of ruminative self-focus (sometimes called 'brooding') implicated in the detrimental consequences of rumination on depressed mood, autobiographical memory, emotional reactivity and problem solving (see review in Watkins, 2008). In contrast, repetitive thinking about negative situations that involves a concrete and specific processing style focused on the contextual details of negative events and emotions has adaptive consequences such as improved problem-solving and reduced emotional reactivity (Watkins, Moberly and Moulds, 2008; Watkins and Moulds, 2005; Watkins and Teasdale, 2001). Recent theoretical work has proposed that unresolved goals produce rumination but also that pathological rumination is a mental habit – an automatic cognitive response conditioned to triggering stimuli such as low mood (Watkins and Nolen-Hoeksema, 2014). Rumination has also been identified as a 'transdiagnostic mechanism' that contributes to the onset and maintenance of not just depression, but also anxiety, substance abuse, eating disorders and psychosis (Aldao, Nolen-Hoeksema and Schweizer, 2010; Nolen-Hoeksema and Watkins, 2011), potentially explaining the co-morbidity between depression and other disorders.

Self-concept in depression

A theme in many of the cognitive models of depression is that of negative views of the self, a deep-seated belief that one is defective, unworthy, unwanted or incapable of obtaining or keeping important sources of meaning and gratification. Such low self-esteem has been suggested as a potential cognitive factor in depression. Different dimensions of self-esteem are potentially important: the overall level of self-worth and self-esteem; the relative stability–instability of self-esteem, that is, how much it varies over short periods of time; and the contingency of self-esteem, that is, how much it depends on self-relevant events, such as validation, approval and success.

A meta-analysis of longitudinal studies found that low self-esteem was predictive of subsequent depression (Sowislo and Orth, 2013). While some reviews have suggested that contingent self-esteem increases vulnerability to depressed mood (Crocker and Park, 2004), one study found that overall level of self-esteem is the strongest predictor of depression (Sowislo, Orth and Meier, 2014). Dysfunctional self-worth and self-esteem is an important construct in social learning and psychodynamic approaches to depression as well as cognitive models.

Evaluating cognitive vulnerability models

There are a number of issues that have been pursued in the empirical evaluation of the cognitive models of depression. The following sections are organised around some of the major questions.

Depression and negative cognitions

Of the hundreds of studies testing the question of whether depressed people think more negatively than do non-depressed comparisons, the great majority have found that depressed patients do report more negative cognition, dysfunctional attitudes and negative attributions (e.g., Clark, Beck and Alford, 1999). Further, relative to non-depressed controls, depressed patients show information-processing biases on tasks assessing memory, interpretative reasoning and attention, including retrieving more negative memories (see seminal papers by Clark and Teasdale, 1982; 1985; review by Dalgleish and Werner-Siedler, 2014) and endorsing more negative interpretations of ambiguous information (e.g., Mogg, Bradbury and Bradley, 2006; Wisco and Nolen-Hoeksema, 2010). Moreover, depressed patients also report experiencing more involuntary memories of past upsetting or traumatic events than controls (Brewin, Gregory, Lipton and Burgess, 2010), illustrating another mechanism whereby past adversity can influence present functioning. Experiments investigating deployment of attention suggest that non-depressed individuals attend away from negative stimuli and towards positive stimuli, whereas depressed patients have a bias in attention towards negative relative to positive stimuli (see meta-analysis by Peckham, McHugh and Otto, 2010). Robust evidence across a range of experimental tasks assessing attentional deployment, memory recall and the ability to remove irrelevant material from working memory, show that depression is characterised by increased elaboration of negative information, by difficulties disengaging from negative material, and by deficits in cognitive control when processing negative information (see reviews by Gotlib and Joormann, 2010; Bistricky, Ingram and Atchley, 2011).

Thus, depressed people do appear to emphasise the negative and to find negative information more accessible – a process that likely contributes to the perpetuation or deepening of their depressed mood. We will examine the evidence for whether negative thinking does actually play a causal role in depression in a later section.

State-dependent cognitions and cognitive reactivity

An important implication of the cognitive vulnerability model is that vulnerable individuals should still have dysfunctional cognitions or schemas that increase risk for future depression when they are not depressed, for example, after recovering from an episode of depression. As such, recovered depressed individuals should demonstrate more negative cognition and information-processing biases than those who have never been depressed. However, the great majority of studies do not find any difference between remitted depressed patients and non-depressed controls on measures of negative cognition including the Attribution Style Questionnaire and the Dysfunctional Attitudes Scale (for detailed reviews see Scher, Ingram and Segal, 2005). The few studies that found elevated cognitive dysfunctions in remitted depressed patients compared to controls involved patients with residual depressive symptoms, suggesting that cognitive dysfunctions may only be found in the presence of depressed mood. Thus, the evidence indicates that depressogenic cognitions are not stable traits but rather that they may be 'latent' and mood-state-dependent, inaccessible unless they are activated or primed by a relevant 'challenge', such as the onset of a negative mood or the experience of a stressful event (Ingram, Miranda and Segal, 1998; Miranda, 1997; Teasdale, 1983), an idea originally proposed by Beck (1967). This process is called 'cognitive reactivity', defined as the extent to which negative cognition is activated in response to negative mood or stress.

Cognitive reactivity approaches hypothesise that although remitted depressed patients do not differ from non-depressed persons when assessed under normal conditions, vulnerable individuals will demonstrate greater negative thinking than controls in the context of negative mood, difficulties and stressful events, because these challenges activate underlying depressogenic schemas. Consistent with this hypothesis, individuals with a history of depression do demonstrate greater dysfunctional attitudes and information-processing biases than controls but only when they are primed (e.g., by negative moods) prior to assessment (for detailed reviews see Ingram et al., 1998; Scher et al., 2005).

The main experimental approach to priming is to induce depressed mood by having subjects read depressive words or phrases, listen to sad music or watch sad films. For example, following such a sad mood induction procedure, there was greater endorsement of dysfunctional attitudes as depressed mood increased for currently non-depressed women with a prior history of depression but not for currently non-depressed women with no prior history (Miranda and Persons, 1988). Thus, the women vulnerable to depression (indicated by previous episodes) appeared to possess underlying negative cognitions that became accessible during mildly depressed mood. Similarly, mood inductions influence information-processing biases in vulnerable groups, whether assessed through dichotic listening tasks or deployment of attention tasks (Ingram, Bernet and Mclaughlin, 1994; Ingram and Ritter, 2000).

Importantly, cognitive reactivity prospectively predicts levels of depression in longitudinal studies (Dent and Teasdale, 1988). For example, a sad mood induction produces greater increases in dysfunctional attitudes in remitted patients treated with pharmacotherapy relative to those treated with cognitive-behavioural therapy (CBT) (Segal et al., 2006), with CBT treatment reducing cognitive reactivity, and the extent of cognitive reactivity predicting relapse over the next 18 months. Hence, the accessibility of the negative thinking during negative mood appears to indicate an underlying cognitive structure that confers vulnerability for depression.

These findings have influenced the development of the underlying models of information processing in depression. Teasdale (1983, 1988) proposed the differential activation hypothesis, which suggested that individuals differ in the extent to which patterns of negative thinking are activated in response to depressed mood and stressors, i.e., that there are individual differences in cognitive reactivity. Borrowing from Bower's (1981) associative network model of moods and memory, Teasdale hypothesised that emotions and associated cognitions are linked in memory, so that when a mood is activated, representations of events and cognitions that are associated with it in memory may also be made accessible. This hypothesis predicts that degree of cognitive reactivity will be a consequence of earlier learning experiences: a negative event such as an interpersonal rejection will activate more negative cognitions, including recollections of previous rejections and self-criticism, for individuals with more negative histories than for individuals with less negative histories. Thus, Teasdale proposed that in response to a sad mood, all individuals will experience an increase in negative thinking, but that for more vulnerable individuals, sad mood activates much more extreme and global negative thoughts, such as 'I am a complete failure', which, in turn, lead to a depressive reaction (Teasdale, 1988).

This model has subsequently evolved into a more complex model, which proposes that depressed mood activates an entire 'mental model' that involves globally negative views of the self, incorporating semantic and procedural knowledge, as well as sensory experience including bodily feelings, rather than a set of individual cognitions (Teasdale and Barnard, 1993). A person vulnerable to depression is believed to have acquired a schematic 'mental model' that contains a global, holistic, dysfunctional sense of the self. Consistent with this hypothesis, when depressed participants completed sentence stems related to social approval or personal achievement (e.g., 'Always to put other's interests before your own is a recipe for . . .'), they made more completions with positive words ('success') that result in dysfunctional meanings than completions with negative words ('disaster') that result in appropriate meanings (e.g., Sheppard and Teasdale, 2004).

Specificity of depressive cognitions

How unique is this negative thinking to depression alone? After all, negative cognition is likely to reflect the presence of distress and psychopathology in general. Negative explanatory style and dysfunctional attitudes are elevated across a range of patient groups (see review in Harvey, Watkins, Mansell and Shafran, 2004), and there is considerable overlap and shared variance for negative cognition across anxiety and depression. Moreover, the high levels of co-morbidity between depression and other disorders make it hard to identify unique patterns of thinking. Further, rumination has been identified as a transdiagnostic process that cuts across disorders (Nolen-Hoeksema and Watkins, 2011). Nonetheless, there may be forms of negative thinking that are unique to depression and not shared with other disorders – the most stringent comparison being with anxious disorders as another internalised, emotional disorder. For example, depression-related thinking is focused more on the past, personal inadequacy and worthlessness, whereas anxiety-related thinking is focused more on the future and potential threat, although, anxiety disorders can involve negative thinking about the past, most notably, the re-experiencing of traumatic events in post-traumatic stress disorder. One cognitive bias specifically associated with depression that prospectively predicts subsequent depression is the tendency to process information in an overgeneralised way (Watkins, 2011; Watkins, 2015), in which a general rule or conclusion is drawn on the basis of isolated incidents and applied across the board to related and unrelated situations, such that one negative event, such as a failure, is interpreted as indicating a global, characterological inadequacy (Beck, 1976; Carver and Ganellen, 1983).

In parallel, depression is characterised by reduced recall of specific autobiographical memories relative to healthy controls and other psychiatric patients (with the exception of patients with post-traumatic stress disorder and schizophrenia, although separating out co-morbid depression is difficult) (Williams et al., 2007). Both depressed patients and formerly depressed patients recall a greater proportion of overgeneral memories characterised by categoric summaries of repeated events (e.g., 'making mistakes' or 'playing golf every week') even when asked to recall specific personal memories that occurred at a particular place and time (e.g., 'beating my friend Paul at golf last Saturday', Williams, 1996; Williams et al., 2007). Increased retrieval of overgeneral memory predicts poorer long-term outcome for depression in prospective studies in adults and adolescents (see reviews, meta-analyses and studies including Dalgleish and Werner-Seidler, 2014; Rawal and Rice, 2012; Sumner, Griffith and Mineka, 2010).

The pathological rumination characteristic of depression is also characterised by an abstract, global thinking style (e.g., asking 'Why?', 'What does this mean about me?' and has been implicated in the development of overgeneral memory recall in depression (Watkins, 2015; Watkins and Teasdale, 2001; Williams et al., 2007) and mediates the effects of overgeneral memory in predicting future depression (Raes et al., 2006).

Negative thinking as a cause of depression

The observed relationship noted earlier between depression and negative thinking could reflect negative thinking causing depressed mood or negative thinking being a consequence of depression, or a bidirectional relationship, or both being related to a common third factor, such as a history of negative life events or early trauma. How can we establish the causal direction?

First, prospective longitudinal studies can demonstrate that cognitive vulnerability at one point in time predicts the onset of a later depressive episode or worsening of depressive symptoms at subsequent points over time, once initial depression level was controlled. Such studies indicate that a cognitive vulnerability precedes and predicts depression in real world settings, suggesting a role for negative cognition in depression, although this cannot prove causality. Second, bidirectional manipulation of cognitive styles through experiment or intervention allows stronger inference about a causal effect: if increasing negative thinking increases depressed mood, while reducing negative thinking reduces depressed mood, there are strong grounds to infer that negative thinking influences mood.

Longitudinal prospective studies

There is growing evidence that cognitive vulnerability predicts the onset of depression using 'behavioural high risk' designs in which individuals are selected on the basis of hypothesised psychological vulnerability to depression. A seminal study is the Temple-Wisconsin Cognitive Vulnerability to Depression (CVD) Study: a large sample of high cognitive risk and low cognitive risk undergraduates, defined in terms of scoring in the upper and lower quartiles respectively of the Dysfunctional Attitude Scale (DAS) and the Cognitive Style Questionnaire (CSQ), were followed up prospectively every six weeks for two years and then every four months for an additional three years. The DAS assesses the endorsement of inflexible, maladaptive and perfectionistic beliefs about the contingencies necessary to demonstrate self-worth, e.g., 'If I do not do well all the time people will not respect me'. The CSQ is an expanded and modified version of the Attributional Style Questionnaire (Seligman, Abramson, Semmel and Baeyer, 1979), which assesses the tendency to make internal, stable and global attributions about positive and negative events. For the first two and a half years of follow-up, the high cognitive risk participants were significantly more likely than low-risk participants to develop a first onset of major depression, even after controlling for initial levels of depression (Alloy et al., 1999; Alloy, Abramson, Whitehouse and Hogan, 2006). Similarly, high cognitive risk participants with a history of prior depression were more likely to develop recurrences than low cognitive risk participants with a history of depression. This finding has been replicated in large-scale prospective studies (Abela et al., 2011; Hankin, 2008; Nusslock et al., 2011) and confirmed in reviews (Jacobs, Reinecke, Gollan and Kane, 2008; Liu, Klerman, Nestor and Cheek, 2015) and meta-analyses (Hu, Zhang and Yang, 2015; Huang, 2015).

As noted above, rumination is a form of repetitive negative thinking that reliably predicts prospective depression (Nolen-Hoeksema, 2000; Spasojevic and Alloy, 2001). In the CVD study, the effect of attributional style on depression was accounted for by its effect on rumination, that is, rumination was found to mediate the effect of negative attributional style on risk for depression (Spasojevic and Alloy, 2001). In parallel, rumination in response to stressful events moderated the effect of attributional style on onset of depression, that is, stressful events were more likely to lead to depression in individuals who tended to ruminate (Robinson and Alloy, 2003). These findings have been replicated in multiple prospective studies (e.g., Abela and Hankin, 2011; Hong et al., 2010)

It is important to note that there is also evidence from longitudinal studies that cognitive vulnerability interacts with negative life events to predict future depression (e.g., Abela and Hankin, 2011; Abela, Parkinson, Stolow and Starrs, 2009; Hankin, Abramson, Miller and Haeffel, 2004; Stange, Hamilton, Abramson and Alloy, 2014). For example, Abela and Hankin (2011) found that rumination alone predicted increased onset of depression in adolescents over two years but also that it moderated (i.e., interacted) with negative life events to predict future depression. Hence, rumination provides a link between cognitive and life stress accounts of depression because ruminative thinking is often about prior stressful events. The relationship between vulnerability and stress will be discussed in more detail later in the chapter.

Cognitive bias modification

A key development within recent years is the use of experimental paradigms to test whether changing negative information processing does influence symptoms. Cognitive bias modification (CBM) experiments involve the use of experimental training paradigms designed to induce cognitive biases, to test whether these biases influence emotional response (Hertel and Mathews, 2011). Although first used to test the role of negative thinking in anxiety, recent studies have confirmed that negative cognitive biases play a causal role in impacting negative mood in depression (see Hallion and Ruscio, 2011 meta-analysis).

For example, a task has been developed to assess and modify inter-pretative bias (CBM-I) in which participants repeatedly work through multiple training trials on a computer, with each trial consisting of an scenario that is emotionally ambiguous, but with the final sentence ending in a word fragment whose completion forces the participant to complete either a positive or negative meaning (Mathews and MacLeod, 2005). On the test version, positive and negative completions occur equally frequently (50 per cent each) and any existing bias can be assessed by examining the relative speed to complete negative versus positive variants. Negative interpretative biases on these tasks are correlated with severity of depression (Lee, Mathews, Shergill and Yiend, 2016) and associated with the tendency to ruminate (Mor, Hertel, Ngo, Shachar and Redak, 2014), confirming that depression is characterised by negative cognitive biases. On the training version, participants repeatedly practice many trials, with the trials set up so that the majority (e.g., 90 per cent) force the participant to make the same type of completion (positive or negative). The individual learns to make that particular response more automatically and rapidly, thus acquiring the respective cognitive bias. Participants trained to make negative interpretations show greater negative affect (e.g., anxiety or sadness) in response to a subsequent experimental stress task (e.g., a speech task or failure task) than those trained to make positive interpretations (Mathews and MacLeod, 2005; Hertel and Mathews, 2011), providing evidence supporting a causal role for such cognitions on symptoms.

Relevant to depression, CBM-I tasks have shown that training negative interpretations relative to benign ones increases negative mood and state rumination to subsequent stressor tasks (Hertel et al., 2014; Koster and Hoorelbeke, 2015). Furthermore, a CBM study manipulated attributional style in an undergraduate sample, by the use of multiple training trials intended to promote a positive attributional style or a negative attributional style (i.e., internal, stable and global attributions for negative events; external, unstable and local attributions for positive events). The training was successful in that those in the positive training condition made fewer self-critical causal attributions on a subsequent difficult anagram task and experienced less depressed mood to this stressor relative to those in the negative training condition (Peters, Constans and Mathews, 2011). Hence, this study provides the first direct evidence that attributional style can influence depressive symptoms, albeit in an analogue non-clinical group.

Likewise, a variant of CBM designed to train participants out of the abstract, global style characteristic of depression has been shown to reduce symptoms of depression in an analogue population (Watkins, Baeyens and Read, 2009) and in patients with major depression (Watkins et al., 2012), relative to an attentional control or usual care, supporting a strong causal inference for the role of abstract, general thinking in maintaining depression.

CBM approaches have also tested the training of attentional bias towards or away from negative versus positive faces and/or words, indicating that shifting these biases can also improve emotional reactivity to a subsequent stressor (Beevers, Clasen, Enock and Schnyer, 2015; Clasen, Wells, Ellis and Beevers, 2013; LeMoult, Joormann, Kircanski and Gotlib, 2016; Yang, Ding, Dai, Peng and Zhang, 2015).

CBM approaches have therefore strengthened the claims that cognition can influence certain (e.g., rumination, low mood) but not all of the symptoms of depression. Some researchers have proposed that extensive CBM could itself provide a treatment for depression and anxiety, although this is more contentious, with recent meta-analyses suggesting weak effects in patient populations (Cristea, Kok and Cuijpers, 2015).

What underpins the development of cognitive vulnerability?

The original cognitive model proposes that the negative self-schemata and associated habits of negative thinking result from difficult early experiences or are learned from critical and rejecting parents. The evidence is broadly consistent with this.

For example, taking rumination as an exemplar of negative cognition, there is evidence that experiences of childhood abuse, especially sexual and emotional abuse, bullying and stressful life events, as well as personality factors such as neuroticism and sensitivity to rejection, are all correlated with and prospectively predict rumination (Kingston, Watkins and O'Mahen, 2013; Michl, McLaughlin, Shepherd and Nolen-Hoeksema, 2013; Pearson, Watkins and Mullan, 2011; Sarin and Nolen-Hoeksema, 2010). Other studies have investigated the role of specific parenting styles on the development of rumination: a longitudinal prospective study that observed positive and aggressive parenting behaviours during laboratory-based interactions completed by mother-adolescent dyads at ages 12 found that low levels of positive maternal behaviour predicted increased rumination at age 15, which in turn predicted depression at age 17 (Gate et al., 2013). Similarly, greater feminine gender role identity among children and encouragement of emotion expression by mothers at age 11 predicted the development of depressive rumination at age 15 in girls, after controlling for rumination at age 11 (Cox, Mezulis and Hyde, 2010).

Similar patterns are found for other negative cognitions. In a three-wave longitudinal study with 998 adolescents (aged 13 to 17), emotional abuse by parents and peers at baseline predicted a worsening of several cognitive vulnerabilities at Time 2 including ruminative brooding and negative attributional style, which mediated between the experiences of abuse and the increase of depressive symptoms at Time 3 (Paredes and Calvete, 2014). Consistent with the cognitive model, peer victimisation and harsh parenting in 12-year-olds predicted negative cognitions one year later, which in turn partially mediated the effect of these difficult experiences on depressive symptoms one year on (Cole et al., 2016), and were also independently correlated with cognitive reactivity in children and adolescents (Cole et al., 2014). In 289 children and their parents followed longitudinally from infancy to 10–11 years old, the interaction of greater maternal negativity and negative life events predicted subsequent negative cognitive styles, as did self-reported maternal anger expression and negative feedback to the child (Mezulis, Hyde and Abramson, 2006).

Overall evaluation of cognitive models of depression

The cognitive models of depression have stimulated very active research programmes over the last 40 years and the body of evidence is now consistent with a modified cognitive vulnerability perspective such that the extent to which extreme, global and overgeneralised negative models of the self, the world and the future, and abstract rumination are activated in response to negative mood and stressful events contribute to vulnerability to depression. Moreover, there is now robust support for a causal role of cognition in the development of depression from many prospective studies that have found that negative cognitive style, rumination, increased cognitive reactivity and overgeneralisation predict the onset, relapse and recurrence of major depression, and from the CBM work that demonstrates that cognitive biases influence mood and symptoms in the laboratory.

However, some important methodological and conceptual issues still require resolution. The relationship between thought content, as assessed by self-report measures, and thought process, as assessed by information processing tasks, is not always clear, although progress is being made, for example, the relationships between self-reported rumination and information processing is being elucidated (Koster, De Lissnyder, Derakshan and De Raedt, 2011). Critically, the schemas hypothesised to underpin depressive vulnerability are inferred on the basis of thought content and thought process, rather than directly assessed.

A further criticism emphasises the over-simplicity of the near-exclusive focus on internal cognition as the major diathesis in depression, to the relative neglect of the environmental and social context in which the person lives. For example, the lives of depressed people are often extremely stressful and deficient in resources (e.g., Coyne, 1992; Hammen, 1992). The role of interpersonal relationships including intimate, social and family relationships has not been fully integrated (e.g., Gotlib and Hammen, 1992), leading many to call for more integrative models that account for biological as well as personality, social, environmental and developmental aspects of depression. In subsequent sections and chapters, these alternative and integrative approaches are discussed.

Stressful events and circumstances and their role in depression

It is a common observation that most depressive episodes are preceded by bad things happening to the individual. In addition to establishing this association empirically, much of the research in recent decades has addressed an additional critical question: because most people do not develop a depressive episode even when negative events occur, why do some people have such reactions while others do not? Moreover, there are questions about what kinds of stress are most likely to trigger depression. There is also great interest in the dynamic relationships between stress and depression over time and course of disorder, and the bidirectional association between stress and depression. Finally, in recent years, much of the current research has begun to address the complex issue of how does stress precipitate depression in those who are vulnerable.

Empirical associations between stressors and depression

Acute negative life events

The observation in ancient and classical writings of a link between life's adversities and depression is as old as history, and certainly represents one of the longest lines of empirical research on predictors of depression.

We start by noting methodological issues about assessment of acute negative life events. Most of the systematic research on the association between stress and depression, which largely emerged in the latter part of the twentieth century, focused on the occurrence of negative life events, mostly including events that had a particular point of occurrence and resolution in the environment (death of a loved one, loss of a job, marital break-up). Improvements in conceptualisation and methods required the actual occurrence of events, not merely the perception or subjective experiences that something was stressful. Questionnaires and checklists of events had been commonly employed to assess stressful life events, but British depression researchers Brown and Harris (1978) argued that such questionnaires were too imprecise in meaning (e.g., different people interpret the item 'death of a loved one' in different ways) and cannot factor in the unique impact of an event given the individual's life circumstances. For example, a questionnaire filled out by a woman endorsing 'death of a spouse' does not reveal whether the death occurred in a devastating context of leaving her with young children and no means of support, or whether it occurred in a spouse long separated from and reviled by the surviving spouse. Brown and Harris (1978) promoted the use of interviews that probe the nature of the context in which the event occurred as a means of understanding its impact. They also pioneered the use of objective measures of how 'objectively' stressful each event would be (for the typical person under identical circumstances) by establishing independent rating teams or scoring guidelines in which the scorers used only contextual information but had no information on how the respondent actually reacted. By contrast, most questionnaire methods ask respondents 'how stressful would you rate each event' on a 7-point scale (or similar metric). Brown and Harris (1978) argued that by definition, individuals who have had depressive reactions are highly negatively biased by depression in their appraisals of stressfulness and may infer the event's severity from its impact on their depression. Thus, the severity of the event and the severity of depression are confounded, obscuring scientific evidence that the event was the cause of the depression.

The majority of empirical studies in the past few decades have focused on negative life events, especially those occurring in the past one to three months. Although questionnaire methods of assessment are still widely used because they are very inexpensive to administer, experts in the field strongly advocate for the use of semi-structured interview measures of the context in which the event occurs, and objective (independent) assessment of the impact of the events given their context (e.g., Hammen, 2016; Harkness and Monroe, 2016).

The empirical association between depressive episodes and the occurrence of a recent acute stressful life event has been demonstrated extensively. Research using such state-of-the-art interview measures of stressful life events has consistently found higher levels of significant stressors prior to onset of major depressive episodes in patient samples compared to controls, and in community samples (e.g., reviewed in Brown and Harris, 1989; Mazure, 1998). Mazure's review noted that stressors were 2.5 times more likely in depressed patients compared to controls, and that in community samples, 80 per cent of depressed cases were preceded by major life events. Figure 5.1 displays results from Mazure's review of community studies in which those

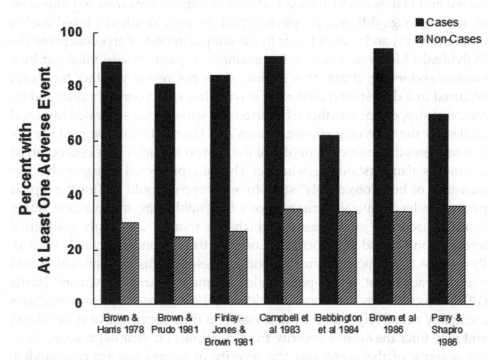

Figure 5.1 Rates of severe stress prior to depression comparing depressed and nondepressed adults in community samples across multiple studies

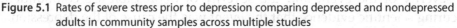

Source: Mazure, C. (1998). Life stressors as risk factors for depression. *Clinical Psychology: Science and Practice, 5*, 291–313. Copyright (1998) the American Psychology Association, reprinted with permission.

who were depressed were compared with similar others who were not depressed, and the depressed group reported substantially more recent severe life events than did the nondepressed. Other studies and reviews have also confirmed the association between prior stressors and subsequent depression (e.g., Hammen, 2005; Kendler and Gardner, 2010). Also, 'natural' experiments that occur when exposure to a negative event is random and independent of depressive outcomes, such as widowhood, or exposure to natural disasters, have also been shown to precipitate depression compared to those not experiencing such events (reviewed in Kessler, 1997). In subsequent sections when discussing different aspects of the stress–depression relationship, most of the research is based on stress defined by acute negative life events.

Chronic life stress

Until recently there has been relative neglect of the effects on depression of ongoing, chronic stressful circumstances. Ironically, animal studies of analogues of depression and anxiety (distress) commonly examine chronic stress exposure as best characterising naturalistic experiences faced by animals involving physical deprivation, predator conditions and social defeat. Chronic stress in humans refers to stressful, challenging or threatening ongoing conditions that typically affect everyday life. Generally, research on the effects of chronic circumstances on symptoms and disorders has focused on the depressive impact of *individual situations*, such as marital distress (Robles, Slatcher, Trombello and McGinn, 2014), poverty (Evans, Li and Whipple, 2013), caretaking for an ill family member (Adelman, Tmanova, Delgado, Dion and Lachs, 2014) and identity discrimination (Schmitt, Branscombe, Postmes and Garcia, 2014). Evidence invariably shows that such chronic stressors are associated with higher levels of distress including depression and anxiety and potentially a myriad of health and behavioural problems.

A small amount of research has systematically assessed chronic stress conditions concurrently across marital, family, income, occupational and health domains, showing that total chronic stress is as predictive of depression as is acute stress (e.g., Hammen, Kim, Eberhart and Brennan, 2009; Vrshek-Schallhorn et al., 2015). Additionally, in their large longitudinal study of women, Hammen and colleagues (2009) found that acute stress is more strongly predictive of depression in those with high versus low chronic stress. Further, the authors argued that chronic stressful conditions in major roles that the individual fulfils in family, work, income and health domains, for example, may be present even if not measured, and that they may be as powerful in the prediction of depressive episodes as acute stressors that are measured (see also Hammen, 2016). Further, chronic stressful conditions and emotional distress symptoms likely have an effect on each other, intensifying or prolonging both. Also, chronic stressors, like acute stressors, may often 'pile up' in the sense that marital difficulties typically portend parenting problems, or economic disadvantage may predict exposure to unsafe neighbourhoods and poor health and diminished access to health care. Clearly, chronic stressful conditions are too important to be neglected in understanding depression.

Exposure to early childhood adversity (ECA)

A specific form of stress exposure that has attracted considerable research attention in recent years is the effect of childhood maltreatment and other severely adverse childhood conditions (such as marital discord or violence, poverty, parental mental illness or criminality) on risk for depression and other disorders. As noted in Chapter 4, information from animal and human studies indicates that exposure to abnormal stress levels and patterns during critical early periods of brain development such as infancy, childhood and early adolescence may lead to long-term changes in neural circuitry and neuroregulatory mechanisms that can have significant negative effects on brain structure and function, thereby affecting many functions and behaviours (Anda et al., 2006; Shonkoff et al., 2012).

Chapter 4 noted that early adversity predicts abnormal levels and functions of cortisol and other neurohormones of the hypothalamic pituitary adrenal (HPA) axis system, leading to maladaptive responses to stress (including depression). Abnormalities of the HPA axis are also likely to negatively influence brain structure and circuitry associated with emotional and cognitive control relevant to depression, and stress exposure may also affect genetic characteristics. In Chapter 6 we will further discuss the effects of early adversity in its typical context of problematic parenting, potentially creating additional risk factors for depression such as dysfunctional inter-personal beliefs about the self in relation to others.

The construct of childhood adversity may refer narrowly to abuse/maltreatment or more broadly to a variety of challenging situations affecting a child's family and living environment. Such adverse conditions are predictive of numerous negative health outcomes, cognitive difficulties and emotional and behavioural disorders (e.g., Miller and Chen, 2010; Pechtel and Pizzagalli, 2011). Green et al. (2010) found that ECAs predicted 26.2 per cent of mood disorders in the National Comorbidity Survey Replication, with most onsets in childhood. Similar analyses in the World Health Organization World Mental Health Surveys reported the population attributable risk proportions of 23 per cent of mood disorders due to childhood adversity exposure (Kessler et al., 2010; see also Anda et al., 2006; St. Clair et al., 2015;

McLaughlin et al., 2012). In all these surveys ECAs were associated strongly with anxiety, substance use and behavioural disorders as well.

As is well-documented across numerous studies, the effects of early adversity exposure are general, with little evidence that specific adversity types are uniquely predictive of particular disorders (e.g., parental death does not uniquely predict depression; Green et al., 2010). Notably also, individuals who experience any adversity are likely to experience more than one; clustering is typical. This is particularly true of what Kessler and colleagues term 'maladaptive family functioning' (parental mental illness, substance misuse, criminality, domestic violence, physical and sexual abuse, neglect; e.g., Kessler et al., 2010; Green et al., 2010). As we note in Chapter 6, such poor family conditions profoundly affect vulnerability to depression through disruption of attachment bonds and formation of negative cognitions about the self and others.

Continuity of stress

Perhaps not surprisingly, stress begets stress, in the sense that those exposed to high levels of stress in childhood are likely to have high rates of stress at other times in their lives. Although obviously some negative events and situations are relatively time-limited and get resolved, chronically stressful circumstances tend to be continuous even if fluctuating in severity over time, and chronic and acute stressors tend to be correlated, with higher levels of each predicting more chronic and acute stress. Individuals' adverse life situations may be constrained to an extent by education, income and other barriers such as racial discrimination, and by the multiple innate and acquired personality and socioemotional, as well as genetic and neurobiological factors that shape reactions to stress. Hence, individuals may be 'stuck' in socioeconomic and family conditions that restrict access to marital, employment and neighbourhood situations that offer pathways to greater comfort and security, and socioemotional satisfaction and adjustment. They may also be 'stuck' in their maladaptive stress reaction styles and coping strategies, including limited sources of support. Although long-term longitudinal studies are rare, Hazel, Hammen, Brennan and Najman (2008) found substantial correlations between several areas of maternal life (income, marital satisfaction and mental health issues) during the first five years of the child's life and at child's age 15 in a longitudinal follow-up of a large sample of depressed and never depressed women and their children. For example, women who reported marital distress in the child's early life tended to report marital distress ten–15 years later even if married to different men; mental health problems continued often despite treatment, and financial hardship also persisted. The same sample of youth was followed from birth to age 20, and Hammen, Hazel, Brennan and Najman (2012) found continuing correlations between early childhood adversity (by age 5), and both acute and chronic youth stress at ages 15 and 20 – finding the expected patterns of stress predicting depression.

Effects of type of stress

Is there any evidence that particular kinds of stressor content are more likely to precipitate depression? Virtually any negative event (or even an imagined event) could trigger depression if personally relevant to the individual's sense of well-being and with severe enough impact. However, research provides additional specification in two ways: there are certain kinds of general themes (such as interpersonal content) that are especially likely to provoke depressive reactions universally; as well, individuals may have particular values and orientations that make them vulnerable to negative events that specifically match those tendencies.

There is a long tradition from psychodynamic theory and other approaches to depression focusing on the unique significance for depression of interpersonal 'loss', which may include bereavement, separations, endings or threats of separation. Paykel (2003) reviewed studies showing that such 'exit' events often precede depression, and may be more common in depressed samples than in other forms of psychopathology. Tennant (2002; Farmer and McGuffin, 2003; see also Kendler et al., 1995; Kendler and Gardner, 2014) also suggested that relationship stressors – many of which are loss or threatened loss events – are common in depression, perhaps especially for women. The concept of loss has sometimes been expanded beyond interpersonal exit events to include loss of self-esteem, role loss or loss of cherished ideas (e.g., Brown, Harris and Hepworth, 1995; Finlay-Jones and Brown, 1981). Life event characteristics involving humiliation and helpless entrapment have also been shown to be especially depressogenic (Brown et al., 1995; Kendler, Hettema, Butera, Gardner and Prescott, 2003). 'Humiliation' in the context of loss refers to separations initiated by another person or rejection/being 'put down' by an authority figure. It is similar to the construct of 'targeted rejection', which has been shown to be more highly predictive of depressive reactions than equally severe but non-rejection events (Slavich, Thornton, Torres, Monroe and Gotlib, 2009). Slavich and Irwin (2014) argue that interpersonal stress and social rejection uniquely drive a biological reaction in the immune system that promotes depressive reactions (the social signal transduction theory of depression); their hypothesis is supported by a number of neural and genetic findings on the role of immune processes in some forms of depression as reviewed in their 2014 article.

There is also evidence that personality styles or values that match event content would be more likely to produce depression than a non-match, also called the 'specific vulnerability' or 'congruency' hypothesis (e.g., Arieti and Bemporad, 1980; Beck, 1983). Specifically, individuals differ in the sources of their self-esteem and sense of mastery, with some individuals experiencing personal worth as deriving from the achievement of highly valued goals and control/autonomy, while others are more likely to invest themselves and their self-definitions in personal relationships with others. The former type is variously termed *autonomous*, dominant goal-oriented or self-critical, while the latter may be termed *sociotropic*, dominant-other oriented or dependent (reviewed in Nietzel and Harris, 1990). Vulnerability, therefore, might consist of personality features or cognitions that include attitudes, beliefs and values such that a major stressor that is *interpreted* as representing a depletion in the specific area of an individual's sense of worth or competence would provoke a depressive reaction. Most of the research on the topic was conducted in the 1990s and early 2000s, largely supporting the model. Zuroff, Mongrain and Santor (2004) noted that dependency-sociotropy is reasonably specifically linked with interpersonal loss events in the prediction of depression, but self-criticism/autonomy has been less clearly supported.

Who gets depressed following stress experiences and what are the mechanisms?
Risk factors, also called vulnerability factors, are the 'diatheses' in the classic diathesis–stress model of disorder. Here we only briefly note major risk factors, as most are discussed in greater detail in different chapters. Among demographic risk factors, female gender is the best known as noted in Chapter 3. Studies have suggested that one reason is women's greater reactivity to interpersonal stressors, such as marital and relational difficulties, deficiencies in close relationships with parents and inadequate social supports (e.g., Kendler and Gardner, 2014). Kuehner's (2016) review notes that environmental stressors ranging from early adversity to violence against women and discrimination may play a role in gender differences in depression. Women are also affected by stressors in the lives of others in their networks. Several theoretical reviews have offered a variety of hypotheses about the mechanisms underlying such patterns, including biological, gender socialisation, and cognitive and coping processes (e.g., Cyranowski, Frank, Young and Shear, 2000; Kuehner, 2016; Nolen-Hoeksema, 2002; Nolen-Hoeksema and Girgus, 1994; Hankin and Abramson, 2001).

Other demographic predictors of depression are younger age (adolescence and adulthood rather than older age), and lower socio-economic status (in higher income nations) and non-married status (e.g., Bromet et al., 2011). Chapter 6 discusses associations between poor marital quality and depression (see also Kendler and Gardner, 2014). Being the child of a depressed parent is also a strong risk factor for developing depression, commonly including a family context of chronic and acute stress along with dysfunctional parenting (e.g., Hammen, Hazel, Brennan and Najman, 2012; see also Chapter 6).

Psychological risk factors include depressive information processing style (negative cognitions) and related constructs such as neuroticism and ruminative response style. Indeed, as discussed earlier in the current chapter, Beck's cognitive model of depression assumes that depression arises as a response to dysfunctional (negative) interpretations of events and circumstances concerning the self, the world and the future. Thus, when negative life events and circumstances occur, it is presumed that individuals with cognitive vulnerabilities will automatically interpret them in ways that emphasise their own lack of worth or competence, inability to resolve the problem and see the future as bleak and uncontrollable.

Ruminative response style, also discussed previously in this chapter, can be characterised not only as a coping style in the face of negative emotions, but also as a maladaptive cognitive style of responding to stressful events that may result in prolonging and intensifying distress and interfering with adaptive coping with the stressor (Nolen-Hoeksema, 2000). Ruminative style is discussed in various chapters. A related construct, trait neuroticism, is also highly predictive of depressive responses to stress (Barlow, Sauer-Zavala, Carl, Bullis and Ellard, 2014; Griffith et al., 2010; Lahey, 2009).

Biological mechanisms that explain how stressors and responses to stressors lead to depression were largely discussed in Chapter 4. The HPA axis shows abnormal cortisol processes that are thought to underlie depressive reactions. Considerable research has been devoted to understanding the origins of maladaptive HPA axis activity. As previously noted, Frodl and O'Keane (2013) summarised research that found evidence of abnormal levels of cortisol in samples of adults and children with histories of maltreatment and other forms of early childhood adversity (see also Heim, Newport, Mletzko, Miller and Nemeroff, 2008; McLaughlin et al., 2015). Abnormalities in the stress response system also may be due to genetic and neural factors that are present at birth or which may be altered during development by exposure to stressful experiences. There have been many studies, for example, of gene–environment interactions. A classic example was illustrated in Chapter 4 on the increased risk of depressive responses to stress by individuals who have short alleles of the serotonin transporter gene (Caspi et al., 2003; see also Starr, Hammen, Conway, Raposa and Brennan, 2014).

Overall, therefore, it is generally understood that the risk factors for depression (e.g., female gender, depressed parents, exposure to maltreatment and adversity, negative cognitive style, temperament, coping and neuroendocrine and genetic factors) all influence the (maladaptive) ways in which individuals respond to stressors.

Nature of stress–depression relationships

While stress and vulnerabilities interact to trigger depressive reactions, a traditional diathesis–stress model of depression is overly simplistic, because the relationship between stress and depression is not one-directional, is not stable and unvarying over time and is most definitely not simple (e.g., Hammen, 2015). Indeed, the relationship is bidirectional and the association is dynamic over time and circumstances as we discuss below.

Effects of depression on stress: stress generation

Most research on stress–depression associations has examined the effects of stressors on depression, but the opposite direction of influence has also been studied, indicating bidirectional relationships. Hammen (1991) observed that women with recurrent depression experienced significantly more interpersonal negative events during a one-year follow-up period than groups of women with bipolar or medical disorders or non-ill controls. Moreover, the unipolar depressed women were especially likely to experience conflict events – interpersonal disputes with a wide variety of others such as friends, spouses, family, employers and teachers. Interpersonal and conflict events are among those that occur at least in part because of the actions or characteristics of the individual. This process has been termed 'stress generation' (Hammen, 1991). The implications of stress generation are significant: some individuals seem to contribute to higher levels of stress occurrence and individuals whose lives are highly stressful are likely to experience recurrences of depression in response to such upsetting events.

The tendency of depressed women and men to contribute to the occurrence of more interpersonal and conflict stressors has been replicated in numerous samples of adults, adolescents and children (reviewed in Hammen, 2006; Liu, 2013; Liu and Alloy, 2010). Most of the research has further indicated that while *current* depression may contribute to greater difficulty in relationships and hence major negative life events such as fights, break-ups, and estrangement, many studies have found that such elevated rates of negative interpersonal events may occur in formerly depressed people even when they are not currently depressed (e.g., Hammen, 1991; Hammen and Brennan, 2002).

What factors are responsible for the generation of stressful interpersonal events? One hypothesis is that individuals select themselves into potentially stressful circumstances, possibly due to characteristics of their environments or to personal vulnerabilities. Thus, for example, due to poverty and low educational attainment, or due to childhood adversities that affect self-esteem and social skills, an individual may be more likely to 'select' (or have available) a marital partner who him or herself may have limited personal or social resources. Under difficult and stressful circumstances the marriage may be more likely to have conflict. Further, the children may be exposed to genetic and social environments that contribute to behavioural and school problems that challenge effective parent–child relationships, possibly creating parent–child conflict. In Chapter 6 we discuss examples of interpersonal character-istics and patterns of conduct associated with depression. Additionally, stress generation extends beyond acute negative life events. As an example of 'creating dysfunctional circumstances' Keenan-Miller, Hammen and Brennan (2007) found that history of depression in youth predicted being a victim of severe intimate partner violence during the teenage years. Also, depressed adolescent women were more likely to become depressed young mothers by age 20, often unmarried and not self-supporting (Hammen, Brennan and Le Brocque, 2011), thus 'selecting' into highly stressful ongoing situations with the potential for continuing stress and depression. In Chapter 6 we discuss various interpersonal traits and behaviours commonly shared by depressed individuals that have the potential for creating stressful situations in social relationships.

Changing relations of stress and depression over time

The stress–depression relationship is not only bidirectional, but is also dyna-mic, changing with circumstances and course of disorder. Based in part on clinical lore and bolstered by animal models of kindling and sensitisation, Post and colleagues (Post, Rubinow and Ballenger, 1984; Post, 1992) hypothesised that recurrent episodes of mood disorders (both depressive and bipolar disorders) may become progressively independent of stressors, as a function of neurobiological changes or psychological changes associated with repeated stressors and repeated episodes. There have been numerous studies testing the kindling model in patient samples, and research has generally supported the hypothesis that *first* episodes are more likely to be triggered by major negative life events compared to recurrent episodes (reviews by Mazure, 1998; Monroe and Harkness, 2005; see Kendler, Thornton and Gardner, 2000). The kindling model has the important implication that effective treatments and interventions early in the course of depression may be especially crucial in changing the course/progression of the disorder than if untreated or minimally treated.

Unfortunately, however, as Monroe and Harkness (2005) point out, the meaning of Post's original hypothesis is highly ambiguous: does stress become irrelevant as depressive episodes occur autonomously later in the course of disorder, or, are episodes triggered by less severe and more minor or even by symbolic (such as thoughts about) negative events? Moreover, much of the research that has been conducted has used methods of assessing life stress that are suboptimal, or was based on conceptual and statistical decisions that are questionable, or had other methodological shortcomings such as heterogeneity of patient populations and unknown information about initial history of depression and stress exposure. Obviously, long-term longitudinal studies with excellent methods are needed to determine whether the 'sensitisation' model (less stress needed) vs. 'autonomy' model (stress becomes irrelevant) is more valid. One of the few projects that examined evidence to compare the sensitisation vs. autonomy models studied young women from 18–23 for five years, Stroud, Davila, Hammen and Vrshek-Schallhorn (2011) found some support for the sensitisation model, in that the impact of less severe events was greater for recurrences than first onsets of major depressive episodes (first onsets were more related to severe life events).

As we have noted elsewhere, early life stress may have a sensitising effect on depressive reactions to negative life events. Hammen, Henry and Daley (2000) found that women who reported higher levels of early adversity exposure were more likely to become depressed following less total stress than women without such adversity. The results could not be accounted for by chronic stress or prior depression. Similar patterns of the impact of childhood adversity and maltreatment have been reported by other investigators (e.g., Harkness, Bruce and Lumley, 2006; McLaughlin, Conron, Koenen and Gilman, 2010).

In an earlier section we also discussed 'moderators' of the effects of stress on depression, those demographic, personality, experiential and biological/genetic factors that appear to make some individuals more likely to develop depression in response to stress, and some of these factors may also show 'sensitisation' (greater likelihood of depression with smaller levels of stress). An example is from a large longitudinal study of twins, in which Kendler, Thornton and Gardner (2001) determined that the increasing independence of stress and depression over repeated episodes was strongest in those with low genetic risk (had no twin with depression). In contrast, those at higher genetic risk (had twin siblings with depression) appeared to be 'prekindled' with weaker associations between stressors and depression, similar to those at low genetic risk who had already experienced at least three episodes. Thus, the stress–depression relationship may vary not only over time with increasing numbers of episodes, but may also differ according to genetic risk for depression.

Further study is needed of the mechanisms of kindling and sensitisation. The neurobiological changes occurring as a result of exposure to stress and depressive episodes, as well as the psychological (cognitive, coping and personality) changes over time with exposure to stress and episodes may help explain alterations in the pattern of associations of stress and depression over the course of disorder (e.g., Segal, Williams, Teasdale and Gemar, 1996; Treadway et al., 2015). Such information is vital to improving treatments to be more effective in disrupting pernicious patterns of recurrence.

Models of the mechanisms in the stress–depression association

The associations between stress and depression are not only bidirectional and changing over the course of illness, they are also very complex. As we have emphasised in this chapter, a big piece of the puzzle is why only some people get depressed even when negative life events and circumstances befall them. We discussed biological aspects in Chapter 4, and will talk about interpersonal aspects of depression in Chapter 6. The 'environmental' piece of the puzzle as discussed in this chapter is increasingly viewed as an essential element, and we also emphasise the increasing promise of studies of human development and maturation that reflect the impact of adverse exposures on the developing brain and the likelihood of dysfunctional neurobiological, emotional and behavioural patterns in response to environmental experiences. Increasingly, therefore, investigators are constructing more and more complex theories of depression that integrate across different levels of analysis. Many of the models are aspirational and have yet to be tested. However, increasingly investigators are collecting and publishing data to test such models. A few examples of complex, multifactorial studies that included stress assessment are reported in Kendler, Gardner and Prescott (2002, 2006), Hammen, Shih and Brennan (2004). Importantly, longitudinal studies more frequently include both complex biological parameters and stress (e.g., Dennison et al., 2016; LeMoult, Ordaz, Kircanski, Singh and Gotlib, 2015; Pagliaccio et al., 2014) and many additional studies are emerging that combine environmental and biological variables. The future of depression research is in the hands of those who conduct complex integrative studies that include environmental, developmental, biological and psychosocial levels of analysis.

Summary

◆ Cognitive models of depression, originating with Beck, emphasise negative thinking as a factor causing or maintaining depression.

◆ Contemporary versions of cognitive models variously emphasise explanatory style, self-schemas, hopelessness, ruminative response style and biased information-processing, among other factors.

◆ Cognitive vulnerability models of depression have stimulated considerable research and discussion of measurement and design issues. Both prospective longitudinal and experimental research has led to improved empirical support for the idea that negative cognitions play an important causal role in the onset and maintenance of depression.

◆ Negative life events play a triggering role in the occurrence of most episodes of depression, but most people who experience stressful events do not get depressed.

◆ Research has attempted to explore what kinds of events and circumstances are most likely to provoke depression, suggesting that loss and interpersonal events are especially prevalent causes of depression, but that individual cognitive and personality factors may determine which kinds of events are most potent predictors for that person.

◆ The relationships between stress and depression are not just unidirectional with stress precipitating depression. Depression and personal characteristics may create stressful events, and also the nature of the stress–depression relationship may change over the course of multiple episodes.

References

Abela, J. R. Z. and Hankin, B. L. (2011). Rumination as a vulnerability factor to depression during the transition from early to middle adolescence: a multiwave longitudinal study. *Journal of Abnormal Psychology, 120*(2), 259–271.

Abela, J. R. Z., Parkinson, C., Stolow, D. and Starrs, C. (2009). A test of the integration of the hopelessness and response styles theories of depression in middle adolescence. *Journal of Clinical Child and Adolescent Psychology, 38*(3), 354–364.

Abela, J. R. Z., Stolow, D., Mineka, S., Yao, S. Q., Zhu, X. Z. and Hankin, B. L. (2011). Cognitive vulnerability to depressive symptoms in adolescents in urban and rural

Hunan, China: a multiwave longitudinal study. *Journal of Abnormal Psychology*, *120*(4), 765–778.

Adelman, R. D., Tmanova, L. L., Delgado, D., Dion, S. and Lachs, M. S. (2014). Caregiver burden: a clinical review. *Journal of the American Medical Association*, *311*(10), 1052–1060.

Abramson, L. Y., Metalsky, G. I. and Alloy, L. B. (1989). Hopelessness Depression: a theory-based subtype of depression. *Psychological Review*, *90*, 358–372.

Abramson, L. Y., Seligman, M. E. P. and Teasdale, J. D. (1978). Learned helplessness in humans: critique and reformulation. *Journal of Abnormal Psychology*, *87*(1), 49–74.

Aldao, A., Nolen-Hoeksema, S. and Schweizer, S. (2010). Emotion-regulation strategies across psychopathology: a meta-analytic review. *Clinical Psychology Review*, *30*(2), 217–237.

Alloy, L. B., Abramson, L. Y., Walshaw, P. D. and Neeren, A. M. (2006). Cognitive vulnerability to unipolar and bipolar mood disorders. *Journal of Social and Clinical Psychology*, *25*(7), 726–754.

Alloy, L. B., Abramson, L. Y., Whitehouse, W. G. and Hogan, M. E. (2006). Prospective incidence of first onsets and recurrences of depression in individuals at high and low cognitive risk for depression. *Journal of Abnormal Psychology*, *115*, 145–156.

Alloy, L. B., Abramson, L. Y., Whitehouse, W. G., Hogan, M. E., Tashman, N. A., Steinberg, D. L. . . . Donovan, P. (1999). Depressogenic cognitive styles: predictive validity, information processing and personality characteristics, and developmental origins. *Behaviour Research and Therapy*, *37*, 503–531.

Anda, R. F., Felitti, V. J., Bremner, J. D., Walker, J. D., Whitfield, C. H., Perry, B. D., . . . Giles, W. H. (2006). The enduring effects of abuse and related adverse experiences in childhood. *European Archives of Psychiatry and Clinical Neuroscience*, *256*(3), 174–186.

Arieti, S. and Bemporad, J. (1980). The psychological organisation of depression. *American Journal of Psychiatry*, *137*, 1360–1365.

Barlow, D. H., Sauer-Zavala, S., Carl, J. R., Bullis, J. R. and Ellard, K. K. (2014). The nature, diagnosis, and treatment of neuroticism: back to the future. *Clinical Psychological Science*, *2*(3), 344–365.

Bebbington, P. E., Sturt, E., Tennant, C. and Hurry, J. (1984). Misfortune and resilience: a replication of the work of Brown and Harris. *Psychological Medicine*, *14*, 347–363.

Beck, A. T. (1967). *Depression: clinical, experimental and theoretical aspects*. New York: Harper and Row.

Beck, A. T. (1976). *Cognitive therapy and emotional disorders*. New York: Meridian.

Beck, A. T. (1983). Cognitive therapy of depression: new perspectives. In P. J. Clayton and J. E. Barrett (eds), *Treatment of depression: old controversies and new approaches* (pp. 265–290). New York: Raven Press.

Beck, A. T. (2008). The evolution of the cognitive model of depression and its neurobiological correlates. *American Journal of Psychiatry*, *165*(8), 969–977.

Beck, A. T. and Haigh, E. A. P. (2014). Advances in cognitive theory and therapy: the generic cognitive model. *Annual Review of Clinical Psychology, 10*, 1–24.

Beevers, C. G., Clasen, P. C., Enock, P. M. and Schnyer, D. M. (2015). Attention bias modification for major depressive disorder: effects on attention bias, resting state connectivity, and symptomchange. *Journal of Abnormal Psychology, 124*(3), 463–475.

Bistricky, S. L., Ingram, R. E. and Atchley, R. A. (2011). Facial affect processing and depression susceptibility: cognitive biases and cognitive neuroscience. *Psychological Bulletin, 137*(6), 998–1028.

Bower, G. H. (1981). Mood and memory. *American Psychologist, 36*, 129–148.

Brewin, C. R., Gregory, J. D., Lipton, M. and Burgess, N. (2010). Intrusive images in psychological disorders: characteristics, natural mechanisms, and treatment implications. *Psychological Review, 117*(1), 210–232.

Bromet, E., Andrade, L., Hwang, I., Sampson, N., Alonso, J., de Girolamo, G., . . . Kessler, R.C. (2011). Cross-national epidemiology of DSM-IV major depressive episode. *BMC Medicine 9*, 90.

Brown, G. W. and Harris, T. (1978). *Social origins of depression: a study of psychiatric disorder in women*. New York: Free Press.

Brown, G. W. and Harris, T. O. (1986). Establishing causal links: the Bedford College studies of depression. In H. Katschnig (ed.), *Life events and psychiatric disorders: controversial issues* (pp. 107–117). Cambridge: Cambridge University Press.

Brown, G. W. and Harris, T. O. (1989). Depression. In G. W. Brown and T. O. Harris (eds), *Life Events and Illness* (pp. 49–93). New York: Guilford Press.

Brown, G. W., Harris, T. O. and Hepworth, C. (1995). Loss, humiliation and entrapment among women developing depression: a patient and non-patient comparison. *Psychological Medicine, 25*(01), 7–21.

Brown, G. W. and Prudo, R. (1981). Psychiatric disorder in a rural and an urban population: 1. Aetiology of depression. *Psychological Medicine, 11*(3), 581–599.

Campbell, E. A., Cope, S. J. and Teasdale, J. D. (1983). Social factors and affective disorder: an investigation of Brown and Harris's model. *The British Journal of Psychiatry, 143*(6), 548–553.

Carver, C. S. and Ganellen, R. J. (1983). Depression and components of self-punitiveness: high standards, self-criticism, and overgeneralisation. *Journal of Abnormal Psychology, 92*, 330–337.

Caspi, A., Sugden, K., Moffitt, T. E., Taylor, A., Craig, I. W., Harrington, H., . . . Poulton, R. (2003). Influence of life stress on depression: moderation by a polymorphism in the 5-HTT gene. *Science, 301*(5631), 386–389.

Clark, D. A., Beck, A. T. and Alford, B. A. (1999). *Scientific foundations of cognitive theory and therapy of depression*. New York: Wiley.

Clark, D. M. and Teasdale, J. D. (1982). Diurnal variation in clinical depression and accessibility of memories of positive and negative experiences. *Journal of Abnormal Psychology, 91*, 87–95.

Clark, D. M. and Teasdale, J. D. (1985). Constraints on the effects of mood on memory. *Journal of Personality and Social Psychology, 48*, 1595–1608.

Clasen, P. C., Wells, T. T., Ellis, A. J. and Beevers, C. G. (2013). Attentional biases and the persistence of sad mood in major depressive disorder. *Journal of Abnormal Psychology, 122*(1), 74–85.

Cole, D. A., Martin, N. C., Sterba, S. K., Sinclair-McBride, K., Roeder, K. M., Zelkowitz, R. and Bilsky, S. A. (2014). Peer victimisation (and harsh parenting) as developmental correlates of cognitive reactivity, a diathesis for depression. *Journal of Abnormal Psychology, 123*(2), 336–349.

Cole, D. A., Sinclair-McBride, K. R., Zelkowitz, R., Bilsk, S. A., Roeder, K. and Spinelli, T. (2016). Peer victimisation and harsh parenting predict cognitive diatheses for depression in children and adolescents. *Journal of Clinical Child and Adolescent Psychology, 45*(5), 668–680.

Cox, S. J., Mezulis, A. H. and Hyde, J. S. (2010). The influence of child gender role and maternal feedback to child stress on the emergence of the gnder difference in depressive rumination in adolescence. *Developmental Psychology, 46*(4), 842–852.

Coyne, J. C. (1992). Cognition in depression: a paradigm in crisis. *Psychological Inquiry, 3*(3), 232–235.

Cristea, I. A., Kok, R. N. and Cuijpers, P. (2015). Efficacy of cognitive bias modification interventions in anxiety and depression: meta-analysis. *British Journal of Psychiatry, 206*(1), 7–16.

Crocker, J. and Park, L. E. (2004). The costly pursuit of self-esteem. *Psychological Bulletin, 130*, 392–414.

Cyranowski, J. M., Frank, E., Young, E. and Shear, K. (2000). Adolescent onset of the gender difference in lifetime rates of major depression. *Archives of General Psychiatry, 57*, 21–27.

Dalgleish, T. and Werner-Seidler, A. (2014). Disruptions in autobiographical memory processing in depression and the emergence of memory therapeutics. *Trends in Cognitive Sciences, 18*(11), 596–604.

Dennison, M. J., Sheridan, M. A., Busso, D. S., Jenness, J. L., Peverill, M., Rosen, M. L. and McLaughlin, K. A. (2016). Neurobehavioural markers of resilience to depression amongst adolescents exposed to child abuse. *Journal of Abnormal Psychology, 125*(8), 1201–1212.

Dent, J. and Teasdale, J. D. (1988). Negative cognition and the persistence of depression. *Journal of Abnormal Psychology, 97*, 29–34.

Evans, G. W., Li, D. and Whipple, S. S. (2013). Cumulative risk and child development. *Psychological Bulletin, 139*(6), 1342–1396.

Farmer, A. E. and McGuffin, P. (2003). Humiliation, loss and other types of life events and difficulties: a comparison of depressed subjects, healthy controls and their siblings. *Psychological Medicine, 33*, 1169–1175.

Finlay-Jones, R. and Brown, G. W. (1981). Types of stressful life event and the onset of anxiety and depressive disorders. *Psychological Medicine, 11*, 803–815.

Frodl, T. and O'Keane, V. (2013). How does the brain deal with cumulative stress? A review with focus on developmental stress, HPA axis function and hippocampal structure in humans. *Neurobiology of disease, 52*, 24–37.

Gate, M. A., Watkins, E. R., Simmons, J. G., Byrne, M. L., Schwartz, O. S., Whittle, S., . . . Allen, N. B. (2013). Maternal parenting behaviours and adolescent depression: the mediating role of rumination. *Journal of Clinical Child and Adolescent Psychology*, 42(3), 348–357.

Gibb, B. E. (2002). Childhood maltreatment and negative cognitive styles – a quantitative and qualitative review. *Clinical Psychology Review*, 22, 223–246.

Gibb, B. E., Alloy, L. B., Abramson, L. Y., Rose, D. T., Whitehouse, W. G., Donovan, P. . . . Tierney, S. (2001). History of childhood maltreatment, negative cognitive styles, and episodes of depression in adulthood. *Cognitive Therapy and Research*, 25, 425–446.

Gotlib, I. H. and Joormann, J. (2010). Cognition and depression: current status and future directions. *Annual Review of Clinical Psychology*, 6, 285–312.

Green, J. G., McLaughlin, K. A., Berglund, P. A., Gruber, M. J., Sampson, N. A., Zaslavsky, A. M. and Kessler, R. C. (2010). Childhood adversities and adult psychiatric disorders in the national comorbidity survey replication I: associations with first onset of DSM-IV disorders. *Archives of General Psychiatry*, 67(2), 113–123.

Griffith, J. W., Zinbarg, R. E., Craske, M. G., Mineka, S., Rose, R. D., Waters, A. M. and Sutton, J. M. (2010). Neuroticism as a common dimension in the internalising disorders. *Psychological Medicine*, 40, 1125–1136.

Hallion, L. S. and Ruscio, A. M. (2011). A meta-analysis of the effect of cognitive bias modification on anxiety and depression. *Psychological Bulletin*, 137(6), 940–958.

Hammen, C. (1992). Cognitive, life stress, and interpersonal approaches to a developmental psychopathology mode of depression. *Development and Psychopathology*, 4(1), 189–206.

Hammen, C. (2005). Stress and depression. *Annual Review of Clinical Psychology*, 1, 293–319.

Hammen, C. (2006). Stress generation in depression: reflections on origins, research, and future directions. *Journal of Clinical Psychology*, 62, 1065–1082.

Hammen, C. (2015). Stress and depression: old questions, new approaches. *Current Opinion in Psychology*, 4, 80–85.

Hammen, C. (2016) Depression and stressful environments: identifying gaps in conceptualisation and measurement. *Anxiety, Stress and Coping*, 29, 335–351.

Hammen, C. and Brennan, P. (2002). Interpersonal dysfunction in depressed women: impairments independent of depressive symptoms. *Journal of Affective Disorders*, 72, 145–156.

Hammen, C. Brennan, P. and Le Brocque, R. (2011). Youth depression and early child-rearing: stress generation and intergenerational transmission of depression. *Journal of Consulting and Clinical Psychology*,79, 353–363.

Hammen, C., Hazel, N., Brennan, P. and Najman, J. (2012). Intergenerational transmission and continuity of stress and depression: depressed women and their offspring in 20 years of follow-up. *Psychological Medicine*, 42, 931–942.

Hammen, C., Henry, R. and Daley, S. (2000). Depression and sensitisation to stressors among young women as a function of childhood adversity. *Journal of Consulting and Clinical Psychology, 68*, 782–787.

Hammen, C., Kim, E., Eberhart, N. and Brennan, P. (2009). Chronic and acute stress and the prediction of major depression in women. *Depression and Anxiety, 26*, 718–723.

Hammen, C., Shih, J. and Brennan, P. (2004). Intergenerational transmission of depression: Test of an interpersonal stress model in a community sample. *Journal of Consulting and Clinical Psychology, 72*, 511–522.

Hankin, B. L. (2008). Cognitive vulnerability–stress model of depression during adolescence: investigating depressive symptom specificity in a multi-wave prospective study. *Journal of Abnormal Child Psychology, 36*(7), 999–1014.

Hankin, B. L. and Abramson, L. Y. (2001). Development of gender differences in depression: an elaborated cognitive vulnerability–transactional stress theory. *Psychological Bulletin, 127*, 773–796.

Hankin, B. L., Abramson, L. Y., Miller, N. and Haeffel, G. J. (2004). Cognitive vulnerability–stress theories of depression: examining affective specificity in the prediction of depression versus anxiety in three prospective studies. *Cognitive Therapy and Research, 28*(3), 309–345.

Harkness, K. L., Bruce, A. E. and Lumley, M. N. (2006). The role of childhood abuse and neglect in the sensitisation to stressful life events in adolescent depression. *Journal of Abnormal Psychology, 115*(4), 730–741.

Harkness, K. L. and Monroe, S. M. (2016). The assessment and measurement of adult life stress: basic premises, operational principles, and design requirements. *Journal of Abnormal Psychology, 125*(5), 727–745.

Harvey, A. G., Watkins, E., Mansell, W. and Shafran, R. (2004). *Cognitive behavioural processes across psychological disorders*. Oxford: Oxford University Press.

Hazel, N., Hammen, C., Brennan, P. and Najman, J. (2008). Early childhood adversity and adolescent depression: mediating role of continued stress. *Psychological Medicine, 38*, 581–589.

Heim, C., Newport, D. J., Mletzko, T., Miller, A. H. and Nemeroff, C. B. (2008). The link between childhood trauma and depression: insights from HPA axis studies in humans. *Psychoneuroendocrinology, 33*(6), 693–710.

Hertel, P. T. and Mathews, A. (2011). Cognitive bias modification: past perspectives, current findings, and future applications. *Perspectives on Psychological Science, 6*(6), 521–536.

Hertel, P. T., Mor, N., Ferrari, C., Hunt, O. and Agrawal, N. (2014). Looking on the dark side: rumination and cognitive bias modification. *Clinical Psychological Science, 2*, 714–726.

Hong, W., Abela, J. R. Z., Cohen, J. R., Sheshko, D. M., Shi, X. T., Van Hamel, A. and Starrs, C. (2010). Rumination as a vulnerability factor to depression in adolescents in mainland China: lifetime history of clinically significant depressive episodes. *Journal of Clinical Child and Adolescent Psychology, 39*(6), 849–857.

Hu, T. Q., Zhang, D. J. and Yang, Z. Z. (2015). The relationship between attributional style for negative outcomes and depression: a meta-analysis. *Journal of Social and Clinical Psychology*, *34*(4), 304–321.

Huang, C. J. (2015). Relation between attributional style and subsequent depressive symptoms: a systematic review and meta-analysis of longitudinal studies. *Cognitive Therapy and Research*, *39*(6), 721–735.

Ingram, R. E. (1990). Self-focused attention in clinical disorders – review and a conceptual model. *Psychological Bulletin*, *107*(2), 156–176.

Ingram, R. E., Bernet, C. Z. and Mclaughlin, S. C. (1994). Attentional allocation processes in individuals at risk for depression. *Cognitive Therapy and Research*, *18*, 317–332.

Ingram, R. E., Miranda, J. and Segal, Z. V. (1998). *Cognitive vulnerability to depression*. New York: Guilford.

Ingram, R. E. and Ritter, J. (2000). Vulnerability to depression: cognitive reactivity and parental bonding in high-risk individuals. *Journal of Abnormal Psychology*, *109*(4), 588–596.

Jacobs, R. H., Reinecke, M. A., Gollan, J. K. and Kane, P. (2008). Empirical evidence of cognitive vulnerability for depression among children and adolescents: a cognitive science and developmental perspective. *Clinical Psychology Review*, *28*(5), 759–782.

Keenan-Miller, D., Hammen, C. and Brennan, P. (2007). Adolescent psychosocial risk factors for severe intimate partner violence in young adulthood. *Journal of Consulting and Clinical Psychology*, *75*, 456–463.

Kendler, K. S. and Gardner, C. O. (2010). Dependent stressful life events and prior depressive episodes in the prediction of major depression: the problem of causal inference in psychiatric epidemiology. *Archives of General Psychiatry*, *67*(11), 1120–1127.

Kendler, K. S. and Gardner, C. O. (2014). Sex differences in the pathways to major depression: a study of opposite-sex twin pairs. *American Journal of Psychiatry*, *171*(4), 426–435.

Kendler, K. S., Gardner, C. O. and Prescott, C. A. (2002). Toward a comprehensive developmental model for major depression in women. *American Journal of Psychiatry*, *159*(7), 1133–1145.

Kendler, K. S., Gardner, C. O. and Prescott, C. A. (2006). Toward a comprehensive developmental model for major depression in men. *American Journal of Psychiatry*, *163*(1), 115–124.

Kendler, K. S., Hettema, J. M., Butera, F., Gardner, C. O. and Prescott, C. A. (2003). Life event dimensions of loss, humiliation, entrapment, and danger in the prediction of onsets of major depression and generalised anxiety. *Archives of General Psychiatry*, *60*(8), 789–796.

Kendler, K. S., Kessler, R. C., Walters, E. E., MacLean, C., Neale, M. C., Heath, A. C. and Eaves, L. (1995). Stressful life events, genetic liability, and onset of an episode of major depression in women. *American Journal of Psychiatry*, *152*, 833–842.

Kendler, K. S., Thornton, L. M. and Gardner, C. O. (2000). Stressful life events and previous episodes in the aetiology of major depression in women: an evaluation of the 'kindling' hypothesis. *American Journal of Psychiatry, 157*(8), 1243–1251.

Kendler, K. S., Thornton, L. M. and Gardner, C. O. (2001). Genetic risk, number of previous depressive episodes, and stressful life events in predicting onset of major depression. *American Journal of Psychiatry, 158*(4), 582–586.

Kessler, R. C. (1997). The effects of stressful life events on depression. *Annual Review of Psychology, 48*, 191–214.

Kessler, R. C., McLaughlin, K. A., Green, J. G., Gruber, M. J., Sampson, N. A., Zaslavsky, A. M., . . . Williams, D. (2010). Childhood adversities and adult psychopathology in the WHO World Mental Health Surveys. *The British Journal of Psychiatry, 197*(5), 378–385.

Kinderman, P., Schwannauer, M., Pontin, E. and Tai, S. (2013). Psychological processes mediate the impact of familial risk, social circumstances, and life events on mental health. *PLOS One, 8*: e76564.

Kingston, R. E. F., Watkins, E. R. and O'Mahen, H. A. (2013). An integrated examination of risk factors for repetitive negative thought. *Journal of Experimental Psychopathology, 4*(2), 161–181.

Koster, E. H. W., De Lissnyder, E., Derakshan, N. and De Raedt, R. (2011). Understanding depressive rumination from a cognitive science perspective: the impaired disengagement hypothesis. *Clinical Psychology Review, 31*(1), 138–145.

Koster, E. H. W. and Hoorelbeke, K. (2015). Cognitive bias modification for depression. *Current Opinion in Psychology, 4*, 119–123.

Kuehner, C. (2016). Why is depression more common among women than among men? *The Lancet Psychiatry, 4*, 146–158.

Kuster, F., Orth, U. and Meier, L. L. (2012). Rumination mediates the prospective effect of low self-esteem on depression: a five-wave longitudinal study. *Personality and Social Psychology Bulletin, 38*(6), 747–759.

Lahey, B. B. (2009). Public health significance of neuroticism. *American Psychologist, 64*(4), 241–256.

Lee, J. S., Mathews, A., Shergill, S. and Yiend, J. (2016). Magnitude of negative interpretation bias depends on severity of depression. *Behaviour Research and Therapy, 83*, 26–34.

LeMoult, J., Joormann, J., Kircanski, K. and Gotlib, I. H. (2016). Attentional bias training in girls at risk for depression. *Journal of Child Psychology and Psychiatry, 57*(11), 1326–1333.

LeMoult, J., Ordaz, S. J., Kircanski, K., Singh, M. K. and Gotlib, I. H. (2015). Predicting first onset of depression in young girls: interaction of diurnal cortisol and negative life events. *Journal of Abnormal Psychology, 124*(4), 850–859.

Liu, R. T. (2013). Stress generation: future directions and clinical implications. *Clinical Psychology Review, 33*(3), 406–416.

Liu, R. T. and Alloy, L. B. (2010). Stress generation in depression: a systematic review of the empirical literature and recommendations for future study. *Clinical Psychology Review, 30*(5), 582–593.

Liu, R. T., Kleiman, E. M., Nestor, B. A. and Cheek, S. M. (2015). The hopelessness theory of depression: a quarter-century in review. *Clinical Psychology-Science and Practice*, 22(4), 345–365.

Lyubomirsky, S., Layous, K., Chancellor, J. and Nelson, S. K. (2015). Thinking about rumination: the scholarly contributions and intellectual legacy of Susan Nolen-Hoeksema. *Annual Review of Clinical Psychology*, 11, 1–22.

McLaughlin, K. A., Conron, K. J., Koenen, K. C. and Gilman, S. E. (2010). Childhood adversity, adult stressful life events, and risk of past-year psychiatric disorder: a test of the stress sensitisation hypothesis in a population-based sample of adults. *Psychological Medicine*, 40(10), 1647–1658.

McLaughlin, K. A., Green, J. G., Gruber, M. J., Sampson, N. A., Zaslavsky, A. M. and Kessler, R. C. (2012). Childhood adversities and first onset of psychiatric disorders in a national sample of US adolescents. *Archives of General Psychiatry*, 69(11), 1151–1160.

McLaughlin, K. A., Sheridan, M. A., Tibu, F., Fox, N. A., Zeanah, C. H. and Nelson, C. A. (2015). Causal effects of the early caregiving environment on development of stress response systems in children. *Proceedings of the National Academy of Sciences*, 112(18), 5637–5642.

Mathews, A. and MacLeod, C. (2005). Cognitive vulnerability to emotional disorders. *Annual Review of Clinical Psychology*, 1, 167–195.

Mazure, C. M. (1998). Life stressors as risk factors in depression. *Clinical Psychology: Science and Practice*, 5, 291–313.

Mccabe, S. B., Gotlib, I. H. and Martin, R. A. (2000). Cognitive vulnerability for depression: deployment of attention as a function of history of depression and current mood state. *Cognitive Therapy and Research*, 24, 427–444.

Mezulis, A. H., Abramson, L. Y., Hyde, J. S. and Hankin, B. L. (2004). Is there a universal positivity bias in attributions? A meta-analytic review of individual, developmental, and cultural differences in the self-serving attributional bias. *Psychological Bulletin*, 130, 711–747.

Mezulis, A. H., Hyde, J. S. and Abramson, L. Y. (2006). The developmental origins of cognitive vulnerability to depression: temperament, parenting, and negative life events in childhood as contributors to negative cognitive style. *Developmental Psychology*, 42(6), 1012–1025.

Michl, L. C., McLaughlin, K. A., Shepherd, K. and Nolen-Hoeksema, S. (2013). Rumination as a mechanism linking stressful life events to symptoms of depression and anxiety: longitudinal evidence in early adolescents and adults. *Journal of Abnormal Psychology*, 122, 339–352.

Miller, G. E. and Chen, E. (2010). Harsh family climate in early life presages the emergence of a proinflammatory phenotype in adolescence. *Psychological Science*, 21, 848–856.

Miranda, J. (1997). Cognitive vulnerability, depression, and the mood-state dependent hypothesis: is out of sight out of mind? *Cognition and Emotion*, 11, 585–605.

Miranda, J. and Persons, J. B. (1988). Dysfunctional attitudes are mood-state dependent. *Journal of Abnormal Psychology, 97*, 76–79.

Mogg, K., Bradbury, K. E. and Bradley, B. P. (2006). Interpretation of ambiguous information in clinical depression. *Behaviour Research and Therapy, 44*, 1411–1419.

Monroe, S. M. and Harkness, K. L. (2005). Life stress, the 'kindling' hypothesis, and the recurrence of depression: considerations from a life stress perspective. *Psychological Review, 112*(2), 417–445.

Mor, N., Hertel, P., Ngo, T. A., Shachar, T. and Redak, S. (2014). Interpretation bias characterises trait rumination. *Journal of Behaviour Therapy and Experimental Psychiatry, 45*(1), 67–73.

Mor, N. and Winquist, J. (2002). Self-focused attention and negative affect: a meta-analysis. *Psychological Bulletin, 128*, 638–662.

Nietzel, M. T. and Harris, M. J. (1990). Relationship of dependency and achievement/ autonomy to depression. *Clinical Psychology Review, 10*, 279–297.

Nolen-Hoeksema, S. (2000). The role of rumination in depressive disorders and mixed anxiety/depressive symptoms. *Journal of Abnormal Psychology, 109*, 504–511.

Nolen-Hoeksema, S. (2002). Gender differences in depression. In I. H. Gotlib and C. L. Hammen (eds), *Handbook of depression* (pp. 492–509). New York: Guilford Press.

Nolen-Hoeksema, S. N. and Girgus, J. S. (1994). The emergence of gender differences in depression during adolescence. *Psychological Bulletin, 115*, 424–443.

Nolen-Hoeksema, S. and Watkins, E. R. (2011). A heuristic for developing trans-diagnostic models of psychopathology: explaining multifinality and divergent trajectories. *Perspectives on Psychological Science, 6*(6), 589–609.

Nolen-Hoeksema, S., Wisco, B. E. and Lyubomirsky, S. (2008). Rethinking rumination. *Perspectives on Psychological Science, 3*(5), 400–424.

Nusslock, R., Shackman, A. J., Harmon-Jones, E., Alloy, L. B., Coan, J. A. and Abramson, L. Y. (2011). Cognitive vulnerability and frontal brain asymmetry: common predictors of first prospective depressive episode. *Journal of Abnormal Psychology, 120*(2), 497–503.

Pagliaccio, D., Luby, J. L., Bogdan, R., Agrawal, A., Gaffrey, M. S., Belden, A. C., . . . Barch, D. M. (2014). Stress-system genes and life stress predict cortisol levels and amygdala and hippocampal volumes in children. *Neuropsychopharmacology, 39*(5), 1245–1253.

Paredes, P. P. and Calvete, E. (2014). Cognitive vulnerabilities as mediators between emotional abuse and depressive symptoms. *Journal of Abnormal Child Psychology, 42*(5), 743–753.

Parry, G., and Shapiro. D. A. (1986). Social support and life events in working class women: stress buffering or independent effects. *Archives General Psychiatry, 43*, 315–323.

Paykel, E. S. (2003). Life events and affective disorders. *Acta Psychiatrica Scandinavica, 108*, 61–66.

Pearson, K. A., Watkins, E. R. and Mullan, E. G. (2011). Rejection sensitivity prospectively predicts increased rumination. *Behaviour Research and Therapy*, *49*(10), 597–605.

Pechtel, P. and Pizzagalli, D. A. (2011). Effects of early life stress on cognitive and affective function: an integrated review of human literature. *Psychopharmacology*, *214*(1), 55–70.

Peckham, A. D., McHugh, R. K. and Otto, M. W. (2010). A meta-analysis of the magnitude of biassed attention in depression. *Depression and Anxiety*, *27*(12), 1135–1142.

Peters, K. D., Constans, J. I. and Mathews, A. (2011). Experimental modification of attribution processes. *Journal of Abnormal Psychology*, *120*(1), 168–173.

Post, R. M. (1992). Transduction of psychosocial stress into the neurobiology of recurrent affective disorder. *American Journal of Psychiatry*, *149*, 999–1010.

Post, R. M., Rubinow, D. R. and Ballenger, J. C. (1984). Conditioning, sensitisation, and kindling: implications for the course of affective illness (pp. 432–466). In R. M. Post and J. C. Ballenger (eds), *Neurobiology of Mood Disorders*. Baltimore: Williams and Wilkins.

Pyszczynski, T. and Greenberg, J. (1987). Self-regulatory perseveration and the depressive self-focussing style – a self-awareness theory of reactive depression. *Psychological Bulletin*, *102*(1), 122–138.

Raes, F., Hermans, D., Williams, J. M. G., Beyers, W., Brunfaut, E. and Eelen, P. (2006). Reduced autobiographical memory specificity and rumination in predicting the course of depression. *Journal of Abnormal Psychology*, *115*, 699–704.

Rawal, A. and Rice, F. (2012). Examining overgeneral autobiographical memory as a risk factor for adolescent depression. *Journal of the American Academy of Child and Adolescent Psychiatry*, *51*(5), 518–527.

Robles, T. F., Slatcher, R. B., Trombello, J. M. and McGinn, M. M. (2014). Marital quality and health: a meta-analytic review. *Psychological Bulletin*, *140*(1), 140–187.

Robinson, M. S. and Alloy, L. B. (2003). Negative cognitive styles and stress-reactive rumination interact to predict depression: a prospective study. *Cognitive Therapy and Research*, *27*, 275–291.

Rose, D. T., Abramson, L. Y., Hodulik, C. J., Halberstadt, L. and Leff, G. (1994). Heterogeneity of cognitive style among depressed inpatients. *Journal of Abnormal Psychology*, *103*(3), 419–429.

Ruscio, A. M., Gentes, E. L., Jones, J. D., Hallion, L. S., Coleman, E. S. and Swendsen, J. (2015). Rumination predicts heightened responding to stressful life events in major depressive disorder and generalised anxiety disorder. *Journal of Abnormal Psychology*, *124*(1), 17–26.

Sarin, S. and Nolen-Hoeksema, S. (2010). The dangers of dwelling: an examination of the relationship between rumination and consumptive coping in survivors of childhood sexual abuse. *Cognition and Emotion*, *24*(1), 71–85.

Scher, C. D., Ingram, R. E. and Segal, Z. V. (2005). Cognitive reactivity and vulnerability: empirical evaluation of construct activation and cognitive diatheses in unipolar depression. *Clinical Psychology Review*, *25*, 487–510.

Schmitt, M. T., Branscombe, N. R., Postmes, T. and Garcia, A. (2014). The consequences of perceived discrimination for psychological well-being: a meta-analytic review. *Psychological Bulletin, 140*(4), 921–948.

Segal, Z. V., Kennedy, S., Gemar, M., Hood, K., Pedersen, R. and Buis, T. (2006). Cognitive reactivity to sad mood provocation and the prediction of depressive relapse. *Archives of General Psychiatry, 63*, 749–755.

Segal, Z. V., Williams, J. M., Teasdale, J. D. and Gemar, M. (1996). A cognitive science perspective on kindling and episode sensitisation in recurrent affective disorder. *Psychological Medicine, 26*(02), 371–380.

Seligman, M. E. P., Abramson, L. Y., Semmel, A. and Baeyer, C. V. (1979). Depressive attributional style. *Journal of Abnormal Psychology, 88*, 242–247.

Sheppard, L. C. and Teasdale, J. D. (2004). How does dysfunctional thinking decrease during recovery from major depression? *Journal of Abnormal Psychology, 113*, 64–71.

Shonkoff, J. P., Garner, A. S., Siegel, B. S., Dobbins, M. I., Earls, M. F., McGuinn, L., . . . Wood, D. L. (2012). The lifelong effects of early childhood adversity and toxic stress. *Pediatrics, 129*(1), e232-e246.

Slavich, G. M. and Irwin, M. R. (2014). From stress to inflammation and major depressive disorder: a social signal transduction theory of depression. *Psychological Bulletin, 140*, 774–815.

Slavich, G. M., Thornton, T., Torres, L. D., Monroe, S. M. and Gotlib, I. H. (2009). Targeted rejection predicts hastened onset of major depression. *Journal of Social and Clinical Psychology, 28*(2), 223–243.

Sowislo, J. F., Orth, U. and Meier, L. L. (2014). What constitutes vulnerable self-esteem? Comparing the prospective effects of low, unstable, and contingent self-esteem on depressive symptoms. *Journal of Abnormal Psychology, 123*(4), 737–753.

Sowislo, J. F. and Orth, U. (2013). Does low self-esteem predict depression and anxiety? A meta-analysis of longitudinal studies. *Psychological Bulletin, 139*(1), 213–240.

Spasojevic, J. and Alloy, L. B. (2001). Rumination as a common mechanism relating depressive risk factors to depression. *Emotion, 1*, 25–37.

Stange, J. P., Hamilton, J. L., Abramson, L. Y. and Alloy, L. B. (2014). A vulnerability-stress examination of response styles theory in adolescence: stressors, sex differences, and symptom specificity. *Journal of Clinical Child and Adolescent Psychology, 43*(5), 813–827.

St. Clair, M. C., Croudace, T., Dunn, V. J., Jones, P. B., Herbert, J. and Goodyer, I. M. (2015). Childhood adversity subtypes and depressive symptoms in early and late adolescence. *Development and Psychopathology, 27*(03), 885–899.

Starr, L., Hammen, C., Conway, C., Raposa, E. and Brennan, P. (2014). Sensitising effect of early adversity on depressive reactions to later proximal stress: moderation by polymorphisms in serotonin transporter and corticotropin releasing hormone receptor genes in a 20-year longitudinal study. *Development and Psychopathology, 26*, 1241–1254.

Stroud, C. B., Davila, J., Hammen, C. and Vrsheck-Schallhorn, S. (2011). Severe and nonsevere events in first onsets and recurrences of depression: evidence for stress sensitisation. *Journal of Abnormal Psychology, 120,* 142–154.

Sumner, J. A., Griffith, J. W. and Mineka, S. (2010). Overgeneral autobiographical memory as a predictor of the course of depression: a meta-analysis. *Behaviour Research and Therapy, 48*(7), 614–625.

Teasdale, J. D. (1983). Negative thinking in depression – cause, effect, or reciprocal relationship. *Advances in Behaviour Research and Therapy, 5,* 3–25.

Teasdale, J. D. (1988). Cognitive vulnerability to persistent depression. *Cognition and Emotion, 2*(3), 247–274.

Teasdale, J. D. and Barnard, P. J. (1993). *Affect, cognition, and change: re-modelling depressive thought.* Hove, UK: Erlbaum.

Tennant, C. (2002). Life events, stress and depression: a review of the findings. *Australian and New Zealand Journal of Psychiatry, 36,* 173–182.

Treadway, M. T., Waskom, M. L., Dillon, D. G., Holmes, A. J., Park, M. T. M., Chakravarty, M. M., . . . Gabrieli, J. D. (2015). Illness progression, recent stress, and morphometry of hippocampal subfields and medial prefrontal cortex in major depression. *Biological Psychiatry, 77*(3), 285–294.

Vrshek-Schallhorn, S., Stroud, C. B., Mineka, S., Hammen, C., Zinbarg, R. E., Wolitzky-Taylor, K., Craske, M. G. (2015). Chronic and episodic interpersonal stress as statistically unique predictors of depression in two samples of emerging adults. *Journal of Abnormal Psychology, 124*(4), 918–932.

Watkins, E. (2011). Dysregulation in level of goal and action identification across psychological disorders. *Clinical Psychology Review, 31*(2), 260–278.

Watkins, E. (2015). Overgeneral autobiographical memories and their relationship to rumination. In Watson, L. A. and Bernsten, D. (eds) *Clinical Perspectives on Autobiographical Memory* (pp. 199–220). Cambridge: Cambridge University Press.

Watkins, E. and Moulds, M. (2005). Distinct modes of ruminative self-focus: impact of abstract versus concrete rumination on problem solving in depression. *Emotion, 5,* 319–328.

Watkins, E. and Teasdale, J. D. (2001). Rumination and overgeneral memory in depression: effects of self-focus and analytic thinking. *Journal of Abnormal Psychology, 110*(2), 353–357.

Watkins, E. R. (2008). Constructive and unconstructive repetitive thought. *Psychological Bulletin, 134*(2), 163–206.

Watkins, E. R., Baeyens, C. B. and Read, R. (2009). Concreteness training reduces dysphoria: proof-of-principle for repeated cognitive bias modification in depression. *Journal of Abnormal Psychology, 118*(1), 55–64.

Watkins, E., Moberly, N. J. and Moulds, M. L. (2008). Processing mode causally influences emotional reactivity: distinct effects of abstract versus concrete construal on emotional response. *Emotion, 8*(3), 364–378.

Watkins, E. R. and Nolen-Hoeksema, S. (2014). A habit-goal framework of depressive rumination. *Journal of Abnormal Psychology, 123*(1), 24–34.

Watkins, E. R., Taylor, R. S., Byng, R., Baeyens, C., Read, R., Pearson, K. and Watson, L. (2012). Guided self-help concreteness training as an intervention for major depression in primary care: a Phase II randomised controlled trial. *Psychological Medicine*, 42(7), 1359–1371.

Williams, J. M. G. (1996). Depression and the specificity of autobiographical memory. In D. C. Rubin (ed.), *Remembering our past: studies in autobiographical memory*. (pp. 244–267). Cambridge: Cambridge University Press.

Williams, J. M. G., Barnhofer, T., Crane, C., Hermans, D., Raes, F., Watkins, E. and Dalgleish, T. (2007). Autobiographical memory specificity and emotional disorder. *Psychological Bulletin*, 133(1), 122–148.

Wisco, B. E., Gilbert, K. E. and Marroquin, B. (2014). Maladaptive processing of maladaptive content: rumination as a mechanism linking cognitive biases to depressive symptoms. *Journal of Experimental Psychopathology*, 5(3), 329–350.

Wisco, B. E. and Nolen-Hoeksema, S. (2010). Interpretation bias and depressive symptoms: the role of self-relevance. *Behaviour Research and Therapy*, 48(11), 1113–1122.

Yang, W. H., Ding, Z. R., Dai, T., Peng, F. and Zhang, J. X. (2015). Attention bias modification training in individuals with depressive symptoms: a randomised controlled trial. *Journal of Behaviour Therapy and Experimental Psychiatry*, 49, 101–111.

Zuroff, D. C., Mongrain, M. and Santor, D. A. (2004). Conceptualising and measuring personality vulnerability to depression: comment on Coyne and Whiffen (1995). *Psychological Bulletin*, 130, 489–511.

6

Social aspects of depression

Most forms of psychological disorder affect individuals' interpersonal lives, with symptoms that alter social behaviours, perceptions of others and the quality of interacting and relating with others. Depression is a prime example, because the symptoms of depression may definitely interfere with normal relationships. But even more importantly, several perspectives emphasise the role of ongoing difficulties and vulnerabilities in relatedness to others as a fundamental causal or risk factor for depression. In this chapter, therefore, various topics are explored. There is no single interpersonal perspective on depression; instead there are diverse topics of study, such as parent–child or marital functioning, attachment security, effects of parental depression on children, the uniquely negative impact of stressful interpersonal life events, and quality of social skills and social support. As we will see, difficulties in social relatedness have been viewed variously as concomitants of being in a depressed state, consequences of depression that have negative side effects and as fundamental causal factors in depression.

Throughout the chapter, the distinction between depression as a cause of interpersonal difficulties and depression as a result of interpersonal problems is somewhat arbitrary. Or perhaps more precisely, the associations are bidirectional: eventually, even if some social difficulties are the result of depression, the interpersonal problems may perpetuate or trigger depression because they are stressful for the depressed or depression-vulnerable person. Vulnerability to depression may arise in the early family environment; the interpersonal consequences of depression might also contribute to further symptomatology; and deficits or maladaptive patterns relevant to social behaviours set the stage for occurrence of stressful events and circumstances that may trigger further depression.

Depression in the family context

Theoretical models of the family origins of depression

Historically speaking, both traditional psychodynamic and more modern social learning models of human development emphasise the importance of experiences in early childhood in the family environment. When those experiences are dysfunctional or when the child lacks crucial experiences such as a close bond with a stable caretaker, he or she may develop in maladaptive ways. Both of these perspectives hypothesise that depression might be a form of psychopathology resulting from certain negative family experiences.

In broad terms, the original Freudian psychodynamic theory emphasised the importance of the early parent–child relationship in general, and loss of the relationship (or threatened loss) as a prime factor in depression. John Bowlby (1978, 1981) articulated a model of the importance of early attachment bonds between the infant and caretaker, which has implications not only for depression, but also for key elements of individual personality and adaptive functioning. Specifically, Bowlby argued that infants have an innate and fundamental tendency to form attachment bonds to a primary caretaker, in the service of protection and survival. Further, the development of a stable and secure attachment bond is essential for healthy development. An infant whose mother or primary caretaker is consistently responsive, accessible and warmly supportive will acquire a 'working model' (that is, mental representations) of the self that is positive, will be able to use the relationship as a 'secure base' from which to explore the environment and acquire essential skills, and will form beliefs and expectations of other people as trustworthy and dependable. If, however, the attachment bond is insecure due to actual disruption or loss, or to caretaker rejection, unresponsiveness or inconsistency, the person may become vulnerable to depression and other disturbances. Insecurely attached children may be highly anxious and needy, or alternatively, may deal with the lack of attachment by being avoidant or rejecting of closeness. In later life, actual or threatened loss of close relationships may trigger not only mourning, but also self-criticism, feelings of abandonment, hopelessness and helplessness, and related depressive symptoms. There is a considerable body of empirical work validating Bowlby's ideas about attachment security in infants and its consequences for healthy or maladaptive development. Studies specifically linking attachment quality and loss to depression are reviewed in a later section.

Based on learning models, the cognitive social learning perspective on the role of early family experiences on depression is more general than the attachment model, and has been less well elaborated as a model specifically of depression than has attachment theory. Its essential tenets are that adaptive social skills and self- and interpersonal attitudes and expectations are acquired through learning during childhood. Because children's early life is centred on and dependent on caretaking, crucial learning occurs in the context of parent–child interactions. In Chapter 5 we discussed the role of negative cognitions in vulnerability to depression. Parent–child interactions that lead a child to have negative, dysfunctional self-schemas or negative explanatory styles set the stage for vulnerability to depression in the face of stress. Several forms of learning in early family life affect depression vulnerability. These may include direct experiences with reward and punishment of the child by parents, as well as learning through observation of the parent. Being treated harshly or subjected to criticism, or not receiving rewards for appropriate socially skilled behaviour, or modelling negative views of the self and world from the parent's own attitudes, may all have a negative effect on a developing child's self-esteem, expectations about others and ability to engage appropriately in relations with others. Because coping with stressors throughout life requires learning appropriate problem-solving and coping skills, deficiencies in these areas might also create vulnerability for depression.

In addition to early childhood family causes of vulnerability to depression, the family context is also important from the opposite perspective: the enormous impact of depression on others in the family. Depressed parents commonly have difficulties in their parenting roles, and such dysfunctions may contribute to the high rates of depression and other disorders in the children. Marital relationships may also suffer as a result of the depression of one of the partners. In other cases, the depressed individual may experience relating to family members as highly stressful, and this stress may contribute to further depression. Research on the relationship between depression and parental and marital functioning is reviewed below.

Parent–child relationships and early environment as potential causes of depression

We turn first to various lines of research investigating the importance of early family experiences on development of depression.

Early loss and depression

Older studies probed the impact of loss of a parent on risk for depression, but many of the studies did not distinguish between types of loss (e.g., death, separation, divorce) or age of occurrence. In general earlier research has shown at best a small or modest association between childhood loss and later adult depression (e.g., Brown and Harris, 1978; Lloyd, 1980). Kendler, Sheth, Gardner and Prescott (2002) found that the risk of depression was greater following maternal death in childhood than death of fathers, and that the risk period was relatively brief, suggesting that the person who develops depression, if at all, experiences depression apparently precipitated by and in close proximity to the death, but had little continuing risk for depression into adulthood.

Increasingly it has been recognised that it is usually not parental loss as such that creates risk for depression, but rather the quality of parental care following the loss. Poor quality of parenting or inconsistent parenting following loss was found to be predictive of later depression (e.g., Bifulco, Brown and Harris, 1987). Other consequences of loss of a parent may include economic hardship, family instability and stressful conditions that contribute to risk for depression. Kendler, Gardner and Prescott (2006) found that parental loss (defined to include death or separation) predicted depression in a sample of adult men in part because of its association with various risk factors including low self-esteem and low educational attainment. The same authors had previously also demonstrated that prediction of depression in women involved multiple interacting risk factors of which childhood parental loss was a small contributor (Kendler, Gardner and Prescott, 2002).

Early adversity and depression

Another approach to the link between early family and learning experiences and risk for depression involves exposure to adverse conditions in childhood. Various kinds of negative experiences that affect a child's safety, well-being and emotional stability have been studied, including loss of a parent, but also events such as child maltreatment, poverty, family instability, parental mental illness and substance abuse, exposure to violence and others.

Among single specific experiences (including loss), one of the most studied is abuse – sexual, physical or emotional maltreatment, typically but not always occurring in the family context. There is ample evidence from mostly retrospective community and clinical studies of a significant association between childhood sexual or physical abuse and adult depression. For example, Lindert, von Ehrenstein, Grashow, Gal, Braehler and Weisskopf (2014) analysed results from 19 studies of over 100,000 adult participants, and found significantly elevated rates of depression and anxiety disorders in those exposed to sexual or physical abuse prior to age 16. Kendler and Aggen (2014) statistically controlled for various potentially confounding environmental and methodological features in their large sample of adult women, and concluded that sexual abuse in childhood has a largely causal relationship to later depression (although other factors also contribute). Childhood maltreatment also predicts an especially pernicious course of depression. Nanni, Uher and Danese (2012), for example, performed meta-analyses of multiple studies, finding that abuse was associated with an elevated risk of both recurrent and persistent (chronic) depression, and worse clinical outcomes (less response to treatment). Chen et al. (2014) found that Chinese women who experienced more severe sexual abuse had more severe and recurrent depression.

Large-scale epidemiological surveys have shown associations between psychiatric disorders including depression and exposure to adverse conditions in childhood for both adult (Kessler et al., 2010) and adolescent samples (McLaughlin et al., 2012). Moreover, adverse conditions tend to aggregate, so that individuals who experience one are likely to experience others as well. Importantly, the cluster of those defining 'maladaptive family functioning' (parental mental illness, substance abuse disorder and criminality; family violence; physical abuse; sexual abuse; and neglect) is particularly strongly predictive of psychological disorders (Green et al., 2010).

Why is early adversity and trauma likely to predict depression? The chapters of this book review a number of mechanisms of risk that are all likely to operate to some extent in childhood in the context of family conflict, poverty and economic crises, exposure to parental drug and alcohol abuse or mental illness and abusive or neglectful parenting. Such risk factors and risk mechanisms include maladaptive psychological and neurobiological stress processes, genetic and gene–environment interaction effects contributed by dysfunctional parents, cognitive mechanisms that contribute to maladaptive information-processing and cognitive control (coping), and disrupted parenting practices that impair nurturance, protection, support, monitoring and teaching functions. Significantly, the impact of harsh environmental conditions, especially for infants and young children, is mediated by the caretaker, usually Mum (Tang, Reeb-Sutherland, Romeo and McEwen, 2014). Thus, quality of *parenting* is likely to be a critical factor. In subsequent sections we discuss in greater detail the example of how parental depression may affect parenting in ways that promote children's insecurities and negative expectations about themselves and the world, and fail to support the children's coping skills in the face of stress and conflict.

Another crucial fact about early life exposure to adversity is its effect on neurobiological development, through genetic, epigenetic and HPA axis and neural processes (as reviewed in Chapter 4) – as well as psychological mechanisms. Individuals exposed to adverse environmental conditions and events showed heightened depressive *sensitivity to stress* in adolescence and adulthood (Essex et al., 2013; Hammen, Henry and Daley, 2000; McLaughlin, Conron, Koenen and Gilman, 2010; Starr, Hammen, Conway, Raposa and Brennan, 2014). As Figure 6.1 illustrates, major depressive episodes (and by comparison post-traumatic stress disorders) are more likely to occur following a major recent stressful life event if the individual has experienced higher numbers of childhood adversities before age 17.

Attachment and depression

In Bowlby's model of infant attachment, the quality of the primary caregiver's (typically the mother's) parenting style and support promotes foundational attitudes the child develops about the self, others and the world, and shapes the child's efforts and comfort with which to explore the environment. Considerable evidence has accumulated that measures of the security of the

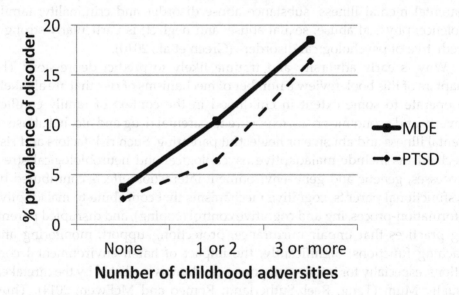

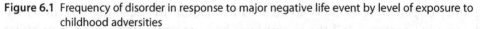

Figure 6.1 Frequency of disorder in response to major negative life event by level of exposure to childhood adversities

Source: Adapted from Table 2, McLaughlin, K. A., Conron, K. J., Koenen, K. C., and Gilman, S. E. (2010). Childhood adversity, adult stressful life events, and risk of past-year psychiatric disorder: a test of the stress sensitisation hypothesis in a population-based sample of adults. *Psychological Medicine*, 40(10), 1647–1658.

child's attachment to the caregiver – as assessed by diverse behavioural methods as well as questionnaires and other ways of measuring the representations of attachment displayed by children and adolescents – are associated with anxiety and depression. Brumariu and Kerns (2010) conducted an extensive review of research literature on attachment, variously measured, in children and adolescents across a wide array of designs in various industrialised nations. Generally, they found evidence that both depression and anxiety – especially in adolescents – was associated with insecure forms of attachment to the parent(s) (see also a meta-analytic review in Madigan, Atkinson, Laurin and Benoit, 2013). Unfortunately, the ideal long-term prospective study to test the link between infant insecurity of attachment to adult depression has yet to be conducted, and very few even short-term longitudinal attachment studies have been published. Moreover, as Brumariu and Kerns (2010) note, the attachment model needs to be expanded to include a variety of factors that might modify the link between insecure attachment and depression, such as high levels of family adversity, aspects of parenting style and characteristics of the child. Also, further work is needed to clarify the mechanisms by which attachment leads to depression, such as the child's cognitive biases, emotion regulation and self-concept. It might be noted that investigators have developed various methods of measuring 'adult attachment' including peer and romantic attachment, including content such as trust, communication, comfort with intimacy and fear of abandonment (reviewed in Ravitz, Maunder, Hunter, Sthankiya and Lancee, 2010). Such measures are generally positively correlated with parent attachment, and predict a wide array of interpersonal outcomes, as well as physical and psychological well-being.

Quality of parent–child relationships and depression

As we have noted, parenting quality is a strong predictor of maladaptive outcomes including depression, and was one of the classic early approaches to understanding depression. Several kinds of research designs have directly investigated the associations between parent–child relationship quality and depression. Retrospective reports by depressed adults (both patients and community samples) described both mothers and fathers as more rejecting, controlling and as demonstrating hostile detachment, and relations with their parents were marked by lack of caring, warmth and acceptance, as well as by stricter control, compared with the reports of the nondepressed controls (e.g., reviewed in Parker and Gladstone, 1996). A particular pattern of 'affectionless control' (Parker, 1983) has commonly been observed: lack of warmth and caring, and psychological control (guilt induction, criticism, intrusiveness) (reviewed in Alloy, Abramson, Smith, Gibb and Neeren, 2006). These authors conclude that depression is relatively more associated with low caring than with high control, and note that these dimensions may also contribute to disruptive behavioural disorders in youth as well as internalising disorders such as depression and anxiety.

In addition to retrospective reports, there is also direct evidence from contemporary reports and observations that depressed children and adolescents experience difficulties in their relationships with parents (e.g., see reviews in Alloy et al., 2006; Kaslow, Deering and Racusin, 1994). True prospective studies collect information about parental behaviour prior to onset of depression in the offspring, and are thus free of potential reporting biases due to current depression and are therefore more able to establish probable causality. Such studies are relatively infrequent, but Weich, Patterson, Shaw and Stewart-Brown (2009) reviewed depression outcomes in 17 studies of 13 cohorts that used diverse measures of family or parenting quality. Eight prospective studies defined as 'high quality' found clear significant effects of depression associated with maltreatment for both sexes, and several studies found effects with sex differences. Several of the studies found parenting quality effects after adjusting for possible confounding risk factors for depression such as family stress, low socioeconomic status and family discord, and only two relatively lower-quality studies failed to find depression associated with parenting issues. Thus, childhood parenting quality emerged as a robust predictor of adolescent and adult depression.

While much of the theoretical link between negative parenting and later depression is based on the assumption that neglect, harsh and punitive discipline, and over-controlling parenting give children a message of not being valued, or of incompetence, research has measured actual negative cognitions children acquire that predispose them to depression when stress occurs. As if echoing a punitive or uncaring parent, the child constantly berates herself or himself, and attacks the self as worthless. Cognitions about worthlessness and unlovability set the stage for depression, as discussed in Chapter 5. Studies have confirmed that higher levels of negative parenting styles that include low warmth and negative feedback are associated with children's negative cognitions such as low self-esteem, negative explanatory style and other dysfunctional schemas (reviewed in Alloy et al., 2006; Liu, 2003). In addition to cognition, neurobiological mechanisms are likely in play. As noted in Chapter 4, neural circuits involving overactivation of the amygdala and hippocampus, along with reduced activity and efficiency in areas of the prefrontal cortex responsible for cognitive control and effective coping with stress, may be shaped by the stress of harsh parenting. In a novel study, for example, Hooley, Gruber, Scott, Hiller and Yurgelun-Todd (2005) examined activation of a brain region thought to be implicated in depression (the dorsolateral prefrontal cortex, DLPFC), while formerly depressed women listened to audio-taped critical or praise comments about them by their own mothers. Even though the women were no longer depressed, they showed significantly less activation of the DLPFC during criticism than did never-depressed controls, but the two groups did not differ on responses to praise. The authors suggest that vulnerability to depression due to criticism may operate in part through brain changes associated with failure to effectively engage the prefrontal cortex responsible for cognitive control (such as distraction or problem-solving) of the negative thoughts. That is, the brain shaped by depression or the brain vulnerable to depression, fails to inhibit or reinterpret negative content during psychosocial threat such as criticism. The resulting reduced cognitive control/coping thus leads to more pronounced negative emotion potentially creating risk for further depression.

Summary

This brief review of research indicates that the quality of early life experiences in the family may contribute to depression. The quality of the attachment bond, the experience of critical, rejecting or overcontrolling parenting and disrupted family life appear to set the stage for depression. Children exposed to such experiences may become depressed, while adults who experienced such events in childhood may be vulnerable to depressive reactions when faced with stressful experiences. Most of the research to date is correlational, however, with little direct evidence of a causal relationship between early negative events and depression due to the paucity of long-term longitudinal studies. Nevertheless, the associations are robust and well replicated, suggesting that disruption of close family relationships may be a critical vulnerability factor for depression. Although research has yet to fully clarify the mechanisms accounting for the associations with depression, it is likely that maladaptive family relationships create children's negative cognitions about the worth and competence of the self, and overwhelm or impair important adaptive skills that would help to avoid or resolve stressful situations. Such experiences contribute to vulnerability to react with depression when a negative event is encountered that is interpreted as a depletion of the self and beyond one's ability to overcome its impact.

Depression and marital relationships

As we noted in Chapter 3 on demographic correlates of depression, marital status issues were the strongest single predictor of major depression in both high-middle and low-income countries (Bromet et al., 2011). Absence of a partner through divorce, separation or death is universally associated with elevated rates of depression and distress – for various reasons, including lack of support, economic status and for many, loss of affection and companionship.

For those who are married, unfortunately, depression and poor marital quality have a powerful, reciprocal effect on each other. At the most basic level, the symptoms of depression may contribute to difficulties in close relationships. Irritability, loss of energy and enjoyment, sensitivity to criticism, pessimistic or even suicidal thoughts may initially elicit concern from others, but eventually may seem burdensome, unreasonable or even willful – sometimes eroding the support of spouses, and causing them distress (Coyne, 1976). There is ample evidence of an association between depression and poor marital adjustment. In their classic book, Weissman and Paykel (1974) were among the first to characterise the marriages of depressed women as fraught with friction, inadequate communication, dependency, overt hostility, resentment and guilt, poor sexual relationships and a lack of affection. Patterns of blame, withdrawal, verbal aggression and lower frequency of positive communications have been confirmed in observational studies of communications between depressed individuals and their spouses (reviewed in Rehman, Gollan and Mortimer, 2008). Meta-analyses of multiple studies show significant associations between depressive symptoms or diagnoses and self-reported poor marital satisfaction (Whisman, 2001).

In addition to correlations between depression and marital dissatisfaction, longitudinal studies have shown both that depression results from marital problems and also that marital problems result from depression. A study of several thousand community women in Australia over a 21-year period showed that depressive symptoms led to a decline in marital quality over time (and the reverse was also true: lower marital satisfaction predicted depressive symptoms) (Najman et al., 2014).

Conflict in a marriage or close relationship, or the ending of a desired intimacy are obviously highly stressful experiences that often precipitate depression. There is fairly strong evidence from longitudinal studies that earlier relationship dissatisfaction predicts later depressive symptoms or episodes. For instance, Whisman and Bruce (1999) examined reported marital dissatisfaction in over 900 non-depressed married adults in an epidemiological sample, and examined occurrence of major depression in the subsequent 12 months. They found that dissatisfied spouses were nearly three times more likely to develop a depressive episode than satisfied spouses, and the effects were similar for men and women.

Research has also confirmed that relationship difficulties affect the course of depression. For instance, spouse expressions of criticism and negative attitudes toward the depressed person (sometimes termed 'expressed emotion') have been shown to predict relapse following treatment or hospitalisation, according to a review by Butzlaff and Hooley (1998). Studies of family functioning of hospitalised depressed patients indicate that those with poorer family functioning were less likely to recover by 12 months and to have worse long-term course of depression (Keitner, Ryan, Miller, Kohn, Bishop and Epstein, 1995; Keitner, Ryan, Miller and Zlotnick, 1997). Overall, therefore, conflict and dissatisfaction in marital relationships may contribute to the onset and continuing course of depressive disorders.

Depression may cause marital difficulties. As noted in discussions of depressive symptoms and cognitions, depression is typically accompanied by characteristically negative interpretations, so that a depressed person might focus on the annoying, less rewarding aspects of the marital relationship that they largely overlook when not depressed, and they may be irritable, withdrawn and generally not pleasant to be around. It appears that the partner's depression may affect the behaviour and attitudes of the well spouse in negative ways, possibly causing or exacerbating marital unhappiness in both partners (Coyne, Thompson and Palmer, 2002; Whisman, Uebelacker and Weinstock, 2004). A four-year longitudinal study of newlywed couples confirmed that depressive symptoms predicted lower marital satisfaction levels over time as much as lower marital satisfaction levels predicted depressive symptoms (Davila, Karney, Hall and Bradbury, 2003). Similarly, longitudinal studies of young adult marriage and relationships reveal predictive associations over time between adolescent depression and later marital/relationship dissatisfaction compared to nondepressed adolescents (Gotlib, Lewinsohn and Seeley, 1998; Rao, Hammen and Daley, 1999). Further, Keenan-Miller, Hammen and Brennan (2007) found that adolescent depression by age 15 predicted being a victim of severe intimate partner violence in a romantic relationship by age 20.

Finally, it should be noted that marital/relationship discord may be somewhat stable over time, perhaps owing to stable traits and maladaptive problem-solving skills. Although the state of being in a depressive episode with heightened levels of symptoms may contribute to marital difficulties, there is substantial evidence that even when treated or no longer depressed, many depressed individuals have persisting interpersonal dysfunction including marital dissatisfaction and conflict (e.g., Billings and Moos, 1985; Hammen and Brennan, 2002; Weissman and Paykel, 1974).

As previously noted, most forms of psychopathology may be associated with disruptions in close relationships. The question arises: Is marital maladjustment more likely to occur with depression than other disorders? Some have speculated that for many people, the vulnerability to develop depression is rooted in dysfunctions in the ability to manage close relationships, possibly originating in insecure attachment bonds or poor parenting in childhood so that the individual has difficulties in trust, closeness, management of conflict and other interpersonal skills and attitudes. Comparative studies have rarely been conducted, but two are noteworthy. Zlotnick, Kohn, Keitner and Della Grotta (2000) used a large epidemiological data base to compare groups of people who were currently depressed, nondepressed and those with other psychiatric disorders on ratings of the quality of relationships with their spouses/partners. The depressed individuals – both men and women – reported significantly fewer positive and more negative interactions with their partners than did the other two groups. Also, in the Gotlib et al. (1998) longitudinal study of adolescents, only the depressed youth – but not those with nondepressive disorders – reported greater relationship dissatisfaction in early adulthood. It must be noted, however, that a large-scale cross-sectional epidemiological study based on adult respondents of all ages did not find significantly higher rates of marital dissatisfaction among those with depression compared to other disorders (such as substance abuse, bipolar disorders, generalised anxiety disorder; Whisman, 2007).

Mechanisms of marital dysfunction in couples with depression

Why is there a strong association between depressive disorders and marital difficulties? Little evidence exists to address the issue but there are several speculative hypotheses. Obviously, the symptoms of depression itself, as noted earlier, may impede marital communication and satisfaction. Furthermore, as Coyne (1976) noted, there may be a deteriorating marital process in which initial concern and caring by the well spouse for the depressed spouse eventually is replaced by resentment and impatience – reactions likely perceived by the depressed person as rejection and lack of sympathy, provoking further depression. Because depression is often misunderstood as largely within the sufferer's control, spouses may be perplexed and frustrated when the depressed partner does not quickly bounce back or take the steps the well partner believes will be fruitful ('don't let things bother you so much', 'go get a new job if this one is causing you distress'). The burden of caring for a depressed person is stressful and often overwhelms the caretaker. Spouses and partners are often especially troubled by the restrictions in social and leisure activities, and the depressed persons' withdrawal, worry and suicidal thoughts (e.g., Coyne et al., 1987; Fadden, Bebbington and Kuipers, 1987).

Vulnerability to depression itself may include personality predispositions, insecure attachment expectations and behavioural styles such as over-dependency on others that create tension in relationships. These vulnerability features may contribute to dysfunctional relationships – and are reviewed elsewhere in the chapter.

Finally, a further hypothesis is that depressed people tend to marry other people with psychological problems, thus increasing the chances of marital disharmony. A review and meta-analysis of several studies of patients with mood disorders confirmed the significant likelihood that individuals with depressive disorders marry others with depression (Mathews and Reus, 2001). In general, mate similarity analyses of different disorders indicate that most psychiatric conditions including depression show patterns of 'non-random mating' in which individuals with a disorder have an elevated rate of marrying someone with the same or another disorder (e.g., Nordsletten et al., 2016). Depressed women patients have also been found to have higher rates of marriage to men with antisocial and substance use disorders (e.g., Galbaud du Fort, Bland, Newman and Boothroyd, 1998; Hammen, 1991a). Research on nonpatient samples also shows spouse similarity for depressive disorders (e.g., Hammen and Brennan, 2002), and wife major depression associated with husband antisocial personality disorder (Galbaud du Fort et al., 1998). While the possible reasons for 'nonrandom mating' are beyond the scope of this chapter, the implications of such marital patterns are clear: marriages in which both partners experience symptoms and vulnerabilities to disorder may give rise to marital discord and instability by contributing to stressful home environments and potentially to limited skills for resolving interpersonal disputes.

Effects of parental depression on children

Over the past two decades research has demonstrated that one of the most profoundly significant effects of depression on the family is the increased risk that children of a depressed parent will develop depressive disorders, or other forms of psychopathology and functional impairment. Reviews of early clinic-based studies of depressed patients suggested that approximately half of the offspring of depressed parents develop disorders (e.g., reviewed in Beardslee, Versage and Gladstone, 1998). It is particularly useful to examine community samples not in treatment, because clinical populations are typically more severe cases not directly generalisable to typical community samples. Numerous studies have been conducted in recent years, and a meta-analysis of 193 studies of both treatment and community samples showed a significant preponderance of both internalising and externalising disorders and symptoms in school-age children of depressed women compared to nondepressed women (Goodman et al., 2011). It should be noted that the great majority of studies have examined the effects of *maternal* depression on offspring largely due to the greater numbers of depressed women with children. However, fathers' depressions also have negative effects on children's adjustment, although possibly they are less pronounced (e.g., Fletcher, Feeman, Garfield and Vimpani, 2011; Kane and Garber, 2004; Wilson and Durbin, 2010).

Longitudinal studies confirm the negative effects of maternal depression across all ages in childhood. In the Avon (England) Longitudinal Study of Parents and Children, 7,500 mother–child pairs were studied between child ages 1½ to 7½ years. The young children of ever-depressed women compared with nondepressed women were found to have significantly higher rates of disorders (1.2 per cent vs. 0.4 per cent were depressed; 4.1 per cent vs. 1.8 per cent showed oppositional defiant disorder; 7.7 per cent vs. 2.6 per cent had anxiety disorders; Barker, Copeland, Maughan, Jaffee and Uher, 2012). A Canadian community study of depression and anxiety symptoms assessed yearly over several years in 1,759 young children between 1½ and 5 years found that those with patterns of high sustained and increasing levels of symptoms compared to those with sustained low levels of symptoms were significantly more likely to have mothers with histories of depression (Côté et al., 2009). Halligan, Murray, Martins and Cooper (2007) followed up children of women who had postpartum depression and found a rate of 40 per cent for any Axis I diagnosis by age 13, including 23 per cent with depressive disorder. The rate of depression was over 30 per cent for youth whose mother had both postpartum and subsequent depression. In a longitudinal study of older community children, Hammen and Brennan (2001) studied 815 pairs of 15-year-old children and their depressed or never-depressed mothers selected from a birth cohort sample in Queensland, Australia. They found that youth of depressed mothers were diagnosed with past or current major depressive episode at the rate of 18.4 per cent vs. 9.85 per cent compared with youth of never-depressed women; 9.6 per cent vs. 4.4 per cent had anxiety disorders; and 4.2 per cent vs. 1.3 per cent had conduct disorder. By age 20, offspring of depressed women had a rate of major depressive episode of 39 per cent compared to 28 per cent of children of never-depressed women. In one small but unique study that followed up offspring of depressed parents for 30 years, Weissman and colleagues (2016) found persisting high rates of depression and other disorders, as well as continuing psychosocial maladjustment, and increased health problems. Weissman et al. (2016) found that the maternal depression specifically predicted early adolescent onset depression, but did not predict first onsets in adulthood (see also Hammen and Brennan, 2016). Thus, it appears that the risk factors stemming from maternal depression operate primarily during childhood promoting early onset depression.

It is important to emphasise that apart from psychological disorders evident in many offspring of depressed parents, the children also commonly display a variety of health, cognitive and social developmental disruptions, which may have enduring effects (Hammen, Brennan, Keenan-Miller and Herr, 2008; Lampard, Franckle and Davison, 2014; NICHD Early Child Care Research Network, 1999; Stein et al., 2014; Wachs, Black and Engle, 2009; Weissman et al., 2006).

While most research on offspring of depressed women has focused on high-income mostly Western countries, there is increasing attention to the impact on children in low- and middle-income countries. Wachs et al. (2009) reviewed studies in low- and middle-income countries, noting high rates of maternal depression and significant associations of depression with children's behavioural problems and depression symptoms, difficult temperament, motor and cognitive delays, as well as medical and developmental issues.

Effects of perinatal maternal depression on children

Investigators have increasingly focused on maternal depression during pregnancy and postpartum. The assumption is that early exposure (prenatal or infancy) might be especially disruptive to important infant developmental and parenting processes, potentially leading to greater impairment compared to later exposure. Also, perinatal depression is commonly chronic or recurrent. There is evidence that mothers' *prenatal* stress, depression and anxiety may put infants at risk for later depression operating through mechanisms such as neuroendocrine abnormalities, reduced blood flow to the fetus, fetal neuro-behavioural development, maternal maladaptive health behaviours, among others (reviewed in Goodman and Lusby, 2014). Stein et al. (2014) reviewed global research on fetal and neonatal outcomes, finding that prenatal depression is associated with premature birth, and low birth-weight especially in low- and middle-income compared with high-income countries (see also Accortt, Cheadle and Dunkel Schetter, 2015; Surkan, Kennedy, Hurley and Black, 2011).

Mechanisms of negative effects of parental depression

The reasons for the negative impact of parental depression on children include a variety of genetic and environmental possibilities. Genetic and neurobio-logical/neurohormonal factors were reviewed in Chapter 4, including gene–environment interactions and gene–environment correlations. It seems clear that whatever modest genetic contributions to offspring depression exist, a considerable amount of the explanation of the effects of parental depression comes from a complex and interacting set of family, environmental stress, cognitive and interpersonal factors. Investigators have observed that depression in a parent typically occurs in the context of marital problems, chronically stressful family and social circumstances, economic disadvantage, difficult parent–child relationships and maladaptive communication patterns, and parental personality, interpersonal and cognitive characteristics that impair the child's acquisition of social and problem-solving skills. Thus, the essential story is 'correlated risk factors'. Several scholars have proposed, and some have tested, complex models (e.g., Barker et al., 2012; Garber and Cole, 2010; Goodman and Gotlib, 1999; Hammen, Shih and Brennan, 2004; Luby, Gaffrey, Tillman, April and Belden, 2014; Rice et al., 2017), but truly comprehensive (complex) biopsychosocial models have yet to be tested and validated.

Despite multiple and complex related contributors to offspring risk, one factor seems critical: adverse environmental conditions affect the young child through the mother (caregiver), as previously noted (Tang et al., 2014). Thus, considerable attention has been directed at quality of parent–child relations in families with a depressed parent. Parenting styles and practices are typically impaired during depressive episodes and conditions, and dysfunctional parenting is likely the most important – and potentially modifiable – risk factor for youth depression (e.g., review in Goodman, 2007). As Goodman notes, depressive symptoms plus underlying emotional, cognitive and social vulnerabilities impede parental warmth, responsiveness, monitoring and discipline that undermine children's well-being and effectiveness. Observational studies have noted that depressed, compared to non-depressed, mothers display more negative behaviours toward children, such as criticism and hostility, and/or more withdrawn, disengaged behaviours (reviewed in Lovejoy, Graczyk, O'Hare and Neuman, 2000). Specific patterns commonly observed among depressed women interacting with their infants include intrusive (harsh, irritated), or withdrawn (disengaged) styles or both (Field, Diego and Hernandez-Reif, 2006; Wang and Dix, 2013). Reising et al. (2013) examined families of depressed parents, and found support for correlated risk factors (economic disadvantage, neighborhood stress and disrupted parenting) predicting both externalising and internalising symptoms. When the stress and economic factors were statistically controlled in regression analyses, parenting problems had a significant independent effect.

While discussion of treatment or preventive intervention is beyond the scope of this chapter, it is noteworthy that increasingly worldwide efforts have begun to appear aimed at identifying depression in pregnant women and new mothers. O'Hara and McCabe (2013) and Beardslee, Solantaus, Morgan, Gladstone and Kowalenko (2012) reported on efforts in many Western nations, and in some jurisdictions in the US, to mandate perinatal screening for depression and provision of treatment/supportive services. However, such efforts are far from adequate, and considerable research is needed to determine the most effective and most enduring interventions and how they can be disseminated successfully in high-risk populations.

Social behaviours of depressed persons

Interpersonal behaviours are affected by depression

In the state of depression, the symptoms of apathy and anhedonia, negative mood including sadness and irritability, social withdrawal, low energy and negative cognitions create obstacles to pleasant and constructive communication and social interaction. Studies have indeed shown that both depressed persons themselves, as well as observers, rate them as less socially skilled than nondepressed persons (e.g., reviewed in Segrin, 2000; Tse and Bond, 2004). When people are depressed they are less verbally fluent and have more monotonous speech and poor eye contact. The content of verbal communications between married couples when one member is depressed, for example, commonly reflects greater negativity and less positivity, although varying by gender and level of marital satisfaction (e.g., Gabriel, Beach and Bodenmann, 2010). Generally, such 'depressive' behaviours elicit negative reactions from others, because they violate certain norms of communication such as responsiveness, politeness and expectations of mutual involvement. Depressed people may fail to engage others and respond with interest and attention, so that interacting with them is aversive and unrewarding. Not only do spouses and children find it difficult to interact with a depressed adult, but also children may have difficulty with peers who are depressed. For example, Kochel, Ladd and Rudolph (2012) followed a group of nearly 500 school-aged children over time, and found that depressive symptoms predicted later peer difficulties. Specifically, depressed children elicit negative attitudes from peers over time, presumably because the depressed children have social deficits or are treated poorly by other children because of social styles such as passivity or fearfulness, leading them to be viewed unfavourably over time.

Even interactions with strangers may have negative consequences for depressed people. A variety of older controlled, simulated laboratory experiments documented that interacting with a simulated depressed person often resulted in negative emotional reactions in the other person, relatively more negative verbal and nonverbal interactions, and indicators of rejection in the form of lack of desire for further contact (e.g., Hammen and Peters, 1978; Segrin and Abramson, 1994; Stephens, Hokanson and Welker, 1987; Strack and Coyne, 1983).

Interpersonal-related vulnerability factors for depression

While depressive symptoms definitely disrupt social functioning, are they simply temporary side effects that disappear when the person is not depressed? Unfortunately, there is considerable evidence of continuing social vulnerability.

Underlying traits

Underlying traits and characteristics that are present even when the person is not in a depressed state may predispose to depression and/or anxiety. One of the most-studied such enduring traits is *neuroticism*, which is a tendency to have negative mood states and typically greater reactivity to and poorer coping with life events. Neuroticism has been linked consistently to both depression and anxiety disorders (e.g., Kendler, Gatz, Gardner and Pedersen, 2006; Klein, Kotov and Bufferd, 2011; Kotov, Gamez, Schmidt and Watson, 2010). While not itself literally about interpersonal behaviours, neuroticism predicts excessive negative cognitions and emotions about interpersonal life events, such as perceptions or expectations of rejection, reassurance-seeking, perceived criticism and the like, which commonly lead to negative behavioural impacts on relationships, such as conflict. *Introversion* (or low extraversion) represents a trait of low amounts of enthusiastic engagement with social activities (and discomfort in such situations), but this trait is less consistently predictive of vulnerability to depressive states (e.g., Klein et al., 2011) – probably depending on the extent to which the person feels lonely or more isolated than they wish to be and believe their isolation is a result of personal shortcomings. A similar construct used by Hames, Hagan and Joiner (2013) is interpersonal inhibition (shyness), often termed behavioural inhibition in children. These authors surveyed studies suggesting that inhibition may be predictive of depressive symptoms especially under conditions of low social support. Katz, Conway, Hammen, Brennan and Najman (2011) found that a similar construct, social withdrawal, in children at age 5 predicted depression by age 20 as mediated by relatively poorer quality of social relationships in early adolescence (see also Gladstone and Parker, 2006).

Interpersonal styles as vulnerabilities

In addition to basic personality traits that portend potential interpersonal difficulties there are several specific (although overlapping) relational behaviour styles that have been demonstrated to predict risk for depression. One is *excessive reassurance-seeking* about one's worth and desirability, first identified by Coyne (1976) as an interactional style likely to elicit rejection (hence, triggering depressive reactions). Considerable evidence has shown that this characteristic does indeed predict depression (e.g., Joiner and Metalsky, 2001), largely because it can be annoying and provokes low social support, and/or generates acute and chronic interpersonal stress including romantic conflict and breakups (Eberhart and Hammen, 2009; Starr and Davila, 2008; Stewart and Harkness, 2015; Stroud, Sosoo and Wilson, 2015). Reassurance-seeking behaviours are especially likely to promote conflict and depression in adult or adolescent romantic relationships, but may also negatively affect depressive symptoms in response to peer relationships in children and adolescents (e.g., Prinstein, Borelli, Cheah, Simon and Aikins, 2005).

Another problematic social style that commonly triggers depression in the face of relationship stressors stems from *insecure attachment* beliefs. As noted earlier, *secure* attachment perceptions, presumed to arise from positive early childhood experiences with caregivers, include beliefs that the self is love-able and that support from others is available. Thus, for example, attachment insecurity might lead to expectations of rejection or abandonment, lack of trust of close others, or dismissive attitudes toward closeness. Such attachment cognitions and associated behaviours have been shown to predict depressive reactions especially due to problems in close romantic relationships (e.g., Eberhart and Hammen, 2009), but also affecting children's and adolescents' peer relationships and mood (e.g., Abela et al., 2005; Lee and Hankin, 2009). A related interpersonal style predictive of depression is *rejection sensitivity* (Downey and Feldman, 1996), which because of its negative expectations and interpretations, shares many features with excessive reassurance-seeking and attachment insecurity.

Interpersonal dependency, also called *sociotropy*, is described as excessive need for close relationships with others and basing self-worth on others' approval and relatedness, and is typically accompanied by inhibition of direct anger and hostility in order to maintain ties. Dependency has been shown to be predictive of depression (e.g., Sanathara, Gardner, Prescott and Kendler, 2003; Shih, 2006). Dependency/sociotropy is also highly related to excessive reassurance-seeking.

Dependency traits are generally more elevated in women than men (Bornstein, 1992). The implications of these findings for excess depression in women are apparent: to the extent that women are relatively more socialised both to orient toward others, to suppress expressions of aggression and seek reassurance of their value to others, they may thereby acquire vulnerabilities to depressive experiences (Cyranowski, Frank, Young and Shear, 2000; Nolen-Hoeksema, 2001).

Interpersonal vulnerability–stress relationships

Most models of depression are 'diathesis–stress' models, positing that stressful life events or circumstances provoke or challenge the person's underlying vulnerabilities, triggering depression. While stress–depression associations have been discussed in various chapters, here we briefly discuss the unique impact of acute and chronic stresses that have interpersonal content, and the ways in which interpersonal vulnerabilities may impair coping with stress.

Specific individual vulnerability to interpersonal stress

One form of vulnerability to depression is due to female gender. As noted, it is generally acknowledged that socialisation and biological mechanisms promote women's heightened affiliative needs for greater orientation to attend to, nurture and promote close relations with others (e.g., Cyranowski et al., 2000). Thus, in general women might be expected to be more reactive to negative, stressful circumstances affecting them and others with whom they are close. As an example, Shih, Eberhart, Hammen and Brennan (2006) found that under identical high levels of recent interpersonal stress, adolescent girls had significantly higher levels of depression than adolescent boys did (see also review in Hammen, 2005). It appears that girls 'care' more about interpersonal difficulties than boys do. Studies of individual differences in level of sociotropic values found that those higher in such values were more likely to become depressed if they experienced stressful life events with interpersonal content but not if they experienced non-interpersonal stressors (reviewed in Hammen, 2005). Women in general tend to score higher on measures of sociotropy – plus in general, life events with social content (such as relationship endings, changes, conflicts affecting self and close others) are relatively more common compared to events signifying achievement failures or impediments to autonomy. Achievement and autonomy values may reflect individual vulnerabilities for some individuals more than others (commonly, men), suggesting in general that different individuals are more vulnerable to different types of stressful events.

Interpersonal aspects of coping with stress

Resources for coping with stress may mitigate the depressive impact of life events and chronic stressful conditions. A considerable body of research indicates that the availability of supportive relationships with others – or the perception of such support – plays an important role in whether individuals will become depressed or experience other negative health outcomes. Quality and quantity of social relationships are strong predictors of increased like-lihood of survival; a meta-analysis of mortality from all causes showed that higher quality of support increased survival rates by 50 per cent (Holt-Lunstad, Smith and Layton, 2010). Depression is associated with lower levels of perceived and actual support, and some studies note that this is especially true for women (Dalgard et al., 2006; Kendler, Myers and Prescott, 2005). Despite some evidence that social support 'buffers' the effects of stress on depression, research findings have not been consistent with this hypothesis. Instead, both high levels of stress regardless of support and low levels of support regardless of stress are associated with development of depression (e.g., Burton, Stice and Seeley, 2004; Wade and Kendler, 2000). The causes of low social support are not fully known, but it is likely that it reflects both effects of depressive (biased) negative cognitions about the actual availability and quality of help available, as well as traits and behaviours described earlier in the chapter that may serve to alienate others (such as insecurity of attachment), resulting in diminished relationships. It is likely that low levels of high quality social relationships are both directly 'depressive' and also provide inad-equate resources with which to combat depression and stressful experiences.

Generation of (interpersonal) stress

'Stress generation' is a term introduced by Hammen (1991b) to indicate the tendency of individuals with histories of depression to have persisting elevated levels of stressful life events when followed up over time. Spe-cifically, the elevations are due to higher frequencies of events to which the individuals have contributed, at least in part, due to their own behaviours and circumstances. Prototypically, such events are frequently, although not invariably, interpersonal in content, including experiences such as conflicts with family members and others, and relationship breakups. Such pile-ups of events tend to promote further depressive episodes, and such patterns portend continuous relatively higher rates of life events over many years (Hammen, Hazel, Brennan and Najman, 2012; Hazel, Hammen, Brennan and Najman, 2008). Unsurprisingly, stress generation is often related to the kinds of enduring traits and interpersonal styles discussed in this chapter: neuro-ticism, excessive reassurance-seeking, attachment insecurity, among other predictors (reviews in Hames et al., 2013; Hammen, 2006; Liu and Alloy, 2010). As an example, in a longitudinal study Eberhart and Hammen (2010) found that interpersonal style variables such as attachment insecurity, dependency and excessive-reassurance seeking predicted the occurrence of romantic relationship stressors, which in turn predicted increases in depressive symptoms. Thus, individuals with depressive vulnerabilities (especially those that affect close relationships) are more likely to react to stressors with depression, but they are also likely to contribute to the occurrence of stressors, thus creating conditions for recurrent and chronic depression.

Summary

- Difficulties in social relationships may be a key element of many depressions: disrupted social connectedness may cause depression, and depression disrupts relationships, potentially causing depression continuation or recurrence.
- Early adverse experiences reflecting disrupted bonds between children and parents appear to be associated with vulnerability for later depression. Early loss, adversity, insecure attachment and difficulties in the parent–child relationship have been linked to vulnerability for later depression.
- Depression affects the family. Not only are the symptoms of depression difficult for other family members to cope with, but also depression takes a toll on marital relationships and parent–child relationships.
- Parental depression is a major risk factor for depression in their offspring, operating through a complex mix of biological (genetic, neurodevelopmental and neuroendocrine) and psychosocial factors (such as parenting difficulties, stressful family life and cognitive and interpersonal dysfunctions).
- The social behaviours of depressed people appear to have a negative impact on others, potentially leading to rejection. While heightened when the person is in a depressed state, some behaviours and traits commonly displayed by depressed people, such as dependency and reassurance-seeking, may persist even when the person is not depressed, creating risk for interpersonal difficulties and further depressive reactions.
- Maladaptive interpersonal styles and vulnerabilities may contribute to the occurrence of stressful life events and chronic difficulties that result in further depression. Furthermore, people who are vulnerable to depression may be deficient in key problem-solving and support-eliciting skills that help them to cope with the effects of stressful life events.

References

Abela, J. R., Hankin, B. L., Haigh, E. A., Adams, P., Vinokuroff, T. and Trayhern, L. (2005). Interpersonal vulnerability to depression in high-risk children: the role of insecure attachment and reassurance seeking. *Journal of Clinical Child and Adolescent Psychology*, 34(1), 182–192.

Accortt, E. E., Cheadle, A. C. and Dunkel Schetter, C. (2015). Prenatal depression and adverse birth outcomes: an updated systematic review. *Maternal and Child Health Journal*, 19(6), 1306–1337.

Alloy, L. B., Abramson, L. Y., Smith, J. M., Gibb, B. E. and Neeren, A. M. (2006). Role of parenting and maltreatment histories in unipolar and bipolar mood disorders: mediation by cognitive vulnerability to depression. *Clinical Child and Family Psychology Review*, 9(1), 23–64.

Barker, E., Copeland, W., Maughan, B., Jaffee, S. and Uher, R. (2012). Relative impact of maternal depression and associated risk factors on offspring psychopathology. *The British Journal of Psychiatry*, 200, 124–129.

Beardslee, W., Solantaus, T., Morgan, B., Gladstone, T. and Kowalenko, N. (2012). Preventive interventions for children of parents with depression: international perspectives. *Medical Journal of Australia, Open 1 Suppl 1*, 23–27.

Beardslee, W. R., Versage, E. M. and Gladstone, T. R. (1998). Children of affectively ill parents: a review of the past 10 years. *Journal of the American Academy of Child and Adolescent Psychiatry*, 37, 1134–1141.

Bifulco, A. T., Brown, G. W. and Harris, T. O. (1987). Childhood loss of parent, lack of adequate parental care and adult depression: a replication. *Journal of Affective Disorders*, 12, 115–128.

Billings, A. G. and Moos, R. H. (1985). Psychosocial processes of remission in unipolar depression: comparing depressed patients with matched community controls. *Journal of Consulting and Clinical Psychology*, 53, 314–325.

Bornstein, R. F. (1992). The dependent personality: developmental, social, and clinical perspectives. *Psychological Bulletin*, 112, 3–23.

Bowlby, J. (1978). Attachment theory and its therapeutic implications. *Adolescent Psychiatry*, 6, 5–33.

Bowlby, J. (1981). Psychoanalysis as a natural science. *International Review of Psychoanalysis*, 8, 243–256.

Bromet, E., Andrade, L., Hwang, I., Sampson, N., Alonso, J., de Girolamo, G., . . . Kessler, R. C. (2011). Cross-national epidemiology of DSM-IV major depressive episode. *BMC Medicine 9*, 90.

Brown, G. W. and Harris, T. O. (1978). *Social origins of depression*. New York: Free Press.

Brumariu, L. E. and Kerns, K. A. (2010). Parent–child attachment and internalising symptoms in childhood and adolescence: a review of empirical findings and future directions. *Development and Psychopathology*, 22(1), 177–203.

Burton, E., Stice, E. and Seeley, J. R. (2004). A prospective test of the stress-buffering model of depression in adolescent girls: no support once again. *Journal of Consulting and Clinical Psychology, 72,* 689–697.

Butzlaff, R. L. and Hooley, J. M. (1998). Expressed emotion and psychiatric relapse. *Archives of General Psychiatry, 55,* 547–552.

Chen, J., Cai, Y., Cong, E., Liu, Y., Gao, J., Li, Y., . . . Flint, J. (2014). Childhood sexual abuse and the development of recurrent major depression in Chinese women. *PLOS One, 9*(1), e87569.

Côté, S., Boivin, M., Liu, X., Nagin, D., Zoccolillo, M. and Tremblay, R. (2009). Depression and anxiety symptoms: onset, developmental course and risk factors during early childhood. *Journal of Child Psychology and Psychiatry, 50,* 1201–1208.

Coyne, J. C. (1976). Depression and the response of others. *Journal of Abnormal Psychology, 85,* 186–193.

Coyne, J. C., Kessler, R. C., Tal, M., Turnbull, J., Wortman, C. B. and Greden, J. F. (1987). Living with a depressed person. *Journal of Consulting and Clinical Psychology, 55*(3), 347–352.

Coyne, J. C., Thompson, R. and Palmer, S. C. (2002). Marital quality, coping with conflict, marital complaints, and affection in couples with a depressed wife. *Journal of Family Psychology, 16,* 26–37.

Cyranowski, J. M., Frank, E., Young, E. and Shear, K. (2000). Adolescent onset of the gender difference in lifetime rates of major depression. *Archives of General Psychiatry, 57,* 21–27.

Dalgard, O. S., Dowrick, C., Lehtinen, V., Vazquez-Barquero, J. L., Casey, P., Wilkinson, G., . . . ODIN Group. (2006). Negative life events, social support and gender difference in depression. *Social Psychiatry and Psychiatric Epidemiology, 41*(6), 444–451.

Davila, J., Karney, B. R., Hall, T. W. and Bradbury, T. N. (2003). Depressive symptoms and marital satisfaction: within-subject associations and the moderating effects of gender and neuroticism. *Journal of Family Psychology, 17,* 557–570.

Downey, G. and Feldman, S. I. (1996). Implications of rejection sensitivity for intimate relationships. *Journal of Personality and Social Psychology, 70*(6), 1327–1343.

Eberhart, N. K. and Hammen, C. L. (2009). Interpersonal predictors of stress generation. *Personality and Social Psychology Bulletin, 35*(5), 544–556.

Eberhart, N. and Hammen, C. (2010). Interpersonal style, stress, and depression: an examination of transactional and diathesis–stress models. *Journal of Social and Clinical Psychology, 29,* 23–38.

Essex, M. J., Boyce, T., Hertzman, C., Lam, L., Armstrong, J., Neumann, S. and Kobor, M. S. (2013). Epigenetic vestiges of early developmental adversity: childhood stress exposure and DNA methylation in adolescence. *Child Development, 84*(1), 58–75.

Fadden, G., Bebbington, P. and Kuipers, L. (1987). Caring and its burdens: a study of the spouses of depressed patients. *British Journal of Psychiatry, 151,* 660–667.

Field, T., Diego, M. and Hernandez-Reif, M. (2006). Prenatal depression effects on the fetus and newborn: a review. *Infant Behaviour and Development*, 29(3), 445–455.

Fletcher, R. J., Feeman, E., Garfield, C. and Vimpani, G. (2011). The effects of early paternal depression on children's development. *Medical Journal of Australia*, 195(11), 685–689.

Gabriel, B., Beach, S. R. and Bodenmann, G. (2010). Depression, marital satisfaction and communication in couples: investigating gender differences. *Behaviour Therapy*, 41(3), 306–316.

Galbaud Du Fort, G., Bland, R. C., Newman, S. C. and Boothroyd, L. J. (1998). Spouse similarity for lifetime psychiatric history in the general population. *Psychological Medicine*, 28(04), 789–802.

Garber, J. and Cole, D. A. (2010). Intergenerational transmission of depression: a launch and grow model of change across adolescence. *Development and Psychopathology*, 22(04), 819–830.

Gladstone, G. and Parker, G. (2006). Is behavioural inhibition a risk factor for depression? *Journal of Affective Disorders*, 95, 85–94.

Goodman, S. (2007). Depression in mothers. *Annual Review of Clinical Psychology*, 3, 107–135.

Goodman, S. and Gotlib, I. (1999). Risk for psychopathology in the children of depressed mothers: a developmental model for understanding mechanisms of transmission. *Psychological Review*, 106, 458–490.

Goodman, S. and Lusby, C. (2014). Early adverse experiences and depression (pp. 220–239). In I. Gotlib and C. Hammen (eds), *Handbook of depression* (3rd edn). New York: Guilford Press.

Goodman, S. H., Rouse, M. H., Connell, A. M., Broth, M. R., Hall, C. M. and Heyward, D. (2011). Maternal depression and child psychopathology: a meta-analytic review. *Clinical Child and Family Psychology Review*, 14, 1–27.

Gotlib, I. H., Lewinsohn, P. M. and Seeley, J. R. (1998). Consequences of depression during adolescence: marital status and marital functioning in early adulthood. *Journal of Abnormal Psychology*, 107(4), 686.

Green, J. G., McLaughlin, K. A., Berglund, P. A., Gruber, M. J., Sampson, N. A., Zaslavsky, A. M. and Kessler, R. C. (2010). Childhood adversities and adult psychiatric disorders in the national comorbidity survey replication I: associations with first onset of DSM-IV disorders. *Archives of General Psychiatry*, 67(2), 113–123.

Halligan, S., Murray, L., Martins, C. and Cooper, P. (2007). Maternal depression and psychiatric outcomes in adolescent offspring: a 13-year longitudinal study. *Journal of Affective Disorders*, 97, 145–154.

Hames, J. L., Hagan, C. R. and Joiner, T. E. (2013). Interpersonal processes in depression. *Annual Review of Clinical Psychology*, 9, 355–377.

Hammen, C. (1991a). *Depression runs in families: the social context of risk and resilience in children of depressed mothers*. New York: Springer-Verlag.

Hammen, C. (1991b). The generation of stress in the course of unipolar depression. *Journal of Abnormal Psychology*, 100, 555–561.

Hammen, C. (2005). Stress and depression. *Annual Review of Clinical Psychology, 1,* 293–319.

Hammen, C. (2006). Stress generation in depression: reflections on origins, research, and future directions. *Journal of Clinical Psychology, 62,* 1065–1082.

Hammen, C. and Brennan, P. (2001). Depressed adolescents of depressed and non-depressed mothers: tests of an interpersonal impairment hypothesis. *Journal of Consulting and Clinical Psychology, 69,* 284–294.

Hammen, C. and Brennan, P. (2002). Interpersonal dysfunction in depressed women: impairments independent of depressive symptoms. *Journal of Affective Disorders, 72,* 145–156.

Hammen, C. and Brennan, P. (2016). *Continuity of stress and depression in 30 years of follow-up.* Association for Behavioural and Cognitive Therapies, New York.

Hammen, C., Brennan, P., Keenan-Miller, D. and Herr, N. (2008). Early onset recurrent subtype of adolescent depression: clinical and psychosocial correlates. *Journal of Child Psychology and Psychiatry, 49,* 433–440.

Hammen, C., Hazel, N., Brennan, P. and Najman, J. (2012). Intergenerational transmission and continuity of stress and depression: depressed women and their offspring in 20 years of follow-up. *Psychological Medicine, 42,* 931–942.

Hammen, C., Henry, R. and Daley, S. E. (2000). Depression and sensitisation to stressors among young women as a function of childhood adversity. *Journal of Consulting and Clinical Psychology, 68*(5), 782–787.

Hammen, C. L. and Peters, S. D. (1978). Interpersonal consequences of depression: responses to men and women enacting a depressed role. *Journal of Abnormal Psychology, 87,* 322–332.

Hammen, C., Shih, J. and Brennan, P. (2004). Intergenerational transmission of depression: test of an interpersonal stress model in a community sample. *Journal of Consulting and Clinical Psychology, 72,* 511–522.

Hazel, N., Hammen, C., Brennan, P. and Najman, J. (2008). Early childhood adversity and adolescent depression: mediating role of continued stress. *Psychological Medicine, 38,* 581–589.

Holt-Lunstad, J., Smith, T. B. and Layton, J. B. (2010). Social relationships and mortality risk: a meta-analytic review. *PLOS Medicine, 7*(7), e1000316.

Hooley, J. M., Gruber, S. A., Scott, L. A., Hiller, J. B. and Yurgelun-Todd, D. A. (2005). Activation in dorsolateral prefrontal cortex in response to maternal criticism and praise in recovered depressed and healthy control participants. *Biological Psychiatry, 57,* 809–812.

Joiner, T. E. and Metalsky, G. I. (2001). Excessive reassurance seeking: delineating a risk factor involved in the development of depressive symptoms. *Psychological Science, 12*(5), 371–378.

Kane, P. and Garber, J. (2004). The relations among depression in fathers, children's psychopathology, and father-child conflict: a meta-analysis. *Clinical Psychology Review, 24,* 339–360.

Kaslow, N. J., Deering, C. G. and Racusin, G. R. (1994). Depressed children and their families. *Clinical Psychology Review*, *14*, 39–59.

Katz, S., Conway, C., Hammen, C., Brennan, P. and Najman, J. (2011). Childhood social withdrawal, interpersonal impairment, and young adult depression: a mediational model. *Journal of Abnormal Child Psychology*, *39*(8), 1227–1238.

Keenan-Miller, D., Hammen, C. and Brennan, P. (2007). Adolescent psychosocial risk factors for severe intimate partner violence in young adulthood. *Journal of Consulting and Clinical Psychology*, *75*, 456–463.

Keitner, G. I., Ryan, C. E., Miller, I. W., Kohn, R., Bishop, D. S. and Epstein, N. B. (1995). Role of the family in recovery and major depression. *American Journal of Psychiatry*, *152*, 1002–1008.

Keitner, G. I., Ryan, C. E., Miller, I. W. and Zlotnick, C. (1997). Psychosocial factors and the long-term course of major depression. *Journal of Affective Disorders*, *44*, 57–67.

Kendler, K. S. and Aggen, S. H. (2014). Clarifying the causal relationship in women between childhood sexual abuse and lifetime major depression. *Psychological Medicine*, *44*(06), 1213–1221.

Kendler, K. S., Gardner, C. O. and Prescott, C. A. (2002). Toward a comprehensive developmental model for major depression in women. *American Journal of Psychiatry*, *159*, 1133–1145.

Kendler, K. S., Gardner, C. O. and Prescott, C. A. (2006). Toward a comprehensive developmental model for major depression in men. *American Journal of Psychiatry*, *163*, 115–124.

Kendler, K. S., Gatz, M., Gardner, C. O. and Pedersen, N. L. (2006). A Swedish national twin study of lifetime major depression. *American Journal of Psychiatry*, *163*(1), 109–114.

Kendler, K. S., Myers, J. and Prescott, C. A. (2005). Sex differences in the relationship between social support and risk for major depression: a longitudinal study of opposite-sex twin pairs. *American Journal of Psychiatry*, *162*(2), 250–256.

Kendler, K. S., Sheth, K., Gardner, C. O. and Prescott, C. A. (2002). Childhood parental loss and risk for first-onset of major depression and alcohol dependence: the time-decay of risk and sex differences. *Psychological Medicine*, *32*, 1187–1194.

Kessler, R. C., McLaughlin, K. A., Green, J. G., Gruber, M. J., Sampson, N. A., Zaslavsky, A. M., . . . Williams, D. (2010). Childhood adversities and adult psychopathology in the WHO World Mental Health Surveys. *The British Journal of Psychiatry*, *197*(5), 378–385.

Klein, D. N., Kotov, R. and Bufferd, S. J. (2011). Personality and depression: explanatory models and review of the evidence. *Annual Review of Clinical Psychology*, *7*, 269.

Kochel, K. P., Ladd, G. W. and Rudolph, K. D. (2012). Longitudinal associations among youth depressive symptoms, peer victimisation, and low peer acceptance: an interpersonal process perspective. *Child Development*, *83*(2), 637–650.

Kotov, R., Gamez, W., Schmidt, F. and Watson, D. (2010). Linking 'big' personality traits to anxiety, depressive, and substance use disorders: a meta-analysis. *Psychological Bulletin*, 136(5), 768–821.

Lampard, A. M., Franckle, R. L. and Davison, K. K. (2014). Maternal depression and childhood obesity: a systematic review. *Preventive Medicine*, 59, 60–67.

Lee, A. and Hankin, B. L. (2009). Insecure attachment, dysfunctional attitudes, and low self-esteem predicting prospective symptoms of depression and anxiety during adolescence. *Journal of Clinical Child and Adolescent Psychology*, 38(2), 219–231.

Lindert, J., von Ehrenstein, O. S., Grashow, R., Gal, G., Braehler, E. and Weisskopf, M. G. (2014). Sexual and physical abuse in childhood is associated with depression and anxiety over the life course: systematic review and meta-analysis. *International Journal of Public Health*, 59(2), 359–372.

Liu, Y. L. (2003). The mediators between parenting and adolescent depressive symptoms: dysfunctional attitudes and self-worth. *International Journal of Psychology*, 38(2), 91–100.

Liu, R. T. and Alloy, L. B. (2010). Stress generation in depression: a systematic review of the empirical literature and recommendations for future study. *Clinical Psychology Review*, 30(5), 582–593.

Lloyd, C. (1980). Life events and depressive disorders reviewed: II. Events as precipitating factors. *Archives of General Psychiatry*, 37, 541–548.

Lovejoy, C. M., Graczyk, P. A., O'Hare, E. and Neuman, G. (2000). Maternal depression and parenting behaviour: a meta-analytic review. *Clinical Psychology Review*, 20, 561–592.

Luby, J. L., Gaffrey, M. S., Tillman, R., April, L. M. and Belden, A. C. (2014). Trajectories of preschool disorders to full DSM depression at school age and early adolescence: continuity of preschool depression. *American Journal of Psychiatry*, 171, 768–776.

Madigan, S., Atkinson, L., Laurin, K. and Benoit, D. (2013). Attachment and internalising behaviour in early childhood: a meta-analysis. *Developmental Psychology*, 49(4), 672–689.

Mathews, C. A. and Reus, V. I. (2001). Assortative mating in the affective disorders: a systematic review and meta-analysis. *Comprehensive Psychiatry*, 42, 257–262.

McLaughlin, K. A., Conron, K. J., Koenen, K. C. and Gilman, S. E. (2010). Childhood adversity, adult stressful life events, and risk of past-year psychiatric disorder: a test of the stress sensitisation hypothesis in a population-based sample of adults. *Psychological Medicine*, 40(10), 1647–1658.

McLaughlin, K. A., Green, J. G., Gruber, M. J., Sampson, N. A., Zaslavsky, A. M. and Kessler, R. C. (2012). Childhood adversities and first onset of psychiatric disorders in a national sample of US adolescents. *Archives of General Psychiatry*, 69(11), 1151–1160.

Najman, J. M., Khatun, M., Mamun, A., Clavarino, A., Williams, G. M., Scott, J., . . . Alati, R. (2014). Does depression experienced by mothers leads to a decline in marital quality: a 21-year longitudinal study. *Social Psychiatry and Psychiatric Epidemiology*, *49*(1), 121–132.

Nanni, V., Uher, R. and Danese, A. (2012). Childhood maltreatment predicts unfavorable course of illness and treatment outcome in depression: a meta-analysis. *American Journal of Psychiatry*, *169*, 141–151.

NICHD Early Child Care Research Network (1999). Chronicity of maternal depressive symptoms, maternal sensitivity, and child functioning at 36 months. *Developmental Psychology*, *35*, 1297–1310.

Nolen-Hoeksema, S. (2001). Gender differences in depression. *Current Directions in Psychological Science*, *10*(5), 173–176.

Nordsletten, A. E., Larsson, H., Crowley, J. J., Almqvist, C., Lichtenstein, P. and Mataix-Cols, D. (2016). Patterns of nonrandom mating within and across 11 major psychiatric disorders. *JAMA Psychiatry*, *73*(4), 354–361.

O'Hara, M. and McCabe, J. (2013). Postpartum depression: current status and future directions. *Annual Review of Clinical Psychology*, *9*, 379–407.

Parker, G. (1983). Parental 'affectionless control' as an antecedent to adult depression: a risk factor delineated. *Archives of General Psychiatry*, *40*(9), 956–960.

Parker, G. and Gladstone, G. (1996). Parental characteristics as influences on adjustment in adulthood. In G. R. Pierce, B. R. Sarason and I. G. Sarason (eds), *Handbook of Social Support and the Family* (pp. 195–218). New York: Plenum Press.

Prinstein, M. J., Borelli, J. L., Cheah, C. S., Simon, V. A. and Aikins, J. W. (2005). Adolescent girls' interpersonal vulnerability to depressive symptoms: a longitudinal examination of reassurance-seeking and peer relationships. *Journal of Abnormal Psychology*, *114*(4), 676.

Ravitz, P., Maunder, R., Hunter, J., Sthankiya, B. and Lancee, W. (2010). Adult attachment measures: a 25-year review. *Journal of Psychosomatic Research*, *69*(4), 419–432.

Rao, U., Hammen, C. and Daley, S. (1999). Continuity of depression during the transition to adulthood: a 5-year longitudinal study of young women. *Journal of the American Academy of Child and Adolescent Psychiatry*, *38*, 908–915.

Rehman, U. S., Gollan, J. and Mortimer, A. R. (2008). The marital context of depression: research, limitations, and new directions. *Clinical Psychology Review*, *28*(2), 179–198.

Reising, M., Watson, K., Hardcastle, E., Merchant, M., Roberts, L., Forehand, R. and Compas, B. (2013). Parental depression and economic disadvantage: the role of parenting in associations with internalising and externalising symptoms in children and adolescents. *Journal of Child and Family Studies*, *22*, 335–343.

Rice, F., Sellers, R., Hammerton, G., Eyre, O., Bevan-Jones, R., Thapar, A. K., . . . Thapar, A. (2017). Antecedents of new-onset major depressive disorder in adolescence: a longitudinal familial high-risk study. *JAMA Psychiatry*, *74*, 153–160.

Sanathara, V. A., Gardner, C. O., Prescott, C. A. and Kendler, K. S. (2003). Interpersonal dependence and major depression: aetiological inter-relationship and gender differences. *Psychological Medicine*, *33*, 927–931.

Segrin, C. (2000). Social skills deficits associated with depression. *Clinical Psychology Review, 20,* 379–403.

Segrin, C. and Abramson, L. Y. (1994). Negative reactions to depressive behaviours: a communication theories analysis. *Journal of Abnormal Psychology, 103,* 655–668.

Shih, J. H. (2006). Sex differences in stress generation: An examination of sociotropy/autonomy, stress, and depressive symptoms. *Personality and Social Psychology Bulletin, 32*(4), 434–446.

Shih, J. H., Eberhart, N., Hammen, C. and Brennan, P. A. (2006). Differential exposure and reactivity to interpersonal stress predict sex differences in adolescent depression. *Journal of Clinical Child and Adolescent Psychology, 35,* 103–115.

Starr, L. R. and Davila, J. (2008). Excessive reassurance seeking, depression, and interpersonal rejection: a meta-analytic review. *Journal of Abnormal Psychology, 117*(4), 762–775.

Starr, L. R., Hammen, C., Conway, C. C., Raposa, E. and Brennan, P. A. (2014). Sensitising effect of early adversity on depressive reactions to later proximal stress: moderation by polymorphisms in serotonin transporter and corticotropin releasing hormone receptor genes in a 20-year longitudinal study. *Development and Psychopathology, 26,* 1241–1254.

Stein, A., Pearson, R., Goodman, S., Rapa, E., Rahman, A., McCallum, M., . . . Pariante, C. (2014). Effects of perinatal mental disorders on the fetus and child. *The Lancet, 384,* 1800–1819.

Stephens, R. S., Hokanson, J. E. and Welker, R. A. (1987). Responses to depressed interpersonal behaviour: mixed reactions in a helping role. *Journal of Personality and Social Psychology, 52,* 1274–1282.

Stewart, J. G. and Harkness, K. L. (2015). The interpersonal toxicity of excessive reassurance-seeking: evidence from a longitudinal study of romantic relationships. *Journal of Social and Clinical Psychology, 34*(5), 392–410.

Strack, S. and Coyne, J. C. (1983). Social confirmation of dysphoria: shared and private reactions to depression. *Journal of Personality and Social Psychology, 44,* 798–806.

Stroud, C. B., Sosoo, E. E. and Wilson, S. (2015). Normal personality traits, rumination and stress generation among early adolescent girls. *Journal of Research in Personality, 57,* 131–142.

Surkan, P., Kennedy, C., Hurley, K. and Black, M. (2011). Maternal depression and early childhood growth in developing countries: systematic review and meta-analysis. *Bulletin of the World Health Organization, 287,* 607–615.

Tang, A., Reeb-Sutherland, B., Romeo, R. and McEwen, B. (2014). On the causes of early life experience effects: evaluating the role of mom. *Frontiers of Neuroendocrinology, 35,* 245–251.

Tse, W. S. and Bond, A. J. (2004). The impact of depression on social skills. *The Journal of Nervous and Mental Disease, 192,* 260–268.

Wachs, T., Black, M. and Engle, P. (2009). Maternal depression: a global threat to children's health, development, and behaviour and to human rights. *Child Development Perspectives, 3,* 51–59.

Wade, T. D. and Kendler, K. S. (2000). Absence of interactions between social support and stressful life events in the prediction of major depression and depressive symptomatology in women. *Psychological Medicine, 30*, 965–974.

Wang, Y. and Dix, T. (2013). Patterns of depressive parenting: why they occur and their role in early developmental risk. *Journal of Family Psychology, 27*, 884–895.

Weich, S., Patterson, J., Shaw, R. and Stewart-Brown, S. (2009). Family relationships in childhood and common psychiatric disorders in later life: systematic review of prospective studies. *The British Journal of Psychiatry, 194*(5), 392–398.

Weissman, M. M., Berry, O. O., Warner, V., Gameroff, M. J., Skipper, J., Talati, A., . . . Wickramaratne, P. (2016). A 30-year study of 3 generations at high risk and low risk for depression. *JAMA Psychiatry, 73*(9), 970–977.

Weissman, M. M. and Paykel, E. S. (1974). *The depressed woman: a study of social relationships*. Oxford: University Chicago Press.

Weissman, M. M., Wickramaratne, P., Nomura, Y., Warner, V., Pilowsky, D. and Verdeli, H. (2006). Offspring of depressed parents: 20 years later. *American Journal of Psychiatry, 163*, 1001–1008.

Whisman, M. A. (2001). The association between depression and marital dissatisfaction. In S. Beach (ed.), *Marital and family processes in depression: a scientific approach* (pp. 3–24). Washington, DC: American Psychological Association.

Whisman, M. A. (2007). Marital distress and DSM-IV psychiatric disorders in a population-based national survey. *Journal of Abnormal Psychology, 116*(3), 638–643.

Whisman, M. A. and Bruce, M. L. (1999). Marital dissatisfaction and incidence of major depressive episode in a community sample. *Journal of Abnormal Psychology, 108*, 674–678.

Whisman, M. A., Uebelacker, L. A. and Weinstock, L. M. (2004). Psychopathology and marital satisfaction: the importance of evaluating both partners. *Journal of Consulting and Clinical Psychology, 72*, 830–838.

Wilson, S. and Durbin, C. E. (2010). Effects of paternal depression on fathers' parenting behaviours: a meta-analytic review. *Clinical Psychology Review, 30*(2), 167–180.

Zlotnick, C., Kohn, R., Keitner, G. and Della Grotta, S. A. (2000). The relationship between quality of interpersonal relationships and major depressive disorder: findings from the National Comorbidity Survey. *Journal of Affective Disorders, 59*, 205–215.

7

Biological treatment
of depression

Stephanie experienced two bouts of major depression that each lasted for about six months. During one episode she sought counselling, but discussions of her life difficulties didn't seem to relieve the symptoms of depression, and she dragged herself through the bleak days and endless nights until the depression just seemed to wear away. Recently, when she began to sink into yet another depressive episode, she sought treatment from a medical doctor who prescribed a common antidepressant medication. Within a week her energy improved and she slept more soundly, and within two weeks her mood was definitely better and she began to feel able to face some of the difficult personal events that had precipitated the depression.

As we discuss in this chapter, there are several well-established biological interventions as well as several more experimental approaches to treatment. This chapter discusses antidepressant medications, omega-3 fatty acids, electroconvulsive therapy (ECT), transcranial magnetic stimulation (TMS), light therapy, sleep deprivation and physical exercise.

Comment on treatment of depression

Before discussing biological or psychotherapy approaches to treating depression, it is important to emphasise a singular fact about treatment in general. The majority of individuals with major depression or persistent depressive disorder do not receive treatment for their condition, either because they do not seek out help, or because it remains undetected, or because treatment is not available or not offered appropriately. For example, of those screening positive for depression (8 per cent) in a large recent survey of US households (46,417 people), only 28.7 per cent received any treatment for depression (Olfson, Blanco and Marcus, 2016).

Similarly, in the UK, it is estimated that of the 130 cases of depression per 1,000 people, only 80 will consult their general practitioner (GP), of whom approximately 49 are not recognised as being depressed on a single appointment, probably because the patient presents with a physical complaint and does not consider themselves mentally unwell. Of those recognised as depressed, 80 per cent are treated in primary care and only 20–25 per cent are referred for specialist mental health services. That is, only around 20 per cent of those with depression will end up receiving treatment.

Furthermore, there is substantial delay between the first onset of depression and initial help seeking, with the delay for those seeking help for mood disorders ranging from six to eight years from initial onset within the National Comorbidity Survey replication (Wang et al., 2005). Unfortunately, as we have seen, the consequences of depression are extremely negative in terms of impaired functioning, reduced health and impact on others. Moreover, individuals whose depression goes unrecognised and untreated may actually burden the primary care sector and inflate health care costs for medical problems (Simon, Ormel, Vonkorff and Barlow, 1995).

The reasons for failure to seek treatment for depression are numerous. Depression is often unrecognised as such by the individual, who might attribute symptoms to medical conditions or to stress and circumstances – leading either to seeking medical treatment or to the expectation that the symptoms are simply an aspect of the stress to be endured. The US National Co-morbidity Survey Replication included questions asking participants their reasons for not seeking treatment (Mojtabai et al., 2011). The most common reason was a low perceived need for any treatment, reported by 44.8 per cent of respondents with a disorder who did not seek treatment, with this more common among those with mild relative to moderate or severe disorders.

Among those who recognised a need, a desire to handle the problem on one's own was the most common reason for not seeking treatment (72.6 per cent) and for dropping out of treatment (42.2 per cent). Alternatively, people may not think anyone can help, or think that the problem will improve by itself or be too embarrassed to discuss it with anyone. Western culture particularly emphasises such self-reliance, and many with depression feel guilty about 'weakness' and forego seeking help because they believe depression requires firmer will or personal effort – 'stiff upper lip' and so forth. Although women are given greater latitude in help-seeking, both women and men typically believe that depression is under their own control (if only they were stronger) or that with the help of friends and family they will get by. An additional factor may be lack of resources with disparities in mental health services in the US disadvantaging those with low income and lack of insurance (e.g., Roll, Kennedy, Tran and Howell, 2013), or negative expectations about the possible outcome of treatment even if it is sought. Depression itself magnifies pessimistic beliefs that treatment cannot help.

Cultural barriers including general stigma towards mental illness and concerns about the implications of a mental health diagnosis on employment, as well as a lack of adaptation of treatment services to reflect cultural and linguistic differences among different ethnic groups and migrant status, can further limit treatment uptake (e.g., Lindert, Schouler-Ocak, Heinz and Priebe, 2008; Manseau and Case, 2014).

As well as the willingness of individuals to seek help, the availability of relevant treatment services is a factor in the proportion of individuals with depression able to access appropriate treatment. In many Western healthcare systems, mental health is a Cinderella service, receiving significantly less funding than physical health compared to their relative prevalence and impact. In the UK, which has experienced a significant increase in treatment capacity for depression through the growth of Improving Access to Psychological Treatments services within the National Health Service, it is estimated that only 15 per cent of relevant patients with depression or anxiety receive specialist therapy.

Antidepressant medications

Antidepressants are now the most commonly prescribed class of medications in the US, with their rates doubling between 1995–2005, with estimates that approximately 10 per cent of the population (27 million people) receive antidepressants (Olfson and Marcus, 2009). There has also been a significant rise in the use of antidepressants in other developed countries, for example, the United Kingdom, where the number of antidepressants prescribed in primary care almost doubled between 1993 to 2005 (Moore et al., 2009). The surge in antidepressant use appears to be associated with a number of factors. Positively, increased prescription may reflect the development of new drugs, increased awareness of their potential usefulness and active efforts to increase the detection of depression in primary care. Less positively, increased use of antidepressants may reflect more direct marketing to the public in the US, and, potentially, their prescription for distress more broadly than just for diagnostic major depression (Olfson et al., 2016).

Despite their increased use, however, antidepressants continue to be *underutilised* among depressed outpatients compared with the frequency of depressive disorders, according to large-scale surveys of patients in treatment. For example, a US household survey study found that less than one third of those screening for depression receive treatment (Olfson et al., 2016), replicating earlier surveys (Wang et al., 2005). Moreover, even when antidepressants are prescribed for patients, they are often administered in sub-therapeutic dosages. Analysis of treatment content in comparison to published treatment guidelines has found that no more than one third of patients in treatment receive even minimally acceptable treatment. For example, only 32 per cent of patients in UK primary care were prescribed a type of antidepressant medication (selective serotonin re-uptake inhibitors, SSRIs) with an adequate dose for at least three months, consistent with treatment recommendations (Dunn, Donoghue, Ozminkowski, Stephenson and Hylan, 1999).

Like many drugs used in the treatment of mental disorders, the discovery of antidepressant medications was partly fortuitous, an observed side effect of drugs used to treat medical conditions. Medications that were known to deplete certain neurotransmitters in the brain appeared to cause depression, while those that increased specific neurotransmitters reduced depression. These early effects were focused largely on the monoamine neurotransmitters norepinephrine (noradrenaline), dopamine and serotonin. In the 1950s, two classes of medications came to be introduced into widespread use, the *tricyclic antidepressants* (TCAs, named for their chemical structure) and the *monoamine oxidase inhibitors (MAOIs)*. Since 1987, a second generation of antidepressants with a different chemical structure has been developed. The most popular of these newer antidepressants are the *selective serotonin reuptake inhibitors (SSRIs)*, such as fluoxetine (Prozac), citalopram (Celexa), escitalopram (Lexapro), sertraline (Zoloft), which block the presynaptic reuptake of serotonin, thereby increasing its availability to the postsynaptic neuron and enhancing serotonergic function.

There are also a number of novel antidepressants with unique action on multiple neurotransmitters (e.g., Bupropion, Venlafaxine, Nefazodone). Two recently introduced antidepressants are agomelatine, which uniquely is an agonist for melatonin, and vortioxetine, an SSRI that targets additional serotonin related receptors (5HT1A, 5HT7).

While most antidepressant medications have a similar action to the SSRIs and target the monoamine transmitters, there has been a big push to develop new products in recognition of the limited benefit of existing medications and the large market of people who experience depression. Because of the extensive evidence of dysfunctional HPA responses to stress in depression, one approach is to develop medications to regulate the HPA response. A recent experimental treatment is the use of antiglucocorticoid drugs as antidepressants. Antiglucocorticoid drugs improve the regulation of the HPA stress response, in particular by reducing the elevated levels of the stress hormone cortisol that are found in depression (see Chapter 4) (Wolkowitz et al., 1999). Although initial evidence suggested that antiglucocorticoid drugs may have potential as an adjunct to other antidepressants (Jahn et al., 2004) and as a treatment for psychotic depression (DeBattista et al., 2006), a recent large-scale clinical trial found no benefit of adding antiglucocorticoid drugs to existing antidepressant treatment for treatment-resistant depression (McAllister-Williams et al., 2016). Further, a systematic review of nine trials suggested that the findings to date were not conclusive (Gallagher et al., 2008).

Another alternative approach builds on emerging evidence that the glutamatergic system may be involved in mood disorders. Both the amino acid glutamate and gamma-aminobutyric acid (GABA) are identified as important neurotransmitters in many synapses. Key among medications targeting this system is ketamine, originally used as an anaesthetic medication, which blocks the glutamate N-methyl-d-aspartate (NMDA) receptor (Krystal, Sanacora and Duman, 2013). Of greatest interest is that ketamine provides proof-of-principle that it is possible to produce a rapid antidepressant response within hours rather than weeks, from a single dose, with benefit persisting for a week (e.g., trials by Zarate et al., 2006; Murrough et al., 2013; meta-analysis of trials by McGirr, Berlim, Bond, Fleck, Yatham and Lam, 2015; Romeo, Choucha, Fossati and Rotge, 2015). However, ketamine remains an experimental treatment that is not approved by the US Food and Drug Administration (FDA) for treating mood disorders. Critically, its effects are short-lived, and there are concerns about the use of repeated doses because of potential long-term side effects and the risk for abuse, given that its 'trance-like' and dissociative qualities have led to ketamine being used as a recreational drug.

Table 7.1 lists several of more than 20 currently available antidepressants.

Table 7.1 Selected antidepressant medications: chemical and brand names

Generic (chemical) name	Brand name
Tricyclic Antidepressants	
Imipramine	Tofranil
Amitriptyline	Elavil
Clomipramine	Anafranil
Desipramine	Norpramin
Monoamine oxidase inhibitors	
Phenelzine	Nardil
Isocarboxazid	Marplan
Selective serotonin reuptake inhibitors	
Fluoxetine	Prozac
Sertraline	Zoloft
Paroxetine	Paxil
Citalopram	Celexa
'Novel' antidepressants	
Buproprion	Wellbutrin
Nefazodone	Serzone
Venlafaxine	Effexor

Use of antidepressants

Antidepressants are especially recommended for moderate-to-severe levels of depression. Some medications are initially taken at low dosages and build up to a therapeutic level over time adjusted for the person's needs and reactions, while some of the newer drugs have a standard dosage for everyone that starts immediately. Although it was previously judged that the positive effects of antidepressants are not seen for at least two weeks, more recent reviews suggest that symptomatic improvement occurs during the first one to two weeks of treatment, and that symptoms continue to improve over the next six weeks but at a decreasing rate (Taylor, Freemantle, Geddes and Bhagwagar, 2006). For example, in one trial, over 50 per cent of all eventual responders to fluoxetine responded within the first two weeks, over 75 per cent started to respond by week 4, and 90 per cent responded by week 6 (Nierenberg et al., 2000). Given the cumulative response to antidepressants over the first two–six weeks, depressed people need to be informed that they will not recover immediately. Furthermore, these findings suggest that if a patient has not responded within four–eight weeks, she is unlikely to respond to continuation of that antidepressant at the same dose.

The treatment of current symptoms is referred to as *acute* treatment, but it is only one phase of the recommended course. Once symptoms have diminished, *continuation* treatment is recommended for at least six–nine months in order to prevent relapse of the current episode, and then the medication may be discontinued by tapering off the dosage (as abrupt discontinuation may cause unpleasant side effects). For example, a meta-analysis of 31 trials found that continuation treatment with antidepressants over six–36 months reduced the risk of relapse from 41 per cent to 18 per cent (Geddes et al., 2003).

A third phase of medication treatment, called *maintenance*, is strongly recommended for individuals who have a history of recurrent episodes of depression. In contrast to the generally agreed period of treatment for continuation, there is less agreement on the ideal duration of maintenance treatment, as no long-term studies have compared the relative efficacy of different durations of maintenance in preventing recurrence, leaving open the question of whether medications should be prescribed indefinitely for those at risk for recurrent depression. Meta-analyses suggest that antidepressants maintained for one year significantly reduced the odds of relapse by at least two thirds relative to placebo (Glue, Donovan, Kolluri and Emir, 2010; Kaymaz, van Os, Loonen and Nolen, 2008), although benefits are less for patients with a history of recurrent episodes. Clinical recommendations are that individuals with a history of recurrent depression should maintain their antidepressant regime, if initially effective, for at least one year, and perhaps two years (Cleare et al., 2015).

It is important to note that the evidence that maintenance antidepressant treatment significantly reduces the risk of relapse comes almost entirely from studies in secondary and tertiary specialist care settings, where patients tend to present with more severe depression than is found in primary care settings (Geddes et al., 2003; Glue et al., 2010; Kaymaz et al., 2008). This has led to concerns that patients in primary care settings may unnecessarily be being prescribed antidepressant medication for long periods. For example, a systematic review of pharmacological and psychological interventions for preventing relapse or recurrence of depression in adults with depression in primary care only found three small studies, none of which showed a statistically significant benefit (Gili, Vicens, Roca, Andersen and McMillan, 2015). There is therefore limited evidence to inform relapse or recurrence prevention strategies in primary care.

Mechanisms of action

The tricyclic drugs have their effects in complex ways, various ones altering functions of norepinephrine (noradrenaline), dopamine, serotonin and related neurotransmitter systems. Depending on their specific mechanisms, they may bind to a receptor site in specific neurons, achieving effects by causing a reaction directly, or by blocking the effects of naturally occurring substances, for example, the MAOIs block the effects of substances that break down the monoamine neurotransmitters, increasing their availability. Alternatively, antidepressant medications may cause the release of more of a particular neurotransmitter, or by blocking the reuptake of a neurotransmitter back into the neuron may thereby increase the amount of the neurotransmitter that is available in the synapse. In some cases, the medication alters the neurotransmitter receptors, by changing their sensitivity or their numbers. The older tricyclic medications often had effects on several different neurotransmitters, as do several of the novel antidepressants, whereas the SSRIs tend to be more selective, only acting on serotonin.

However, it is now clear that the therapeutic effects of antidepressants are not simply due to increasing levels of neurotransmitter as originally hypothesised because the effects on neurotransmitter levels are relatively immediate after the first dose of antidepressant, whereas patients do not show any therapeutic benefit for one to two weeks. One proposed mechanism of antidepressant action is that increased levels of neurotransmitters in the synapse activate an intracellular signalling cascade, which ultimately influences neurogenesis, which is the ability of neurons in key brain areas to grow and form new connections. The neurotransmitters activate secondary messenger proteins and transcription factors (e.g., cAMP response element binding protein, CREB), which in turn regulate the expression of specific target genes, including the increased expression of neurotrophic factors (e.g., brain derived neurotrophic factor, BDNF) necessary for the survival, differentiation, growth and function of particular neurons (Duman, Heninger and Nestler, 1997; Duman and Monteggia, 2006).

In animal models, the expression of neurotrophic factors in key limbic brain regions implicated in depression (e.g., hippocampus, amygdala) is increased by the administration of antidepressants at a time course consistent with that required for the observed antidepressant effect in humans (Hashimoto, Shimizu and Iyo, 2004) and appears necessary for the behavioural effects of antidepressants (Santarelli et al., 2003). Furthermore, antidepressant medications, ECT, TMS and exercise all increase the up-regulation of BDNF, whereas adult depression is associated with reduced BDNF, whether assessed through the analysis of post-mortem hippocampus or through blood serum levels in antidepressant-naïve patients. A meta-analysis of 1,000s of patients found that BDNF concentrations were lower in antidepressant-free patients with depression relative to antidepressant-treated patients and healthy controls (Molendijk et al., 2014).

It has been proposed that it may not be neurogenesis per se but rather the increase in neuronal plasticity, that is, the growth, formation and remodelling of synaptic connections, underlying learning and memory, that is critical to the effects of antidepressants (Castren, 2013; Castren and Rantamaki, 2010; Maya-Vetencourt et al., 2008; McEwen, 2012). For example, in rat models, the therapeutic benefits of antidepressants are maintained even when neurogenesis is blocked, suggesting that the reestablishment of neuronal plasticity in the hippocampus and prefrontal cortex may underlie the treatment benefit (Bessa et al., 2009). We know that exposure to stress decreases the ability to learn from the environment, and, in contrast, it is proposed that antidepressants act to facilitate the effect of environmental impacts on modifying neuronal networks so that they are better adapted to the environment.

In parallel, an alternative account of the effect of antidepressants is a neuropsychological one, which proposes that antidepressants work by altering some of the cognitive biases found in depression (see Chapter 5), potentially involving neurogenesis or neuroplasticity (Harmer and Cowen, 2013; Harmer, Hill, Taylor, Cowen and Goodwin, 2003; Harmer et al., 2009). For example, a number of studies have shown that acute administration of antidepressants ameliorates the negative cognitive biases typically found in patients with depression, such as reduced recognition of positive facial expressions and slower endorsement and recall of positive self-related adjectives, relative to patients who are administered placebo (Harmer et al., 2009). These changes occur well before clinical improvement in symptoms and mood, leading to the hypothesis that it takes time for the change in bias induced by antidepressants to lead to mood changes, by learning new more positive emotional associations through several weeks of interacting with the environment with the relatively more positive cognitive bias.

Effectiveness of antidepressants

All of the current antidepressant medications are about equally effective, and the efficacy of antidepressants are broadly on a par with treatments used in medicine as a whole (Leucht, Hierl, Kissling, Dold and Davis, 2012). A network meta-analysis of 117 randomised control trials (RCTs) that compared at least two of 12 new-generation antidepressants (mainly SSRIs) suggested that escitalopram and sertraline had the highest response rates coupled with fewer discontinuations than other medications (Cipriani et al., 2009). A subsequent meta-analysis assessed 234 studies of second-generation antidepressants, of which 118 were head-to-head comparisons (Gartlehner et al., 2011) and found no significant differences between different drugs.

Therefore, the consideration of which drug to take depends on previous response to medications, the type of symptoms displayed, life circumstances, as well as side effects. *Individuals* may respond significantly better to one than another, and therefore sometimes a period of trial-and-error is needed to find an effective drug.

How effective are antidepressants in the treatment of acute depression?

Previous reviews have indicated a substantial benefit of antidepressants relative to placebo in controlled *blind* trials. For example, where treatment response is defined as 50 per cent or more decrease in symptoms on a clinical interview, response rates for a single antidepressant are on average 60–70 per cent versus 30 per cent for placebo. However, more recent reviews have suggested a weaker although still significant effect, as a consequence of identifying unpublished trials that had less positive findings. For example, a study of placebo-controlled RCTs of antidepressants that had been registered with the US FDA, a statutory requirement for conducting such trials, found that 31 per cent of studies, mainly those with negative findings were not published (Turner, Matthews, Linardatos, Tell and Rosenthal, 2008). In the published literature, 94 per cent of trials had positive findings, whereas across all registered trials only 51 per cent were positive, leading to an overestimation of the benefits of antidepressants relative to pill placebo. Using the FDA data, a meta-analysis suggested that antidepressants only outperformed placebo in the most severely depressed patients (Kirsch et al., 2008). This study in turn has been criticised for selective reporting, and a re-analysis of the same data concluded that there is a genuine drug effect at all levels of severity, whereas the effect of placebo is only stronger for milder depression (Fountoulakis, Veroniki, Siamouli and Moller, 2013). In a meta-analysis of 56 published and unpublished trials submitted for marketing approval in Sweden, response rates for antidepressants were 47 per cent relative to 32 per cent for placebo (Melander, Salmonson, Abadie and van Zwieten-Boot, 2008).

The priority of antidepressant treatment is to achieve full remission from the episode of depression, defined as minimal levels of symptoms on clinical interview, as even patients who respond may still have significant residual symptoms, which in turn are associated with greater functional disability and increased risk of relapse (Hardeveld, Spijker, De Graaf, Nolen and Beekman, 2010; Judd et al., 1998; Paykel et al., 1995). Short-term treatment produces remission rates of 35–50 per cent with antidepressants, relative to 25–35 per cent for placebo (Gibbons, Hur, Brown, Davis and Mann, 2012), with approximately one third of patients still having residual symptoms of depression after acute treatment (Paykel et al., 1995). Furthermore, 30–40 per cent of patients show no or only partial response to antidepressants (Hirschfeld et al., 2002).

Therefore, an important issue concerns the choice of treatment for patients who do not fully respond to the initial treatment. For non-responders, the clinical recommendation is to *switch* to another antidepressant with a different mode of action (Hirschfeld et al., 2002), whereas for partial responders, the clinical recommendation is to first increase antidepressant dose, followed by *augmentation* of the antidepressant with another medication that facilitates the action of the original drug without itself being an antidepressant (e.g., lithium) or the addition of another antidepressant *(combination therapy)* (Cleare et al., 2015). However, these treatment recommendations have rarely been tested in RCT and there is not definitive evidence to support them. The largest prospective (over 3,600 patients initially recruited), multi-site, multi-step, complex, randomised controlled trial investigating this issue is the Sequenced Treatment Alternative to Relieve Depression (STAR*D) trial, which tested the efficacy of switching and augmenting treatment for outpatients who did not initially respond to the SSRI citalopram (Rush et al., 2006; Trivedi et al., 2006). Within the STAR*D project, stepped trials have suggested that augmentation (Trivedi et al., 2006) and switching to another antidepressant (Rush et al., 2006) can have clinical benefits after unsuccessful treatment with citalopram, producing remission rates of approximately 25 per cent, although there was no placebo control condition. A meta-analysis of four RCTs found that switching SSRI non-responders to another antidepressant class led to a significantly higher remission rate than those switched to another SSRI, but that it was small and unlikely to be clinically significant (Papakostas, Fava and Thase, 2008).

There is good evidence that augmentation by atypical antipsychotic medication improves response and remission rates relative to antidepressant monotherapy, including meta-analyses of 16 trials (Nelson and Papakostas, 2009) and of 14 trials where augmentation was compared to antidepressant plus placebo (Spielmans et al., 2013). Similarly, there is evidence indicating that lithium augmentation can be beneficial, as identified in a systematic review of 30 open-label trials and 10 placebo-controlled trials, although the overall effects are relatively modest, most studies have small numbers and test the augmentation of tricyclic antidepressants rather than SSRIs (Bauer, Adli, Ricken, Severus and Pilhatsch, 2014).

Research reviews suggest that combination therapy can be a useful treatment for otherwise treatment-refractory patients, particularly if the antidepressants act on different neurotransmitter systems (Dodd, Horgan,

Malhi and Berk, 2005; Henssler, Bschor and Baethge, 2016; Rocha, Fuzikawa, Riera and Hara, 2012), although concerns were raised about the quality and number of relevant trials. As discussed in Chapter 8, there is also evidence that combining antidepressants with psychological treatments may improve outcomes for severe or treatment-resistant depression.

There is increasing evidence for the effectiveness of long-term, or *maintenance*, psychopharmacology to prevent depressive relapse or recurrence, especially in individuals at greater risk because of previous episodes of depression. A number of randomised placebo-controlled trials using tricyclics (Frank et al., 1990; Kupfer et al., 1992), SSRIs (Keller et al., 1998; Kornstein, Bose, Li, Saikali and Gandhi, 2006; Lepine et al., 2004; Lustman et al., 2006) and novel antidepressants such as venlafaxine (Montgomery et al., 2004) and nefazodone (Gelenberg et al., 2003) compared the maintenance of antidepressant medication for between one and five years after a clinically significant response versus pill placebo for patients with recurrent or chronic depression. In all of these trials, patients receiving placebo were at least twice as likely to experience recurrence as patients on maintenance antidepressant. A meta-analysis confirmed that second generation antidepressants continued for 12 months reduced relapse (22 per cent pooled rate) relative to placebo (42 per cent) (Hansen et al., 2008). Similarly, an analysis of 15 maintenance antidepressant trials registered with the US FDA found that average reduction in relapse rates for maintenance antidepressants was 52 per cent relative to placebo (Borges et al., 2014). However, only a limited number of trials have examined the effects of maintenance beyond one–two years, thereby limiting definitive conclusions (Frank et al., 1990; Kupfer et al., 1992).

As a final issue when considering effectiveness, it has been proposed that between 60–80 per cent of the response to antidepressants may be duplicated by placebo treatment (Khan, Detke, Khan and Mallinckrodt, 2003), which if the effects of medication and placebo are additive, would suggest that much of the effectiveness of antidepressants is due to a placebo effect, with the medication only having a relatively small direct biological effect. It has been hypothesised that positive expectations and hope associated with belief in the medication working could itself produce beneficial treatment effects (Rutherford and Roose, 2013). Furthermore, the awareness of side effects could itself enhance the placebo effect by promoting positive expectancy of treatment response, because the experience of a side effect could lead to attributions that the medication has a powerful biological effect. Thus, one limitation of existing antidepressant trials is that there is a greater frequency of side effects in the medication condition than in the inert pill placebo condition, confounding antidepressant effects with placebo effects. This analysis suggests that trials require an active placebo comparison that produces side effects mimicking those of antidepressants. As noted earlier, meta-analyses of the FDA data have been interpreted as indicating that much of the treatment effect is due to placebo (Kirsch et al., 2008), although this was disputed by Fountoulakis and Moller (2011).

An individual patient-level analysis of trials comparing antidepressants versus placebo for outpatients with depression found that the benefit of medication relative to placebo increases as the severity of depressive symptoms increases, with little difference at milder levels of depression (Fournier et al., 2010), suggesting that there is only a clear difference between antidepressants and placebo for more severe depression. However, a further analysis of individual patient data failed to replicate this significant effect of severity on the relative benefit of antidepressants relative to placebo, albeit this analysis was limited by the data being constrained in a moderate to severe depression range (Gibbons et al., 2012). Meta-analyses that evaluated studies that compared different antidepressant medications against each other as well as against active and inert placebos provide a partial answer to this issue. The results suggested that drug effects were considerably more modest than previously claimed – and indeed, only mildly more effective than active placebo (Moncrieff, Wessely and Hardy, 1998), although these conclusions are disputed (Quitkin, Rabkin, Gerald, Davis and Klein, 2000).

Side effects

Common side effects include dry mouth, nausea, blurry vision, weight gain and sexual dysfunction (e.g., erectile difficulties). Some drugs are sedating (causing drowsiness, being slowed down), and some are stimulating (causing anxiety, tremor, rapid heartbeat, insomnia). Some antidepressants can be lethal if taken if in overdose. It has therefore been recommended that an antidepressant should be chosen to optimise the fit between potential side effects and the symptoms and needs of the individual patient. For example, it would be logical to prescribe stimulating medications to lethargic and psychomotor-retarded patients, and sedating medications to anxious, agitated and insomniac patients, although no added benefit of matching antidepressant with symptom profile on these dimensions has been found (Rush et al., 2001; Simon, Heiligenstein, Grothaus, Katon and Revicki, 1998). However, in the GENDEP study of 800 patients with depression, the SSRI escitalopram improved mood and cognitive symptoms more than nortriptyline, whereas the reverse effect was found for neurovegetative symptoms such as disturbed sleep and appetite (Uher et al., 2009).

At the most serious extreme, a few medications may cause seizures in rare cases, or cardiac irregularities or other problems. Constant medical evaluation is important; however, most antidepressant medications do not have known therapeutic levels in the blood that can be monitored. MAOI drugs have a unique and potentially life-threatening side effect; suddenly increased blood pressure, stroke or even death may occur if the person taking such medications also ingests foods or other drugs containing *tyramine*. Tyramine is an amino acid found in many aged foods such as cheese, smoked or pickled fish or meats, red or fortified wines, and other foods and medications. Thus, people on MAOI drugs must restrict their diets accordingly.

The SSRI drugs have become popular because of their *relatively milder* side effects, although there is no evidence that they are any more effective than any other antidepressants. There has been considerable media attention about fluoxetine (Prozac), with it attracting extreme claims that on the one hand it is a 'wonder drug' but that on the other hand it causes suicidal feelings and behaviours. Given these concerns, the safety of antidepressants was reviewed by the US FDA, who issued a public health advisory in 2004, recommending close observation for the emergence of suicidal thoughts and behaviours in all patients treated with antidepressants, especially when treatment starts or dose is increased. This advisory acknowledged that the available evidence did not indicate any increase in suicide risk in adults treated with antidepressants but noted that the early activating effects of antidepressants can sometimes transiently increase suicide risk. An update in 2007 specifically recommended that antidepressants labelling include warnings about increased risks of suicidal thinking and behaviour in young adults ages 18 to 24 during the first one to two months of treatment.

Meta-analyses of the data from pharmacotherapy trials have found no difference between antidepressants and placebo in risk of suicide for adults, arguing against antidepressants causally increasing suicide risk (Brent, 2016; Carpenter et al., 2011; Fergusson et al., 2005; Sharma, Guski, Freund and Gotzsche, 2016), although it is noted that many studies have discrepancies in reporting, such that harms may be underreported. Attempts to compare different antidepressants, across trials or within large-scale cohort studies typically find little difference in suicidal behaviour between medications (Schneeweiss et al., 2010; Valenstein et al., 2012), although a cohort study of 238,963 patients in UK primary care found that mirtazapine, venlafaxine and trazodone had higher suicide and attempted suicide rates than other SSRIs and TCAs, albeit on small incidence rates (Coupland et al., 2015).

However, because clinical trials typically exclude those at high risk for suicide, it is possible that such trials underestimate the risk for suicide.

To address this issue, a seminal study used computerised records from a large prepaid health plan in the US (over 65,000 people) to examine the relationship between antidepressant use in the community and suicide attempts assessed by hospitalisations and death certificates (Simon, Savarino, Operskalski and Wang, 2006). This study found that the risk of suicide was one in 3,000 for patients receiving antidepressants and that there was no increase in suicide risk during the first month of antidepressant treatment, although there was an increase in suicide risk during the month preceding the start of anti-depressants, perhaps because increased suicidal ideation and behaviour lead to the initiation of treatment. The SSRIs had no greater risk of suicide than the older antidepressants. A recent retrospective new user cohort study found similar effects across antidepressant prescriptions after statistically controlling for potential covariates (propensity-matching) (Valuck et al., 2016).

An additional 'side effect' of medications is noncompliance. At least 40 per cent of patients prescribed antidepressants discontinue them within the first month and only 25 per cent continued antidepressant medication for more than 90 days (Olfson, Marcus, Tedeschi and Wan, 2006; Rossom et al., 2016). Given the evidence that continuation of medication is import-ant for full acute response and for preventing relapse, many patients are reducing their chances of staying well. Reasons for noncompliance range from unpleasant side effects to psychological concerns about reluctance to use chemicals to control moods or resistance to defining oneself as having a psychiatric problem. There is some evidence that treatment compliance is higher for SSRIs than for MAOIs and tricyclics, perhaps reflecting their milder side effects (e.g., Olfson et al., 2006).

Predicting response

Can we tell who will respond well to antidepressants? There are currently few robust indicators to predict treatment response (Cleare et al., 2015). As noted earlier, it may be that patients with more severe symptoms respond better to antidepressants relative to placebo (Fournier et al., 2010). There is little evidence that particular subtypes of depression ('melancholic' or 'atypical') predict treatment response (Arnow et al., 2015) or that antidepres-sant response is better for patients with more of the physical symptoms of depression (i.e., 'endogenous' depression) rather than patients with depres-sion associated with psychological causes.

In recent years, advances in the genetic understanding of depression (see Chapter 4) have led to the hope that it may be possible to determine genetic markers or other biomarkers that indicate differential antidepressant treat-ment responsiveness and susceptibility to side effects, for example by assessing gene markers of enzymes involved in metabolising specific anti-depressants (e.g., Strawbridge, Young and Cleare, 2017). However, to date, attempts to do this have had limited success. The GENDEP study genotyped the serotonin transporter gene (5HTTLPR) in 795 adults with depression treated with SSRI escitalopram or nortriptyline, and found that the 5HTTLPR genotype moderated the effect of escitalopram, with individuals with long alleles improving more than those with short alleles (Huezo-Diaz et al., 2009). In contrast, an analysis of a database of nearly 2,000 European-ancestry individuals with major depressive disorder, for whom there were pros-pectively measured treatment outcomes with SSRI or SNRIs as well as available genome-wide genotyping, failed to find any genetic markers that significantly predicted response to antidepressants overall or differentially (Katherine et al., 2012). Similarly, a meta-analysis of three large genome-wide antidepressant studies found no reliable polygenic predictors of antidepres-sant outcome (Uher et al., 2013).

Finally, it should be recalled that relatively few depressions arise 'endogenously' in the absence of personally significant life difficulties. Consequently, while medications might be useful to reduce the depression that itself is debilitating, they have little effect on the underlying 'depressive' circumstances. Thus, many individuals may need psychotherapeutic inter-ventions to deal with such problems. In Chapter 8 the effectiveness of therapies for depression is discussed, including research that has pitted anti-depressants and psychotherapy against each other to study their comparative effects.

Antidepressants in treatment of children and adolescents

There is debate as to the relative pros and cons for antidepressant medication in adolescents, and suggestions that this balance may vary by particular antidepressants. A Cochrane review of 19 trials comparing antidepressants against placebo indicated that newer-generation antidepressants, principally SSRIs, outperformed placebo (remission of 45 per cent versus 38 per cent) (Hetrick, McKenzie, Cox, Simmons and Merry, 2012), whereas a review of TCAs found no effect on response rates relative to placebo (Hazell and Mirzaie, 2013). In particular, there is a suggestion that of the antidepressants, fluoxetine may be most suitable for children and younger adolescents: a network meta-analysis of 34 trials found that only fluoxetine out-performed placebo and other antidepressants and had the best tolerability of all antidepressants (Cipriani et al., 2016).

However, there is a need for caution in the use of antidepressants with children and adolescents because of potentially dangerous side effects including cardiac complications and increased suicide risk. Both the British Medicine and Healthcare products Regulatory Agency (MHRA) and the US FDA have issued warnings about the potential risk of suicide for children treated with SSRIs, with the MHRA recommending against the use of all SSRI antidepressants except fluoxetine in children and adolescents. Meta-analyses of controlled drug trials in children and adolescents have found that SSRIs can increase suicidal ideation or behaviours, for example, 4 per cent for SSRIs vs 2.5 per cent for placebo in Hetrick et al. (2012) and with SSRIs doubling the likelihood of suicidal behaviour and aggressiveness in the studies meta-analysed by Sharma et al. (2016). Nonetheless, care needs to be taken in interpreting these findings given the low levels of suicidality reported, and, because suicidal ideation does not necessarily lead to a suicide attempt.

St John's wort

Over the last 30 years, there has been increasing interest in complementary medicine approaches to depression (Ernst, Rand and Stevinson, 1998), particularly in the use of extracts of the herb St John's wort (*hypericum perforatum*) as an antidepressant. A meta-analysis of 29 randomised trials with 5,489 patients (18 compared against placebo; 17 against antidepressant medication) found that St John's wort outperformed placebo (28 per cent better in the larger more methodologically rigorous trials) and had similar effects to antidepressants, while having fewer drop-outs due to adverse effects and side-effects (Linde, Berner and Kriston, 2008). For example, a large trial of 251 adult patients with depression in Germany found that St John's wort had similar efficiancy (was non-inferior) to paroxetine in the treatment of depression (Szegedi, Kohnen, Dienel and Kieser, 2005). A recent network meta-analysis of 66 studies and 15,161 patients of treatment in primary care including antidepressants and St John's wort found that St John's wort was superior to placebo and no different in outcome from TCAs and SSRIs (Linde et al., 2015).

Omega-3 fatty acids

Omega-3 fatty acids are polyunsaturated fatty acids (PUFAs), with eicosapentaenoic acid (EPA) and docosahexaenoic acid (DHA) the two most relevant to human physiology, which are most commonly found in fish and fish oils. Because these long-chain omega-3 fatty acids have anti-inflammatory properties and elevated inflammation has been implicated in depression (see Chapter 4) and because depression is associated with lower levels of total PUFAs, EPA and DHA (Lin, Huang and Su, 2010), omega-3 fatty acids have been proposed as a potential treatment or treatment adjunct for depression.

Recent meta-analyses of RCTs have suggested that omega-3 fatty acid supplementation in which EPA (but not DHA) predominates (doses in range 0.6–4.4g) is efficacious relative to placebo in reducing depressive symptoms in patients with depression (Grosso et al. 2014; Hallahan et al., 2016), although concerns have been raised about publication bias (i.e., only significant findings published) (Bloch and Hannested, 2012). A trial directly comparing EPA versus DHA versus placebo failed to find any significant benefit for either omega-3 fatty acid (Mischoulon et al., 2015). Other trials have examined the use of omega-3 fatty acid supplements as adjuncts to antidepressant medication, typically SSRIs, relative to antidepressants plus pill placebo (e.g., olive oil supplements). Several trials find that adding omega-3 fatty acids to antidepressant improves outcomes (e.g. Gertsik et al., 2012; Peet and Horrobin, 2002).

Non-pharmacological biological treatments

Additional biological interventions sometimes used to treat depression include electroconvulsive therapy, transcranial magnetic stimulation and phototherapy for seasonal affective disorder, sleep deprivation and exercise.

Electroconvulsive therapy (ECT)

ECT often strikes people as a barbaric, inhumane treatment that should be entirely abolished. Indeed, in past decades it was misused, applied to many patient groups without evidence of effectiveness, and caused physical damage to many people. Nowadays its use in the US and Europe is subject to stringent restrictions and highly variable according to location, hospital and patient characteristics, reflecting the ambivalence that many psychiatrists experience about it.

Use and effectiveness

ECT has not disappeared for one very good reason. It is extremely effective in the treatment of severe, otherwise-untreatable, depressions. It is the treatment of choice where there are prominent psychotic features of depression and especially where severe depression has not responded to medication, and in life-threatening situations where rapid response is needed (Heijnen, Birkenhager, Wierdsma and van den Broek, 2010; Kellner et al., 2012). A meta-analysis of controlled short-term trials (typically of four weeks treatment) concluded that ECT is significantly more effective than placebo (in the form of simulated or sham ECT, six trials) and more effective than antidepressants (18 trials) (Carney et al., 2003).

ECT is currently administered under medically safe conditions, in which patients are first given sedatives, muscle relaxants or other agents to control potentially damaging physical side effects. The typical course averages six to nine treatments spaced two or three times per week. The electrical current must be supplied above a threshold necessary to induce an epileptic seizure in order to achieve therapeutic effects. There has been some debate as to whether ECT delivered to both hemispheres of the brain simultaneously (bilateral) is more effective than ECT delivered to one hemisphere only (unilateral) (Carney et al., 2003). A study comparing bilateral versus unilateral placements did not find any significant differences in remission rates (Kellner et al., 2010). A meta-analysis compared ECT administered once per week, twice per week and thrice per week, and concluded that there was no outcome difference between twice weekly versus thrice weekly ECT and that thrice weekly was better than once a week (Charlson et al., 2012).

Despite its short-term efficacy, one limitation of ECT is that it has high relapse rates. A meta-analysis of 32 studies with up to two years of follow-up (Jelovac, Kolshus and McLoughlin, 2013) found that maintenance anti-depressant medication after ECT halved the risk of relapse compared with placebo in the first six months. Even then, approximately half of all patients had relapsed within 12 months, most within the first six months. Similar relapse rates were found for continuation ECT. The use of continuation anti-depressants following a course of ECT is therefore recommended to reduce relapse.

How does ECT work?

Its mechanisms are not fully understood, but the principal models of its action are similar to those proposed for antidepressant medication, for example, by increasing neurotransmitter availability, changing receptor sensitivity or facilitating neurogenesis. In addition, it is hypothesised that the therapeutic effects of ECT are related to anticonvulsant effects including the observation that seizure thresholds increase over the course of ECT as well as evidence of changes in neurohormones and GABA. Evidence indicates that ECT, like antidepressants, influences the intracellular signalling cascade and neurogenesis through the up-regulation of factors such as BDNF (Brunoni, Baeken, Machado-Vieira, Gattaz and Vanderhasselt, 2014; Duman and Monteggia, 2006; Inta et al., 2013; Schloesser et al., 2015).

Side effects of ECT

A major issue in the use of ECT is whether it causes damage to the recipient, in terms of functions or structure of the brain. ECT typically produces impairments in autobiographical memory during the period of treatment, which sometimes persist for three–six months post-treatment. The amnesia typically improves during the months after treatment, although amnesia for events that immediately preceded the ECT often remains. Reviews summarising the findings of neuroimaging of the brains of ECT recipients, controlled animal studies of neuronal consequences of ECT administration, and long term follow-ups of patients with repeated assessment of cognitive performance conclude that there is no evidence that ECT causes structural brain damage or long-term memory deficits (Devanand, Dwork, Hutchinson, Bolwig and Sackeim, 1994; Maric et al., 2016). For example, a study of 199 patients followed over ten years found no evidence of cumulative cognitive deficits (Kirov et al., 2016).

Transcranial magnetic stimulation (TMS)

In TMS, high intensity current is pulsed through electromagnetic coils placed on the scalp, producing a time-varying high intensity magnetic field, which induces an electric current in brain neural tissue (George, Lisanby and Sackeim, 1999). Thus, like ECT, TMS induces electrical stimulation in the brain, although it has the advantages of being more focal and localised than ECT, since magnetic fields are not deflected or weakened by intervening scalp and tissue. Furthermore, TMS does not require anaesthesia, muscle relaxants or analgesics. Single pulses of TMS can be used to excite or inhibit localised brain function, temporarily influencing behaviour and cognition, and it is therefore a useful tool for mapping brain function.

For the treatment of mood disorders, repeated, rhythmic pulses of TMS are used, called repetitive TMS (rTMS). There is some evidence that rTMS has a small to moderate antidepressant effect, although most trials are limited by small sample size, the lack of a long-term follow-up and the lack of a double-blind – even when a sham is used, few studies report blinding success, all limitations noted in meta-analyses. One of the larger trials randomised 190 patients with major depression not currently receiving medication to rTMS versus to sham TMS, where the coils are held at an angle to the scalp that prevents any active effect, and found a significant if mild treatment benefit for rTMS (remission rate of 14 per cent versus 5 per cent) (George et al., 2010). Several meta-analyses confirm that active rTMS outperforms sham; for example, in patients who had failed to respond to previous treatment (remission rates 9 per cent versus 6 per cent) (Lam, Chan, Wilkins-Ho and

Yatham, 2008), in patients with treatment-resistant depression (Gaynes et al., 2014) and for bilateral rTMS (Berlim, Van den Eynde and Daskalakis, 2013). There is evidence that both high frequency rTMS of the left DLPFC and low frequency rTMS of the right DLPFC reduce depressive symptoms when compared to sham rTMS. Since high frequency stimulation is hypothesised to have an excitatory effect on cortical activity, whereas low frequency stimulation is hypothesised to have an inhibitory effect, both forms of rTMS may work by increasing left DLPFC cortical activity relative to right DLFPC activity. The principal side effect of rTMS is muscle-tension headaches, caused by the stimulation of facial and scalp muscles, found in 5–25 per cent of patients and is usually only temporary. In addition, high frequency rTMS only may increase the risk of epileptic seizures.

Phototherapy for seasonal mood disorders

Phototherapy, or light therapy, is a treatment for the Seasonal Affective Disorder subtype of depression. Speculating that SAD may be a 'hibernation-like' response resulting from circadian rhythm dysfunction during diminished exposure to light during winter, it was reasoned that increasing exposure to bright light might reverse the depressive symptoms. The basic treatment consists of having the depressed person sit near a source of bright (5,000–10,000 lux) light for at least one hour daily, typically in the morning. An initial review and meta-analysis of 13 controlled trials in SAD found that light therapy was an efficacious treatment compared with placebo (Golden et al., 2005). Light therapy is also as effective as fluoxetine in patients with winter SAD, although with the advantages of an earlier response onset and fewer side effects (Lam et al., 2006). Although improvements in symptoms occur relatively rapidly (within a few days or a week), the benefit is temporary, such that people with SAD may need to continue the treatments through-out the winter. A recent review of the evidence was more critical, noting that there were many limitations in the data, making it hard to reach an unequivocal conclusion, including lack of double-blind, small sample sizes and short-term follow-up (Martensson, Pettersson, Berglund and Ekselius, 2015). Similarly in a review for the UK National Institute for Health and Clinical Excellence (2009) Clinical Guideline for Depression, it was concluded that when the higher quality studies were examined, there was a large effect of phototherapy relative to waiting list control, but only a small effect against attentional controls and no difference relative to active control treatments.

A recent trial of 177 patients with SAD compared six weeks of CBT versus six weeks of bright light therapy and found no difference in post-treatment remission (47 per cent), but when followed up over two subsequent winters, CBT resulted in fewer recurrences of depression than light therapy (27 per cent versus 45 per cent) (Rohan et al., 2015; Rohan et al., 2016).

The mechanism of action of phototherapy is assumed to relate to circadian rhythm dysregulation. Consistent with the hypothesis that winter depressions are triggered by phase delays in the circadian system with respect to the sleep–wake or light–dark cycle, exposure to morning light appears to achieve antidepressant effects by phase-advancing the circadian rhythm, whereas evening exposure, which produces delays in the melatonin rhythm, has less antidepressant effect (LeGates, Fernandez and Hattar, 2014; Lewy et al., 1998; Lewy, Lefler, Emens and Bauer, 2006; Schnell, Albrecht and Sandrelli, 2014).

Recent studies have examined the value of light therapy for non-seasonal depression. A meta-analysis of nine trials suggests that there is evidence of efficacy, while noting that patients are not blinded, samples are small and follow-ups are short-term (Al-Karawi and Jubair, 2016). A controlled trial compared bright light therapy, fluoxetine, their combination and placebo in the treatment of 122 patients with non-seasonal depression: combination treatment and phototherapy, but not fluoxetine, outperformed placebo (Lam et al., 2016).

Sleep deprivation (SD)

SD is an experimental treatment based on the association between sleep disturbances and depression, as well as atypical rapid eye movement (REM) sleep patterns in some depressed patients (Dallaspezia, Suzuki and Benedetti, 2015). Manipulations of the sleep–wake cycle, including total or partial sleep deprivation, in which depressed patients are kept awake throughout the night; and phase advance, in which the sleep cycle is advanced by six hours, produces marked mood improvements the night of SD or on the following day in 40–60 per cent of patients with mood disorders (Giedke and Schwarzler, 2002). However, these positive benefits are very temporary, with 50–80 per cent of responders relapsing after a night's sleep or even after naps. It may be that these treatment benefits can be maintained by the combination of SD with antidepressants or light therapy, although approximately 50 per cent of medicated patients still relapse after SD. To date, SD has not been examined in large-scale controlled studies, and is not a commonplace or established treatment. The therapeutic effect of SD is postulated to be linked to changes in disturbed circadian and disturbed sleep–wake dependent phase relationships.

Effects of physical exercise on depression

Increasing attention has focused on the beneficial effects of exercise in treating depression. Although this research is included in this chapter on biological treatments, it must be emphasised at the outset that the actual mechanisms accounting for the positive effects of exercise might be psychological (rewarding effects of positive activity, social contact, distraction, improved self-esteem, changes in cognitions, sense of agency and control) as well as due to actual physical changes in energy, endorphin and monoamine concentrations, and physical arousal.

A meta-analysis of 37 RCTs of physical exercise on depression found that exercise had a moderate effect size in reducing symptoms of depression relative to no treatment or a control condition (Cooney et al., 2013). However, when only the six trials with better quality methods (i.e., adequate concealment of treatment allocation, intention-to-treat analysis and blinded outcome assessment) were considered, exercise did not significantly differ from control. A more recent meta-analysis concludes that exercise can be an effective intervention (Kvam, Kleppe, Nordhus and Hovland, 2016).

Among the better studies, a well-controlled randomised trial with participants with major depression found that 12 weeks of individual supervised moderate-to-high dose aerobic exercise reduced symptoms of depression significantly more than a low dose exercise programme or a placebo control consisting of flexibility exercise (Dunn, Trivedi, Kampert, Clark and Chambliss, 2005). In contrast, the TREAD trial randomised 361 adults with depression to facilitated physical activity, in which face-to-face and telephone sessions were used to encourage physical activity, rather than directly supervised exercise, in addition to usual care versus usual care in the UK (Chalder et al., 2012). There was no benefit for the facilitation group relative to usual care. These studies suggest that exercise may be beneficial for mild-to-moderate depression but that it needs to exceed a threshold level of intensity to be of value.

Summary

◆ Antidepressant medication use has greatly increased in use in recent years, but antidepressants continue to be frequently misadministered in terms of dosage and application to suitable cases.
◆ There is solid evidence of therapeutic effectiveness of antidepressant medications, although all have about the same level of demonstrated effectiveness. Rates of 'success' differ,

however, depending on how outcomes are defined, and many people continue to have residual symptoms and incomplete recovery.

◆ There are concerns about the acceptability of antidepressants to patients, with recognised unpleasant side effects and low rates of continuation of medication.

◆ Based on research findings, treatment guidelines recommend that antidepressants be continued for up to six months after recovery to prevent relapse, and that antidepressant treatment be maintained long term or indefinitely for patients with histories of recurrent depression.

◆ The efficacy of antidepressants is not proof of underlying biochemical aetiology of depression.

◆ Other biological treatments for depression include electroconvulsive therapy, transcranial magnetic stimulation, light therapy, sleep deprivation and, possibly, physical exercise.

References

Al-Karawi, D. and Jubair, L. (2016). Bright light therapy for nonseasonal depression: meta-analysis of clinical trials. *Journal of Affective Disorders, 198*, 64–71.

Arnow, B. A., Blasey, C., Williams, L. M., Palmer, D. M., Rekshan, W., Schatzberg, A. F., . . . Rush, A. J. (2015). Depression subtypes in predicting antidepressant response: a report from the iSPOT-D trial. *American Journal of Psychiatry, 172*(8), 743–750.

Bauer, M., Adli, M., Ricken, R., Severus, E. and Pilhatsch, M. (2014). Role of Lithium augmentation in the management of Major Depressive Disorder. *CNS Drugs, 28*(4), 331–342.

Berlim, M. T., Van den Eynde, F. and Daskalakis, Z. J. (2013). A systematic review and meta-analysis on the efficacy and acceptability of bilateral repetitive transcranial magnetic stimulation (rTMS) for treating major depression. *Psychological Medicine, 43*(11), 2245–2254.

Bessa, J. M., Ferreira, D., Melo, I., Marques, F., Cerqueira, J. J., Palha, J. A., . . . Sousa, N. (2009). The mood-improving actions of antidepressants do not depend on neurogenesis but are associated with neuronal remodeling. *Molecular Psychiatry, 14*(8), 764–773.

Bloch, M. H. and Hannestad, J. (2012). Omega-3 fatty acids for the treatment of depression: systematic review and meta-analysis. *Molecular Psychiatry, 17*(12), 1272–1282.

Borges, S., Chen, Y. F., Laughren, T. P., Temple, R., Patel, H. D., David, P. A., . . . Khin, N. A. (2014). Review of maintenance trials for Major Depressive Disorder: a

25-year perspective from the US Food and Drug Administration. *Journal of Clinical Psychiatry*, 75(3), 205–214.

Brent, D. A. (2016). Antidepressants and suicidality. *Psychiatric Clinics of North America*, 39(3), 503–510.

Brunoni, A. R., Baeken, C., Machado-Vieira, R., Gattaz, W. F. and Vanderhasselt, M. A. (2014). BDNF blood levels after electroconvulsive therapy in patients with mood disorders: a systematic review and meta-analysis. *World Journal of Biological Psychiatry*, 15(5), 411–418.

Carney, S., Cowen, P., Geddes, J., Goodwin, G., Rogers, R., Dearness, K., . . . Scott, A. (2003). Efficacy and safety of electroconvulsive therapy in depressive disorders: a systematic review and meta-analysis. *Lancet*, 361(9360), 799–808.

Carpenter, D. J., Fong, R., Kraus, J. E., Davies, J. T., Moore, C. and Thase, M. E. (2011). Meta-Analysis of efficacy and treatment-emergent suicidality in adults by psychiatric indication and age subgroup following initiation of paroxetine therapy: a complete set of randomized placebo-controlled trials. *Journal of Clinical Psychiatry*, 72(11), 1503–1514.

Castren, E. (2013). Neuronal network plasticity and recovery from depression. *JAMA Psychiatry*, 70(9), 983–989.

Castren, E. and Rantamaki, T. (2010). The role of BDNF and its receptors in depression and antidepressant drug action: reactivation of developmental plasticity. *Developmental Neurobiology*, 70(5), 289–297.

Chalder, M., Wiles, N. J., Campbell, J., Hollinghurst, S. P., Haase, A. M., Taylor, A. H., . . . Lewis, G. (2012). Facilitated physical activity as a treatment for depressed adults: randomised controlled trial. *British Medical Journal*, 344.

Charlson, F., Siskind, D., Doi, S. A. R., McCallum, E., Broome, A. and Lie, D. C. (2012). ECT efficacy and treatment course: a systematic review and meta-analysis of twice vs thrice weekly schedules. *Journal of Affective Disorders*, 138(1–2), 1–8.

Cipriani, A., Furukawa, T. A., Salanti, G., Geddes, J. R., Higgins, J. P. T., Churchill, R., . . . Barbui, C. (2009). Comparative efficacy and acceptability of 12 new-generation antidepressants: a multiple-treatments meta-analysis. *Lancet*, 373(9665), 746–758.

Cipriani, A., Zhou, X. Y., Del Giovane, C., Hetrick, S. E., Qin, B., Whittington, C., . . . Xie, P. (2016). Comparative efficacy and tolerability of antidepressants for major depressive disorder in children and adolescents: a network meta-analysis. *Lancet*, 388(10047), 881–890.

Cleare, A., Pariante, C. M., Young, A. H., Anderson, I. M., Christmas, D., Cowen, P. J., . . . British Assoc, P. (2015). Evidence-based guidelines for treating depressive disorders with antidepressants: a revision of the 2008 British Association for Psychopharmacology guidelines. *Journal of Psychopharmacology*, 29(5), 459–525.

Cooney, G. M., Dwan, K., Greig, C. A., Lawlor, D. A., Rimer, J., Waugh, F. R., . . . Mead, G. E. (2013). Exercise for depression. *Cochrane Database of Systematic Reviews*, (9), 160.

Coupland, C., Hill, T., Morriss, R., Arthur, A., Moore, M. and Hippisley-Cox, J. (2015). Antidepressant use and risk of suicide and attempted suicide or self harm in people aged 20 to 64: cohort study using a primary care database. *British Medical Journal*, *350*, 13.

Dallaspezia, S., Suzuki, M. and Benedetti, F. (2015). Chronobiological Therapy for Mood Disorders. *Current Psychiatry Reports*, *17*(12), 11.

DeBattista, C., Belanoff, J., Glass, S., Khan, A., Horne, R. L., Blasey, C. et al. (2006). Mifepristone versus placebo in the treatment of psychosis in patients with psychotic major depression. *Biological Psychiatry*, *60*, 1343–1349.

Devanand, D. P., Dwork, A. J., Hutchinson, E. R., Bolwig, T. G. and Sackeim, H. A. (1994). Does ECT alter brain structure. *American Journal of Psychiatry*, *151*(7), 957–970.

Dodd, S., Horgan, D., Malhi, G. S. and Berk, M. (2005). To combine or not to combine? A literature review of antidepressant combination therapy. *Journal of Affective Disorders*, *89*(1–3), 1–11.

Duman, R. S., Heninger, G. R. and Nestler, E. J. (1997). A molecular and cellular theory of depression. *Archives of General Psychiatry*, *54*(7), 597–606.

Duman, R. S. and Monteggia, L. M. (2006). A neurotrophic model for stress-related mood disorders. *Biological Psychiatry*, *59*(12), 1116–1127.

Dunn, A. L., Trivedi, M. H., Kampert, J. B., Clark, C. G. and Chambliss, H. O. (2005). Exercise treatment for depression – efficacy and dose response. *American Journal of Preventive Medicine*, *28*(1), 1–8.

Dunn, R. L., Donoghue, J. M., Ozminkowski, R. J., Stephenson, D. and Hylan, T. R. (1999). Longitudinal patterns of antidepressant prescribing in primary care in the UK: comparison with treatment guidelines. *Journal of Psychopharmacology*, *13*(2), 136–143.

Ernst, E., Rand, J. I. and Stevinson, C. (1998). Complementary therapies for depression – an overview. *Archives of General Psychiatry*, *55*(11), 1026–1032.

Fergusson, D., Doucette, S., Cranley, K., Glass, K. C., Shapiro, S., Healy, D., . . . Hutton, B. (2005). Association between suicide attempts and selective serotonin reuptake inhibitors: systematic review of randomised controlled trials. *British Medical Journal*, *330*(7488), 396–399.

Fountoulakis, K. N., Veroniki, A. A., Siamouli, M. and Moller, H. J. (2013). No role for initial severity on the efficacy of antidepressants: results of a multi-meta-analysis. *Annals of General Psychiatry*, *12*, 10.

Fournier, J. C., DeRubeis, R. J., Hollon, S. D., Dimidjian, S., Amsterdam, J. D., Shelton, R. C. and Fawcett, J. (2010). Antidepressant drug effects and depression severity A patient-level meta-analysis. *JAMA-Journal of the American Medical Association*, *303*(1), 47–53.

Frank, E., Kupfer, D. J., Perel, J. M., Cornes, C., Jarrett, D. B., Mallinger, A. G., . . . Grochocinski, V. J. (1990). Three-year outcomes for maintenance therapies in recurrent depression. *Archives of General Psychiatry*, *47*(12), 1093–1099.

Gallagher, P., Malik, N., Newham, J., Young, A. H., Ferrier, I. N. and Mackin, P. (2008). Antiglucocorticoid treatments for mood disorders. *Cochrane Database of Systematic Reviews*, (1), 64.

Gartlehner, G., Hansen, R. A., Morgan, L. C., Thaler, K., Lux, L., Van Noord, M., . . . Lohr, K. N. (2011). Comparative benefits and harms of second-generation antidepressants for treating Major Depressive Disorder: an updated meta-analysis. *Annals of Internal Medicine*, 155(11), 772–785.

Gaynes, B. N., Lloyd, S. W., Lux, L., Gartlehner, G., Hansen, R. A., Brode, S., . . . Lohr, K. N. (2014). Repetitive Transcranial Magnetic Stimulation for treatment-resistant depression: a systematic review and meta-analysis. *Journal of Clinical Psychiatry*, 75(5), 477–489.

Geddes, J. R., Carney, S. M., Davies, C., Furukawa, T. A., Kupfer, D. J., Frank, E. and Goodwin, G. M. (2003). Relapse prevention with antidepressant drug treatment in depressive disorders: a systematic review. *Lancet*, 361(9358), 653–661.

Gelenberg, A. J., Trivedi, M. H., Rush, A. J., Thase, M. E., Howland, R., Klein, D. N., . . . Keller, M. B. (2003). Randomized, placebo-controlled trial of nefazodone maintenance treatment in preventing recurrence in chronic depression. *Biological Psychiatry*, 54(8), 806–817.

George, M. S., Lisanby, S. H., Avery, D., McDonald, W. M., Durkalski, V., Pavlicova, M., . . . Sackeim, H. A. (2010). Daily left prefrontal transcranial magnetic stimulation therapy for Major Depressive Disorder: a sham-controlled randomized trial. *Archives of General Psychiatry*, 67(5), 507–516.

George, M. S., Lisanby, S. H. and Sackeim, H. A. (1999). Transcranial magnetic stimulation: applications in neuropsychiatry. *Archives of General Psychiatry*, 56(4), 300–311.

Gertsik, L., Poland, R. E., Bresee, C. and Rapaport, M. H. (2012). Omega-3 fatty acid augmentation of citalopram treatment for patients with Major Depressive Disorder. *Journal of Clinical Psychopharmacology*, 32(1), 61–64.

Gibbons, R. D., Hur, K., Brown, C. H., Davis, J. M. and Mann, J. J. (2012). Benefits from antidepressants synthesis of 6-week patient-level outcomes from double-blind placebo-controlled randomized trials of Fluoxetine and Venlafaxine. *Archives of General Psychiatry*, 69(6), 572–579.

Giedke, H. and Schwarzler, F. (2002). Therapeutic use of sleep deprivation in depression. *Sleep Medicine Reviews*, 6(5), 361–377.

Gili, M., Vicens, C., Roca, M., Andersen, P. and McMillan, D. (2015). Interventions for preventing relapse or recurrence,of depression in primary health care settings: a systematic review. *Preventive Medicine*, 76, S16-S21.

Glue, P., Donovan, M. R., Kolluri, S. and Emir, B. (2010). Meta-analysis of relapse prevention antidepressant trials in depressive disorders. *Australian and New Zealand Journal of Psychiatry*, 44(8), 697–705.

Golden, R. N., Gaynes, B. N., Ekstrom, R. D., Hamer, R. M., Jacobsen, F. M., Suppes, T., . . . Nemeroff, C. B. (2005). The efficacy of light therapy in the treatment of mood disorders: a review and meta-analysis of the evidence. *American Journal of Psychiatry*, 162(4), 656–662.

Grosso, G., Pajak, A., Marventano, S., Castellano, S., Galvano, F., Bucolo, C., . . . Caraci, F. (2014). Role of omega-3 fatty acids in the treatment of depressive disorders: a comprehensive meta-analysis of randomized clinical trials. *PLOS One*, 9(5), 18.

Hallahan, B., Ryan, T., Hibbeln, J. R., Murray, I. T., Glynn, S., Ramsden, C. E., . . . Davis, J. M. (2016). Efficacy of omega-3 highly unsaturated fatty acids in the treatment of depression. *British Journal of Psychiatry*, 209(3), 192–201.

Hansen, R., Gaynes, B., Thieda, P., Gartlehner, G., Deveaugh-Geiss, A., Krebs, E. and Lohr, K. (2008). Meta-analysis of major depressive disorder relapse and recurrence with second-generation antidepressants. *Psychiatric Services*, 59(10), 1121–1130.

Hardeveld, F., Spijker, J., De Graaf, R., Nolen, W. A. and Beekman, A. T. F. (2010). Prevalence and predictors of recurrence of major depressive disorder in the adult population. *Acta Psychiatrica Scandinavica*, 122(3), 184–191.

Harmer, C. J. and Cowen, P. J. (2013). 'It's the way that you look at it' – a cognitive neuropsychological account of SSRI action in depression. *Philosophical Transactions of the Royal Society B-Biological Sciences*, 368(1615), 8.

Harmer, C. J., Hill, S. A., Taylor, M. J., Cowen, P. J. and Goodwin, G. M. (2003). Toward a neuropsychological theory of antidepressant drug action: increase in positive emotional bias after potentiation of norepinephrine activity. *American Journal of Psychiatry*, 160(5), 990–992.

Harmer, C. J., O'Sullivan, U., Favaron, E., Massey-Chase, R., Ayres, R., Reinecke, A., . . . Cowen, P. J. (2009). Effect of acute antidepressant administration on negative affective bias in depressed patients. *American Journal of Psychiatry*, 166(10), 1178–1184.

Hashimoto, K., Shimizu, E. and Iyo, M. (2004). Critical role of brain-derived neurotrophic factor in mood disorders. *Brain Research Reviews*, 45, 104–114.

Hazell, P. and Mirzaie, M. (2013). Tricyclic drugs for depression in children and adolescents. *Cochrane Database of Systematic Reviews*, (6), 50.

Heijnen, W. T., Birkenhager, T. K., Wierdsma, A. I. and van den Broek, W. W. (2010). Antidepressant pharmacotherapy failure and response to subsequent electroconvulsive therapy: a meta-analysis. *Journal of Clinical Psychopharmacology*, 30(5), 616–619.

Henssler, J., Bschor, T. and Baethge, C. (2016). Combining antidepressants in acute treatment of depression: a meta-analysis of 38 studies including 4511 patients. *Canadian Journal of Psychiatry-Revue Canadienne De Psychiatrie*, 61(1), 29–43.

Hetrick, S. E., McKenzie, J. E., Cox, G. R., Simmons, M. B. and Merry, S. N. (2012). Newer generation antidepressants for depressive disorders in children and adolescents. *Cochrane Database of Systematic Reviews*, (11), 157.

Hirschfeld, R. M. A., Montgomery, S. A., Aguglia, E., Amore, M., Delgado, P. L., Gastpar, M., . . . Versiani, M. (2002). Partial response and nonresponse to antidepressant therapy: current approaches and treatment options. *Journal of Clinical Psychiatry*, 63(9), 826–837.

Huezo-Diaz, P., Uher, R., Smith, R., Rietschel, M., Henigsberg, N., Marusic, A., . . . McGuffin, P. (2009). Moderation of antidepressant response by the serotonin transporter gene. *British Journal of Psychiatry*, 195(1), 30–38.

Inta, D., Lima-Ojeda, J. M., Lau, T., Tang, W. N., Dormann, C., Sprengel, R., . . . Gass, P. (2013). Electroconvulsive Therapy induces neurogenesis in frontal rat brain areas. *PLOS One*, 8(7), 5.

Jahn, H., Schick, M., Kiefer, F., Kellner, M., Yassouridis, A. and Wiedemann, K. (2004). Metyrapone as additive treatment in major depression – A double-blind and placebo-controlled trial. *Archives of General Psychiatry*, *61*(12), 1235–1244.

Jelovac, A., Kolshus, E. and McLoughlin, D. M. (2013). Relapse following successful electroconvulsive therapy for major depression: a meta-analysis. *Neuropsychopharmacology*, *38*(12), 2467–2474.

Judd, L. L., Akiskal, H. S., Maser, J. D., Zeller, P. J., Endicott, J., Coryell, W., . . . Keller, M. B. (1998). A prospective 12-year study of subsyndromal and syndromal depressive symptoms in unipolar major depressive disorders. *Archives of General Psychiatry*, *55*(8), 694–700.

Kaymaz, N., van Os, J., Loonen, A. J. M. and Nolen, W. A. (2008). Evidence that patients with single versus recurrent depressive episodes are differentially sensitive to treatment discontinuation: a meta-analysis of placebo-controlled randomized trials. *Journal of Clinical Psychiatry*, *69*(9), 1423–1433.

Keller, M. B., Kocsis, J. H., Thase, M. E., Gelenberg, A. J., Rush, A. J., Koran, L., . . . Sertraline Chronic Depression Study, G. (1998). Maintenance phase efficacy of sertraline for chronic depression – a randomized controlled trial. *Journal of the American Medical Association*, *280*(19), 1665–1672.

Kellner, C. H., Greenberg, R. M., Murrough, J. W., Bryson, E. O., Briggs, M. C. and Pasculli, R. M. (2012). ECT in treatment-resistant depression. *American Journal of Psychiatry*, *169*(12), 1238–1244.

Kellner, C. H., Knapp, R., Husain, M. M., Rasmussen, K., Sampson, S., Cullum, M., . . . Petrides, G. (2010). Bifrontal, bitemporal and right unilateral electrode placement in ECT: randomised trial. *British Journal of Psychiatry*, *196*(3), 226–234.

Khan, A., Detke, M., Khan, S. R. F. and Mallinckrodt, C. (2003). Placebo response and antidepressant clinical trial outcome. *Journal of Nervous and Mental Disease*, *191*(4), 211–218.

Kirov, G. G., Owen, L., Ballard, H., Leighton, A., Hannigan, K., Llewellyn, D., . . . Atkins, M. (2016). Evaluation of cumulative cognitive deficits from electroconvulsive therapy. *British Journal of Psychiatry*, *208*(3), 266–270.

Kirsch, I., Deacon, B. J., Huedo-Medina, T. B., Scoboria, A., Moore, T. J. and Johnson, B. T. (2008). Initial severity and antidepressant benefits: a meta-analysis of data submitted to the food and drug administration. *PLOS Medicine*, *5*(2), 260–268.

Kornstein, S. G., Bose, A., Li, D., Saikali, K. G. and Gandhi, C. (2006). Escitalopram maintenance treatment for prevention of recurrent depression: a randomized, placebo-controlled trial. *Journal of Clinical Psychiatry*, *67*(11), 1767–1775.

Krystal, J. H., Sanacora, G. and Duman, R. S. (2013). Rapid-acting glutamatergic antidepressants: the path to Ketamine and beyond. *Biological Psychiatry*, *73*(12), 1133–1141.

Kupfer, D. J., Frank, E., Perel, J. M., Cornes, C., Mallinger, A. G., Thase, M. E., . . . Grochocinski, V. J. (1992). Five-year outcome for maintenance therapies in recurrent depression. *Archives of General Psychiatry*, *49*(10), 769–773.

Kvam, S., Kleppe, C. L., Nordhus, I. H. and Hovland, A. (2016). Exercise as a treatment for depression: a meta-analysis. *Journal of Affective Disorders, 202,* 67–86.

Lam, R. W., Chan, P., Wilkins-Ho, M. and Yatham, L. N. (2008). Repetitive transcranial magnetic stimulation for treatment-resistant depression: a systematic review and metaanalysis. *Canadian Journal of Psychiatry-Revue Canadienne De Psychiatrie, 53*(9), 621–631.

Lam, R. W., Levitt, A. J., Levitan, R. D., Enns, M. W., Morehouse, R., Michalak, E. E. and Tam, E. M. (2006). The can-SAD study: a randomized controlled trial of the effectiveness of light therapy and fluoxetine in patients with winter seasonal affective disorder. *American Journal of Psychiatry, 163*(5), 805–812.

Lam, R. W., Levitt, A. J., Levitan, R. D., Michalak, E. E., Cheung, A. H., Morehouse, R., . . . Tam, E. M. (2016). Efficacy of bright light treatment, fluoxetine, and the combination in patients with nonseasonal Major Depressive Disorder: a randomized clinical trial. *JAMA Psychiatry, 73*(1), 56–63.

LeGates, T. A., Fernandez, D. C. and Hattar, S. (2014). Light as a central modulator of circadian rhythms, sleep and affect. *Nature Reviews Neuroscience, 15*(7), 443–454.

Lepine, J. P., Caillard, V., Bisserbe, J. C., Troy, S., Hotton, J. M., Boyer, P. and Investigators, P. (2004). A randomized, placebo-controlled trial of sertraline for prophylactic treatment of highly recurrent major depressive disorder. *American Journal of Psychiatry, 161*(5), 836–842.

Leucht, S., Hierl, S., Kissling, W., Dold, M. and Davis, J. M. (2012). Putting the efficacy of psychiatric and general medicine medication into perspective: review of meta-analyses. *British Journal of Psychiatry, 200*(2), 97–106.

Lewy, A. J., Bauer, V. K., Cutler, N. L., Sack, R. L., Ahmed, S., Thomas, K. H., . . . Jackson, J. M. L. (1998). Morning vs evening light treatment of patients with winter depression. *Archives of General Psychiatry, 55*(10), 890–896.

Lewy, A. J., Lefler, B. J., Emens, J. S. and Bauer, V. K. (2006). The circadian basis of winter depression. *Proceedings of the National Academy of Sciences of the United States of America, 103*(19), 7414–7419.

Lin, P. Y., Huang, S. Y. and Su, K. P. (2010). A meta-analytic review of polyunsaturated fatty acid compositions in patients with depression. *Biological Psychiatry, 68,* 40–147.

Linde, K., Berner, M. M. and Kriston, L. (2008). St John's wort for major depression. *Cochrane Database of Systematic Reviews,* (4), 147.

Linde, K., Kriston, L., Rucker, G., Jamil, S., Schumann, I., Meissner, K., . . . Schneider, A. (2015). Efficacy and acceptability of pharmacological treatments for depressive disorders in primary care: systematic review and network meta-Analysis. *Annals of Family Medicine, 13*(1), 69–79.

Lindert, J., Schouler-Ocak, M., Heinz, A. and Priebe, S. (2008). Mental health, health care utilisation of migrants in Europe. *European Psychiatry, 23,* 14–20.

Lustman, P. J., Clouse, R. E., Nix, B. D., Freedland, K. E., Rubin, E. H., McGill, J. B., . . . Ciechanowski, P. S. (2006). Sertraline for prevention of depression recurrence in diabetes mellitus – a randomized, double-blind, placebo-controlled trial. *Archives of General Psychiatry, 63*(5), 521–529.

Manseau, M. and Case, B. G. (2014). Racial-ethnic disparities in outpatient mental health visits to US physicians, 1993–2008. *Psychiatric Services*, 65(1), 59–67.

Maric, N. P., Stojanovic, Z., Andric, S., Soldatovic, I., Dolic, M. and Spiric, Z. (2016). The acute and medium-term effects of treatment with electroconvulsive therapy on memory in patients with major depressive disorder. *Psychological Medicine*, 46(4), 797–806.

Martensson, B., Pettersson, A., Berglund, L. and Ekselius, L. (2015). Bright white light therapy in depression: a critical review of the evidence. *Journal of Affective Disorders*, 182, 1–7.

Maya-Vetencourt, J. F., Sale, A., Viegi, A., Baroncelli, L., De Pasquale, R., O'Leary, O. F., . . . Maffei, L. (2008). The antidepressant fluoxetine restores plasticity in the adult visual cortex. *Science*, 320(5874), 385–388.

McAllister-Williams, R. H., Anderson, I. M., Finkelmeyer, A., Gallagher, P., Grunze, H. C. R., Haddad, P. M., . . . Team, A. D. D. S. (2016). Antidepressant augmentation with metyrapone for treatment-resistant depression (the ADD study): a double-blind, randomised, placebo-controlled trial. *Lancet Psychiatry*, 3(2), 117–127.

McEwen, B. S. (2012). The ever-changing brain: cellular and molecular mechanisms for the effects of stressful experiences. *Developmental Neurobiology*, 72(6), 878–890.

McGirr, A., Berlim, M. T., Bond, D. J., Fleck, M. P., Yatham, L. N. and Lam, R. W. (2015). A systematic review and meta-analysis of randomized, double-blind, placebo-controlled trials of ketamine in the rapid treatment of major depressive episodes. *Psychological Medicine*, 45(4), 693–704.

Melander, H., Salmonson, T., Abadie, E. and van Zwieten-Boot, B. (2008). A regulatory Apologia – a review of placebo-controlled studies in regulatory submissions of new-generation antidepressants. *European Neuropsychopharmacology*, 18(9), 623–627.

Mischoulon, D., Nierenberg, A. A., Schettler, P. J., Kinkead, B. L., Fehling, K., Martinson, M. A. and Rapaport, M. H. (2015). A double-blind, randomized controlled clinical trial comparing eicosapentaenoic acid versus docosahexaenoic acid for depression. *Journal of Clinical Psychiatry*, 76(1), 54–61.

Mojtabai, R., Olfson, M., Sampson, N. A., Jin, R., Druss, B., Wang, P. S., . . . Kessler, R. C. (2011). Barriers to mental health treatment: results from the National Comorbidity Survey Replication. *Psychological Medicine*, 41(8), 1751–1761.

Molendijk, M. L., Spinhoven, P., Polak, M., Bus, B. A. A., Penninx, B. and Elzinga, B. M. (2014). Serum BDNF concentrations as peripheral manifestations of depression: evidence from a systematic review and meta-analyses on 179 associations (N=9484). *Molecular Psychiatry*, 19(7), 791–800.

Moncrieff, J., Wessely, S. and Hardy, R. (1998). Meta-analysis of trials comparing antidepressants with active placebos. *British Journal of Psychiatry*, 172, 227–231.

Montgomery, S. A., Entsuah, R., Hackett, D., Kunz, N. R., Rudolph, R. L. and Venlafaxine 335 Study Group. (2004). Venlafaxine versus placebo in the preventive treatment of recurrent major depression. *Journal of Clinical Psychiatry*, 65(3), 328–336.

Moore, M., Yuen, H. M., Dunn, N., Mullee, M. A., Maskell, J. and Kendrick, T. (2009). Explaining the rise in antidepressant prescribing: a descriptive study using the general practice research database. *British Medical Journal, 339,* 7.

Murrough, J. W., Losifescu, D. V., Chang, L. C., Al Jurdi, R. K., Green, C. E., Perez, A. M., . . . Mathew, S. J. (2013). Antidepressant efficacy of Ketamine in treatment-resistant major depression: a two-site randomized controlled trial. *American Journal of Psychiatry, 170*(10), 1134–1142.

National Institute for Health and Clinical Excellence (NICE). (2009). *Depression: the treatment and management of depression in adults* (updated edn). National Clinical Practice Guideline 90. Retrieved 20 July from 2017 from https://nice.org.uk/guidance/cg90.

Nelson, J. C. and Papakostas, G. I. (2009). Atypical antipsychotic augmentation in major depressive disorder: a meta-analysis of placebo-controlled randomized trials. *American Journal of Psychiatry, 166*(9), 980–991.

Nierenberg, A. A., Farabaugh, A. H., Alpert, J. E., Gordon, J., Worthington, J. J., Rosenbaum, J. F. and Fava, M. (2000). Timing of onset of antidepressant response with fluoxetine treatment. *American Journal of Psychiatry, 157*(9), 1423–1428.

Olfson, M., Blanco, C. and Marcus, S. C. (2016). Treatment of adult depression in the United States. *JAMA Internal Medicine, 176*(10), 1482–1491.

Olfson, M. and Marcus, S. C. (2009). National patterns in antidepressant medication treatment. *Archives of General Psychiatry, 66*(8), 848–856.

Olfson, M., Marcus, S. C., Tedeschi, M. and Wan, G. J. (2006). Continuity of antidepressant treatment for adults with depression in the United States. *American Journal of Psychiatry, 163*(1), 101–108.

Papakostas, G. I., Fava, M. and Thase, M. E. (2008). Treatment of SSRI-resistant depression: a meta-analysis comparing within-versus across-class switches. *Biological Psychiatry, 63*(7), 699–704.

Paykel, E. S., Ramana, R., Cooper, Z., Hayhurst, H., Kerr, J. and Barocka, A. (1995). Residual symptoms after partial remission – an important outcome in depression. *Psychological Medicine, 25*(6), 1171–1180.

Peet, M. and Horrobin, D. F. (2002) A dose-ranging study of the effects of ethyl-eicosapentaenoate in patients with ongoing depression despite apparently adequate treatment with standard drugs. *Archives of General Psychiatry, 59,* 913–919.

Quitkin, F. M., Rabkin, J. G., Gerald, J., Davis, J. M. and Klein, D. F. (2000). Validity of clinical trials of antidepressants. *American Journal of Psychiatry, 157*(3), 327–337.

Rocha, F. L., Fuzikawa, C., Riera, R. and Hara, C. (2012). Combination of anti-depressants in the treatment of major depressive disorder: a systematic review and meta-analysis. *Journal of Clinical Psychopharmacology, 32*(2), 278–281.

Rohan, K. J., Mahon, J. N., Evans, M., Ho, S. Y., Meyerhoff, J., Postolache, T. T. and Vacek, P. M. (2015). Randomized trial of Cognitive-Behavioral Therapy versus light therapy for Seasonal Affective Disorder: acute outcomes. *American Journal of Psychiatry, 172*(9), 862–869.

Rohan, K. J., Meyerhoff, J., Ho, S. Y., Evans, M., Postolache, T. T. and Vacek, P. M. (2016). Outcomes one and two winters following cognitive behavioral therapy or light therapy for Seasonal Affective Disorder. *American Journal of Psychiatry*, *173*(3), 244–251.

Roll, J. M., Kennedy, J., Tran, M. and Howell, D. (2013). Disparities in unmet need for mental health services in the United States, 1997–2010. *Psychiatric Services*, *64*(1), 80–82.

Romeo, B., Choucha, W., Fossati, P. and Rotge, J. Y. (2015). Meta-analysis of short- and mid-term efficacy of ketamine in unipolar and bipolar depression. *Psychiatry Research*, *230*(2), 682–688.

Rossom, R. C., Shortreed, S., Coleman, K. J., Beck, A., Waitzfelder, B. E., Stewart, C., . . . Simon, G. E. (2016). Antidepressant adherence across diverse populations and healthcare settings. *Depression and Anxiety*, *33*(8), 765–774.

Rush, A. J., Batey, S. R., Donahue, R. M. J., Ascher, J. A., Carmody, T. J. and Metz, A. (2001). Does pretreatment anxiety predict response to either bupropion SR or sertraline? *Journal of Affective Disorders*, *64*(1), 81–87.

Rush, A. J., Trivedi, M. H., Wisniewski, S. R., Nierenberg, A. A., Stewart, J. W., Warden, D., . . . Fava, M. (2006). Acute and longer-term outcomes in depressed outpatients requiring one or several treatment steps: a STAR*D report. *American Journal of Psychiatry*, *163*(11), 1905–1917.

Rutherford, B. R. and Roose, S. P. (2013). A model of placebo response in antidepressant clinical trials. *American Journal of Psychiatry*, *170*(7), 723–733.

Santarelli, L., Saxe, M., Gross, C., Surget, A., Battaglia, F., Dulawa, S., . . . Hen, R. (2003). Requirement of hippocampal neurogenesis for the behavioral effects of antidepressants. *Science*, *301*(5634), 805–809.

Schloesser, R. J., Orvoen, S., Jimenez, D. V., Hardy, N. F., Maynard, K. R., Sukumar, M., . . . Martinowich, K. (2015). Antidepressant-like effects of electroconvulsive seizures require adult neurogenesis in a neuroendocrine model of depression. *Brain Stimulation*, *8*(5), 862–867.

Schneeweiss, S., Patrick, A. R., Solomon, D. H., Mehta, J., Dormuth, C., Miller, M., . . . Wang, P. S. (2010). Variation in the risk of suicide attempts and completed suicides by antidepressant agent in adults: a propensity score-adjusted analysis of 9 years' data. *Archives of General Psychiatry*, *67*(5), 497–506.

Schnell, A., Albrecht, U. and Sandrelli, F. (2014). Rhythm and mood: relationships between the circadian clock and mood-related behavior. *Behavioral Neuroscience*, *128*(3), 326–343.

Sharma, T., Guski, L. S., Freund, N. and Gotzsche, P. C. (2016). Suicidality and aggression during antidepressant treatment: systematic review and meta-analyses based on clinical study reports. *British Medical Journal*, *352*, 10.

Simon, G. E., Heiligenstein, J. H., Grothaus, L., Katon, W. and Revicki, D. (1998). Should anxiety and insomnia influence antidepressant selection: a randomized comparison of fluoxetine and imipramine. *Journal of Clinical Psychiatry*, *59*(2), 49–55.

Simon, G., Ormel, J., Vonkorff, M. and Barlow, W. (1995). Health-care costs associated with depressive and anxiety disorders in primary-care. *American Journal of Psychiatry*, 152, 352–357.

Simon, G. E., Savarino, J., Operskalski, B. and Wang, P. S. (2006). Suicide risk during antidepressant treatment. *American Journal of Psychiatry*, 163(1), 41–47.

Spielmans, G. I., Berman, M. I., Linardatos, E., Rosenlicht, N. Z., Perry, A. and Tsai, A. C. (2013). Adjunctive atypical antipsychotic treatment for Major Depressive Disorder: a meta-analysis of depression, quality of life, and safety outcomes. *PLOS Medicine*, 10(3), 24.

Strawbridge, R., Young, A. H. and Cleare, A. J. (2017). Biomarkers for depression: recent insights, current challenges and future prospects. *Neuropsychiatric Disease and Treatment*, 13, 1245–1262

Szegedi, A., Kohnen, R., Dienel, A. and Kieser, M. (2005). Acute treatment of moderate to severe depression with hypericum extract WS 5570 (St John's wort): randomised controlled double blind non-inferiority trial versus paroxetine. *British Medical Journal*, 330(7490), 503–506.

Tansey, K., Guipponi, M., Perroud, N., Bondolfi, G., Domenici, E., Evans, D., . . . Uher, R. (2012). Genetic predictors of response to serotonergic and noradrenergic antidepressants in major depressive disorder: a genome-wide analysis of individual-level data and a meta-analysis. *PLOS Medicine*, 9(10), 10.

Taylor, M. J., Freemantle, N., Geddes, J. R. and Bhagwagar, Z. (2006). Early onset of selective serotonin reuptake inhibitor antidepressant action – systematic review and meta-analysis. *Archives of General Psychiatry*, 63(11), 1217–1223.

Trivedi, M. H., Fava, M., Wisniewski, S. R., Thase, M. E., Quitkin, F., Warden, D., . . . Team, S. D. S. (2006). Medication augmentation after the failure of SSRIs for depression. *New England Journal of Medicine*, 354(12), 1243–1252.

Turner, E. H., Matthews, A. M., Linardatos, E., Tell, R. A. and Rosenthal, R. (2008). Selective publication of antidepressant trials and its influence on apparent efficacy. *New England Journal of Medicine*, 358(3), 252–260.

Uher, R., Gendep Investigators, Mars Investigators and STAR-D Investigators. (2013). Common genetic variation and antidepressant efficacy in Major Depressive Disorder: a meta-analysis of three genome-wide pharmacogenetic studies. *American Journal of Psychiatry*, 170(2), 207–217.

Uher, R., Maier, W., Hauser, J., Marusic, A., Schmael, C., Mors, O., . . . McGuffin, P. (2009). Differential efficacy of escitalopram and nortriptyline on dimensional measures of depression. *British Journal of Psychiatry*, 194(3), 252–259.

Valenstein, M., Kim, H. M., Ganoczy, D., Eisenberg, D., Pfeiffer, P. N., Downing, K., . . . McCarthy, J. F. (2012). Antidepressant agents and suicide death among US Department of Veterans Affairs patients in depression treatment. *Journal of Clinical Psychopharmacology*, 32(3), 346–353.

Valuck, R. J., Libby, A. M., Anderson, H. D., Allen, R. R., Strombom, I., Marangell, L. B. and Perahia, D. (2016). Comparison of antidepressant classes and the risk and time course of suicide attempts in adults: propensity matched, retrospective cohort study. *British Journal of Psychiatry, 208*(3), 271–279.

Wang, P. S., Berglund, P., Olfson, M., Pincus, H. A., Wells, K. B. and Kessler, R. C. (2005). Failure and delay in initial treatment contact after first onset of mental disorders in the national comorbidity survey replication. *Archives of General Psychiatry, 62*(6), 603–613.

Wolkowitz, O. M., Reus, V. I., Keebler, A., Nelson, N., Friedland, M., Brizendine, L. and Roberts, E. (1999). Double-blind treatment of major depression with dehydroepiandrosterone. *American Journal of Psychiatry, 156*(4), 646–649.

Zarate, C. A., Singh, J. B., Carlson, P. J., Brutsche, N. E., Ameli, R., Luckenbaugh, D. A., . . . Manji, H. K. (2006). A randomized trial of an N-methyl-D-aspartate antagonist in treatment-resistant major depression. *Archives of General Psychiatry, 63*(8), 856–864.

8

Psychological treatments

There are now many systematically tested and effective psychological treatments for depression, providing optimism for both therapists and patients. RCTs have confirmed that most bona fide psychological treatments for depression, that is, treatments with a good rationale for treating depression, outperform no treatment and waiting list control conditions, indicating that the treatments work, and that they are of similar efficacy to each other and to antidepressant medication (see Chapter 7) (Cuijpers, van Straten, Andersson and van Oppen, 2008; Cuijpers, van Straten, van Oppen and Andersson, 2008). This chapter will review the methods, effectiveness, applications and mechanisms of psychological treatment by focusing on three illustrative, distinct treatments: *Behavioural Activation (BA)*, *CBT* and *Interpersonal Therapy (IPT)*.

In addition, this chapter will consider some key challenges and questions for psychological treatments. One major challenge is that despite being efficacious, psychological treatments still only produce sustained and full recovery in approximately 30–40 per cent of patients with depression, indicating scope for significant improvement. Further, treatment outcomes have not significantly improved for over 40 years since the development of CBT, raising the question of how to improve the effectiveness of therapy. A second related challenge is that we still don't know exactly how psychological treatments work or what their active ingredients are. A third major challenge is how to make evidence-based treatments accessible and available to as many people with depression as possible given the high prevalence of depression worldwide (see Chapter 2) and the relatively limited number of therapists. This chapter reviews several proposed solutions including digital and self-help treatments, stepped care healthcare models and improving prevention of the onset and relapse of depression.

Psychotherapy approaches to depression

Behavioural treatments

Behavioural interventions for depression are based on learning theory principles that depression is characterised by an understandable attempt to escape or to avoid aversive situations or emotional states (e.g., withdrawing from others when feeling low; doing less when tired; minimising risk of failure or embarrassment). However, such avoidance is proposed to maintain and exacerbate depression because it narrows the range of an individual's behaviour and reduces contact with the positively reinforcing events that can improve mood (Ferster, 1973). Behavioural treatments therefore focus on reducing avoidance and building up approach and positive activities, consistent with a common-sense view that being active leads to rewards that are an antidote to depression (Kanter, Puspitasari, Santos and Nagy, 2012). Behavioural approaches are an integral part of CBT but have also been developed into a stand-alone psychological therapy in its own right called Behavioural Activation (BA; Martell, Addis and Jacobson, 2001).

One BA approach, commonly used within CBT, is to build up positive activities, through activity scheduling and graded task assignment. Depressed individuals often decrease previously enjoyable activities because of a loss of interest and pleasure, or they anticipate that activity would be too difficult, take too much energy or fail to produce pleasure. The therapist and client collaborate to identify potentially pleasurable or meaningful activities and make plans for the client to engage in these activities, typically starting with small steps and building up to more difficult tasks, and anticipate and plan for possible actual or cognitive obstacles to undertaking them. Monitoring pleasure and mastery, a weekly activity schedule, task rehearsal and role-playing are used to assess and then influence how changes in behaviour are related to changes in mood. The client is encouraged to experiment with activity and test the hypothesis that engagement in activities that provide a sense of mastery or pleasure improves mood. Graded task assignments help clients to engage in successively more rewarding yet demanding activities that lead to increased pleasure or mastery experiences; such activities can also tackle current problems (e.g., lack of rewarding job, relationship difficulties) that contribute to depression. BA is especially likely to be employed to treat symptoms directly, usually at the initial stages of treatment.

A second approach, more often used within stand-alone BA, focuses on the context and functions of thoughts and behaviours rather than their form or content, concentrating on variability in feelings and behaviour across situations in order to determine what differences in environment and behaviour influence the patient's mood and their success at achieving goals. The key technique here is functional analysis, which is the analysis of antecedents, consequences and variability in behaviour in order to formulate the triggers and reinforcers for behaviours and, thereby, to plan behavioural change (Martell et al., 2001).

The elaboration of BA as a stand-alone therapy resulted from a seminal dismantling study, which found no significant difference between BA alone, BA plus modification of negative thoughts, and full 'CBT' for depressed outpatients post-treatment and at two-year follow-up (Gortner, Gollan, Dobson and Jacobson, 1998; Jacobson et al., 1996). In other words, the BA component was as efficacious a treatment as full CBT, although the trial may have been underpowered to detect any difference between active treatments.

Cognitive-behavioural treatment of depression

Developed by Aaron Beck, a psychoanalytically trained psychiatrist, the theory behind CBT emphasises the role of maladaptive cognitions in the origin, maintenance and worsening of depression (Beck, 1967), as described in Chapter 5. When people think negatively, they feel depressed, and therefore therapy attempts to identify and alter the negative thoughts and beliefs, while also altering dysfunctional behaviours that might contribute to depression.

CBT is intended to be time-limited, relatively brief (approximately 20 sessions over 16 weeks), active, collaborative and here-and-now focused on current problems and current dysfunctional thinking (as described in Beck, Rush, Shaw and Emery, 1979). Homework assignments are used between sessions to practice skills necessary to master the techniques of the treatment, observe thoughts and behaviour, test hypotheses and acquire new skills. CBT has two core components: behavioural approaches as described above; and cognitive approaches that are directly focused on changing the negative thinking hypothesised to contribute to the maintenance of depression. The two approaches are complementary to each other, for example, in the form of behavioural experiments, in which plans to try certain activities are made to deliberately test out the negative thoughts and beliefs held by depressed patients.

Identifying and challenging 'automatic negative thoughts' is the fundamental tool for changing maladaptive, depressogenic thoughts. Clients are taught to observe the link between thoughts and feelings, and to clarify their own emotion-related thoughts. Using a written form typically divided into columns, individuals keep records of emotion-arousing experiences, the automatic negative thoughts associated with them, and their realistic thoughts or challenges to the maladaptive thoughts. Several techniques are taught to clients to challenge each negative thought, focused on evaluating the evidence for and against a negative thought (e.g., asking 'is there a distortion?', 'what's the evidence?'), and looking at alternative explanations (e.g. 'is there another way to look at it?', 'what if (the worst is really true)?'). Usually, one or more of these challenges helps the client to replace the dysfunctional thought with a more realistic one.

Often the realistic thoughts lead to specific behavioural activities to try out new ways of behaving or to collect behavioural data to test one's beliefs ('behavioural experiments'). The negative thoughts are hypothesised to occur at different levels, ranging from surface level interpretations of events ('if he didn't call me it means he doesn't like me'), to deeper, pervasive, core beliefs and assumptions ('if someone doesn't like me it means I'm no good'). Later stages of therapy focus on addressing the deeper level assumptions and schemas.

CBT is intended not only to alleviate the symptoms of depression and resolve immediate difficulties in the client's environment, but also to teach skills that can be used to resolve problems or deal with emerging depressive symptoms. Thus, an important goal of the therapy is to reduce the likelihood of recurrence of depression, which is further discussed later in the chapter.

Interpersonal Psychotherapy

IPT is based on the interpersonal therapy model of Harry Stack Sullivan, which assumes that depression can result from, and lead to, difficulties in the interpersonal relationships among depressed persons and their significant others (Klerman, Weissman, Rounsaville and Chevron, 1984). IPT, therefore, attempts both to alleviate depressive symptoms and to improve interpersonal functioning by 'clarifying, refocusing, and renegotiating the interpersonal context associated with the onset of depression' (Weissman and Klerman, 1990). IPT is a brief, weekly time-limited therapy of 12 to 16 weeks, administered individually. The first few sessions are devoted to assessment and forming treatment goals. During this first phase, the patient is taught the 'sick role', learning about depression as an illness and receiving encouragement to continue regular activities but without the expectation of performing normally. The second phase identifies and targets interpersonal problems thought to contribute to the depression, and the third, or termination phase, focuses on consolidating what has been learned and anticipating using the skills during times of future difficulty. The therapy is oriented toward the here-and-now, rather than the early origins of depressive vulnerabilities or interpersonal difficulties.

Improving the depressed patient's interpersonal functioning is accomplished by exploring with the patient one or more of the following problem areas commonly associated with the onset of depression: *grief, role disputes, role transition or interpersonal deficits*. Klerman et al. (1984) discuss specific goals and procedures to deal with each of the four problem areas. *Grief* refers to abnormal bereavement (distorted, delayed or chronic) and the need to resolve loss by accurate perception and by replacing some of the lost activities or resources. *Role disputes* and *role transitions* refer to difficulties with others in managing or changing important areas of functioning and self-definition, such as marital conflict, occupational difficulties, dealing with a child moving out of the home and the like. The therapy aims at identification of the problem, clarification of expectations, negotiation of disputes and improvement of communication. *Interpersonal deficits* refer to relatively depression-related problems in interpersonal functioning, such as communication or forming friendships; therapy helps the person identify the problem and its consequences and acquire new behaviours. In general, IPT therapists make use of nondirective exploration, encourage expression of affect, teach the patient more effective methods of interpersonal communication, and attempt to alter depressive behaviours through insight, providing information and role-playing.

As an example of IPT, a woman might report depression occurring in the context of dealing with a rebellious teenage daughter; she feels upset because the teenager is disrespectful and disobedient, and the mother cannot control her actions, causing great worry. The woman also feels that her husband ignores the problem and does not support her. IPT would draw a link between the depression and the woman's goals and disputes in the parental role. Through exploration, support and problem-solving activity, IPT helps the woman to see the extent to which her own self-esteem is tied to the approval of her daughter and the daughter's achievements. The mother is encouraged to have realistic expectations for her child's behaviour and to pursue alternative means of bolstering her own self-esteem (such as working outside the home). She is aided in developing reasonable standards of conduct for her daughter, and consistency in disciplining the girl (instead of being lenient as a way to avoid the child's anger at her).

Evaluating the outcome of psychological treatments

Meta-analyses have indicated that bona fide treatments such as BA, CBT and IPT are effective treatments, superior to non bona fide treatments (i.e., those with no specific good reason to treat depression e.g., non-directive supportive counselling) but of equivalent treatment efficacy to each other and to anti-depressant medication (Cuijpers, Cristea, Karyotaki, Reijnders and Huibers, 2016; Cuijpers, van Straten, Andersson et al., 2008; Cuijpers, van Straten, van Oppen et al., 2008; Driessen, Hollon, Bockting, Cuijpers and Turner, 2015; Tolin, 2010; Wampold, Minami, Baskin and Tierney, 2002). However, treatment effects may be overestimated because of potential publication bias, allegiance bias and poor study quality.

Meta-analyses of controlled trials of CBT find that CBT is an effective treatment for depression, significantly superior to no-treatment control groups, waiting list or placebo control groups (e.g., Gloaguen, Cottraux, Cucherat and Blackburn, 1998; Robinson, Berman and Neimayer, 1990). Similarly, meta-analyses have confirmed that BA alone has significant treatment effects for depression, of similar efficacy to other active treatments such as CBT (Ekers, Richards and Gilbody, 2008; Ekers et al., 2014). A meta-analysis of 38 studies confirmed that IPT is an empirically valid treatment for depression, with an average overall moderate effect size relative to control groups (Cuijpers et al., 2011).

A recent methodological innovation is the use of network meta-analyses, which combine direct calculations of effect sizes between treatments compared in existing studies (e.g., CBT vs medication; CBT vs IPT) to also estimate indirect comparisons that have not been so frequently compared (e.g., IPT vs CBT). A network meta-analysis of psychotherapy for depression (Barth et al., 2013) found that both CBT and IPT were significantly more effective than waiting list control.

The best individual RCTs with large sample sizes and superior method-ology confirm these results, finding similar rates of acute recovery from depression for CBT, IPT and BA, ranging from 32–43 per cent and that these bona fide therapies are active treatments better than pill placebo (e.g., DeRubeis et al., 2005; Dimidjian et al., 2006; Elkin et al., 1989; Hollon et al., 1992).

Psychological treatments compared to medication

The comparison of psychotherapy with pharmacotherapy is of critical importance, since antidepressant medications represent the standard treatment
option of persons with clinically significant depression (see Chapter 7).
Outcome studies comparing psychological treatments with pharmacotherapy
need to include a pill placebo control condition in order to determine whether
the pharmacotherapy has produced an efficacious response.

A number of methodologically sophisticated trials have affirmed the
efficacy of CBT, IPT and BA when compared to antidepressants and pill
placebo. IPT is as effective as pharmacotherapy in reducing depressive symptomatology, and is more effective than pharmacotherapy in improving
social functioning both acutely and at one-year follow-up (Weissman, 1979;
Weissman, Klerman, Prusoff, Sholomskas and Padian, 1981). A large-scale
RCT of patients with moderate to severe depression across two treatment sites,
found that after eight weeks, CBT and pharmacotherapy (paroxetine) were
not significantly different (43 per cent vs. 50 per cent response rates) with both
superior to pill placebo (25 per cent) (DeRubeis et al., 2005). At 16 weeks, the
rates of recovery were 46 per cent for pharmacotherapy and 40 per cent for
CBT, indicating that CBT can be as effective as antidepressants. An RCT of
241 patients with major depression compared CBT, BA, pharmacotherapy
(paroxetine) or pill placebo (Dimidjian et al., 2006). For patients with more
severe depression only, antidepressant medication produced significantly
greater improvement per treatment week than pill placebo, confirming
that pharmacotherapy was adequately implemented. For patients with less
severe depression, CBT, BA and antidepressants all produced significant
improvements and were equally efficacious. However, for patients with more
severe depression, BA and antidepressant medication produced significantly
more improvement than CBT, with BA and antidepressant medication not
differing.

The seminal NIMH Treatment of Depression Collaborative Research
Program (TDCRP; Elkin et al., 1989) randomly allocated 250 outpatients with
major depression to CBT, IPT, imipramine plus clinical management (brief
support and advice to patients along with the pills) or pill placebo plus clinical
management, in a multi-site study. There were few differences between CBT
and IPT, and it appeared that overall both were as effective as medication.

Combined psychological treatment with medication

Another important comparison is between antidepressants alone versus antidepressants plus psychological treatment. This comparison is of particular
relevance to patients with severe or treatment-resistant depression, who do

not respond to either antidepressants alone or to psychotherapy alone. A systematic review of 16 RCTs comparing combined pharmacotherapy and psychological treatment versus pharmacotherapy alone for depression found that combined treatment improved outcomes significantly more than medication treatment alone, in part due to a reduction in patients dropping out of therapy (Pampallona, Bollini, Tibaldi, Kupelnick and Munizza, 2004). Eleven of these trials featured CBT as the psychological treatment, suggesting additional benefit from combining both medication and CBT. A meta-analysis of 32 trials of depressive disorders found a moderate effect size in favour of combined treatment (psychotherapy plus antidepressants) relative to antidepressant alone (Cuijpers et al., 2014).

An important US trial compared the effects of antidepressant medication alone or with the addition of CBT, with treatment continuing up to 42 months, for 452 adult outpatients with severe or chronic major depression (Hollon et al., 2014). Combined treatment was found to enhance recovery (81.3 per cent recovery) relative to antidepressants alone (51.7 per cent), with this effect found for those patients for severe but not chronic depression. A similar pattern of results was found in the UK based CoBaLT trial, which found that using CBT as an adjunct to antidepressant medication in patients with treatment-resistant depression improved outcomes and was cost-effective, even after a variable three–five years' follow-up (Wiles et al., 2013; Wiles et al., 2016). Combination treatment is therefore recommended for patients who do not respond to single modality treatment, especially for severe depression (Craighead and Dunlop, 2014).

Comparing psychotherapies

As noted previously, the seminal TDCRP trial found few differences between CBT and IPT. Similarly, a Dutch RCT of 182 patients with major depression found no differential effects between IPT and CBT, with both producing significantly more improvement than waiting list control, with effects sustained at one-year follow-up (Lemmens et al., 2015).

Trials comparing CBT with short-term psychodynamic-interpersonal therapy (which uses psychodynamic methods such as interpretations) found the two psychotherapies equally effective in symptom reduction, albeit often with relatively small sample size and no medication or pill placebo control arm (e.g., Shapiro et al., 1994). A recent non-inferiority trial in a community health centre compared 16 sessions of short-term psychodynamic therapy versus CBT in 237 adult outpatients with depression. A non-inferiority trial is designed to compare a treatment to an established active treatment (e.g., CBT) with a view to testing that it is not clinically worse with regards to a maximum difference between treatments at which the test treatment is not to be considered inferior. If a 95 per cent confidence interval for the difference between treatments means lies on the appropriate side of this non-inferiority margin, then non-inferiority is deemed to have been established. Typically, non-inferiority trials require larger sample sizes than superiority trials that test whether one treatment is better than another, because the difference between treatments needed to establish significance is considerably smaller. This trial found that psychodynamic therapy was not inferior to CBT, with both treatments significantly reducing symptoms of depression (Gibbons et al., 2016).

A recent large-scale UK-based non-inferiority trial (the COBRA trial) randomised 440 adult outpatients with major depression to receive up to 20 sessions of either BA from junior mental health workers (psychological wellbeing practitioners) or CBT from psychological therapists (Richards et al., 2016). BA was non-inferior to CBT, and because the workforce providing the BA was less costly than the workforce providing the CBT, was found to be more cost-effective, although the ability of junior workers to deliver CBT was not tested.

Relapse prevention and residual depression

Given that relapse and recurrence is a major problem for patients with major depression (Judd, 1997), we are not only interested in the acute short-term effects of psychotherapy but also whether treatments can produce sustained recovery and prevent relapse and recurrence into future episodes of depression. For example, since CBT and BA teach patients skills to manage their depression, they might protect against further episodes of depression. Psychotherapy for a current episode of depression may successfully treat the acute symptoms and then provide ongoing benefit after the therapy is discontinued (*prophylactic* effects of acute-phase treatment). Psychotherapy may also be used as a sequential intervention to teach self-management skills following a successful acute response to pharmacotherapy or another treatment. A recent meta-analysis confirmed that psychological interventions, and in particular CBT, may prolong recovery after prior successful psychological or antidepressant treatment (Clarke, Mayo-Wilson, Kenny and Pilling, 2015). Psychotherapy may also be used as an adjunctive treatment when there is a limited or partial response to the initial treatment, typically antidepressant medication (that is, to *target treatment-resistant depression or residual depression*). Finally, following successful acute-phase psychological treatment, further sessions may maintain the treatment gains longer term (i.e., *maintenance* or continuation therapy).

Acute-phase prophylaxis

Research reviews conclude that CBT has enduring *prophylactic* effects that reduce the risk of symptom return following the end of treatment (Bockting, Hollon, Jarrett, Kuyken and Dobson, 2015; Hollon, 2016; Hollon, Stewart and Strunk, 2006). Because it appears that early discontinuation of antidepressant medication after remission of symptoms leaves patients open to relapse of symptoms (see Chapter 7), trials studying relapse prevention require a long-enough follow-up period and treatment conditions that include discontinuation of antidepressants as well as maintenance of antidepressants. In these trials, those patients who respond to the initial pharmacotherapy are typically randomised to continuation antidepressants or to withdrawal onto pill placebo and compared to those who completed acute-phase psychotherapy. Such trials with one or two-year follow-up consistently find that acute-phase CBT produces similar rates of relapse to continuation of antidepressants across the follow-up period (approximately 30 per cent) and reduces rates of relapse compared to when antidepressants are withdrawn and replaced with pill placebo when acute-phase CBT ends (approximately 60 per cent) (e.g., Hollon et al., 2005, the 12-month follow-up to the DeRubeis et al. (2005) trial).

Prevention after recovery: mindfulness-based CBT and CBT

Another approach specifically targets patients at high risk of relapse because they have a history of recurrent depression (e.g., three or more previous episodes), who are currently well following natural remission or successful treatment, whether via pharmacotherapy or psychotherapy. Group treatment is favoured because of its efficiency and cost-effectiveness for helping more patients for the same amount of therapist time. The most significant variant of CBT used specifically for relapse prevention is mindfulness-based CBT (MBCT; Teasdale, Segal and Williams, 1995). MBCT combines standard CBT principles with elements of a mindfulness-based stress reduction programme (Kabat-Zinn, 1990) that incorporates mindfulness meditation, based on the hypothesis that meditation is antithetical to depressive rumination. MBCT is delivered in weekly group training sessions, in which participants practice and develop a moment-by-moment non-judgemental awareness of sensations, thoughts and feelings, through the use of formal and informal meditation exercises, such as focusing attention on the breath, with daily homework practice (see Segal, Williams and Teasdale, 2002 for treatment details). Instead of 'challenging' negative thoughts, MBCT emphasises acceptance of one's thoughts and feelings, and the development of a broader perspective in which thoughts and feelings are viewed as 'mental events' rather than 'realities'.

The initial RCTs of MBCT for patients with a history of three or more episodes of major depression were positive, finding that MBCT significantly reduced risk of relapse over one year compared to usual care (typically nothing or maintenance antidepressants) (Ma and Teasdale, 2004; Teasdale et al., 2000), and apparently performing at least as well as maintenance anti-depressants in preventing relapse over one-year follow-up (Kuyken et al., 2008). However, further well-conducted trials have been less encouraging (e.g., Segal et al., 2010). An RCT that randomised 274 individuals with a history of at least three episodes of depression currently in remission to TAU, or TAU plus group MBCT or to TAU plus a control treatment of group cognitive psychological education, which provided the same information and group sessions as MBCT but without training in meditation, found no difference between the three treatments in risk of relapse over the next year (Williams et al., 2014). A further UK-based trial of 424 patients with a history of recurrent depression currently taking antidepressant medication failed to find evidence consistent with the study hypothesis that MBCT with tapering of medication would be superior to maintenance antidepressants in pre-venting recurrence of depression over 24 months follow-up (Kuyken et al., 2015). However, in post-hoc analyses, both trials found that there were differential benefits of MBCT versus TAU or antidepressant continuation for those reporting greater history of childhood trauma. A Dutch trial found no benefit of adding MBCT to maintenance antidepressants relative to main-tenance antidepressants alone (Huijbers et al., 2015). In sum, these more rigorous trials indicate that MBCT may not be as effective as originally thought, but may be of value in groups with elevated vulnerability.

Other group CBT treatments have also significantly reduced relapse in recurrently depressed patients in remission relative to TAU, over a two year follow-up compared to TAU (72 per cent to 46 per cent) for those with five or more previous episodes (Bockting et al., 2005), with these effects maintained up to ten years (Bockting et al., 2015). It may be that provision of CBT-based psychoeducation in a group format is sufficient for relapse prevention in high-risk groups.

Treatment-resistant and residual depression

CBT approaches have proven to be useful adjuncts to pharmacotherapy to address *residual and treatment-resistant depression*, and, thereby, prevent future relapse. Residual symptoms of depression predict increased risk of relapse and therefore targeting such symptoms may well help reduce future episodes of depression. In patients with recurrent depression (≥ three episodes of depression) following a course of pharmacotherapy and withdrawal from medication, CBT that targeted residual symptoms and increasing well-being resulted in significantly fewer residual symptoms post-intervention and significantly less relapse and recurrence over up to six-year follow-ups than standard clinical management (Fava, Rafanelli, Grandi, Canestrari and Morphy, 1998; Fava et al., 2004). In parallel, in a large-scale RCT, compared to TAU (antidepressants with clinical management), TAU plus CBT reduced relapse over the subsequent two years in 158 patients with residual depression following pharmacotherapy (Paykel et al., 1999). CBT has been adapted to specifically target rumination, identified as an important mechanism in the onset and maintenance of depression (see Chapter 5), by using BA approaches including functional analysis and repeated practice of alternative coping behaviours to tackle rumination as a mental habit (Watkins and Nolen-Hoeksema, 2014), and by training patients to adopt a more helpful concrete thinking style, rather than the abstract style characteristic of rumination (Watkins, 2008). In patients with residual depression, the addition of individual rumination-focused cognitive behavioural therapy (RFCBT) to ongoing antidepressant medication (TAU) significantly outperformed TAU and significantly improved rates of recovery (60 per cent versus 25 per cent) (Watkins et al., 2011). A partial replication using a group variant confirmed that RFCBT outperformed TAU in treating residual depression with effects maintained over one year (Teismann et al., 2014).

Maintenance treatment

Several studies have investigated the value of continuation CBT for patients who successfully responded to acute-phase CBT. In medication-free patients, continuation CBT significantly reduced relapse and recurrence compared to the assessment control condition (10 per cent vs. 31 per cent) over eight months, with benefits maintained over two-year follow-up (Jarrett et al., 2001). However, a further trial of patients with recurrent major depression treated with acute-phase CBT and at high risk because of residual symptoms, failed to find any difference in relapse rates over a two-year follow-up between continuation-CBT and fluoxetine, during active treatment and after discontinuation, with both outperforming pill placebo (Jarrett, Minhajuddin, Gershenfeld, Friedman and Thase, 2013; Jarrett, Minhajuddin, Vittengl, Clark and Thase, 2016). However, both active continuation-phase treatments reduced the elevated likelihood of relapse found for high-risk residual depression patients down to that observed for the lower-risk patients who responded in full to the acute-phase CBT.

The use of maintenance IPT after successful medication treatment reduced relapse rates over three years, with the mean survival time without relapse greatest for patients in the combined IPT plus medication treatment, while patients who received only monthly IPT stayed well almost twice as long as patients receiving only pill placebo (Frank et al., 1990). Similarly, for patients older than 59 years, over a three-year follow-up, maintenance antidepressant, antidepressant plus monthly maintenance IPT, pill placebo and monthly maintenance IPT all increased the time to recurrence relative to pill placebo alone, with combined IPT and medication superior to IPT alone (Reynolds et al., 1999).

Challenges for psychological treatments

Improving the sustained efficacy of treatment for depression

The evidence cited above demonstrates that CBT, IPT and BA are effective treatments, but also indicates that there is a significant need to further improve the efficacy of treatment, since recovery rates are only around 40 per cent and even after psychological treatment, relapse and recurrence rates can be as high as 50 per cent. Improving the efficacy of treatment depends on knowing more about how psychotherapy works. Identifying the key active mechanisms in therapy would enable therapy to be made more potent and effective.

There has been considerable debate as to the mechanisms of psychological treatment. Based on similar efficacy across bona fide treatments, and the difficulty in finding significant benefit relative to control conditions that are matched for structure, therapist contact and plausible rationale (Baskin, Tierney, Minami and Wampold, 2003), it has been argued that the benefits of therapy are due to elements common to all bona fide therapies. These elements, sometimes called non-specific effects, include the provision of a credible treatment rationale, an understanding and supportive therapist, and a structured approach to problems (see Frank and Frank, 1991). In part, it is hypothesised that therapy engenders positive expectations, hope and remoralisation, which improve the patient's mood. This hypothesis parallels the discussion of placebo effects in Chapter 7, where positive patient expectancy for pill placebo (and medication) is proposed to have some treatment effect. Some theorists also emphasise the importance of therapeutic alliance in improving mood. In contrast, other models of mechanisms-of-change, most notably in CBT and BA, hypothesise that in addition to non-specific effects, there are specific mechanisms-of-change, such as learning new coping skills, reducing avoidance and reducing negative thinking.

To date, it has been hard to resolve this issue of specific versus nonspecific effects, mainly because the majority of the evidence is correlational and few studies have evaluated simultaneously the relevant constructs necessary to contrast the different models. For example, investigators measure change in identified constructs from before therapy to post-therapy and evaluate how changes are correlated with symptom improvement. Correlation does not test causation. Moreover, many changes in process and symptoms occur quickly in therapy and thus repeated measurement session by session is needed for sufficient sensitivity to detect effects, rather than only assessing change from beginning to end of therapy. These methodological shortcomings need to be overcome in order to evaluate truly causal processes and how they unfold over time.

The strongest evidence for a specific effect comes from studies examining CBT. The cognitive model predicts that CBT should produce specific changes on measures of cognitions, that these changes in cognitions are unique to CBT and that these changes in cognitions should predict symptomatic improvement. However, the current evidence suggests that CBT does not work by changing underlying cognitive schemata and beliefs or causing such maladaptive schemas to be deactivated (Barber and DeRubeis, 1989). For example, although a recent review concluded that cognitive change, however achieved, is associated with symptom improvement, it was not unique to CBT (Lorenzo-Luaces, German and DeRubeis, 2015). Indeed, there is evidence that several psychological treatments and antidepressant medications may alter cognitive biases associated with depression (Roiser, Elliott and Sahakian, 2012): a meta-analysis of trials that measured dysfunctional attitudes found that there was a consistent effect of CBT on reducing negative attitudes to a greater effect than control conditions but that this effect did not significantly differ from other treatments (Cristea et al., 2015). These results suggest that cognitive change alone is not causally sufficient to produce symptom change and that it may be a consequence of symptom improvement.

Nonetheless, there is good evidence for the hypothesis that CBT teaches a new set of skills that help individuals to deal with negative thoughts when they do arise (Barber and DeRubeis, 1989). First, the specific and concrete techniques taught during therapy, including setting an agenda, structuring the session, asking for specific examples and adherence to cognitive methods such as labelling cognitive errors and examining evidence, predicted subsequent symptom reduction when assessed early in CBT treatment (DeRubeis and Feeley, 1990; Feeley, DeRubeis and Gelfand, 1999; Strunk, Brotman and

DeRubeis, 2010). However, neither the therapeutic alliance nor more abstract approaches, such as exploring the meaning of thoughts, predicted improvement.

Second, as noted in Chapter 5, patients who recovered through pharmacotherapy showed greater increases in dysfunctional attitudes following a negative mood induction than those who recovered through CBT, with such 'cognitive reactivity' predicting relapse over the next 18 months (Segal et al., 2006). The association between depressive symptoms and negative cognition post-treatment was weaker for patients who received CBT (in addition to pharmacotherapy) than for patients who did not receive additional CBT, suggesting that CBT teaches skills that weaken the link between negative mood and negative thinking (Beevers and Miller, 2005). Change in patient's learning of coping skills was negatively correlated with their cognitive reactivity (Strunk, Adler and Hollars, 2013).

How to improve psychological treatments for depression?

Understanding how treatment works

Related to not knowing the active mechanisms of therapy, we also don't know the active ingredients of psychological treatments. Treatments like CBT are complex interventions consisting of many elements (therapist factors, specific techniques, organising principles, modes of delivery). We still don't know which ingredients are active in causing improvement, inert or potentially unhelpful, leading to a call for more research into how CBT and other effective treatments work (Holmes, Craske and Graybiel, 2014). One approach is the use of innovative trial designs, such as factorial designs, which enable a robust examination of the active components within therapy, by manipulating different treatment components (Watkins et al., 2016). This will enable us to parse out the most effective elements within therapy to systematically build briefer and more potent therapy, as well as to separate specific from non-specific treatment effects.

Matching treatments to individuals – personalised care

Another way to improve treatment outcomes is to try and better match the right treatment to each individual patient. To do this, we need to know what patient characteristics predict whether someone will respond to treatment (a *prognostic indicator*) and whether someone will respond better to one treatment (e.g., CBT) than to another treatment (a *prescriptive indicator*).

Individual patient data meta-analyses have pooled the individual pre- and post-treatment data from all patients across a number of relevant trials to examine the relationship between severity of depression and treatment response. These meta-analyses either show that there is no effect of baseline severity on treatment outcome between CBT and antidepressants (Weitz et al., 2015) or in some cases that psychological treatment is more effective for patients with more severe baseline symptoms (Driessen, Cuijpers, Hollon and Dekker, 2010). This later pattern (also found for antidepressant medication) may reflect non-specific and placebo treatment effects being sufficient for recovery from mild depression, such that more active treatments including CBT are only shown to be differentially efficacious for more severe depression.

A general set of variables predict poor outcome to CBT (see review by Hamilton and Dobson, 2002), including increased chronicity of the depression, younger age at onset, greater number of previous episodes, not being married and perfectionistic beliefs, although these variables tend to predict poor outcome for all interventions. It is much harder to find reliable prescriptive indicators of who will do better or worse in CBT. Married patients appear to do better with CBT than single patients (Jarrett et al., 1991), whereas single patients do better in IPT than in CBT (Barber and Muenz, 1996). A treatment trial found that marriage, unemployment and having experienced a greater number of recent life events each predicted superior response to cognitive therapy relative to antidepressant medication (Fournier et al., 2009). There is some evidence in favour of psychological treatments relative to antidepressant medication alone for patients with histories of early difficulties or trauma (Nemeroff et al., 2003; Williams et al., 2014).

Instead of looking for individual moderators of treatment outcome, it may be more effective to create algorithms incorporating multiple moderators to predict which of two treatments (e.g., CBT vs antidepressants; CBT vs IPT) an individual may do better with based on his or her demographics and clinical presentations. Using existing data sets, such approaches suggest that when individuals receive their indicated treatment rather than the non-indicated treatment, there are significant treatment gains, although this approach has not yet been tested prospectively with participants randomised to the indicated or non-indicated treatment (DeRubeis et al., 2014; Huibers et al., 2015).

Targeting underlying pathological mechanisms

Another way to improve the efficacy of treatments is to target known psychological pathological mechanisms identified in the onset and maintenance of depression. As discussed in Chapter 5, one important mechanism is rumination, which has been targeted in treatment, with encouraging effects, by CBT adapted to reduce dysfunctional rumination (Watkins et al., 2011). Another potential mechanism is the relative absence of self-compassion.

Individuals prone to depression have a tendency towards self-criticism and self-shaming and are less good at self-soothing than those less prone to depression (Baiao, Gilbert, McEwan and Carvalho, 2015), leading to suggestions that training individuals to become more self-compassionate may aid recovery from depression (Gilbert, 2014). There is evidence that training in self-compassion can enhance the efficacy of subsequent use of cognitive reappraisal to challenge negative thoughts in patients with major depression (Diedrich, Hofmann, Cuijpers and Berking, 2016) and preliminary positive evidence for compassion training, whether delivered face-to-face (Gilbert and Procter, 2006) or via virtual reality (Falconer et al., 2014). However, compassion has yet to be properly evaluated in a RCT in patients with major depression. A third example is based on increasing evidence that intrusive unwanted memories of past upsetting or traumatic events are common in depression and contribute to the maintenance of symptoms (Brewin, Gregory, Lipton and Burgess, 2010). Preliminary evidence suggests that directly targeting such intrusive memories can be beneficial (Brewin et al., 2009).

Improving the accessibility and availability of psychological treatments

How do we make effective therapy as widely available as possible? This is a critical issue because of the high prevalence of depression and the need to make evidence-based treatment accessible and available to all the people who need or want therapy. With approximately one in five people experiencing depression, traditional face-to-face psychotherapy can never be sufficiently widely available to reduce the global burden of depression, as there would never be sufficient therapists. This suggests a need for alternative delivery methods that can increase access and availability (Kazdin and Blasé, 2011) such as computerised and internet-delivered therapies, or interventions that shift more responsibility to the individual, such as guided self-help. Digital interventions are more accessible, by being available at any time of day and anywhere the patient has access to the internet, and more convenient by not requiring a scheduled therapy appointment or visit to a treatment centre. Moreover, given the financial impact of depression and the significant costs of providing psychological treatments, there is also an imperative in health service systems to find cost-effective ways to provide evidence-based therapies.

Another approach to increase access to psychological interventions for anxiety and depression and to improve cost-effectiveness is to use a Stepped

Care service model in which interventions demanding less resource are offered first where clinically appropriate (Bower and Gilbody, 2005). A world-leading example is the Improving Access to Psychological Treatments (IAPT) programme initiated in 2008 in the English National Health Service (Clark et al., 2009). This involved the national rollout in England of primary care delivery sites to provide evidence-based psychological interventions, pre-dominantly CBT, as recommended by the National Institute of Health and Care Excellence (NICE), the public body that evaluates the efficiancy and cost-effectiveness of treatments for the English National Health Service. High intensity treatments are psychological therapies such as CBT or IPT that are provided by a therapist face-to-face over an extended duration of sessions, with flexibility based on therapist judgement. High intensity therapists are typically already qualified mental health professionals who undergo an extensive period of supervised practice. Low-intensity treatments typically involve briefer, more structured and more generic treatment protocols such as guided written or audio-recorded self-help materials, computerised or internet-delivered CBT, or group-delivered psychoeducation, supported by a practitioner specifically trained to competency for only those materials. In IAPT, a new workforce of Psychological Wellbeing Practitioners (PWPs), typically psychology graduates trained for six months was created to deliver low intensity interventions. Because low-intensity treatment is briefer and PWPs are a more junior role, their introduction enabled more patients to be treated at lower overall cost. In England, IAPT has enabled many more people to access and complete psychological treatment on the NHS than pre-viously (now over 500,000 people per year, and over 3 million people since 2008) with over two thirds seen within four weeks, and with average recovery rates of just under 50 per cent. One argument for the rollout of IAPT was an economic one – that despite its increased treatment costs, it would pay for itself in terms of reduced social care costs and increased return to work and productivity for its recipients (Fonagy and Clark, 2015; Layard and Clark, 2015). This is consistent with arguments from statistical modelling approaches that indicate that better provision for mental health, while expensive, would be good value for money because of the resulting savings in health and social care and increased productivity (Chisholm et al., 2016). Nonetheless, IAPT still only meets an estimated 15 per cent of the need for common mental health problems in adults in England.

A further means to disseminate therapy is by shifting its delivery from professionals to lay practitioners. This approach may be particularly valuable in countries where there is less established mental health infrastructure. As a good example of the benefits of this approach, a simple variant of BA called the Healthy Activity Programme delivered by lay counsellors was more effective than enhanced usual primary care for patients with moderately severe depression in primary care in India, where there is limited access to psychological treatments (Patel et al., 2017).

Mode of treatment delivery: does it matter how psychological treatment is delivered?

In general, the evidence indicates that alternative means of delivering CBT can be as effective as traditional face-to-face therapy. Meta-analyses and direct comparisons suggest that patients find computer or internet-based treatment acceptable and they manifest degrees of clinical recovery of similar magnitude to those who have face-to-face therapy (Andersson, 2009; Andersson, Cuijpers, Carlbring, Riper and Hedman, 2014; Andersson, Hesser, Hummerdal, Bergman-Nordgren and Carlbring, 2013; Andrews, Cuijpers, Craske, McEvoy and Titov, 2010). Computerised CBT (C-CBT) or internet CBT (i-CBT) can be delivered either with minimal therapist involvement (unguided) or with guidance and support from a therapist (guided) typically through secure written communications in the website, sometimes when logged on with the patient (synchronous like live texting) or at a separate time from when the patient is logged on (asynchronous). It can also be used to augment face-to-face therapy to improve efficiency per therapist hour ('blended' therapy). Meta-analyses suggest that guided variants of C-CBT and i-CBT have much better outcomes and treatment retention for patients with depression than unguided self-help versions, in part due to much better levels of motivation and activity when there is an involved therapist (Andrews, Cuijpers, Craske, McEvoy and Titov, 2010; Richards and Richardson, 2012). Notable trials include the first trial showing that internet CBT with only brief therapist contact outperformed a discussion group alone for patients with major depression (Andersson et al., 2005), the first trial showing that self-help internet CBT treatment (MoodGYM) outperformed placebo control in reducing depressive symptoms (Mackinnon, Griffiths and Christensen, 2008), and synchronous online CBT delivered in real time though written messaging by a therapist outperforming TAU in primary care (Kessler et al., 2009). However, a recent large RCT with 691 patients in the UK failed to find any differential benefit in primary care of a C-CBT called Beating the Blues versus MoodGYM, each with minimal telephone support, versus usual GP care (Gilbody et al., 2015).

Guided self-help CBT include patients being encouraged to work through self-help books or specially prepared workbooks, with professionals providing limited but useful supportive or facilitative contact, often via telephone.

Again, guided self-help is more efficacious for depression than completely unguided self-help (Gellatly et al., 2007), although reviews suggest that even relatively low levels of support can be beneficial (Farrand and Woodford, 2013; Newman, Szkodny, Llera and Przeworski, 2011). Repeated practice with audio-recorded mental exercises can be helpful, for example, training to think in a more concrete style significantly reduced depression relative to usual care for patients with major depression in primary care (Watkins et al., 2012). Meta-analyses suggest that guided self-help for depression has similar effect sizes to face-to-face psychotherapy for depression (Cuijpers, Donker, van Straten, Li and Andersson, 2010) and that larger effect sizes are found for higher levels of initial depression severity (Bower et al., 2013). Nonetheless, some patients may express a preference for face-to-face therapy.

Prevention of depression

Given the recurrent and persistent life-long nature of depression, there is an increasing focus on preventing the initial onset of depression, and such prevention is a critical part of reducing the overall global burden of depression (Munoz, Beardslee and Leykin, 2012). Because initial onset of depression is typically between the ages of 16–20, this requires interventions to prevent depression in childhood through to young adulthood, although prevention can be usefully targeted at other high-risk groups, such as pregnant women and recent mothers (Brugha, Morrell, Slade and Walters, 2011) or adults with sub-syndromal symptoms (Buntrock et al., 2016).

Selective prevention targets individuals who manifest some vulnerability or risk factor for depression, such as children of depressed parents or individuals with an elevated tendency towards worry and rumination (Topper, Emmelkamp and Ehring, 2010). Indicated prevention targets individuals who have already demonstrated sub-syndromal symptoms of depression. Universal prevention targets all individuals in a particular population unselected for risk status, with the advantage that it is more broadly accessible, less stigmatising, and has fewer drop-outs, but the disadvantage that the intervention may be delivered to a large proportion of individuals at low risk for depression who do not need any additional help.

There is robust evidence for the efficacy of psychological interventions at preventing the onset of depression summarised in meta-analyses and reviews (Cuijpers, van Straten, Smit, Mihalopoulos and Beekman, 2008; Muñoz et al., 2012; Muñoz, Cuijpers, Smit, Barrera and Leykin, 2010; Stice, Shaw, Bohon, Marti and Rohde, 2009; Stockings et al., 2016), including school-based interventions (Merry et al., 2011) and online and computer-based interventions (Clarke, Kuosmanen and Barry, 2015). These reviews conclude that school-based interventions and online interventions can prevent depression and that selective interventions may do better than universal interventions at 12 months follow-up. However, nearly all evidence is limited to six–12 month follow-ups, with less evidence of longer-term efficacy. Unfortunately, while some studies do examine the prevention of the new onset of an episode of major depression, many still focus on the reduction in depressive symptoms, i.e., a treatment effect rather than a prevention effect.

One noteworthy group-based intervention ('Coping with Stress') is focused on techniques to identify and challenge dysfunctional thoughts (Clarke et al., 1995) and has been effective in lowering rates of major depression more than usual care in three selective and indicated prevention trials: in adolescents selected for high self-reported depression scores followed over 12 months (Clarke et al., 1999; 14.5 per cent vs. 25.7 per cent); in adolescent children of depressed patients followed for two years (Clarke et al., 2001; 9.3 per cent vs. 28.8 per cent); in adolescents with at least one parent with current or past depression and who themselves had a history of depression and/or elevated depressive symptoms, followed at six months (Garber et al., 2009), and up to six years (Brent et al., 2015). For this later study, the effects of the prevention were moderated by parental depression: the benefits of the intervention groups were not found relative to usual care when a parent was actively depressed at baseline.

IPT has also been investigated in indicated prevention studies of adolescents with elevated depressive symptoms (Young et al., 2016; Young, Mufson and Gallop, 2010). In 186 adolescents, group-format IPT skills training reduced depressive symptoms more than group counselling but did not differentially reduce onset of major depressive episodes over six months (Young et al., 2016).

Universal prevention approaches to adolescent depression have often used large samples (from 1,500 to 5,634 students), CBT-based classroom-based interventions delivered by teachers incorporating training in problem-solving and emotional regulation, and two–four years follow-ups (Spence, Sheffield and Donovan, 2005). All effectively found no significant difference between the active intervention and the control condition (monitoring or no intervention) for depressive symptoms or onset of major depression at or beyond 12 months follow-up (Sawyer, Harchak et al., 2010; Sawyer, Pfeiffer et al., 2010; Sheffield et al., 2006). A large-scale cluster RCT in eight UK secondary schools of 5,030 students aged 12–16-year-old students found no difference on symptoms of depression at 12 months between students randomised to the Resourceful Adolescent classroom-based CBT programme, attentional control or usual school provision, even in the adolescents with subsyndromal symptoms (Stallard et al., 2012). A large-scale universal prevention study across 30 schools (1,477 students) found that the online self-directed CBT MoodGYM treatment (Calear, Christensen, Mackinnon, Griffiths and O'Kearney, 2009) reduced symptoms of anxiety but not depression posttreatment and at six months, relative to a waiting list control, with significant reductions in depression only observed in male students.

Thus, the evidence favours selective or indicated interventions targeted for higher-risk adolescents relative to universal prevention programmes, although it is not yet resolved whether this is because targeted interventions are more efficacious or simply have more power to detect an effect because of the increased base rate of incidence of depression in high risk groups.

Treating children and adolescents

CBT and IPT have been adapted to treat children and adolescents, using the same core techniques and approaches as for adults, but modified to make therapy accessible for children and to target common issues in youngsters such as social and academic difficulties, emotion regulation, maladaptive family relationships and poor self-esteem. Treatments can actively involve parents, with parents participating in concurrent *parent-training* in which they learn the same rationales, tasks and skills at the same time as the child. *Family intervention* can also be an essential component, since many of the children's difficulties may originate in families where parents are themselves experiencing psychological disturbances, or dysfunctional interactions.

In general, trials examining CBT administered in school settings for depressed children find that CBT is superior to no treatment or waiting-list controls, with a moderate effect size relative to placebo treatments, summarised in meta-analyses and reviews (Arnberg and Ost, 2014; Weisz, 2014; Weisz, McCarty and Valeri, 2006). However, many trials are limited in having relatively small sample sizes, comparing CBT to no-treatment or waiting list control groups rather to an active control condition, and lacking long-term follow-ups. A network meta-analysis of psychotherapy for depression in children and adolescents found that only CBT and IPT were more effective than control conditions post-treatment and at follow-up (Zhou et al., 2015).

One proven approach is the Coping with Depression (CWD) programme, a group psycho-education course teaching effective behavioural activation and social problem-solving skills, including a parent programme (Lewinsohn, Clarke, Hops and Andrews, 1990), which outperformed waiting list control, with improvements maintained for two years (Clarke, Rohde, Lewinsohn, Hops and Seeley, 1999). Further trials have shown that adding brief individual CBT to TAU improved diagnostic recovery in 12–18-year-olds who declined or stopped antidepressant medication (Clarke et al., 2016) and that adding CBT to continued antidepressants in youths aged 7–18 with residual depression halved the risk of relapse (36 per cent) through a 18-month follow-up relative to medication management alone (62 per cent) (Emslie et al., 2015; Kennard et al., 2014). An important RCT for adolescents with major depression showed that there was no difference between individual CBT and pill placebo in treatment effect, medication alone was superior to CBT alone, and combined CBT-medication treatment was significantly better than placebo, with these effects maintained at one-year naturalistic follow-up (Treatment for Adolescents with Depression Study) (March et al., 2009).

IPT was adapted for use with depressed adolescents by adding a focus on single-parent families to the existing foci (Moreau, Mufson, Weissman and Klerman, 1991). In four RCTs with varying populations and control conditions, IPT for major depression produced significantly better outcomes, whether in comparison to clinical monitoring for predominantly female and Latino adolescents (Mufson, Weissman, Moreau and Garfinkel, 1999), or in comparison to waiting list control for Puerto Rican adolescents (Rossello and Bernal, 1999) or to TAU in school-based health clinics (Mufson et al., 2004) or to TAU from school based mental health workers for those adolescents who reported a high level of conflict with their mothers or peers (Gunlicks-Stoessel, Mufson, Jekal and Turner, 2010).

Summary

- ◆ Cognitive-behavioural treatment of depression stresses changing maladaptive cognitions, as well as behavioural methods to reduce depression and to improve dysfunctional skills and problem solving.
- ◆ CBT and BA are significantly more effective than no treatment, and appear to equal medication and IPT in reducing depression in the acute phase; CBT appears to be more successful than medication in the long-term prevention of relapse and recurrence, although there is still scope for improvement given that most patients show a return of depression.

◆ The mechanism that makes CBT successful appears to be helping patients to learn compensatory skills that break the link between negative mood and negative thinking.

◆ IPT for depression is focused on exploring the role of interpersonal problems as the cause of depression, working through unresolved emotions associated with losses, transitions and bereavements, and on making active changes in relationships.

◆ IPT is significantly more effective than no treatment, and appears to be the equal of medication and CBT in achieving short-term results. IPT has been shown to have maintenance effects in preventing recurrence.

◆ There is preliminary evidence that combined medication and psychotherapy is superior to either alone, particularly for severe depression.

◆ Both CBT and IPT have been extended to treat depression in child and adolescent depression, with some mild-to-moderate success.

◆ There is evidence that selective and indicated approaches may be more effective than universal approaches to preventing depression.

References

Andersson, G. (2009). Using the internet to provide cognitive behaviour therapy. *Behaviour Research and Therapy*, 47(3), 175–180.

Andersson, G., Bergstrom, J., Hollandare, F., Carlbring, P., Kaldo, V. and Ekselius, L. (2005). Internet-based self-help for depression: randomised controlled trial. *British Journal of Psychiatry*, 187, 456–461.

Andersson, G. and Cuijpers, P. (2009). Internet-based and other computerized psychological treatments for adult depression: a meta-analysis. *Cognitive Behaviour Therapy*, 38(4), 196–205.

Andersson, G., Cuijpers, P., Carlbring, P., Riper, H. and Hedman, E. (2014). Guided Internet-based vs. face-to-face cognitive behavior therapy for psychiatric and somatic disorders: a systematic review and meta-analysis. *World Psychiatry*, 13(3), 288–295.

Andrews, G., Cuijpers, P., Craske, M. G., McEvoy, P. and Titov, N. (2010). Computer therapy for the anxiety and depressive disorders is effective, acceptable and practical health care: a meta-analysis. *PLOS One*, 5(10), 6.

Arnberg, A. and Ost, L. G. (2014). CBT for children with depressive symptoms: a meta-analysis. *Cognitive Behaviour Therapy*, *43*(4), 275–288.

Baiao, R., Gilbert, P., McEwan, K. and Carvalho, S. (2015). Forms of self-criticising/attacking and self-reassuring scale: psychometric properties and normative study. *Psychology and Psychotherapy: Theory Research and Practice*, *88*(4), 438–452.

Barber, J. P. and DeRubeis, R. J. (1989). On second thoughts: where the action is in cognitive therapy. *Cognitive Therapy and Research*, *13*, 441–457.

Barber, J. P., and Muenz L. R. (1996). The role of avoidance and obsessiveness in matching patients to cognitive and interpersonal psychotherapy: empirical findings from the Treatment for Depression Collaborative Research Program. *Journal of Consulting and Clinical Psychology*, *64*(5), 951–958.

Barth, J., Munder, T., Gerger, H., Nuesch, E., Trelle, S., Znoj, H., . . . Cuijpers, P. (2013). Comparative efficacy of seven psychotherapeutic interventions for patients with depression: a network meta-analysis. *PLOS Medicine*, *10*(5), 17.

Baskin, T. W., Tierney, S. C., Minami, T. and Wampold, B. E. (2003). Establishing specificity in psychotherapy: a meta-analysis of structural equivalence of placebo controls. *Journal of Consulting and Clinical Psychology*, *71*, 973–979.

Beck, A. T. (1967). *Depression: clinical, experimental and theoretical aspects*. New York: Harper and Row.

Beck, A. T., Rush, A. J., Shaw, B. F. and Emery, G. (1979). *Cognitive therapy of depression*. New York: Guilford Press.

Beevers, C. G. and Miller, I. W. (2005). Unlinking negative cognition and symptoms of depression: evidence of a specific treatment effect for cognitive therapy. *Journal of Consulting and Clinical Psychology*, *73*, 68–77.

Bockting, C. L., Hollon, S. D., Jarrett, R. B., Kuyken, W. and Dobson, K. (2015). A lifetime approach to major depressive disorder: the contributions of psychological interventions in preventing relapse and recurrence. *Clinical Psychology Review*, *41*, 16–26.

Bockting, C. L. H., Schene, A. H., Spinhoven, P., Koeter, M. W. J., Wouters, L. F., Huyser, J. and Kamphuis, J. H. (2005). Preventing relapse/recurrence in recurrent depression with cognitive therapy: a randomized controlled trial. *Journal of Consulting and Clinical Psychology*, *73*, 647–657.

Bockting, C. L. H., Smid, N. H., Koeter, M. W. J., Spinhoven, P., Beck, A. T. and Schene, A. H. (2015). Enduring effects of Preventive Cognitive Therapy in adults remitted from recurrent depression: a 10 year follow-up of a randomized controlled trial. *Journal of Affective Disorders*, *185*, 188–194.

Bower, P. and Gilbody, S. (2005). Stepped care in psychological therapies: access, effectiveness and efficiency – narrative literature review. *British Journal of Psychiatry*, *186*, 11–17.

Bower, P., Kontopantelis, E., Sutton, A., Kendrick, T., Richards, D. A., Gilbody, S., . . . Liu, E. T. H. (2013). Influence of initial severity of depression on effectiveness of low intensity interventions: meta-analysis of individual patient data. *British Medical Journal*, *346*, 11.

Brent, D. A., Brunwasser, S. M., Hollon, S. D., Weersing, V. R., Clarke, G. N., Dickerson, J. F., . . . Garber, J. (2015). Effect of a cognitive-behavioral prevention program on depression 6 years after implementation among at-risk adolescents: a randomized clinical trial. *JAMA Psychiatry*, 72(11), 1110–1118.

Brewin, C. R., Gregory, J. D., Lipton, M. and Burgess, N. (2010). Intrusive images in psychological disorders: characteristics, neural mechanisms, and treatment implications. *Psychological Review*, 117(1), 210–232.

Brewin, C. R., Wheatley, I., Patel, T., Fearon, P., Hackmann, A., Wells, A., . . . Myers, S. (2009). Imagery rescripting as a brief stand-alone treatment for depressed patients with intrusive memories. *Behaviour Research and Therapy*, 47(7), 569–576.

Brugha, T. S., Morrell, C. J., Slade, P. and Walters, S. J. (2011). Universal prevention of depression in women postnatally: cluster randomized trial evidence in primary care. *Psychological Medicine*, 41(4), 739–748.

Buntrock, C., Ebert, D. D., Lehr, D., Smit, F., Riper, H., Berking, M. and Cuijpers, P. (2016). Effect of a web-based guided self-help intervention for prevention of major depression in adults with subthreshold depression: a randomized clinical trial. *JAMA-Journal of the American Medical Association*, 315(17), 1854–1863.

Calear, A. L., Christensen, H., Mackinnon, A., Griffiths, K. M. and O'Kearney, R. (2009). The YouthMood Project: a cluster randomized controlled trial of an online cognitive behavioral program with adolescents. *Journal of Consulting and Clinical Psychology*, 77(6), 1021–1032.

Chisholm, D., Sweeny, K., Sheehan, P., Rasmussen, B., Smit, F., Cuijpers, P. and Saxena, S. (2016). Scaling-up treatment of depression and anxiety: a global return on investment analysis. *Lancet Psychiatry*, 3(5), 415–424.

Clark, D. M., Layard, R., Smithies, R., Richards, D. A., Suckling, R. and Wright, B. (2009). Improving access to psychological therapy: initial evaluation of two UK demonstration sites. *Behaviour Research and Therapy*, 47(11), 910–920.

Clarke, A. M., Kuosmanen, T. and Barry, M. M. (2015). A Systematic review of online youth mental health promotion and prevention interventions. *Journal of Youth and Adolescence*, 44(1), 90–113.

Clarke, G., DeBar, L. L., Pearson, J. A., Dickerson, J. F., Lynch, F. L., Gullion, C. M. and Leo, M. C. (2016). Cognitive behavioral therapy in primary care for youth declining antidepressants: a randomized trial. *Pediatrics*, 137(5), 13.

Clarke, G. N., Hawkins, W., Murphy, M., Sheeber, L. B., Lewinsohn, P. M. and Seeley, J. R. (1995). Targeted prevention of unipolar depressive disorder in an at-risk sample of high-school adolescents – a randomized trial of group cognitive intervention. *Journal of the American Academy of Child and Adolescent Psychiatry*, 34, 312–321.

Clarke, G. N., Hornbrook, M., Lynch, F., Polen, M., Gale, J., Beardslee, W., . . . Seeley J. (2001). A randomized trial of a group cognitive intervention for preventing depression in adolescent offspring of depressed parents. *Archives of General Psychiatry*, 58, 1127–1134.

Clarke, G. N., Rohde, P., Lewinsohn, P. M., Hops, H. and Seeley, J. R. (1999). Cognitive-behavioral treatment of adolescent depression: efficacy of acute group treatment and booster sessions. *Journal of the American Academy of Child and Adolescent Psychiatry*, 38, 272–279.

Clarke, K., Mayo-Wilson, E., Kenny, J. and Pilling, S. (2015). Can non-pharmacological interventions prevent relapse in adults who have recovered from depression? A systematic review and meta-analysis of randomised controlled trials. *Clinical Psychology Review*, 39, 58–70.

Craighead, W. E. and Dunlop, B. W. (2014). Combination psychotherapy and antidepressant medication treatment for depression: for whom, when, and how. *Annual Review of Psychology*, 65, 267–300.

Cristea, I. A., Huibers, M. J. H., David, D., Hollon, S. D., Andersson, G. and Cuijpers, P. (2015). The effects of cognitive behavior therapy for adult depression on dysfunctional thinking: a meta-analysis. *Clinical Psychology Review*, 42, 62–71.

Cuijpers, P., Cristea, I. A., Karyotaki, E., Reijnders, M. and Huibers, M. J. H. (2016). How effective are cognitive behavior therapies for major depression and anxiety disorders? A meta-analytic update of the evidence. *World Psychiatry*, 15(3), 245–258.

Cuijpers, P., Donker, T., van Straten, A., Li, J. and Andersson, G. (2010). Is guided self-help as effective as face-to-face psychotherapy for depression and anxiety disorders? A systematic review and meta-analysis of comparative outcome studies. *Psychological Medicine*, 40(12), 1943–1957.

Cuijpers, P., Geraedts, A. S., van Oppen, P., Andersson, G., Markowitz, J. C. and van Straten, A. (2011). Interpersonal Psychotherapy for depression: a meta-analysis. *American Journal of Psychiatry*, 168(6), 581–592.

Cuijpers, P., Sijbrandij, M., Koole, S. L., Andersson, G., Beekman, A. T. and Reynolds, C. F. (2014). Adding psychotherapy to antidepressant medication in depression and anxiety disorders: a meta-analysis. *World Psychiatry*, 13(1), 56–67.

Cuijpers, P., van Straten, A., Andersson, G. and van Oppen, P. (2008). Psychotherapy for depression in adults: a meta-analysis of comparative outcome studies. *Journal of Consulting and Clinical Psychology*, 76(6), 909–922.

Cuijpers, P., van Straten, A., Smit, F., Mihalopoulos, C. and Beekman, A. (2008). Preventing the onset of depressive disorders: a meta-analytic review of psychological interventions. *American Journal of Psychiatry*, 165(10), 1272–1280.

Cuijpers, P., van Straten, A., van Oppen, P. and Andersson, G. (2008). Are psychological and pharmacologic interventions equally effective in the treatment of adult depressive disorders? A meta-analysis of comparative studies. *Journal of Clinical Psychiatry*, 69(11), 1675–1685.

DeRubeis, R. J., Cohen, Z. D., Forand, N. R., Fournier, J. C., Gelfand, L. A. and Lorenzo-Luaces, L. (2014). The Personalized Advantage Index: translating research on prediction into individualized treatment recommendations. A demonstration. *PLOS One*, 9(1), 8.

DeRubeis, R. J. and Feeley, M. (1990). Determinants of change in cognitive therapy for depression. *Cognitive Therapy and Research, 14*, 469–482.

DeRubeis, R. J., Hollon, S. D., Amsterdam, J. D., Shelton, R. C., Young, P. R., Salomon, R. M. et al. (2005). Cognitive therapy vs medications in the treatment of moderate to severe depression. *Archives of General Psychiatry, 62*, 409–416.

Diedrich, A., Hofmann, S. G., Cuijpers, P. and Berking, M. (2016). Self-compassion enhances the efficacy of explicit cognitive reappraisal as an emotion regulation strategy in individuals with major depressive disorder. *Behaviour Research and Therapy, 82*, 1–10.

Dimidjian, S., Hollon, S. D., Dobson, K. S., Schmaling, K. B., Kohlenberg, R. J., Addis, M. E. et al. (2006). Randomized trial of behavioral activation, cognitive therapy, and antidepressant medication in the acute treatment of adults with major depression. *Journal of Consulting and Clinical Psychology, 74*, 658–670.

Driessen, E., Cuijpers, P., Hollon, S. D. and Dekker, J. J. M. (2010). Does pretreatment severity moderate the efficacy of psychological treatment of adult outpatient depression? A meta-analysis. *Journal of Consulting and Clinical Psychology, 78*(5), 668–680.

Driessen, E., Hollon, S. D., Bockting, C. L. H., Cuijpers, P. and Turner, E. H. (2015). Does publication bias inflate the apparent efficacy of psychological treatment for major depressive disorder? A systematic review and meta-analysis of US National Institutes of Health-funded trials. *PLOS One, 10*(9), 23.

Ekers, D., Richards, D. and Gilbody, S. (2008). A meta-analysis of randomized trials of behavioural treatment of depression. *Psychological Medicine, 38*(5), 611–623.

Ekers, D., Webster, L., Van Straten, A., Cuijpers, P., Richards, D. and Gilbody, S. (2014). Behavioural activation for depression: an update of meta-analysis of effectiveness and sub group analysis. *PLOS One, 9*(6).

Elkin, I., Shea, M. T., Watkins, J. T., Imber, S. D., Sotsky, S. M., Collins, J. F. . . . Docherty, J. P. (1989). National Institute of Mental Health treatment of depression collaborative research program: General effectiveness of treatments. *Archives of General Psychiatry, 46*, 971–982.

Emslie, G. J., Kennard, B. D., Mayes, T. L., Nakonezny, P. A., Moore, J., Jones, J. M., . . . King, J. (2015). Continued effectiveness of relapse prevention Cognitive-Behavioral Therapy following fluoxetine treatment in youth with major depressive disorder. *Journal of the American Academy of Child and Adolescent Psychiatry, 54*(12), 991–998.

Falconer, C. J., Slater, M., Rovira, A., King, J. A., Gilbert, P., Antley, A. and Brewin, C. R. (2014). Embodying compassion: a virtual reality paradigm for overcoming excessive self-criticism. *PLOS One, 9*(11), 7.

Farrand, P. and Woodford, J. (2013). Impact of support on the effectiveness of written cognitive behavioural self-help: a systematic review and meta-analysis of randomised controlled trials. *Clinical Psychology Review, 33*(1), 182–195.

Fava, G. A., Rafanelli, C., Grandi, S., Canestrari, R. and Morphy, M. A. (1998). Six-year outcome for cognitive behavioral treatment of residual symptoms in major depression. *American Journal of Psychiatry*, *155*, 1443–1445.

Fava, G. A., Ruini, C., Rafanelli, C., Finos, L., Conti, S. and Grandi, S. (2004). Six-year outcome of cognitive behavior therapy for prevention of recurrent depression. *American Journal of Psychiatry*, *161*, 1872–1876.

Feeley, M., DeRubeis, R. J. and Gelfand, L. A. (1999). The temporal relation of adherence and alliance to symptom change in cognitive therapy for depression. *Journal of Consulting and Clinical Psychology*, *67*, 578–582.

Ferster, C. B. (1973). A functional analysis of depression. *American Psychologist*, *28*, 857–870.

Fonagy, P. and Clark, D. M. (2015). Update on the Improving Access to Psychological Therapies programme in England. *Psychiatric Bulletin*, *39*(5), 248–251.

Fournier, J. C., DeRubeis, R. J., Shelton, R. C., Hollon, S. D., Amsterdam, J. D. and Gallop, R. (2009). Prediction of response to medication and cognitive therapy in the treatment of moderate to severe depression. *Journal of Consulting and Clinical Psychology*, *77*, 775–787.

Frank, E., Kupfer, D. J., Perel, J. M., Cornes, C., Jarrett, D. B., Mallinger, A. G. . . . Grochocinski, V. J. (1990). 3-year outcomes for maintenance therapies in recurrent depression. *Archives of General Psychiary*, *47*, 1093–1099.

Frank, J. D. and Frank J. B. (1991). *Persuasion and healing: a comparative study of psychotherapy* (3rd edition). London: John Hopkins Press.

Garber, J., Clarke, G. N., Weersing, V. R., Beardslee, W. R., Brent, D. A., Gladstone, T. R. G., . . . Iyengar, S. (2009). Prevention of depression in at-risk adolescents: a randomized controlled trial. *JAMA-Journal of the American Medical Association*, *301*(21), 2215–2224.

Gellatly, J., Bower, P., Hennessy, S., Richards, D., Gilbody, S. and Lovell, K. (2007). What makes self-help interventions effective in the management of depressive symptoms? Meta-analysis and meta-regression. *Psychological Medicine*, *37*(9), 1217–1228.

Gibbons, M. B. C., Gallop, R., Thompson, D., Luther, D., Crits-Christoph, K., Jacobs, J., . . . Crits-Christoph, P. (2016). Comparative effectiveness of Cognitive Therapy and Dynamic Psychotherapy for major depressive disorder in a community mental health setting: a randomized clinical noninferiority trial. *JAMA Psychiatry*, *73*(9), 904–911.

Gilbert, P. (2014). The origins and nature of compassion focused therapy. *British Journal of Clinical Psychology*, *53*(1), 6–41.

Gilbert, P. and Procter, S. (2006). Compassionate mind training for people with high shame and self-criticism: overview and pilot study of a group therapy approach. *Clinical Psychology and Psychotherapy*, *13*(6), 353–379.

Gilbody, S., Littlewood, E., Hewitt, C., Brierley, G., Tharmanathan, P., Araya, R., . . . REEACT Team. (2015). Computerised cognitive behaviour therapy (cCBT) as treatment for depression in primary care (REEACT trial): large scale pragmatic randomised controlled trial. *British Medical Journal, 351*, 13.

Gloaguen, V., Cottraux, J., Cucherat, M. and Blackburn, I. M. (1998). A meta-analysis of the effects of cognitive therapy in depressed patients. *Journal of Affective Disorders, 49*, 59–72.

Gortner, E. T., Gollan, J. K., Dobson, K. S. and Jacobson, N. S. (1998). Cognitive-behavioral treatment for depression: relapse prevention. *Journal of Consulting and Clinical Psychology, 66*, 377–384.

Gunlicks-Stoessel, M., Mufson, L., Jekal, A. and Turner, J. B. (2010). The impact of perceived interpersonal functioning on treatment for adolescent depression: IPT-a versus treatment as usual in school-based health clinics. *Journal of Consulting and Clinical Psychology, 78*(2), 260–267.

Hamilton, K. E. and Dobson, K. S. (2002). Cognitive therapy of depression: pretreatment patient predictors of outcome. *Clinical Psychology Review, 22*, 875–893.

Hollon, S. D. (2016). The efficacy and acceptability of psychological interventions for depression: where we are now and where we are going. *Epidemiology and Psychiatric Sciences, 25*(4), 295–300.

Hollon, S. D., DeRubeis, R. J., Evans, M. D., Wiemer, M. J., Garvey, M. J., Grove, W. M. and Tuason, V. B. (1992). Cognitive Therapy and pharmacotherapy for depression – singly and in combination. *Archives of General Psychiatry, 49*, 774–781.

Hollon, S. D., DeRubeis, R. J., Fawcett, J., Amsterdam, J. D., Shelton, R. C., Zajecka, J., . . . Gallop, R. (2014). Effect of Cognitive Therapy with antidepressant medications vs antidepressants alone on the rate of recovery in Major Depressive Disorder: a randomized clinical trial. *JAMA Psychiatry, 71*(10), 1157–1164.

Hollon, S. D., DeRubeis, R. J., Shelton, R. C., Amsterdam, J. D., Salomon, R. M., O'Reardon, J. P. . . . Gallop, R. (2005). Prevention of relapse following cognitive therapy vs medications in moderate to severe depression. *Archives of General Psychiatry, 62*, 417–422.

Hollon, S. D., Stewart, M. O. and Strunk, D. (2006). Enduring effects for cognitive behavior therapy in the treatment of depression and anxiety. *Annual Review of Psychology, 57*, 285–315.

Holmes, E. A., Craske, M. G. and Graybiel, A. M. (2014). A call for mental-health science. *Nature, 511*(7509), 287–289.

Huibers, M. J. H., Cohen, Z. D., Lemmens, L., Arntz, A., Peeters, F., Cuijpers, P. and DeRubeis, R. J. (2015). Predicting optimal outcomes in Cognitive Therapy or Interpersonal Psychotherapy for depressed individuals using the Personalized Advantage Index approach. *PLOS One, 10*(11), 16.

Huijbers, M. J., Spinhoven, P., Spijker, J., Ruhe, H. G., van Schaik, D. J. F., van Oppen, P., . . . Speckens, A. E. M. (2015). Adding mindfulness-based cognitive therapy to maintenance antidepressant medication for prevention of relapse/recurrence in major depressive disorder: randomised controlled trial. *Journal of Affective Disorders, 187*, 54–61.

Jacobson, N. S., Dobson, K. S., Truax, P. A., Addis, M. E., Koerner, K., Gollan, J. K. . . . Prince, S. E. (1996). A component analysis of cognitive-behavioral treatment for depression. *Journal of Consulting and Clinical Psychology, 64*, 295–304.

Jarrett, R. B., Eaves, G. G., Grannemann, B. D. and Rush, A. J. (1991). Clinical, cognitive, and demographic predictors of response to Cognitive Therapy for depression – a preliminary report. *Psychiatry Research, 37*, 245–260.

Jarrett, R. B., Kraft, D., Doyle, J., Foster, B. M., Eaves, G. G. and Silver, P. C. (2001). Preventing recurrent depression using cognitive therapy with and without a continuation phase – a randomized clinical trial. *Archives of General Psychiatry, 58*, 381–388.

Jarrett, R. B., Minhajuddin, A., Gershenfeld, H., Friedman, E. S. and Thase, M. E. (2013). Preventing depressive relapse and recurrence in higher-risk Cognitive Therapy responders: a randomized trial of continuation phase Cognitive Therapy, Fluoxetine, or matched pill placebo. *JAMA Psychiatry, 70*(11), 1152–1160.

Jarrett, R. B., Minhajuddin, A., Vittengl, J. R., Clark, L. A. and Thase, M. E. (2016). Quantifying and qualifying the preventive effects of acute-phase Cognitive Therapy: pathways to personalizing care. *Journal of Consulting and Clinical Psychology, 84*(4), 365–376.

Judd, L. L. (1997). The clinical course of unipolar major depressive disorders. *Archives of General Psychiatry, 54*, 989–991.

Kabat-Zinn, J. (1990). *Full catastrophe living: using the wisdom of your body and mind to face stress, pain, and illness.* New York: Dell Publishing.

Kanter, J. W., Puspitasari, A. J., Santos, M. M. and Nagy, G. A. (2012). Behavioural activation: history, evidence and promise. *British Journal of Psychiatry, 200*(5), 361–363.

Kazdin, A. E. and Blase, S. L. (2011). Rebooting psychotherapy research and practice to reduce the burden of mental illness. *Perspectives on Psychological Science, 6*(1), 21–37.

Kennard, B. D., Emslie, G. J., Mayes, T. L., Nakonezny, P. A., Jones, J. M., Foxwell, A. A. and King, J. (2014). Sequential treatment with fluoxetine and relapse-prevention CBT to improve outcomes in pediatric depression. *American Journal of Psychiatry, 171*(10), 1083–1090.

Kessler, D., Lewis, G., Kaur, S., Wiles, N., King, M., Weich, S., . . . Peters, T. J. (2009). Therapist-delivered internet psychotherapy for depression in primary care: a randomised controlled trial. *Lancet, 374*(9690), 628–634.

Klerman, G. L., Weissman, M. M., Rounsaville, B. J. and Chevron, E. (1984). *Interpersonal psychotherapy of depression.* New York: Basic Books.

Kuyken, W., Byford, S., Taylor, R. S., Watkins, E., Holden, E., White, K., . . . Teasdale, J. D. (2008). Mindfulness-based Cognitive Therapy to prevent relapse in recurrent depression. *Journal of Consulting and Clinical Psychology, 76*(6), 966–978.

Kuyken, W., Hayes, R., Barrett, B., Byng, R., Dalgleish, T., Kessler, D., . . . Byford, S. (2015). Effectiveness and cost-effectiveness of mindfulness-based cognitive therapy compared with maintenance antidepressant treatment in the prevention of depressive relapse or recurrence (PREVENT): a randomised controlled trial. *Lancet*, *386*(9988), 63–73.

Layard, R. and Clark, D. M. (2015). Why more psychological therapy would cost nothing. *Frontiers in Psychology*, *6*, 3.

Lemmens, L., Arntz, A., Peeters, F., Hollon, S. D., Roefs, A. and Huibers, M. J. H. (2015). Clinical effectiveness of cognitive therapy v. interpersonal psychotherapy for depression: results of a randomized controlled trial. *Psychological Medicine*, *45*(10), 2095–2110.

Lewinsohn, P. M., Clarke, G. N., Hops, H. and Andrews, J. (1990). Cognitive-Behavioral Treatment for depressed adolescents. *Behavior Therapy*, *21*, 385–401.

Lorenzo-Luaces, L., German, R. E. and DeRubeis, R. J. (2015). It's complicated: the relation between cognitive change procedures, cognitive change, and symptom change in cognitive therapy for depression. *Clinical Psychology Review*, *41*, 3–15.

Ma, S. H. and Teasdale, J. D. (2004). Mindfulness-based cognitive therapy for depression: replication and exploration of differential relapse prevention effects. *Journal of Consulting and Clinical Psychology*, *72*, 31–40.

Mackinnon, A., Griffiths, K. M. and Christensen, H. (2008). Comparative randomised trial of online cognitive-behavioural therapy and an information website for depression: 12-month outcomes. *British Journal of Psychiatry*, *192*(2), 130–134.

March, J., Silva, S., Curry, J., Wells, K., Fairbank, J., Burns, B., . . . Bartoi, M. (2009). The Treatment for Adolescents With Depression Study (TADS): outcomes over 1 year of naturalistic follow-up. *American Journal of Psychiatry*, *166*(10), 1141–1149.

Martell, C. R., Addis, M. E. and Jacobson, N. S. (2001). *Depression in context: strategies for guided action*. New York: Norton.

Merry, S. N., Hetrick, S. E., Cox, G. R., Brudevold-Iversen, T., Bir, J. J. and McDowell, H. (2011). Psychological and educational interventions for preventing depression in children and adolescents. *Cochrane Database of Systematic Reviews*, (12), 277.

Moreau, D., Mufson, L., Weissman, M. M. and Klerman, G. L. (1991). Interpersonal psychotherapy for adolescent depression – description of modification and preliminary application. *Journal of the American Academy of Child and Adolescent Psychiatry*, *30*, 642–651.

Mufson, L., Dorta, K. P., Wickramaratne, P., Nomura, Y., Olfson, M. and Weissman, M. M. (2004). A randomized effectiveness trial of interpersonal psychotherapy for depressed adolescents. *Archives of General Psychiatry*, *61*, 577–584.

Mufson, L., Weissman, M. M., Moreau, D. and Garfinkel, R. (1999). Efficacy of interpersonal psychotherapy for depressed adolescents. *Archives of General Psychiatry*, *56*, 573–579.

Muñoz, R. F., Beardslee, W. R. and Leykin, Y. (2012). Major depression can be prevented. *American Psychologist*, *67*(4), 285–295.

Muñoz, R. F., Cuijpers, P., Smit, F., Barrera, A. Z. and Leykin, Y. (2010). Prevention of Major Depression. *Annual Review of Clinical Psychology*, *6*, 181–212.

Nemeroff, C. B., Heim, C. M., Thase, M. E., Klein, D. N., Rush, A. J., Schatzberg, A. F. . . . Keller, M. B. (2003). Differential responses to psychotherapy versus pharmacotherapy in patients with chronic forms of major depression and childhood trauma. *Proceedings of the National Academy of Sciences of the United States of America, 100,* 14293–14296.

Newman, M. G., Szkodny, L. E., Llera, S. J. and Przeworski, A. (2011). A review of technology-assisted self-help and minimal contact therapies for anxiety and depression: is human contact necessary for therapeutic efficacy? *Clinical Psychology Review, 31*(1), 89–103.

Pampallona, S., Bollini, P., Tibaldi, G., Kupelnick, B. and Munizza, C. (2004). Combined pharmacotherapy and psychological treatment for depression – a systematic review. *Archives of General Psychiatry, 61,* 714–719.

Patel, V., Weobong, B., Weiss, H. A., Anand, A., Bhat, B., Katti, B., . . . Fairburn, C. G. (2017). The Healthy Activity Program (HAP), a lay counsellor-delivered brief psychological treatment for severe depression, in primary care in India: a randomised controlled trial. *Lancet, 389*(10065), 176–185.

Paykel, E. S., Scott, J., Teasdale, J. D., Johnson, A. L., Garland, A., Moore, R. . . . Pope, M. (1999). Prevention of relapse in residual depression by cognitive therapy – a controlled trial. *Archives of General Psychiatry, 56,* 829–835.

Reynolds, C. F., Frank, E., Perel, J. M., Imber, S. D., Cornes, C., Miller, M. D. . . . Kupfer, M. D. (1999). Nortriptyline and interpersonal psychotherapy as maintenance therapies for recurrent major depression – a randomized controlled trial in patients older than 59 years. *JAMA-Journal of the American Medical Association, 281,* 39–45.

Richards, D. and Richardson, T. (2012). Computer-based psychological treatments for depression: a systematic review and meta-analysis. *Clinical Psychology Review, 32*(4), 329–342.

Richards, D. A., Ekers, D., McMillan, D., Taylor, R. S., Byford, S., Warren, F. C., . . . Finning, K. (2016). Cost and Outcome of Behavioural Activation versus Cognitive Behavioural Therapy for Depression (COBRA): a randomised, controlled, non-inferiority trial. *Lancet, 388*(10047), 871–880.

Robinson, L. A., Berman, J. S. and Neimeyer, R. A. (1990). Psychotherapy for the treatment of depression – a comprehensive review of controlled outcome research. *Psychological Bulletin, 108,* 30–49.

Roiser, J. P., Elliott, R. and Sahakian, B. J. (2012). Cognitive mechanisms of treatment in depression. *Neuropsychopharmacology, 37*(1), 117–136.

Rossello, J. and Bernal, G. (1999). The efficacy of cognitive-behavioral and interpersonal treatments for depression in Puerto Rican adolescents. *Journal of Consulting and Clinical Psychology, 67,* 734–745.

Sawyer, M. G., Harchak, T. F., Spence, S. H., Bond, L., Graetz, B., Kay, D., . . . Sheffield, J. (2010). School-based prevention of depression: a 2-year follow-up of a randomized controlled trial of the beyondblue Schools Research Initiative. *Journal of Adolescent Health, 47*(3), 297–304.

Sawyer, M. G., Pfeiffer, S., Spence, S. H., Bond, L., Graetz, B., Kay, D., . . . Sheffield, J. (2010). School-based prevention of depression: a randomised controlled study of the beyondblue schools research initiative. *Journal of Child Psychology and Psychiatry, 51*(2), 199–209.

Segal, Z. V., Bieling, P., Young, T., MacQueen, G., Cooke, R., Martin, L., . . . Levitan, R. D. (2010). Antidepressant monotherapy vs sequential pharmacotherapy and mindfulness-based cognitive therapy, or placebo, for relapse prophylaxis in recurrent depression. *Archives of General Psychiatry, 67*(12), 1256–1264.

Segal, Z. V., Kennedy, S., Gemar, M., Hood, K., Pedersen, R. and Buis, T. (2006). Cognitive reactivity to sad mood provocation and the prediction of depressive relapse. *Archives of General Psychiatry, 63,* 749–755.

Segal, Z. V., Williams, J. M. G. and Teasdale, J. D. (2002). *Mindfulness-based cognitive therapy for depression: a new approach to preventing relapse.* New York: Guilford Press.

Shapiro, D. A., Barkham, M., Rees, A., Hardy, G. E., Reynolds, S. and Startup, M. (1994). Effects of treatment duration and severity of depression on the effectiveness of Cognitive-Behavioral and Psychodynamic Interpersonal Psychotherapy. *Journal of Consulting and Clinical Psychology, 62,* 522–534.

Sheffield, J. K., Spence, S. H., Rapee, R. M., Kowalenko, N., Wignall, A., Davis, A. and McLoone, J. (2006). Evaluation of universal, indicated and combined cognitive-behavioral approaches to the prevention of depression among adolescents. *Journal of Consulting and Clinical Psychology, 74,* 66–79.

Spence, S. H., Sheffield, J. K. and Donovan, C. L. (2005). Long-term outcome of a school-based, universal approach to prevention of depression in adolescents. *Journal of Consulting and Clinical Psychology, 73,* 160–167.

Stallard, P., Sayal, K., Phillips, R., Taylor, J. A., Spears, M., Anderson, R., . . . Montgomery, A. A. (2012). Classroom based cognitive behavioural therapy in reducing symptoms of depression in high risk adolescents: pragmatic cluster randomised controlled trial. *British Medical Journal, 345,* 13.

Stice, E., Shaw, H., Bohon, C., Marti, C. N. and Rohde, P. (2009). A meta-analytic review of depression prevention programs for children and adolescents: factors that predict magnitude of intervention effects. *Journal of Consulting and Clinical Psychology, 77*(3), 486–503.

Stockings, E. A., Degenhardt, L., Dobbins, T., Lee, Y. Y., Erskine, H. E., Whiteford, H. A. and Patton, G. (2016). Preventing depression and anxiety in young people: a review of the joint efficacy of universal, selective and indicated prevention. *Psychological Medicine, 46*(1), 11–26.

Strunk, D. R., Adler, A. D. and Hollars, S. N. (2013). Cognitive therapy skills predict cognitive reactivity to sad mood following Cognitive Therapy for depression. *Cognitive Therapy and Research, 37*(6), 1214–1219.

Strunk, D. R., Brotman, M. A. and DeRubeis, R. J. (2010). The process of change in cognitive therapy for depression: predictors of early inter-session symptom gains. *Behaviour Research and Therapy, 48*(7), 599–606.

Teasdale, J. D., Segal, Z. and Williams, J. M. G. (1995). How does cognitive therapy prevent depressive relapse and why should attentional control (mindfulness) training help. *Behaviour Research and Therapy, 33,* 25–39.

Teasdale, J. D., Segal, Z. V., Williams, J. M. G., Ridgeway, V. A., Soulsby, J. M. and Lau, M. A. (2000). Prevention of relapse/recurrence in major depression by mindfulness-based cognitive therapy. *Journal of Consulting and Clinical Psychology, 68*, 615–623.

Teismann, T., Von Brachel, R., Hanning, S., Grillenberger, M., Hebermehl, L., Hornstein, I. and Willutzki, U. (2014). A randomized controlled trial on the effectiveness of a rumination-focused group treatment for residual depression. *Psychotherapy Research, 24*(1), 80–90.

Tolin, D. F. (2010). Is cognitive-behavioral therapy more effective than other therapies? A meta-analytic review. *Clinical Psychology Review, 30*(6), 710–720.

Topper, M., Emmelkamp, P. M. G. and Ehring, T. (2010). Improving prevention of depression and anxiety disorders: repetitive negative thinking as a promising target. *Applied and Preventive Psychology, 14*(1–4), 57–71.

Wampold, B. E., Minami, T., Baskin, T. W. and Tierney, S. C. (2002). A meta-(re)analysis of the effects of cognitive therapy versus 'other therapies' for depression. *Journal of Affective Disorders, 68*, 159–165.

Watkins, E., Newbold, A., Tester-Jones, M., Javaid, M., Cadman, J., Collins, L. M., . . . Mostazir, M. (2016). Implementing multifactorial psychotherapy research in online virtual environments (IMPROVE-2): study protocol for a phase III trial of the MOST randomized component selection method for internet cognitive-behavioural therapy for depression. *BMC Psychiatry, 16*, 13.

Watkins, E. R. (2008). Constructive and unconstructive repetitive thought. *Psychological Bulletin, 134*(2), 163–206.

Watkins, E. R., Mullan, E., Wingrove, J., Rimes, K., Steiner, H., Bathurst, N., . . . Scott, J. (2011). Rumination-focused cognitive-behavioural therapy for residual depression: phase II randomised controlled trial. *British Journal of Psychiatry, 199*(4), 317–322.

Watkins, E. R. and Nolen-Hoeksema, S. (2014). A habit-goal framework of depressive rumination. *Journal of Abnormal Psychology, 123*(1), 24–34.

Watkins, E. R., Taylor, R. S., Byng, R., Baeyens, C., Read, R., Pearson, K. and Watson, L. (2012). Guided self-help concreteness training as an intervention for major depression in primary care: a Phase II randomized controlled trial. *Psychological Medicine, 42*(7), 1359–1371.

Weissman, M. M. and Klerman, G. L. (1990). Interpersonal psychotherapy for depression. In B. B. Wolman and G. Stricker (eds), *Depressive disorders: facts, theories, and treatment methods* (pp. 379–395). New York: Wiley.

Weissman, M. M. (1979). Psychological treatment of depression – evidence for the efficacy of psychotherapy alone, in comparison with, and in combination with pharmacotherapy. *Archives of General Psychiatry, 36*, 1261–1269.

Weissman, M. M., Klerman, G. L., Prusoff, B. A., Sholomskas, D. and Padian, N. (1981). Depressed outpatients – results one year after treatment with drugs and/or Interpersonal Psychotherapy. *Archives of General Psychiatry, 38*, 51–55.

Weisz, J. R. (2014). Building robust psychotherapies for children and adolescents. *Perspectives on Psychological Science, 9*(1), 81–84.

Weitz, E. S., Hollon, S. D., Twisk, J., van Straten, A., Huibers, M. J. H., David, D., ... Cuijpers, P. (2015). Baseline depression severity as moderator of depression outcomes between Cognitive Behavioral Therapy vs Pharmacotherapy: an Individual Patient Data meta-analysis. *JAMA Psychiatry, 72*(11), 1102–1109.

Weisz, J. R., McCarty, C. A. and Valeri, S. M. (2006). Effects of psychotherapy for depression in children and adolescents: a meta-analysis. *Psychological Bulletin, 132*(1), 132–149.

Wiles, N., Thomas, L., Abel, A., Ridgway, N., Turner, N., Campbell, J., ... Lewis, G. (2013). Cognitive behavioural therapy as an adjunct to pharmacotherapy for primary care based patients with treatment resistant depression: results of the CoBalT randomised controlled trial. *Lancet, 381*(9864), 375–384.

Wiles, N. J., Thomas, L., Turner, N., Garfield, K., Kounali, D., Campbell, J., ... Hollinghurst, S. (2016). Long-term effectiveness and cost-effectiveness of cognitive behavioural therapy as an adjunct to pharmacotherapy for treatment-resistant depression in primary care: follow-up of the CoBalT randomised controlled trial. *Lancet Psychiatry, 3*(2), 137–144.

Williams, J. M. G., Crane, C., Barnhofer, T., Brennan, K., Duggan, D. S., Fennell, M. J. V., ... Russell, I. T. (2014). Mindfulness-based Cognitive Therapy for preventing relapse in recurrent depression: a randomized dismantling trial. *Journal of Consulting and Clinical Psychology, 82*(2), 275–286.

Young, J. F., Benas, J. S., Schueler, C. M., Gallop, R., Gillham, J. E. and Mufson, L. (2016). A randomized depression prevention trial comparing Interpersonal Psychotherapy-adolescent skills training to group counseling in schools. *Prevention Science, 17*(3), 314–324.

Young, J. F., Mufson, L. and Gallop, R. (2010). Preventing depression: a randomized trial of interpersonal psychotherapy – adolescent skills training. *Depression and Anxiety, 27*(5), 426–433.

Zhou, X. Y., Hetrick, S. E., Cuijpers, P., Qin, B., Barth, J., Whittington, C. J., ... Xie, P. (2015). Comparative efficacy and acceptability of psychotherapies for depression in children and adolescents: a systematic review and network meta-analysis. *World Psychiatry, 14*(2), 207–222.

Index

Note: *italics* indicate figures; **bold** indicates tables.